**This book is to be returned on or before
the last date stamped below.**

10/10

Titchmarsh, Alan

The Nature of Britain

The Nature of Britain

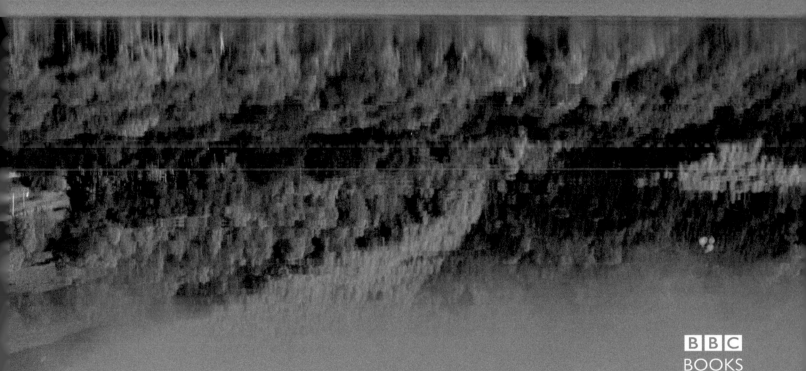

The Nature of Britain
Alan Titchmarsh

BBC
BOOKS

Contents

Foreword

Growing up in the Yorkshire Dales was an idyllic start for a lad who was interested in wildlife and nature. I lived there for the first 20 years of my life and for all that time it remained a constant source of fascination. My chosen career path, as a gardener, grew out of my interest in nature – the back garden being the closest bit of 'nature' to our house – but wildlife and the land that sustains it have always been my greatest interest in life. I still find any excuse to get out into the Hampshire countryside that now surrounds me, as well as to

Yorkshire, Cornwall or the Isle of Wight – my favourite spots – with boots and binoculars.

So I've felt doubly privileged to have worked on two BBC TV series about Britain – one on the origins of its scenery and the second on its natural history. They have taken me to some of Britain's loveliest locations, brought me face to face with spectacular wildlife and have allowed me to meet any number of knowledgeable, passionate and delightful people.

It's true to say that most people's interest in natural history starts early; it's often on family days out in the countryside or at the seaside when you first show curiosity for what's all around you – worms in the garden, frogspawn in country ponds and crabs in rock pools are most children's first encounters with nature, and as their knowledge grows they have fun putting names to new sightings and expanding their interest from small mammals and birds to insects and plants. But in others the enthusiasm dwindles. It might be that opportunities to get out and encounter plants and animals are limited, but often it is because identifying wildlife can be a frustrating business. A lot of field guides are really intended as 'aides memoires' for experts rather than a good starting point for the beginner.

Beginners do far better by getting to know the commoner and more easily identified species first, without bogging themselves down in a lot of academic detail or technical terms. So in putting this book together I've concentrated on the key wildlife you can expect to see in various habitats all round the country, plus the more outstanding or otherwise interesting oddities that are worth looking out for – the feathers in your natural-history cap.

The aim of this book, and of the TV series, is to make you aware of the rich diversity of wildlife that inhabits our beautiful islands, and how interdependent are the plants and animals that live side by side. If we know what they are we are on our way to understanding them, and if we understand them we can better help to ensure their future.

Conservation is not a gloomy, pessimistic pursuit. Well, it shouldn't be. To be effective it needs to be joyous and celebratory. So get out there, and enjoy the countryside and its inhabitants – birds, mammals, flowers, insects… yes, even the creepy-crawlies, otherwise known as invertebrates. Some of the humblest have private lives that will leave you reeling, but each and every one of them – however humble, however ugly, and however lowly – deserves your interest and your protection.

Introduction

Wherever you live in Britain, whether it be in the heart of a big city or in the depths of the countryside, there will be more living creatures within a few feet of you than you could ever imagine. However insignificant they may seem to humans, they all have a vital role to play in the natural history of the British Isles.

Britain's natural history

In wildlife circles, you'll hear a lot of talk about 'native' and 'introduced' species. Well, in a sense all the wildlife in the British Isles is introduced – including man himself – since at different times in our history the slate has been wiped clean by various natural occurrences which, if anyone had been around at the time to witness them, we'd have viewed as catastrophes. We've been repeatedly dunked under water, then allowed to dry out again, as ancient sea levels rose and fell by as much as 300 feet. We've experienced extreme climatic changes, from arid desert to tropical swamp to arctic temperatures. It was the last of these – the ice age (which was actually a whole series of fluctuating warm and cold spells) – that scoured all but the southern end of the mainland with ice, removing virtually all the life, and creating a blank canvas of bare landscape onto which a covering of plants and the insects and other creatures that lived off them appeared. They all jostled for position, finding out by trial and error the best places for survival.

As the balance of species has altered over many centuries, some have been more successful than others. Today some are widespread and capable of living easily in all sorts of different habitats, while others are confined to small areas where particular conditions are found. Centuries of isolation often meant that island species developed their own characteristics, quite different from those of their mainland relatives, since they lacked the usual competition, so you sometimes find oddities such as the blond Alderney hedgehog and unusual mice or wildflowers that were left 'stranded' on remote islands. Not surprisingly, a good many species depend on complex inter-relationships. There are certain plants and animals that must exist in conjunction with each other, for example the parasitic plant dodder, which mostly lives off gorse and heather, and the large blue butterfly, whose caterpillars are 'adopted' by red-ant colonies. But in general the most successful species are those that are the most versatile, can adapt to new habitats and have a broad diet.

The most dramatic thing to hit the British landscape in 30 billion years was man, who altered the landscape and the balance of species living on it by his activities, chiefly farming. Early man introduced our first weeds along with arable crops from the warm, dry plains of the near east, and slowly rearranged the landscape to suit cultivated grains that need well-drained growing conditions. Many common weeds of medieval cornfields (such as weasel's snout) are now virtually extinct, while others (such as corncockle) have reappeared in virtually unaltered form as hardy annual cottage-garden flowers.

Most recently, the Industrial Revolution of the eighteenth and nineteenth centuries, the start of forestry in wartime with its acres of conifers, and twentieth-century road-building and urban sprawl have had an even bigger impact. Today there's hardly a square inch of our islands that isn't under human control, which has in turn impacted on our native wildlife. However, some kinds have proved surprisingly adaptable and have learnt how to take advantage of new man-made habitats. House martins and swallows use our buildings on which to make their nests; pigeons and doves have found that towns give them a better living than the sea cliffs they originally inhabited, and even unusual species such as peregrines now nest in quarries and on city skyscrapers instead of their original cliffs. In cities peregrines find plenty of their favourite food – feral pigeons – which nowadays often nest in window boxes and hanging baskets. Worked-out gravel pits fill with water and turn into waterfowl sanctuaries, while gulls favour rubbish dumps for easy meals. Motorway verges are a great unsung wildlife reserve, so kestrels have been quick to find an abundant supply of mice within their confines. Even unlikely places such as golf courses, cemeteries and wasteland behind factory units play host to wildlife.

Although man has undoubtedly been quite destructive, he is slowly but surely making amends. Conservationists are employing the most natural means possible to re-establish or maintain sensitive habitats, reinstating rare ancient breeds of grazing animals and protecting endangered species. 'Lost' species are being reintroduced, such as the great bustard to Salisbury Plain and the white-tailed eagle to Scotland.

While 'foreign' wildlife may include larger and seemingly more exciting animals and plants, once you're aware of what's around you in the British Isles you'll see there's plenty going on to keep you fascinated on home territory – often quite literally on your doorstep.

PREVIOUS PAGES A picturesque valley north of Lake Thirlmere, in the Lake District National Park, Cumbria.

OPPOSITE The River Ant flanked by wooded banks near How Hill, in the Norfolk Broads.

Watching wildlife

When you first start out watching wildlife, all you need is a sharp pair of eyes for spotting and identifying wildflowers, woody plants, fungi, butterflies, bees and other insects, and the sort of birds that come fairly close – garden birds, and those that visit bird-feeders at nature reserves. But as you grow more interested, you'll find some gear comes in handy. The first piece of serious kit worth investing in is a pair of binoculars ('bins') – they are the only way to get a decent view of more distant birds and animals. They are also good for identifying flowers that you can't easily get close to on foot – for instance, when they are on the far side of a river or on a rocky ledge. Go for a lightweight, compact pair that you won't mind carrying on long walks. Binoculars are rated by two numbers, for example 8 x 40 (which is a good all-round set for naturalists). The first number tells you the magnification – 8 times life size in the example above; anything greater than 9 or 10 makes binoculars difficult to hold steady. The second number tells you how good at light-gathering that particular lens is: the higher the number, the better you'll be able to see in lowish light conditions.

If you go out and about looking at wildlife in all weathers, it is vital that you keep warm, dry and comfortable. Wildlife-watching should be fun, not an exercise in endurance. It's worth kitting yourself out with good walking boots, warm outdoor clothes, lightweight waterproofs with good-sized pockets and a spare pair of socks; a small backpack is also handy. Take maps (go for the largest-scale ordnance survey ones), a compass and current tide tables if you're walking by the coast (you don't want to get cut off by rising tide as we did in Devon). You might also want to consider taking a magnifying glass, which is helpful for identifying flowers and insects, a small digital camera, a notebook and pencil (which works better than a biro in damp conditions) and pocket identification guides. If you are going out into rugged and remote places, a torch, whistle and mobile phone give you extra security; it also makes good sense to let someone back home know where you are going and when you expect to get back.

OPPOSITE Small skipper butterflies, seen here on foxglove seedheads, are found in southern England and Wales.

How to identify wildlife

It looks very easy when you see an expert in action. They take a quick glance and confidently announce the name of whatever they've just spotted, leaving you wondering how on earth they could tell. It boils down to experience: a mixture of knowing what key features to look for and what to expect in a particular place at a certain season, so the more nature-watching you do, the better you get at it.

The first 'rule' of identifying any wildlife is to *assume it's something common*. It usually is. So learn your common birds, flowers and butterflies first – they are the ones likeliest to turn up – and then use them as benchmarks to compare size, colour and markings with sightings of things you don't know.

Rule number two is *shorten the odds*. If you're visiting a reserve, pick up the leaflets detailing what lives there and noting points of interest along the marked nature trails. Look at the sightings board near the entrance to the visitor centre, if there is one (RSPB reserves are especially good at this). If you get the chance, go out spotting with an expert – look out for special events organized at reserves.

Rule number three is *be observant*. Try to take a mental snapshot of anything moving so you fix distinguishing features in your mind quickly. Spend longer studying something that stays still, such as a flower, an insect or a fungus, and look for important features (shape, size, colour) so you can look it up later. If possible, take photos or make a quick sketch of anything new and make a note of time of year, location and behaviour. Keep a nature diary of where you've been, when, and what you saw; it all adds up, and in any case it's fun to reminisce over good days out later.

Where to see wildlife

You'll often spot all sorts of interesting things on country walks and from the car. If you're planning a special trip, road atlases and ordnance survey maps often show sites of special interest for birds or wildflowers. The various national parks round the country are great places to see wildlife in spectacular habitats – for instance, the National Trust (www.nationaltrust.org.uk) owns some superb stretches of coastline and wild areas beyond the gardens at its stately homes, and large privately owned parklands, gardens and arboreta are also good places to see wildlife, so always take your 'bins' and this book with you on the off-chance,

wherever you go. When you want to be sure of seeing a good range and concentration of wildlife reliably, it's always worth visiting reserves. RSPB (www.rspb.org.uk) and county naturalist trusts (www.wildlifetrusts.org) are dotted all over the British Isles, and there are also a few Wildfowl and Wetlands Trust Reserves (www.wwt.org.uk) – find them on the internet, and collect leaflets about them when visiting other wildlife reserves or at tourist centres and build up your own file of places to go.

Try to visit a few of your local places regularly, as you'll see a gradual change as the seasons revolve. If you're making longer trips in the hope of seeing something in particular, it's well worth doing your homework first and checking out the best time and place for seeing what you're interested in to avoid disappointment – for instance, there are very few Bewick's swans at Slimbridge in summer!

Watching birds

Learn your garden birds first, since they are easier to observe close-to (putting out food helps); even so, binoculars make it easier to see fascinating small details that might otherwise be missed – the 'frown' of a greenfinch, the 'whiskers' on long-tailed tits. Get to know the everyday countryside birds in your local area, as they, again, are quite easy to see. Common birds such as sparrows, crows, pigeons and blackbirds make useful 'rough-and-ready' guides to estimating the size of new birds you're attempting to identify.

When faced with something you don't recognize, try to get a good look at a bird standing or perching, especially in

ABOVE Town cemeteries, with plenty of trees and vegetation, are surprisingly good places to spot wildlife, such as foxes.

OPPOSITE A seabird colony congregates on Staple Island, one of the Farne Islands, off the coast of Northumberland.

profile, when it's keeping still. It's much more difficult to identify all but the most familiar birds in flight, as they are often in silhouette and moving too fast to focus binoculars. There's seldom time to check details in a book. Many kinds of birds have colourful males and camouflage-pattern females (especially ducks) or drab-coloured juvenile birds (which often look like small females), so look for the colourful males in any group, as their bold features make them easiest to identify, and rely on close contact, matched body language or courtship display in order to identify their less decorative partners.

In general, it's very difficult to identify birds by their song, but with practice you learn the sounds of the birds you see often – such as robins, wrens, blackbirds or great tits. If you hear *and* see birds at the same time it's easier to 'learn' the calls that go with the appearance – it helps if you have a musical ear, but it's not essential.

Estuaries and salt marshes in winter are the best places to see waders, as huge numbers of migrants such as Brent geese arrive from the far north (including Russia and Siberia), where they spend the summer. Small birds such as dunlin – our commonest wader – begin feeding as soon as the tide starts going out, but bigger birds wait until it has gone out further and has uncovered larger food. A couple of hours after high tide is usually the best time to see the greatest variety of waders. In summer, most waders have moved on to their summer breeding grounds, but herons, egrets and a few other 'regulars' are resident in the British Isles throughout the year.

Spring is by far the best time to see woodland birds, since males stop being so secretive and put on a show of song and territorial display to attract mates; if you hear a bird singing loudly, it will often be found at the top of a tree or on a high twig outlined against the sky, where you can get a good view. Woodland birds are easiest to see before late spring – February or March are good months – before the trees come back into full leaf and obscure the view.

In summer, you can still see and hear a wide range of birds, including summer visitors and waders that are still with us. This is especially the case along the coast and on remote islands, where there is little vegetation to hide them. A shallow pool is a particularly good place to spot them drinking or bathing.

Wildlife-watching rules and tips

● Don't dig up wild plants or flowers, although you can allow children to pick some of the commonest. I reckon this is vital if their interest is to be fostered. Get them to press and dry the flowers between sheets of newspaper or in a special press, then stick them in a scrapbook and label them.

● If you catch butterflies or other insects, treat them very carefully and release them after you've had a look. And don't take home live creatures, even from the sea or rivers, although empty shells or empty egg cases are okay. Replace rocks if you turn them over to see what's beneath, and don't wade around in rock pools, as inhabitants are fragile and easily damaged.

● Don't take eggs, disturb nesting birds or try to rescue 'abandoned' baby birds and animals – one of the parents is bound to be nearby and will know how to cope.

● Keep to public footpaths or marked nature trails at reserves. Use stiles – don't push through hedges or climb over fences – and close gates behind you. Keep clear of areas sectioned off by tape, strings or warning signs, where ground-nesting birds or new marram-grass dunes or other plants are being protected.

● Never drop litter or light fires.

● Don't wear brightly coloured clothes. My red anorak makes it easier for the camera to see me, but generally it's best to stick to greens, browns or beiges, or camouflage patterns. Avoid the sort of fabrics that rustle when you move, and don't take any kit that is likely to rattle or creak.

● Keep quiet and stay as still as possible. Use hides if there are any. Keep your voice down and don't bang the door or make sudden movements, and don't hog space for ages if others are waiting for their turn.

● When there isn't a hide, stay low against a dark background of bushes or trees so you blend in (it's also more sheltered). You can make your own mini-hide by sitting down on a folding camping stool with a green kagoul draped over yourself, like a tent, with just your head sticking out – that way you look less like a person and more like a clump of countryside.

● If you spot something interesting from the road when travelling in the car, pull over, stay inside and take a better look with the binoculars – if you open the doors or get out, the sudden movement will very often frighten off the thing you are looking at.

Watching animals and insects

Try to get a view that allows you to look at animals in profile and butterflies and insects from above, so you can see all the key features. Compare anything new with something you already know to estimate size and colour and look it up while the details are fresh in your mind. A quick sketch in a notebook helps enormously when you need to look up butterflies and insects later.

Frogs are most visible in early spring, usually around February, when they are spawning in ponds; newts live in ponds only in spring and summer. Snakes and lizards are more likely to be seen in spring and summer, as they are more active when the weather is warmer.

Some common mammals such as rabbits may be seen at almost any time of day all year round; hares, stoats and weasels are probably more likely to be seen in spring when they are, in the case of hares, chasing each other round, or, in the case of stoats and weasels, hunting more than usual to feed their young. Foxes can be heard barking at night in winter (the mating season), and in spring when they have cubs to feed they are often out during the day looking for extra food; urban foxes regularly sunbathe on shed roofs by day. Deer are most often seen at dusk or dawn, although they are becoming less shy than they used to be. Nocturnal creatures such as badgers and hedgehogs are usually about only after dark. Look for tell-tale footprints or droppings, even if you don't see the animal.

Looking at wildflowers and trees

The great thing about plants is that they stay still: you can usually get up close, have a good look and take time comparing them to illustrations in books. Get to know the wildflowers and trees that live near your home, in hedges and ditches, on roadside verges and on wasteland – they'll be common kinds that are reasonably widespread all round the country. Once you start looking at them with a new interest, you'll be amazed how many plants there are surrounding you that most people totally overlook.

With anything new, don't just look at the colour of the flowers, look at the leaf shape too, and in the case of trees look at the fruits, nuts or seeds, and also the bark (maybe do a bark rubbing to compare with book illustrations later). Ask yourself, does the plant you are looking at have any similarity to something you already know, in which case it may belong to the same family? It all helps.

Spring and early summer are the best time to see the biggest range of flowers, among them wild orchids, on light, well-drained soils, including sandy sites and chalky downlands. This is also true in deciduous woodlands, before the canopy of leaves casts the ground into deep shade, at which point many woodland plants become dormant for the summer. Woodland edges can be a good place for all sorts of wildlife including birds, flowers and fungi in summer and autumn, when the interior is too dark for good spotting. Wetlands and meadows have a fair range of flowers throughout the summer. Don't overlook trees and native shrubs. Autumn is the very best season for looking at woody plants, since the leaves are changing colour and the fruit and berries are a good aid to identification. In winter, bark patterns and the general shapes of trees are easier to appreciate.

Using this book

Although the dictionary definition says that Great Britain is made up England, Scotland and Wales, in this book I've taken a certain amount of liberty by including a lot of the wildlife also found in Ireland and the Isle of Man, since they are so close to us and their flora and fauna overlap so much with ours. And although we visited the Channel Islands for the making of the TV series, much of their wildlife is more closely allied to that of France, so I've not mentioned their wildlife unless it also appears on mainland Britain. It was hard enough picking 800 key species from the thousands that inhabit us as it was!

Since so many species of plants, animals and insects live in more than one single habitat, you'll find the main entry for each one in the chapter covering what experts generally agree is its main habitat, with its full description, illustration and any interesting observations. At the end of each chapter are lists of other key species found in that habitat cross-referenced to their main entry elsewhere in the book.

I've given identification details for the view you are likely to get. Birds are easiest to see when they are sitting or standing, so the size given is from beak to tip of tail. In the case of large birds you are most likely to spot in flight I have added wingspan.

Unless otherwise stated, all birds are resident. The time of arrival and departure of migrants will vary slightly from season to season depending on weather conditions – some summer visitors may remain here until November when the climate is favourable. Occasionally, freak weather conditions will blow what we consider to be rare or unusual birds off course and they appear here 'out of season', to the delight of keen 'birders'. Nest and egg details are given when a bird breeds in the British Isles and similar birds and variations are described when appropriate.

OPPOSITE The Brecon Beacons with the Black Mountains looming in the background, South Wales.

Coasts and islands

The British Isles are surrounded by approximately 10,000 miles of coastline, if you include the little offshore islands. Unlike the rest of the Great British landscape, every inch of which has been formed or altered to some extent by man's farming activities, our coastline is the only feature to have been shaped mainly by natural agents – the wind, the waves and the weather.

The maritime environment

There's something basic about the edge of the land that tugs at the heart of every member of the British Isles, though in some this instinct might be buried more deeply than in others. Wherever you stand in Great Britain you are never more than 70 miles from the coast, and our climate is greatly affected by our proximity to the sea. We all joke about our rotten weather, but think how much worse it should be. Our islands sit on roughly the same latitude as Newfoundland, so by rights we ought to share their same long, cold, snowy winters and cool, dull summers. The reason we don't is the Gulf Stream, a 'river' of warm water that starts out on the coast of Mexico and works its way across the Atlantic, then runs up our west coasts from Cornwall via southern Ireland to the west of Scotland, acting like a central-heating system.

The sea also gives us the regular rain that keeps Britain green and is why Ireland is known as the Emerald Isle. Since our prevailing wind comes from the south-west, warm(ish) air reaches us after passing over 3000 miles of open ocean, picking up humidity *en route*. A lot of this drops out of the air as rain where it first strikes landfall, which is why Cornwall is warm and moist, while over on the other side of the country East Anglia has our lowest rainfall. In fact, the climate changes quite considerably as you move round the coast of Britain, from the lush, subtropical Isles of Scilly and the surfing beaches of Cornwall, to the storm-tossed islands of Shetland and Orkney, off the north coast of Scotland, which are so cold and windswept that few trees (if any) can grow there.

But nowhere is the effect of our maritime climate so pronounced as right round the coastline itself, and for a couple of miles inland. This is where winter gales are strongest, and summer sunlight is brightest, partly since coasts lack the atmospheric pollution created inland by traffic fumes and industry, and partly because the light is reflected back off the sea – hence the high-factor suntan lotion you need on the beach. The sea also has a big stabilizing effect on seasonal temperature fluctuations along the coast, because it soaks up the sun's heat in summer and then lets it out slowly again in winter – just like a huge radiator.

Our diverse coastal geography – from cliffs to sandy beaches, salt marshes, rock pools and shingle – provides a unique range of specialist habitats for wildlife. But it's no easy ride. Coastal wildlife must be able to tolerate wind, salt spray and exposure, and for animals and plants that live right on the beach itself, there are two tides a day bringing fast,

sweeping changes of conditions. For wildlife prepared to stick at it, the reward of coastal living is the presence of good food supplies – coastal birdlife and mammals have accessible fish stocks, and smaller life forms enjoy the variety of crustaceans, marine worms and abundant saltwater plant life.

Rocky coastlines and islands

As the weather warmed up and the land thawed out after the last ice age around 10,000 years ago, the British Isles were slowly restocked with plants and animals that reached us from the Continent. But as the glaciers melted, the sea levels rose and finally cut us off, roughly 8000 years ago. Whatever wildlife had arrived while we were still linked by a land bridge largely stayed, but from then on it was much harder for new species to reach Britain, which is why Europe boasts a number of plants and mammals that aren't native here. It's also why Ireland – which was cut off from England sooner than England was separated from France – doesn't have snakes. They didn't have time to slither that far before Ireland became an island. Ireland also lacks our moles, weasels and several species of rodent.

At the same time as mainland Britain was being detached from Europe, hundreds of small offshore islands were being

created all round our new coastline – they are the tips of long-lost mountain peaks, cut off by rising sea levels. Meanwhile, the entire coast began to disintegrate and cliffs were being formed – a result of thousands of years of battering from the wind and waves, which eroded mountains and subsequently caused landslips and rock falls, exposing flat, rocky cliff faces studded with ledges. The coasts of mainland Britain and its many smaller offshore islands are well stocked with cliffs and erosion is still happening. It can literally change the shape of the coastal landscape overnight.

The famous Undercliff on the Isle of Wight was created by a huge rock fall in early Victorian times, and something similar happened at Axmouth, Devon, in 1839 – what's left in both cases are very sheltered mini-microclimates, which have

PREVIOUS PAGES Aerial view of the white cliffs at Beachy Head, East Sussex (main picture), and marram grass (small picture).
BELOW LEFT Blakeney Point, Norfolk. A network of marshy creeks meet at Blakeney Point, a vast spit of shingle and sand dunes, with salt marshes and mud flats on the landward side. It is a superb natural wildlife sanctuary.
BELOW CENTRE Doulus Bay, at Valentia Island, off south-west Ireland.
BELOW RIGHT Ammonite fossils eroded by the sea on the beach at Lyme Regis, Dorset, part of our Heritage Coast.

since been colonized by semi-tropical species, quite different from what's found in surrounding areas. Rock falls at cliffs along Dorset's Heritage Coast and on the Isle of Wight are well known for exposing fossils, and even dinosaur skeletons, revealing part of Britain's natural historic past. Rock falls plus regular erosion are what keep the White Cliffs of Dover pure white. Being made of soft, porous chalk, the exposed vertical cliff face slowly turns a dirty grey owing to millions of tiny algae, but the regular scouring action of wind and waves grinds away the 'dirty' outer layer, exposing clean chalk underneath – the downside is that the cliffs are being eaten away at a rate of about 3 feet each year.

Sandy beaches and dune systems

Sand is simply rock that has been pummelled to powder by the action of many millions of years' worth of weather and wave action, and then swept up by the sea and deposited by the tides on a gently shelving stretch of coast to make a beach. As any yachtsman knows, sand banks are constantly shifting, and any change in the sea currents can alter the way

sand is deposited or removed from beaches. Councils may spend a fortune putting in groynes to preserve sandy beaches for tourists, and conservation organizations do the same to save sandy spits, such as Spurn Point in Yorkshire and East Head in Sussex, but sand is meant to shift and changes made to one part of the coast often have an effect further along. Although sandy beaches are glorious for holidaymakers, they can be less good for wildlife, as they can be rather barren compared to other types of coastline. However, depending on sediment particle grade, some sandy beaches are incredibly rich in organic material, supporting an equally rich infauna.

Dunes are a bit different; they create a rolling, desert-like landscape that can extend well back from the high-tide mark, and though they look dramatic to us, they support a distinctly limited range of species. Sand dunes form on an exposed, windy beach with fine sand, in very much the same way as they do in a desert. Starting at the high-water mark, where the sand stays relatively dry, a strong onshore wind whips up loose sand so it runs along the beach and piles up round any little obstacles from pebbles upwards, forming mounds. More sand blows along and adds to existing mounds, but some goes over the top and lands on the leeward side, where it's sheltered, so small dunes grow slowly bigger, and bigger dunes slowly 'march' away from the shore and take over adjacent land.

The constantly shifting sand makes it very difficult for coastal plants to get a grip, which is why marram grass is often deliberately planted to stabilize dunes. The unexciting, tough, wiry tussocks hide a secret weapon – a vast underground network of fine, fibrous roots that mesh together and lock the sand in place. And it works – as long as very high tides don't undermine the sand and expose unprotected grains to the wind, allowing erosion to start up again. Burrowing rabbits, scrabbling dogs or children digging with their buckets and spades – anything that makes a gap in the fragile marram network – can do the same thing.

But if marram or any of the other very few dune colonizers can get a hold, decomposing plant remains build up small stocks of organic matter in the sand that allow further plants to move in, and pave the way for more in turn. It all depends on getting the ball rolling, which is why you'll often find areas of sand dunes cordoned off where new planting has taken place.

Pebble shores and shingle spits

Stony beaches may look a lot more solid than dunes, but they are still not very stable. Shingle is easily shifted around by currents, much like sand banks, and even large pebbles are tossed right up the shore on stormy winter nights, so that the next morning they are banked up along the top of the beach or all over the road. Waves slowly 'grade' pebbles, leaving the biggest at the top of the beach and the smallest close to the water, and if the coastal currents mean waves strike a pebble beach at an angle instead of head-on, the force of the water slowly sorts the pebbles in order of size right along its length. This is what's happened at Chesil Beach, in Dorset, where one end is cobbles and the other is shingle. The shingle has shifted to form a natural lagoon called the Fleet, which makes a sheltered haven for seabirds and houses Britain's only swannery, at Abbotsbury. It's an amazing sight – hundreds of semi-domesticated mute swans living in a great flock; usually they are far too aggressive to tolerate such close neighbours.

The constant shifting of stony beaches makes it hard for plants to survive. A wide, pebbly beach may accommodate a few interesting species, such as the yellow-horned poppy and sea kale, both of which grow well above the high-tide mark, where they stand a chance of getting their roots safely embedded. Sea beet, though not spectacular, is a curiosity if only because it's the ancestor of the spinach and beetroot we grow in our gardens; interestingly, both these vegetables can still tolerate a certain amount of salt in their soil.

Also to watch out for on stony beaches are ground-nesting birds such as terns and ringed plovers. Rather than make nests they simply deposit their perfectly camouflaged eggs on the ground, where they look just like the surrounding pebbles. Colonies are often roped off as they can be easily disturbed by walkers or dogs, so if you visit stony coasts, do please respect temporarily unavailable areas during the breeding season.

OPPOSITE Chesil Beach, Dorset, a linear shingle beach stretching from Bridport to the Isle of Portland and sheltering the Fleet lagoon.

BELOW The coast around Lulworth Cove, Dorset, on the Jurassic Coast, is remarkable for its folded, crumpled rocks and natural arches.

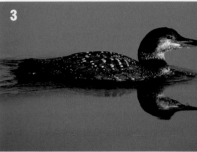

1 Red-throated diver
Gavia stellata

This is our smallest and most common diver, although it is still relatively scarce. It is usually seen on the water; look for a long, low, lean diving bird, with uptilted head and slender beak (unlike other divers), very dark grey-brown back and wings and a dove-grey neck and head. The white of the breast below the bright red throat patch extends across the belly. In the breeding season, males 'walk on water', racing side by side, like penguins, often making goose-like honks to ward off rivals in territorial displays.

HABITAT Remote places, usually seen feeding round the north coast of Scotland, Orkney and the Shetland Islands, or near its nest sites round small lochs or moorland pools in those areas. In winter it occurs off all shores of Britain and Ireland.

SIZE 55–70cm (22–28in)

EGGS 1–2, dark beige with darker brown speckles

NEST Flattish heap of vegetation on the ground near water.

FOOD Mainly fish, some crustaceans and insects.

SIMILAR TO Other divers, but also similar to cormorants and grebes when swimming.

VARIATIONS In winter, adults lack the red throat patch and have dark, white-speckled backs (the only divers that do). The dark eyes are separated from the dark top of the head by white areas on the rest of the head; the neck is also white.

2 Black-throated diver
Gavia arctica

The black-throated diver is a rare bird with a typical long, low, lean diver shape and a sturdy, dagger-like beak held level with the water when swimming. Look for a black-and-white-chequered upper back, black-and-white-speckled sides/folded wings, a dove-grey head and back of neck with bright red eyes, and a black throat patch above the white breast patch. It makes croaking and wailing calls in the breeding season. The males rush over the water with wings angled out sideways and necks arched back to make territorial displays.

HABITAT Summer: breeds in larger Scottish lochs. Winter: round many coastlines in Britain and some in Ireland.

SIZE 58–72cm (23–29in)

EGGS 1–2, greenish brown with blackish speckles

NEST Flattish heap of vegetation on the ground near water.

FOOD Mainly fish, some crustaceans and insects.

SIMILAR TO Other divers, but also cormorants and grebes when swimming. The black-throated diver usually has a prominent white thigh patch visible just above the water line, near the rear of the body (not seen in either red-throated or great northern divers).

VARIATIONS The black-and-white markings on the back and the black throat are lost in winter, when the bird looks dark grey above, contrasting with white on the lower 'cheeks', foreneck and most of the underparts.

3 Great northern diver
Gavia immer

This is our largest diver, seen in Britain and Ireland mostly in winter. Look for a big head with a steep forehead and flat crown, a thick neck and a massive, dagger-like beak. In winter, the dark crown (extending just below the eye) contrasts with the prominent pale eye ring and there is a hint of a dark collar at the base of the neck with a white indentation above.

HABITAT Most occur in the British Isles on coastal waters, with just a few at inland lakes and reservoirs.

SIZE 70–90cm (28–36in)

FOOD Mainly fish, some crabs and marine molluscs.

SIMILAR TO Other divers, cormorant.

VARIATIONS In summer, the head and neck are black, apart from a collar formed from narrow, vertical white stripes on the lower neck, with a tiny crescent of white stripes above it; fine black-and-white stripes lead into the chequered pattern of black and white on the bird's back.

4 Red-necked grebe
Podiceps grisegena

A very scarce winter visitor, this diving bird is difficult to identify as it swims some distance offshore and bobs out of sight between waves. It makes a long, low, lean shape – similar to but smaller than the great crested grebe – with a large, more wedge-shaped or rounded head. The slightly shorter beak is dark but with a yellow base. The bird's back and back of neck are dirty grey, the eyes are dark brown and the 'cheeks' are white. The black cap extends to eye-level.

HABITAT Mainly seen in eastern and southern coastal waters, but very occasionally on large, reedy lakes and reservoirs.

SIZE 40–50cm (16–20in)

FOOD Fish.

SIMILAR TO Slavonian grebe and great crested grebe (which is sometimes on estuaries and sheltered coastlines in winter).

VARIATIONS Summer plumage is sometimes seen on birds arriving in early autumn, or shortly before returning in spring. They look the same as in winter but with a bright chestnut-red neck and breast.

5 Slavonian grebe
Podiceps auritus

This is a scarce, predominantly winter visitor that is hard to see, as it usually swims too far offshore for us to get a good look, even with binoculars, especially when it's bobbing among the waves. It is more like a little grebe than a great crested grebe in shape, though it's almost half as big again as the little grebe. Given a good view, you may see the blackish back, wings, back of neck and upper half of head, the bright red eyes, a white face and front of neck, and broad white flanks speckled faintly with grey, with clear-cut dividing lines between black and white areas.

HABITAT October–March: round the more sheltered coasts of the British Isles, including large estuaries; also in inland lakes and reservoirs. Summer: a few breed in far north-eastern Scottish lochs.

SIZE 31–38cm (12–15in)

EGGS 3–5, white

NEST Pile of floating water weeds.

FOOD Fish and mainly insects in the breeding season.

SIMILAR TO Red-necked grebe and black-necked grebe; the latter is very similar in winter plumage but is smaller and dumpier, with a shorter neck.

VARIATIONS Summer plumage (sometimes seen in early autumn or late spring) is very striking, with a bright chestnut-red neck, breast and flanks, black wings and a black head with bright yellow ear-tufts extending from the bright red eyes up to the back of the head.

6 Black-necked grebe
Podiceps nigricollis

This scarce breeding bird, passage migrant and winter visitor has the dumpy, rounded shape of the little grebe but has black and grey colouring that is very similar to that of the Slavonian grebe. However, in the black-necked grebe the edges of the black and white areas are less clear-cut than in the Slavonian grebe, there is less white on the face, the black cap extends below eye-level and the 'cheeks' are dusky. The black-necked grebe also has a more angular, high-peaked forehead than the Slavonian grebe, and its beak turns slightly upwards towards the tip, creating a rather quizzical expression.

HABITAT Winter: mostly along southern coasts, especially in sheltered inlets and estuaries as well as large inland lakes and reservoirs. Summer: occasionally breeds at a few lakes in Scotland and England.

SIZE 28–34cm (11–13in)

EGGS 3–4, white

NEST Pile of water weeds on banks or floating on water.

FOOD Fish.

SIMILAR TO Red-necked grebe and Slavonian grebe in winter.

VARIATIONS Adults in summer plumage are black with bright chestnut-red on the flanks, sometimes extending to the neck, and bright gold and yellow ear-tufts just behind the eyes.

How to spot a diver

Swimming divers resemble grebes or cormorants from a distance, especially at sea when the water is rough and visibility poor. Divers spend a lot of time underwater – they often stay under for far longer than they are seen floating on top, and when they dive they often reappear some distance away. The great northern diver, the largest species, is mostly seen in winter in Britain, where it is usually silent. A diver on a large Scottish loch in summer is most likely to be a black-throated diver. The red-throated diver (above), which is smaller and more slender than the others, is more likely to be seen at small lochs or pools or feeding in the sea, swimming with uptilted head and beak. Divers slip neatly under the water when they dive, without curving dolphin-like into the water like a shag, or jumping out of the water to arch in like a grebe. They have short tails compared to a swimming cormorant, and shorter, thicker necks than grebes. Territorial displays of male red-throated and black-throated divers are very different; the great northern does not nest in Britain, so you will not see it performing. Divers may sometimes be seen in small groups migrating eastwards round the south coast of England in May. Make sure you don't disturb these scarce birds at their breeding sites – they will desert their nest easily, leaving eggs vulnerable to predators.

7 Manx shearwater
Puffinus puffinus

This is a summer visitor, normally seen only on the wing over the sea. Look for a black-and-white bird, shaped like a plus sign, flying with a few stiff wing-beats followed by a long glide, usually close to the surface of the sea. Birds appear to glint as they characteristically tilt from one side to another in flight, showing alternate black and white sides. Because of its inaccessibility, you usually need a special boat trip to see this bird.

HABITAT Summer: breeds on offshore islands in the Western Isles, especially on Rhum, and a few other islands in north-western and far northern Scotland, as well as off west Wales and Ireland. However, spends most of its time from spring to autumn far out at sea round the north and west coasts of Britain. Winter: ranges widely across North-west Atlantic, but most end up off South America.

SIZE 35cm (14in)

EGGS 1, white

NEST In colonies, using old rabbit burrows or burrows they make for themselves on offshore islands, but adult birds return only at night after gathering in large, floating 'rafts' at sea, to avoid predatory birds, especially large gulls.

FOOD Small fish, squid and other marine animals.

8 Gannet
Morus bassanus

If seen in flight from a distance, adults of this very large, distinctive seabird look entirely sparkling

white with black wing-tips. Closer up, you can see the yellowish wash on the head and back of the neck and the reptilian-looking eyes and beak. To feed, gannets fold their wings and make spectacular, steep, plunging dives into the water from great heights (typically 9m/30ft), which can carry them to depths of up to 30m (100ft) at speeds of around 100km (70 miles) per hour or more. On shore, the shape is like a resting cormorant's, but without the outstretched wings.

HABITAT Spring–autumn: all round the coast, but breeds on islands on cliffs, most notably St Kilda, Bass Rock and Hermaness, Shetland. Many winter in the British Isles.

SIZE 1m (3ft); wingspan 1.7–1.9m (5½–6¼ft)

EGGS 1, translucent pale blue, soon turning white

NEST Big pile of seaweed, in colonies on rocky islands or cliffs round the mainland.

FOOD Fish.

SIMILAR TO Gulls; dark juveniles resemble cormorants.

VARIATIONS Juveniles take up to 4 years to mature, during which time they change from dark grey to a dirty brown-grey to piebald, then finally patchy white with a yellow-tinged head.

9 Cormorant
Phalacrocorax carbo

This common bird, with a black, white and yellow face, may be seen singly or in large or small groups. It stands more or less upright on rocks or posts close to the shore, often with wings held half-open to dry, which gives it a rather prehistoric appearance. On the water, the cormorant looks long, low and lean, and mostly slides under the water cleanly when diving for fish. It is quite pterodactyl-like in flight, but groups travel in rather orderly,

V-shaped skeins – not unlike polite geese. In close-up, you can see the white 'cheeks' behind the yellow face, extending into a long, yellow beak, hooked at the tip. Around the eyes and beak there is an area of bare skin, without feathers. The long, narrow, streamlined head is little wider than its neck, giving it a snake-like look.

HABITAT Summer: mainly coasts and estuaries around the British Isles, but also inland, on lakes and rivers. Winter: usually seen inland.

SIZE 1m (3ft); wingspan 1.3–1.5m (4¼–5ft)

EGGS 3–4, pale blue or green

NEST Coastal breeders nest on cliff edges or among rocks on stacks. Inland breeders build their nests in trees close to fish-rich lakes or near rivers.

FOOD Fish (including eels).

SIMILAR TO Shag, which is smaller with no white 'cheeks' or yellow face (though it has thin yellow 'lips' outlining the base of the beak) and at breeding time has a

mohican-like crest on top of its head and glistening green plumage. Bare patches around the eyes and beak confirm it is a cormorant – the shag has feathers there. The shag also lacks the white thigh patch of the cormorant in the breeding season.

VARIATIONS In breeding plumage, the head, underparts and tail are mainly glossy blue-black or bluish purple (with a tinge of green) and there is a distinctive white patch on each thigh. The wings have a bronzy gloss and the feathers have black edges. Juveniles are the same shape as adults but a dirty brown colour with paler underparts.

10 Shag
Phalacrocorax aristotelis
Once also known as the green cormorant, this common coastal bird stands upright on land, often on rocks or posts with wings held half-open to dry, but looks long, low and lean when swimming, and half-jumps out of the water to dive down for fish, like a porpoise. It flies low, close to the surface of the sea, alone or in twos or threes, and tends to be far more solitary than the cormorant.
HABITAT Rocky coasts, islands, bays and tidal inlets, mostly in the north, north-west and south-west of Britain and Ireland, but not often seen in East Anglia or the south-east. May venture slightly inland during very severe weather, but it is rare in fresh water.
SIZE 72cm (29in)
EGGS 3, pale blue covered with whitish chalky deposit
NEST Pile of seaweed on wide ledges on rocky cliffs, just inside caves, or sometimes among big boulders at the base of a beach.
FOOD Fish.
SIMILAR TO Cormorant.
VARIATIONS Juvenile is the same shape as the adult, but a dirty oily-brown colour. Adult shags in the breeding season have a yellow 'gape' at the base of the beak, a curly, forward-pointing crest on top of the head, and the plumage has an oily-green sheen (like petrol floating on water).

11 Storm petrel
Hydrobates pelagicus
The storm petrel is our smallest seabird and is normally seen only on the wing over the sea. Look for a black bird with a body about the size of a sparrow's but with wings about twice as long, with a white rump and narrow white line up the central underside of each wing. It glides briefly, like a bat, close to the sea surface and dabbles its feet in the water or dips its beak in the water to feed. This petrel is most likely to be seen in stormy conditions, often criss-crossing the wake of ships.
HABITAT Usually out at sea, mainly off north and west coasts. Nests in colonies on offshore islands in the west and far north of Britain.
SIZE 15cm (6in); wingspan 38cm (15in)
EGGS 1, white
NEST In old rabbit burrows and crevices in stone walls or between boulders; returns only at night.
FOOD Small fish, plankton, small squid, crustaceans, food refuse from ships.
SIMILAR TO House martin.

12 Fulmar
Fulmarus glacialis
The fulmar is one of our most long-lived birds, capable of turning 50, and some are thought to be even older. A common seabird, it looks like a short, fat seagull at first glance but has virtually no neck – the head usually seems to sit straight on the shoulders. It spends most of its time at sea in flocks, floating on water bobbing over waves like a cork, or following fishing boats, but it is most easily seen on and around cliffs during the nesting season. In close-up, look for the short, fat, bottle-shaped beak in grey and pale yellow – given a very good view, you can see raised nostrils above a hooked upper beak; the upper and lower parts of the beak fit together like a pair of stacked teaspoons. In flight, look for the chunky body, straight, stiff wings and lack of neck. The flight style of fulmars is distinctive: they glide on very stiff wings held straight out (not kinked like gulls'), occasionally making a burst of shallow, stiff, fast wing-beats, then gliding again. Juveniles are rarely seen after leaving the nest as they spend several years at sea. Fulmars have a novel method of self-defence, so if visiting fulmar colonies, beware of their habit of regurgitating foul-smelling stomach contents over intruders: the smell lingers for ages.
HABITAT Breeds around all British and Irish coasts where there are suitable cliffs; rarely seen inland.
SIZE 50cm (20in)
EGGS 1, white
NEST On rocky ledges on cliffs, or occasionally on the ground, among grass, dunes or rocks.
FOOD Small fish, crustaceans, carrion, refuse from fishing boats.
SIMILAR TO Most similar-sized gulls, but the lack of neck, chunky shape and short, fat beak distinguish the fulmar.

Watching seabirds
Special bird-watching boat trips are the best way to see ocean-going birds such as petrels, shearwaters, skuas and gannets, and they are also the best way to get a good view of nesting gull or puffin colonies, which are usually sited on steep, inaccessible cliffs. (Note that the breeding season in early summer is the best time to see seabird colonies – birds are usually away at sea for the rest of the year.) Check out details of boat trips via the internet before visiting, especially if you have a long way to travel, and book early to avoid disappointment.

13 Mediterranean gull
Larus melanocephalus

This very scarce gull is often seen in a flock of black-headed gulls, from which it is distinguishable only with difficulty. In summer, it is virtually identical to a black-headed gull but lacks the black tips to the primary feathers along the trailing edges of the wing-tips: also, the summer hood of a Mediterranean gull is jet-black and extends right to the back of the head, while the partial hood of the black-headed gull is dark chocolate-brown. In winter, both gulls lose their dark heads and show just dark smudges around the eyes, but the red beak of the Mediterranean gull turns dark while that of the black-headed gull becomes brighter red. Also, the wings of the adult Mediterranean gull remain entirely white in winter, while the ends of the wing-tip feathers of the black-headed gull remain black.
HABITAT Mainly round the coast of east and southern England, with a few in Scotland, Wales and Ireland. Breeds mainly around lagoons or on marshes on or near the coast; some nest in grassy fields near inland lakes or in wetlands.
SIZE 38cm (15in)
EGGS 3, pale cream or buff with darker markings
NEST Shallow scrape lined with grass and feathers, on bare ground or among vegetation.
FOOD Fish, shellfish, scraps.

14 Black-headed gull
Larus ridibundus

In summer, this very common, medium-sized gull is easily identified by the neat, dark chocolate-brown hood over the front of the head (which often looks black from a distance). The body is white and the wings are very pale grey, with a distinctive white flash along the leading edges of the wing-tips, and black tips to the primary feathers along the trailing edges. The legs are deep blackish red, as is the beak. Usually seen in flocks, black-headed gulls follow fishing boats, swoop down into the garden for scraps, follow the plough in farmland for worms and visit rubbish dumps and outdoor cafés in search of food.
HABITAT All round the British coast, but equally common inland on lakes, reservoirs, farmland and pastures as well as in urban areas. Nests both inland and on coasts.
SIZE 35cm (14in)
EGGS 2–3, blotchy, colour variable
NEST Heap of vegetation on the ground, sometimes in water.
FOOD Fish, food scraps, crabs, worms, insects.
SIMILAR TO Mediterranean gull.
VARIATIONS In winter, adults lose their dark hood but retain a smudgy dark marking behind and above each eye. Juveniles have mottled ginger-brown colouring on the wings, head and breast until they moult at the end of summer, and a dull, pale pinkish beak and legs; as they mature, the brown area gradually diminishes at the same time as the brighter red beak and leg colour develops.

15 Common gull
Larus canus

Despite its name, the common gull is actually not the most common British gull. It looks like a herring gull but is smaller (closer to the black-headed gull in size) and more elegant, with a white head and body and darker, more blue-grey wings than black-headed gulls. If viewing a standing bird at close quarters, you can see black wing-tips with a row of white spots down them, also greenish yellow legs and matching beak, and black eyes, giving it a gentle expression. Location and feeding habits are a useful identification aid: common gulls breed overwhelmingly in the north of England and especially Scotland, with small numbers in Ireland and very few in southern England and Wales. They are more widespread in winter, as many Continental birds overwinter here.
HABITAT Winter: sheltered coasts, coves and creeks, coastal moorlands, fields and sports grounds. Spring: breeds on northern coasts and moorlands.
SIZE 40cm (16in)
EGGS 3, greenish brown, blotchy
NEST Mound of vegetation or seaweed, sited on the ground among low vegetation or sometimes on cliff-tops or roofs.
FOOD Worms, birds' eggs, insects, fish, rubbish-tip scraps.
SIMILAR TO Herring gull, which is bigger and more aggressive-looking, but the herring gull's bright yellow beak (with a red spot near the tip), cold, pale yellow eyes and pale pink legs are the most obvious differences.
VARIATIONS In winter, adults have fine, dusky streaks on the head, running from beak to neck. Juveniles are brown-mottled all over, like those of most gulls, and start changing to adult plumage from the head downwards, so you may see strangely piebald immature birds with a paler head and shoulders with fine brown streaks all over, and part-grey/part-brown, mottled wings. Juveniles have dull pinkish legs and a matching beak with a blackish tip, quite different from that of adult birds.

16

16 Herring gull
Larus argentatus

Large and common, the herring
gull has a white head, neck and
body and a very pale grey back and
wings with black tips, dotted with
white. Given a good view, you can
also see bright pink legs, a rather
fierce facial expression, pale
lemon-yellow eyes surrounded by
a narrow yellow or orange ring,
and a bright yellow beak with a red
dot near the tip. Birds can be quite
bold, especially in summer,
approaching fairly close to people.
They will follow fishing boats and
can become pests at outdoor cafés
– in winter, they will swoop down
into gardens after scraps.
HABITAT Coast, also inland
reservoirs, farmland and rubbish
dumps all year round; many move

inland in winter. Also in towns and
cities, especially near the sea.
SIZE 55cm (22in)
EGGS 3, creamy green with grey and
brown blotches
NEST Large mound of vegetation
or seaweed on rocky ledges,
sometimes on the ground in
moorland or on rooftops.
FOOD Fish, eggs and young of other
birds, small mammals, carrion,
food refuse, scraps.
SIMILAR TO Common gull, lesser
black-backed gull.
VARIATIONS In winter, an adult gull's
back turns a shade darker than
usual. The head and neck are
heavily streaked with grey.
Juveniles are a uniform dappled
brown, turning paler with maturity.

17 Lesser black-backed gull
Larus fuscus

The lesser black-backed gull is a
common gull with a white head,
neck, breast and underparts, yellow
legs and eyes, and a yellow beak
with a red spot at the tip. The
wings are dark grey with black
wing-tips; there is a row of white
spots along the tips of the wings.
HABITAT Coast, lakes and reservoirs,
rubbish tips, towns and cities.
Breeds along coasts, among sand

dunes, on shingle islands and on
upland moors inland.
SIZE 50cm (20in)
EGGS 3, brown, mottled
NEST Large mound of vegetation or
seaweed, on the ground, often near
long, dense vegetation.
FOOD Fish, eggs and young of other
birds, small mammals, carrion,
food refuse, scraps.
SIMILAR TO Herring gull, which has
pink legs and pale grey wings; the
lesser black-backed gull has yellow
legs and dark grey wings.
VARIATIONS Juveniles are a mottled
dirty brown, similar to juvenile
herring gulls.

18 Great black-backed gull
Larus marinus

This is the largest gull in the world,
as big as a goose, with an
aggressive attitude and a 'bad-
tempered' expression. In flight, it is
nearly twice the size of the black-
headed gull and it flies slowly and
deliberately. The entire body is
white, apart from the long black
wings, which have small white tips.
Look also for the heavy, strongly
hooked, bright yellow beak with a
red spot at the tip and pink legs.
Unlike other gulls, it quite often
nests solitarily or in small groups
rather than in big colonies.
HABITAT Rugged coasts, cliff-tops,
harbours, inlets and following big

18

fishing boats. Sometimes seen
further inland on rubbish dumps.
SIZE 65cm (26in)
EGGS 2–3, buff with brown and
grey blotches
NEST Large mound of vegetation or
seaweed, on islands, rocky cliffs
and stacks. Some on moorland.
FOOD Fish, other birds and eggs,
carrion, refuse, small mammals.
VARIATIONS Juveniles are mottled
dirty brown all over, very similar
to young herring gulls but bigger
and turn darker as they mature
(herring gulls turn lighter).

Identifying gulls

Most gulls look superficially
similar; when trying to identify
the different species, always look
for the beak and leg colours first,
then compare size with an 'easy'
gull you know well – the black-
headed gull (small) or herring gull
(large), for instance – and work
your way through likely candidates
from the commonest first, using
a process of elimination. A good
view of a standing bird is easiest,
but with practice it's possible to
identify a few of the most
common species in flight as they
are often moving slowly and close
to you. Juvenile gulls are difficult
to identify, so always look for the
adults in a flock.

17

19 Kittiwake
Rissa tridactyla

Named after its distinctive call, 'kitti-a-waaake', this is a pigeon-sized gull in sparkling white, with black legs and a dove-grey back and wings. The wing-tips are black and triangular. It has a gentle, dove-like facial expression (compared to larger gulls'), with round black eyes; the relatively slender yellow beak is slightly down-curved at the tip. At rest, the head looks to be one size too big for the body, but in flight this isn't noticeable. A superb flier, it balances effortlessly on wind currents and copes well with gusty conditions and gales, when it rises and falls in long arcs.
HABITAT Spring–summer: sea cliffs and offshore close to the coast. Winter: far out at sea.
SIZE 40cm (16in)
EGGS 2, pale grey blotched brown and darker grey
NEST In large, noisy, active colonies on rocky ledges up cliffs or sometimes on lofty bridges or ledges of buildings; the nest itself is just a little seaweed, mud and vegetation perched on the ledge.
FOOD Fishes at sea and follows fishing boats for scraps.
SIMILAR TO Several other gulls, but the kittiwake is identified by its black legs, pure black wing-tips (without white spots), its call and lack of scavenging habits.
VARIATIONS Juvenile kittiwakes have a bold black 'W' pattern on the wings, a white body with a black collar and small black 'ear-blotches' on the head.

20 Great skua
Stercorarius skua

A summer visitor, sometimes nicknamed the 'bonxie', the great skua is a big, bulky, herring-gull-sized bird, all-over dirty brown with a large white flash near the outer edge of each wing when seen in flight. It is a predatory seabird, notorious for harassing or killing smaller birds near seabird breeding colonies on cliffs. The great skua also attacks other birds, including ducks, gulls, auks and even much larger gannets, which are forced to give up food they are carrying in their crops or are killed.
HABITAT Summer: breeds on northern Scottish islands, especially Orkney and Shetland, on remote moors near the coast and on rocky islands. Spring and autumn: round all British and Irish coasts. Winter: most adults winter in the Bay of Biscay, off the Atlantic coast of Iberia and western Mediterranean; immatures often travel as far as the Atlantic coast off West Africa or even South and North America.
SIZE 55cm (22in)
EGGS 2, dark speckled
NEST Hollow in the ground.
FOOD Fish disgorged by chased seabirds, as well as seabirds themselves and their eggs.
SIMILAR TO Arctic skua, which is smaller and more elegant and usually has a white underside – the great skua is all brown, apart from large white wing-flashes.

21 Arctic skua
Stercorarius parasiticus

This is a medium-sized, dark brown, gull-like seabird that is a summer visitor, roughly halfway in size between a herring gull and a black-headed gull, usually with white underparts (brown in some) and a small, whitish flash towards the wing-tips. Seen in close-up, the adult Arctic skua has a 'spike' that projects backwards from the centre of the tail. This bird is usually seen cruising steadily over the sea, or close to shore chasing puffins, kittiwakes and terns, with aerobatic twisting-and-turning manoeuvres, forcing them to drop their load of fish, which is then snapped up by the skua. The birds will dive-bomb walkers who approach their nests and young.
HABITAT April–October: breeds in colonies along far northern coasts of Scotland and its offshore islands, particularly Shetland and Fair Isle; around all British and Irish coasts on spring and autumn migration. Winter: South Africa and elsewhere.
SIZE 45cm (17½in)
EGGS 2, brownish
NEST Shallow hollow in the ground.
FOOD Fish.
SIMILAR TO Great skua, which is larger, lacks white on the body and attacks larger prey.
VARIATIONS Juveniles are lighter brown and have only minimal tail points.

22 Sandwich tern
Sterna sandvicensis

This is Britain's largest tern. It is mainly white, except for a large black cap that forms a shaggy-spiky black crest at the back of the head, grey wings with faint blackish-smudged wing-tips, black legs and a long spike of a black beak with a tiny yellow tip.
HABITAT April–September/October: along most of the British coastline, including lagoons. Winter: West Africa or South Africa.
SIZE 38cm (15in)
EGGS 1–2, pale grey speckled black and brown
NEST On the ground, in sand.
FOOD Sand eels and small fish.

Rocky coasts

Rocky cliffs provide some of our most spectacular coastal scenery, much of which is easily accessed by footpaths. The Cornish coastal footpath and the Heritage Coast of Dorset have particularly stunning views.

A lot of the more rugged cliffs, especially those around north Cornwall and the north and west of Scotland and its offshore islands, provide safe fortresses for seabirds. Where there are no natural predators apart from skuas and large gulls, vast numbers can often build up, leaving the rocks white with guano. On narrow ledges, crowded with birds, rounded eggs could easily roll off and get

A colony of seabirds – guillemots and kittiwakes – nesting on Staple Island, one of the Farne Islands, off the coast of Northumberland.

smashed. Some seabird species lay eggs that are quite elongated – with one wide end and one narrow end – so instead of rolling away in any direction, which might take them over the edge, they can only go round in a circle.

The wildlife along the top of cliffs is also well worth looking at; you'll see gulls wheeling around on the thermals, and in spring and autumn cliff-tops can be good places to spot rare birds blown off course by strong winds. Also, a wealth of wildflowers and the butterflies that rely on them can be

seen only a few feet back from the edge. Cliffs can crumble, so don't get too close.

On low-lying rocky shores it's worth looking for rock pools. They form when large slabs of rock have been weathered away in places to make natural basins, although sometimes they can be found on sandy shores where seams of rocky strata push through and weather unevenly so the hollows fill with water. Half the fun of a seaside holiday when I was a lad was simply catching crabs in rock pools, but they are also fascinating for more ambitious wildlife spotters. They house a huge variety of small fish, seaweeds, shrimps and crabs, and the deeper rock pools sometimes contain creatures that normally live way out to sea and which you'd usually need scuba-diving gear to see. Rock pools are like self-sustaining aquariums: each time the tide comes in they are automatically sluiced out and refilled with fresh seawater. The water carries food and oxygen (dissolved from the air by splashing waves), which help keep small creatures in the pools alive. However, each new tide also brings a sudden rush of cold water, after the rock pool has spent a day warming up in the sun, so temperatures vary alarmingly, and salt can concentrate as a heated rock pool evaporates on a sunny day. These extreme conditions mean that only the toughest creatures survive.

As well as looking inside rock pools, examine the rocks surrounding the pools for interesting seaweeds, winkles and limpets. Observant wildflower-spotters may also notice that there's a strict progression of plant life up a rocky shore – from seaweeds, which are exposed only at low tides, right through to salt- and sand-proof flowering plants in the 'splash zone', way up beyond the high-tide mark, which receive only flung spray except at particularly high tides.

23 Common tern
Sterna hirundo

This is the tern most often seen in southern England, either along the coast or inland. It has an orange-red, black-tipped beak, a black cap, red legs and a white body. It also has a dark wedge along the tip of each wing; on a standing bird with folded wings, it looks like a darker tail as the wing-tips are so long. The dark coloration is not so marked when the birds arrive in spring but becomes darker. The common tern often rises slightly in the air before hovering and then diving to catch fish.

HABITAT April–September/October: coasts, offshore islands, also inland at flooded gravel pits, rivers and canals. Winter: West Africa.

SIZE 33cm (13in)

EGGS 2–3, cream or buff with darker mottling

NEST On the ground, preferably on small islands (these are often created artificially in lakes at reserves for protection).

FOOD Mainly small fish.

24 Arctic tern
Sterna paradisaea

This is the tern most likely to be seen in northern Britain. With its bright red beak, black cap and red legs, it looks very like a common tern but the body colour is slightly deeper grey, the wing-tips have only a thin black trailing edge (so a standing bird does not appear to have a blackish tail) and the legs

are considerably shorter than those of the common tern.

HABITAT Spring and autumn: along coasts of Britain and Ireland. Summer: nest in Orkney, Farne Islands, Shetland and on the Irish coast. Winter: around Antarctica; some reach Australia.

SIZE 33cm (13in)

EGGS 2, cream or buff, spotted brown or black

NEST On gravelly or stony beaches.

FOOD Mainly small fish.

25 Little tern
Sterna albifrons

Britain's smallest tern, this scarce and declining summer visitor has a white body and very light grey wings, orange legs, a yellow beak with a tiny black tip, a white forehead and a black eye-stripe leading to a black 'tonsure' on the back of the head.

HABITAT April–September/October: sandy, shingly or pebbly coasts round Britain and Ireland. Winter: West Africa.

SIZE 25cm (10in)

EGGS 2–3, buff with darker speckles

NEST On the ground, in sand or shingle, usually at holiday beaches.

FOOD Mainly small fish.

26 Guillemot
Uria aalge

Present in the British Isles only during the breeding season, this intensely gregarious, penguin-like bird stands tall, thin and upright

on land and forms a long, low, horizontal figure when afloat. Look for a black or dark chocolate-brown head and neck and a white breast and underparts; the wings, upperparts, beak and feet are all black. Guillemots 'fly' underwater in flocks, chasing fish, and on the surface may gang up to encircle a shoal of fish. They nest in large, quarrelsome colonies, often stabbing at neighbouring birds with their beaks as space is so tight, but breeding pairs may preen each other. Within 21 days of hatching, the chick jumps down from its ledge and is met at the bottom by its father. The male and chick then swim out to sea; the father cares for his offspring until it is about 12 weeks old.

HABITAT March–July: on coastal cliffs, especially around Scotland; spends rest of the year out at sea.

SIZE 40cm (16in)

EGGS 1, pale blue, green, reddish, ochre or brown, sometimes with darker speckles and 'scribbling'

NEST On rocky cliff ledges.

FOOD Mainly fish.

SIMILAR TO Razorbill, which has a much thicker, white-striped beak.

VARIATIONS Juveniles look fluffier, with white on the face and chin.

27 Razorbill
Alca torda

Like the guillemot, this seabird is present only in the breeding season and is black and white and penguin-like. However, the razorbill is scarcer and more thickset than the guillemot, with a proportionately thicker neck, and its beak is broader and more flattened, like a penknife blade; a thin white line runs forward from the eye along the top of the beak and there is a white band around its tip. Its call is a throaty 'gurrr'. When the chick is ready to leave its nest at around 18 days old, it jumps down from its ledge and is met by its father, who continues to care for his offspring for a while.

HABITAT April–July: nests in mainly small colonies (less dense than guillemot colonies) on coastal cliffs, especially around Scotland, but is otherwise out at sea.

SIZE 40cm (16in)

EGGS 1, pale grey or buff with dark brown blotches

NEST In nooks and crannies among rocks on cliff ledges or among boulders at foot of cliffs.

FOOD Mainly fish.

SIMILAR TO Guillemot, which has a more pointed, all-black beak.

VARIATIONS Juveniles are similar but appear slightly fluffier, with white on the face and chin.

28 Black guillemot
Cepphus grylle

This seabird is easily distinguished from the guillemot in summer by its entirely jet-black body, a large, conspicuous white flash on each wing, and its bright red legs. Unlike guillemots and razorbills, black guillemots are usually seen singly or in small groups, not colonies. On the water, they look much more slender and elegant than guillemots or razorbills.

HABITAT Rocky coasts and offshore, mostly round the north and west of Scotland (Shetland, Orkney, Western Isles) and western Ireland, but nests at only a very few sites elsewhere in Britain, notably Anglesey and the Isle of Man.

SIZE 30cm (12in)

EGGS 1–2, whitish with dark brown speckles

NEST Between boulders or flotsam on a stony beach or in caves; occasionally it will nest in walls or other structures.

FOOD Fish.

SIMILAR TO Guillemots in summer, but in winter birds can look rather like grebes or divers.

VARIATIONS Winter plumage is off-white with a dark grey, mottled back and a dark tail, but the large white wing-flash is still evident.

29 Little auk
Alle alle

This is an Arctic seabird that visits the British Isles only in autumn and winter, when driven south by very cold conditions or strong, northerly gales. Look for a small, dumpy, starling-sized but puffin-shaped black-and-white bird, with a short, round head and a stubby, finch-like bill. In winter plumage, the back, wings, tail, back of neck and top of head (down to just below the eyes) are charcoal-black, with white underparts. When floating on water or standing on land it looks hunched and has a rather frog-like head.

HABITAT Usually far out at sea, but sometimes closer inland, where birds may be visible from boats or cliff-tops on the Orkney and Shetland Islands, in northern Scotland or north-east England. It has been known for little auks to be blown on to land.

SIZE 20cm (8in)

FOOD Plankton.

Identifying terns

It is reasonably easy to tell gulls and terns apart: terns are smaller and far more elegant – with their long, pointed heads and beaks and their narrow, pointed wings and forked tails, they are more like animated paper darts. They hover, unlike gulls, and they hunt rather like kingfishers, diving into the water and coming up with a small fish. They mostly fish individually, and are not as noisy and aggressive as gulls. Unlike the commoner gulls, they are also summer visitors – you won't see them in winter.

To tell terns apart is more difficult: look at the beak colour first, then the legs. Standing or floating birds are easiest to identify, but a hovering bird also allows a good look, through binoculars. Common terns (below) and Arctic terns are very difficult to tell apart, though location is a big clue.

Terns lay their eggs directly on the ground and the eggs are well camouflaged. That's why tern colonies at popular beaches are roped off during the breeding season – please respect them and don't let dogs loose.

30 Puffin
Fratercula arctica

Probably our most popular and easily recognized seabird, the puffin is black and white, like a short, fat penguin, with a white, clown face and a colourful, parrot-like beak gaily striped in greyish blue, red and yellow, and bright orange-red webbed feet. The black 'eye make-up', thin red ring round the eye and black stripe behind the eye are visible only close up. Very gregarious birds, puffins nest in colonies and swim in groups on the sea near their nest sites. They sleep at sea at night, floating with their head tucked under one wing, and 'fly' underwater, using their wings as flippers, chasing fish.

HABITAT Summer: seen during the breeding season (which peaks in July), in or near nesting colonies on sea cliffs of islands off northern Scotland, especially St Kilda, also parts of the Irish coast, mainly the west, and several in Wales, including big ones at Skomer and Skokholm, off Pembrokeshire; there are still a few colonies in England, including Lundy in the Bristol Channel (the name of the island is from the Old Norse 'lund-eye', meaning 'Puffin Island'). March–August: also seen at sea in those areas. Winter: far out at sea.

SIZE 30cm (12in)

EGGS 1, off-white with speckling in pale grey

NEST In colonies on offshore islands – mostly on grassy slopes, usually in burrows they dig themselves or take over from rabbits or Manx shearwaters.

FOOD Mainly small fish such as sand eels.

VARIATIONS Juveniles have darker faces with a large black blob around each eye; the beak is much slimmer – it slowly widens and takes on colour gradually, as the birds mature. Winter adults have greyer faces, instead of the sparkling white of their breeding plumage, and the beak is far less colourful in winter.

31 White-tailed eagle
Haliaeetus albicilla

Also known as the sea eagle, this enormous bird of prey – almost twice the size of a buzzard – is the largest eagle in Europe. It resembles its close relative the American bald eagle, with very long, wide wings that flare out into widely open 'fingers' at the tips, and a fan-shaped tail, which is conspicuously white even when seen in silhouette from a distance. Given a good view, you can see the massive, bright yellow, hooked beak and yellow eyes, and the brown body and brown wings with darker brown to black trailing edges. It hunts by swooping down and grabbing prey with its claws. The white-tailed eagle, which is rare in the British Isles, was recently reintroduced after becoming extinct by 1916, and started breeding in Britain again only in 1985.

HABITAT Rocky coasts, sheltered shores and estuaries of north-west Scotland, including offshore islands, especially Rhum, Skye and Mull.

SIZE 80–90cm (31–36in); wingspan 2–2.5m (6½–8ft)

EGGS 2, white

NEST Very large nest of sticks and driftwood high up in trees or on inaccessible cliff ledges.

FOOD Mostly fish, ducks and seabirds, but also takes small mammals, such as rabbits and hares, and a good deal of carrion.

SIMILAR TO Golden eagle, which is less bulky and has a longer tail.

VARIATIONS Juveniles lack the diagnostic white tail, which develops later – they may show white streaks on the tail, but immature golden eagles (which are also brown all over) have a conspicuous white flash on each wing and the tail is white with a dark band across the end.

OPPOSITE A pair of mating shags in summer breeding plumage, complete with eye-catching head crests, in the Farne Islands, off Northumberland.

32 Rock dove
Columba livia

The rock dove is usually seen in flight or standing on rocks or on the ground (it rarely perches in trees). If you can get a close-up view, look for a blue-grey body with 2 black bars on each wing, dark grey wing-tips, a tail with a black tip and a white rump patch. The head and beak are dark grey with a white blob on the bridge of the nose, and there is iridescent pink on the shoulders and an iridescent blue 'thumbprint' up either side of the neck. The beady eyes and the legs are bright red. In flight, the white undersides of the wings are visible. The pure rock dove, which is now scarce, is one of the ancestors of the feral pigeon. This is now almost a pest in many towns and cities.
HABITAT Northern rocky cliffs and islands.
SIZE 33cm (13in)
EGGS 2, white
NEST Loose construction of grasses and seaweed in holes on rock ledges or in sea caves.
FOOD Seeds, buds, grass, grain.
SIMILAR TO Woodpigeon, which has a similar shape but is distinctly larger and stockier, with a longer tail, a darker grey back, a bright orange-yellow beak, a white ring around the back of the neck and

white-fringed black wing-tips with a large white flash across the middle of each upper wing. Feral pigeons are often very similar, but their colours and patterns are very varied. The stock dove is similar, but it lacks the white rump of pure wild rock doves and rock-dove-type feral pigeons and is a farmland and parkland bird, not found near coastal rocks.

33 Shore lark
Eremophila alpestris

This is a very scarce, chaffinch-sized winter visitor with dappled, pinkish brown upperparts, off-white underparts, a white-flecked, blackish 'bib' at the throat and a short black or grey beak. The face is yellow with black markings on the crown and curving down the front of each 'cheek'. The legs and feet are black. The shore lark is frequently seen associating with snow buntings.
HABITAT Winter: salt marshes, sandy or shingly shores, marshy coastal fields, mostly along the east coast of England, especially north Norfolk. Summer: the Arctic, very occasionally on Scottish mountain tops, where it has attempted to breed on a few occasions.
SIZE 16cm (6¼in)
EGGS 4, greenish white, speckled
NEST Hollow in the ground, lined with vegetation.
FOOD Seeds and small invertebrates.
VARIATIONS More colourful in summer, when the head is bright yellow, except for a black 'eye mask', black beak and 2 short,

backward-facing black 'horns' on top of the head, joined by a black 'V' across the forehead.

34 Rock pipit
Anthus petrosus

A sparrow-sized bird with a thin, dark beak, a speckled, dull-brown back, head and tail, heavily speckled buff underparts, a white throat and eye-stripe and dark legs. It is usually seen feeding among rocks or sorting through seaweed along the strand-line of stony shores, singly, in pairs or in family groups in summer. In spring, males display by flying straight up into the air from a rock and then parachuting down.
HABITAT Rocky coastlines all round the British Isles; spends winter in estuaries and salt marshes.

SIZE 17cm (6¾in)
EGGS 4–6, white, speckled brown
NEST Among rocks on the ground, in sheltered inlets near the shore.
FOOD Small invertebrates, such as flies and snails, and some seeds.
SIMILAR TO Meadow pipit, which is smaller and not so dark, has buff to dull orange-red legs and is seen only occasionally on rocky shores.

35 Chough
Pyrrhocorax pyrrhocorax

This is an unusual, small, elegant crow, a bit larger than a jackdaw, with all-black plumage, red legs and a slender, down-curved red beak. It breeds and flies about among cliffs but feeds on nearby heathland and short-grass pasture by probing the ground with its slim, sharp beak for invertebrates.
HABITAT Sea cliffs and cliff-tops of western Ireland, also west Wales, the Isle of Man and a few Inner Hebridean islands. A few pairs have recently recolonized Cornwall.
SIZE 40cm (16in)
EGGS 3–6, off-white speckled grey
NEST Made of sticks and plant stems, lined with hair and wool; under rocky ledges and in high crevices or caves.
FOOD Mainly insects and their larvae living in soil; also spiders.
VARIATIONS Juveniles have shorter, dull orange-yellow beaks.

36

38

36 Barnacle goose
Branta leucopsis

In certain localized areas of the British Isles, wild barnacle geese are reasonably common winter visitors. They are a little bigger than Brent geese and have black-and-white markings arranged as if wearing black-tie evening dress, with black legs, white underparts and blue-grey to lavender-grey upperparts (seen in close-up, the grey is actually patterned with vertical black-and-white bars). Look also for a black cap, a black and creamy white face with contrasting black eyes, a small, neat black beak, and a black neck and breast ending in a straight line across the chest.

HABITAT Late September–April: salt marshes and marshy coastal meadows round northern and western Scotland (especially on Islay and the Solway Firth) and coastal areas in Ireland. Also sometimes seen in north Norfolk, north Kent and the Severn estuary, at Slimbridge. Summer: Arctic (Siberia, Greenland, Spitsbergen).

SIZE 65cm (26in)

FOOD Marshland vegetation, grass, roots, flowers.

SIMILAR TO Brent or Canada geese, which also have black-and-white markings, but the white face of the barnacle goose is a useful distinguishing feature.

37 Brent goose
Branta bernicla

Flocks of Brents are common winter visitors to shores and coastal farmland. They are small, relatively short-necked geese with short beaks. From a distance, they look dark grey with a white lower rump. In close-up, you can see the black head, neck and breast with a broken white neck patch, a dark grey-black back and wing-tips and a wide white stripe along the rear end, from the legs to the tip of the tail. They feed in small groups or large flocks on coastal farmland, as well as in very shallow water in muddy estuaries and salt marshes near the sea. Brent geese fly, feed and roost in often large, tightly packed flocks. In flight, these form long, wavering lines or shapeless masses rather than 'Vs', and typically fly fast and low. The noise from a big flock swells to a very loud crescendo as they take off.

HABITAT October–April: coastal mud flats, salt marshes and sheltered estuaries, mainly in southern and eastern England and all round Ireland. Summer: Siberia, Greenland, Canada, Spitsbergen.

SIZE 60cm (24in)

FOOD Vegetation, mostly eel grass, algae, soft shoots of winter wheat, grass and marshland plants.

SIMILAR TO Canada goose, which is much bigger (1m/3ft) and taller, with a long neck and distinctive black head and neck, with a large white throat patch, and black tail. The rest of the body has brown upperparts and beige underparts. Canada geese have different, harsh, honking calls. They usually live inland, though are increasingly seen near some coasts.

VARIATIONS There are several races of Brent geese. The most common in Britain come from Siberia and winter in southern England – these are very dark birds with dark bellies. There are also races of paler-bellied birds: those from Greenland and eastern Canada, which winter in Ireland, and those that breed in Spitsbergen and winter on Northumberland's coast.

37

38 Shelduck
Tadorna tadorna

Easy to identify, as well as common and widespread, this large, goose-shaped duck is white with a greenish black head, neck and wing-flash, a chestnut band round the breast and on the wings, pale pink legs and a blood-red beak. It feeds by dabbling in mud and very shallow water. Sleeping birds, with their head under their wing, are less easy to identify. They are present all year round except in late summer, when most migrate to remote North Sea estuaries to moult, since – like all wildfowl – they cannot fly for about a month until their new feathers grow.

HABITAT Estuaries and salt marshes all round the coastline, as well as nearby fields, and sometimes on reservoirs and flooded gravel pits.

SIZE 65cm (26in)

EGGS 8–10, white

NEST In a rabbit burrow or hollow tree, in a hole in a building, under bramble bushes or in a stack of dried vegetation.

FOOD Invertebrates, including molluscs, crustaceans and mud-living worms.

VARIATIONS In spring, the male has a brilliant red beak with a large red knob above the base. Juveniles have the same patterns as adults, but in grey and white; the colours develop slowly.

39 Wigeon
Anas penelope

The wigeon is a medium-sized duck that is far more numerous in winter, when birds arrive from northern Europe. It is smaller than the mallard, with a very finely striped grey back and flanks, a pinkish breast, a white belly, black wing-tips and a triangular black rear end. Look for a white stripe along the flanks, below the closed wing (in flight this appears as a big white patch at the front of each inner wing) and a cream-yellow stripe along the top of the forehead, standing out against a rich chestnut-orange head. A very gregarious bird, it is often seen feeding in large, close flocks, all walking slowly in the same direction. The high-pitched whistling call of the drake ('wheee-ooo') is very distinctive.

HABITAT September–March: edges of well-sheltered, muddy estuaries, and on salt marshes or marshy coastal pastureland. Also in large, inland wetland reserves, especially in East Anglia. Summer: mostly in northern Europe, but a few hundred pairs breed in the British Isles, mainly Scotland.

SIZE 50cm (20in)

EGGS 8–9, creamy white

NEST On the ground, lined with vegetation and soft, downy feathers.

FOOD Stems, roots, leaves of grasses, buttercups, pondweed, eel grass.

40

SIMILAR TO Males could be confused from a distance with the male teal (which is smaller and has a dark green eye-patch).

VARIATIONS Females have a reddish or greyish mottled brown head, neck, breast and body, with a white belly and a speckled buff tail and rear end. They are often redder and more mottled than females of other common dabbling ducks such as mallards and teals. Juveniles look like females.

40 Common scoter
Melanitta nigra

The common scoter, a winter visitor, is Britain's blackest duck. It usually swims a considerable distance offshore. Males are entirely black, except for a yellow patch on top of the beak. Scoters might be mistaken for other offshore diving birds, such as divers, cormorants or grebes. However, these have a longer, leaner body shape, while scoters are more rounded, often with a cocked tail, and are very buoyant, bouncing over the waves like bath-time rubber ducks. Unlike divers and grebes, scoters normally float or fly in large, tight groups out at sea. Their call consists of various whistling sounds that carry over the water on still days.

HABITAT Winter: all round the coastline, especially in large bays and firths. Also, sometimes appears fleetingly at large inland reservoirs, staying near the centre. Summer: a very few breed by remote Scottish and Irish lakes, but most return to Russia or Scandinavia.

SIZE 50cm (20in)

EGGS 6–8, pale buff

NEST Hollow lined with grass, moss and female's down, close to water.

FOOD Mainly marine molluscs.

VARIATIONS Female is dark brown with a darker cap, pale 'cheeks' and an olive-brown to black beak.

41 Long-tailed duck
Clangula hyemalis

This is a locally common, small piebald or skewbald diving duck with a very long, slender spike of a tail (in males only). Present only in winter, it is seen in small groups that usually stay well out to sea, which makes identification difficult. Look for them flying around rather more than many other diving sea ducks, when their tail is very obvious. Males in winter plumage are blackish brown and white with a black tail, white head with blackish brown 'cheeks' and a black-and-pink beak.

41

HABITAT Winter: offshore waters of Britain and Ireland, especially around Shetland and the Western Isles, also in sea lochs and firths in mainland Scotland. Smaller numbers occur as far south as England's south coast. Summer: mostly north of the Arctic Circle.

SIZE 45cm (17½in)

FOOD Mainly marine molluscs.

SIMILAR TO The drake pintail is the only other duck with a long, thin tail; pintails are found on estuaries, close inshore and on large inland waters, not out at sea, and they up-end to feed but do not usually dive. Coloration is also different but is hard to see from a distance.

VARIATIONS Females, young and males at other times of year have changing patterns of grey-brown to black-and-white markings, with a dark grey to black beak. Females and immature males lack the distinctive long tail.

39

42 Eider
Somateria mollissima

Reasonably common and easy to identify, the male eider is a large, thickset, black-and-white duck with a white front half and upperparts, black underparts and rear end, and a big, wedge-shaped white head with a black cap and a divided lime-green patch on the side at the rear. The face looks Roman-nosed, owing to the yellow 'bridge' to the beak, and it has a 'pouting' expression caused by the slightly bulging white 'cheeks'. Eiders feed on rocky beaches, especially among exposed seaweed and rock pools at low tide, or in sheltered water close to the shore, floating in groups (often in a row) on the surface, then diving for deeper prey. Eiders are particularly numerous in winter in Britain.
HABITAT Breeds on sea coasts, mostly in Scotland, northern England and northern Ireland; more widespread in winter around coasts of England and south Wales.
SIZE 60–70cm (24–28in)
EGGS 4–6, grey green
NEST Hollow in the ground, among rocks, lined thickly with fluffy 'eider down'.

FOOD Molluscs, small crabs.
VARIATIONS Female is an entirely drab mottled-brown colour, for camouflage. Juveniles look similar to the female at first, but young males gain more of their characteristic markings and coloration at each moult, passing through several 'piebald' stages.

43 Oystercatcher
Haematopus ostralegus

This is a widespread and easily identified, chunky, black-and-white, medium-to-large wader with a long, straight, stout, bright orange-red beak, red-rimmed eyes and deep pink legs. The back, head, neck and 'bib' on the upper breast are black, contrasting sharply with the pure white underparts. It is usually seen singly or in small groups, walking along the shore or in shallow water, probing deeply with its beak for food. Its call is a loud 'kleep-kleep'.
HABITAT Coasts and estuaries throughout the British Isles.
SIZE 45cm (17½in)
EGGS 2–3, light beige with darker brown spots
NEST Shallow scrape in shingle or coastal fields.

FOOD Opens shellfish (cockles, mussels) with its strong beak, also feeds on marine worms and earthworms on wet farmland.
SIMILAR TO Avocet, which has a much longer, slimmer beak, longer legs, a more elegant shape and upturned beak, and lacks the conspicuous red legs and beak of the oystercatcher.

44 Avocet
Recurvirostra avosetta

A striking and easily recognized medium-sized wader, the avocet has a white-and-black body, long blue-grey legs and a very slender, longish black bill, which is noticeably upturned at the tip. Standing birds look mostly white with black 'trim' – their wings are edged black, and their neck and top of head are also black. They are often seen feeding in muddy water, walking slowly forwards, making rapid, side-to-side swishing motions with their beak.
HABITAT Summer: breeds mainly along coasts of East Anglia, south-east England and the Humber estuary. Winter: mainly in south-west England, especially the Exe and Tamar estuaries, and some in East Anglia and Kent.
SIZE 45cm (17½in)
EGGS 4, light beige with darker brown spots
NEST Scrape on the ground, in dry mud or stones.
FOOD Small shrimps and other small invertebrates.
SIMILAR TO Oystercatcher.

45 Ringed plover
Charadrius hiaticula

This small, plump, almost tail-less, short-legged wader is always on the go – it feeds in damp sand at the water's edge, runs a few steps, stops and looks, then has a quick peck before moving on swiftly. It has orange-yellow legs and a matching beak with a black tip. Its back is brown and the underparts are white, with a distinctive black 'bib' running right round the throat below a white collar. The head has a brown cap and a broad black 'mask' over the 'cheeks', eyes and forehead, with white 'eyebrows' and a white blob between the eyes. The ringed plover is present in the British Isles throughout the year, but numbers are greatest in spring and autumn, when migrants join our own residents, and in winter when many stay here.
HABITAT Sandy and shingly areas of seashores and estuaries all round the British Isles' coastline, but also on many inland reservoirs and flooded gravel pits.
SIZE 20cm (8in)
EGGS 3–4, variable in ground colour but spotted darker
NEST Bare scrape on the ground, in shingle.
FOOD Small marine invertebrates.
SIMILAR TO Little ringed plover, which is a scarce breeder on inland waters and rarely seen on the coast; its legs are pale olive-green, not orange, and its beak is all-black. Also, the little ringed plover has a yellow ring around its eyes and a faint white line across its forehead, above the black 'mask', connecting the 'eyebrows' – both features that are absent from the ringed plover.

46 Grey plover
Pluvialis squatarola

This is a relatively common wader with a dumpy, rather squat, plump and hunched-looking, medium-sized body with a large, round head. Its grey back is semi-dappled, the underparts are paler than the upperside, with the breast and flanks faintly streaked over a grey-buff wash, and it has grey-black legs. The eyes are big and round and the beak is black. The grey plover feeds on mud flats, moving slowly with individual birds well spaced out, even when there are quite a few in the same area. A few non-breeders stay in summer, but numbers are greatest in winter.
HABITAT Sandy or muddy estuaries, beaches and salt marshes, especially around southern, eastern and north-western England. Visitors to Britain breed in Russia.
SIZE 30cm (12in)
FOOD Mainly seashore molluscs and worms.
SIMILAR TO Knot and several other greyish waders are fairly similar, but the feeding style and slow movements easily distinguish the grey plover from other similar waders, which are generally gregarious and faster-moving.
VARIATIONS Summer plumage (April–September) has a bold, very striking, black-grey-and-white pattern, with a large black area covering the face, breast and belly.

47 Dunlin
Calidris alpina

Of all the small waders found in the British Isles, this is the most common and widespread. Halfway in size between a sparrow and a blackbird, in winter the dunlin has a greyish brown back, a paler head and breast streaked the same shade of grey-brown, fading down to off-white, faintly streaky underparts. The legs and beak (which is roughly the same length as the bird's head from beak-base to back) are both black. Given a good view, the beak may be seen to droop slightly downwards at the tip. The bird has a fairly dumpy, hunched shape when standing still, though less so than the grey plover. Dunlins are active birds, usually seen in flocks. Some are present and nest here all year, but numbers are far greater in winter.
HABITAT Mostly muddy estuaries, but also other seashores and even around inland lakes. Breeds on wet upland moors in Scotland, Wales and England and in western Ireland (also far north of Europe).
SIZE 16–22cm (6¼–8¾in)
EGGS 4, pale beige with darker brown markings
NEST Grass-lined hollow hidden in dense undergrowth.
FOOD Various seashore invertebrates and small molluscs.
SIMILAR TO A lot of small, grey-brown waders, but suspect dunlin before others as it's so common, then use a process of elimination.
VARIATIONS Summer plumage is

much brighter, with chestnut-brown 'chevron' markings on the back and top of the head, and a pale speckled head and breast, with a large black patch on the belly, from breast to legs, with a white undertail. (Dunlin is the only small wader to have a black belly in summer – the grey plover does too but is larger and easily distinguished by its shape and lone behaviour, whereas dunlin live in flocks.) Juveniles look like summer birds but with streaky brown underparts in place of the black patch, and with back feathers darker and outlined in chestnut, giving a slightly filigree effect.

48 Curlew sandpiper
Calidris ferruginea

A short-term visitor, this wader drops in temporarily during its autumn migration from Siberia to Africa. Similar in colour to the dunlin, but more elegant-looking,

with a longer neck and legs and a longer, finer, more down-curved beak, the curlew sandpiper has a speckly buff and grey-black back, off-white underparts and a buff head and neck with a bold white stripe above the eyes. It also has a bold, all-white rump, visible in flight. The curlew sandpiper often mixes with flocks of dunlin and feeds like the curlew, standing in deepish water and plunging its long, slightly down-curved black beak into the mud underneath.
HABITAT Occurs on most muddy coasts around Britain and eastern and southern Ireland, but mostly seen on mud flats in estuaries and inlets round south and east coasts of Britain.
SIZE 20cm (8in)
FOOD Marine worms and other small invertebrates.

49 Sanderling
Calidris alba

This is a reasonably common, small wader that is usually seen in winter, when it has a very pale, pearly grey back, shining white underparts, a contrasting, short black beak and shortish black legs. Another key distinguishing feature in winter is the dark smudge at the bend of the wing. In flight, a prominent, wide white wing-bar is visible, as well as white on either side of the dark rump and grey tail. Behaviour is also a good aid to identification: sanderlings occur in small groups, darting up and down the beach, snatching food from the edge of the breaking waves.
HABITAT Sandy and shingle beaches throughout the British Isles, particularly around the Ribble and Alt estuaries, and in some of the Western Isles and the Orkney Islands. Breeds in the Arctic.
SIZE 20cm (8in)
FOOD Very small shrimps.
SIMILAR TO Other small shoreline waders. Sanderlings are often found with dunlin, which usually appear in larger flocks and are much browner.

50 Knot
Calidris canutus

This is a common grey wader seen in large flocks in winter. The head and back are light grey, with almost-white underparts, a straight, quite short (but variable) black beak and short, buff-olive-green legs. Knot tend to flock together tightly on the ground, and in the air form similar dense, swirling clouds to starlings, though they appear much paler.

HABITAT August–April: big estuaries, especially with sandy edges or mud flats alongside. Summer: breeds in the Arctic.
SIZE 25cm (10cm)
FOOD Small molluscs.
SIMILAR TO On the ground, looks similar to several other shoreline waders, especially dunlin (which is slightly smaller and browner, with a slightly shorter beak). In the air, huge, tight flocks and aerial manoeuvres are characteristic; you can tell airborne flocks from lapwings by their steady, light grey colour – lapwings appear to flash black and white, while flocks of starlings are made up of noticeably smaller, darker-coloured, shorter-winged birds.

51 Purple sandpiper
Calidris maritima

A locally distributed winter visitor, this wader has a marked preference for picking through seaweed on rocks and man-made structures such as groynes, pier footings and the base of harbour walls, or in seaweed along the strand-line, where its dark colouring makes it hard to see. Look for a squat, plump, short-legged and short-necked wader, slightly smaller than a blackbird, with a slightly streaky, dark, grey-brown back, dark, speckled breast and paler underparts; it has a medium-long, slightly down-curved dark beak, yellow at the base, and short orange or yellow legs. The purple sandpiper is seen in small groups, often associating with turnstones, which have similar behaviour.
HABITAT October/November–March: most numerous round the north-east coast of Scotland, Shetland, Orkney. Summer: birds that winter in the British Isles breed in Iceland, Scandinavia, Russia, even Greenland and Canada.
SIZE 20cm (8in)
FOOD Various marine invertebrates.

52 Turnstone
Arenaria interpres

Most easily identified by their behaviour, turnstones are squat, short-legged waders that scurry in small flocks over pebbly ground, turning over stones, piles of seaweed and shells, looking for food underneath. Far less wary than most waders, they don't fly off unless you approach fairly close, and then often just move further down the beach. Some are present year round, but they are mostly seen in winter. They breed in the Arctic.
HABITAT All round the British Isles' coastline, especially on rocky or pebbly shores.
SIZE 20–24cm (8–9½in)
FOOD Small seaside invertebrates.
VARIATIONS Winter plumage is quite dull, with a mottled grey-brown back, head, neck and breast, contrasting with pure white underparts (apart from a dull, dark mottled breast band), and with a short black beak and dull orange legs. Summer plumage (shown above) is more colourful – look for the black breast, head, neck and breast bands and bright, orange/chestnut-and-black-patterned back.

53 Redshank
Tringa totanus

The long, orange-red legs and matching straight beak (blackish towards the tip) are the redshank's best identification features. Its back is brown and speckled, its head and breast are paler and buff-speckled (greyer in winter) and its underparts are whiter. Common and widespread, this very wary wader walks around, actively probing into mud for food, and calls loudly – a distinctive, noisy 'teu-heu-heu' – when alarmed.

HABITAT Throughout the British Isles. Winter: along seashores, estuaries and salt marshes. Summer: nests in wet meadows, marshes and boggy moorland inland and on coastal salt marshes.
SIZE 28cm (11in)
EGGS 3–5, buff, spotted with reddish brown
NEST Simple hollow among rushes or other vegetation.
FOOD Worms, crustaceans and other invertebrates.
VARIATIONS Juveniles have yellow-orange legs and paler buff-brown edges to the back and wing feathers, creating a more contrasting, chequered pattern.

54 Spotted redshank
Tringa erythropus

A scarce wader, this is a very slightly bigger and more elegant version of the redshank, with longer legs and a much longer, thinner beak with a slightly down-turned tip. The coloration also differs – in non-breeding plumage, the spotted redshank is pale pearly grey all over, with a darker and rather speckled dove-grey back and wings. Look also for the bold white eye-stripe (not found in redshanks) and the beak, which is red only on the lower half (the redshank has a wholly red beak). The bird stands in deepish water to feed by probing around with its beak; it often runs after prey and is seen swimming and even up-ending like a duck in shallow water near the shore. Its call is a distinctive, loud 'chew-it'.

HABITAT Spring and autumn: mostly along the south and eastern coasts, on mud flats round estuaries and creeks or muddy edges of inland lakes. Winter: small numbers stay, mainly in the south. Summer: breeds in Scandinavia and Russia.
SIZE 30cm (12in)
FOOD Invertebrates, small fish.

55 Greenshank
Tringa nebularia

This wader is similar in shape to the redshank but is slightly larger, taller, slimmer, more elegant and longer-legged, with a much longer, sturdier beak, a grey back, lighter streaks and speckles on the head and breast and whitish underparts.

The legs are greenish and the beak is slightly upcurved. Like a redshank, it is usually seen wading in mud or water, probing for food or chasing small fish. Its call is a loud, ringing 'tew-tew-tew'.

HABITAT Spring–summer: some breed on remote moors in north Scotland. Autumn: seashores, estuaries, salt marshes, also inland lakes and reservoirs throughout the British Isles. Winter: some are present in south-west Britain and Ireland, many winter in Africa.
SIZE 32cm (13in)
EGGS 4, olive with darker spots
NEST Hollow in the ground.
FOOD Invertebrates, fish.
SIMILAR TO Redshank, but the greenshank has a buff beak instead of red, and greenish legs rather than orange-red ones.

56 Curlew
Numenius arquata

The largest of all our waders, the curlew is a relatively common, big, chunky bird with streaked and barred greyish brown, blackish and warm buff plumage fading off into a white belly and undertail. The very long, down-curved beak is a great distinguishing feature. The curlew strides slowly and confidently in mud and shallow water, probing deeply for food. The beautiful bubbling song is a well-known sound of moors, estuaries and marshland, as is the melancholy 'cour-leee' call that gives the bird its name. Birds feed alone on mud flats at low tide, but at high tide they often retire to nearby farmland, sometimes in large flocks.

HABITAT Throughout the British Isles. Winter: in estuaries, creeks, salt marshes and farmland along the coast. Summer: breeds mainly on moors and rough pasture inland.
SIZE 55cm (22in)
EGGS 4, greenish to brownish, speckled brown
NEST Hollow among vegetation on the ground.
FOOD Invertebrates, such as worms, crabs and molluscs, in mud or soil.
SIMILAR TO Whimbrel, which is much less common. The whimbrel is 10–15cm (4–6in) smaller than the curlew and has alternate dark and light stripes on the head. The curlew has a plain brown head and a longer, more strongly down-curved beak.

57 Whimbrel
Numenius phaeopus

This is a large, rather scarce, dark brown, curlew-like wader, with white underparts, a medium-long, down-curved beak (with the curve less pronounced and beginning nearer the tip) and medium-long, grey-brown legs. The dark-brown-and-buff-striped head is the chief distinguishing feature. The whimbrel feeds by probing its beak deeply into soft mud for worms. If with curlews, it can be seen to be smaller and less wary. The whimbrel has a highly distinctive call – a rapid, rippling series of whistling notes (usually 7).

HABITAT Spring and autumn: salt marshes, wet meadows and mud flats around estuaries in most of the British Isles, as it passes through on its annual migration between Iceland and Africa. Summer: most breed in the far north of Europe but about 500 pairs breed in Shetland.
SIZE 40cm (16in)
EGGS 4, olive-green to buff, with brown spots and blotches
NEST Shallow depression in the ground among vegetation.
FOOD Worms, molluscs and other invertebrates.
SIMILAR TO Curlew.

58 Bar-tailed godwit
Limosa lapponica

This winter visitor is a large, long-legged wader with an extended, slightly upturned beak, pinkish at the base if you get a good view. Look for a grey-brown, boldly streaked back and wings, a slightly paler head and neck fading into white underparts, and black legs. The tip of the tail is barred black and brown-grey and the white rump extends far up the back as a wedge. Numbers vary from small groups to larger flocks, though birds usually feed some distance apart from one another.

HABITAT Autumn–winter: sandy coastal estuaries, though sometimes seen in muddy ones, round most of the British Isles. Summer: breeds in the Arctic.
SIZE 38cm (15in)
FOOD Various invertebrates, mainly marine worms and molluscs.
SIMILAR TO Black-tailed godwit, which has a square white rump and upper tail ending in a broad black band (there is no white on the wings of the bar-tailed godwit). The curlew is slightly larger and has a very long, down-curved beak.
VARIATIONS In summer, the head, breast and underparts of the male turn deep brick-red. The back is dark, almost black, streaked with red. The female is less colourful.

59 Black-tailed godwit
Limosa limosa

This is a very large, leggy wader with an extremely long, straight beak that is pinkish at the base (orange in spring and summer). In winter, when most are seen in the British Isles, it has a plain, pale greyish brown back with a slightly paler neck and head, white

underparts, a distinctive white tail ending in a broad black band, and black legs. Numbers vary from a small group to larger flocks; birds usually feed some distance apart.

HABITAT Autumn–winter: muddy coastal estuaries, creeks and salt marshes, mainly round the southern half of England. Summer: breeds in Holland or Iceland; also, small numbers (about 45–50 pairs) breed each year in wetland nature reserves in the British Isles.
SIZE 38–44cm (15–17in)
EGGS 4, olive-green ground colour with brown markings
NEST Flattened hollow in the ground, hidden among grass tussocks in wet grassland.
FOOD Various invertebrates, especially worms and snails; insects in summer.
SIMILAR TO Bar-tailed godwit.
VARIATIONS In summer or early spring, the head, neck and breast turn chestnut-red, fading out into a series of black-and-red bars on the side and belly. The undertail is all-white and the tail tip remains solid black. The back is grey-brown, variably mottled black and bright chestnut-red. The female is a duller version of the male.

60 Little egret
Egretta garzetta

This striking and easily identified newcomer is increasingly evident in coastal estuaries, mud flats, salt marshes and creeks throughout much of the British Isles, and it is now common around the southern half of the British Isles. It is a large, mainly silent, snowy-white member of the heron family, with a black beak and long black legs ending in bright yellow feet. In flight, it looks like a much smaller but more elegant white version of the common grey heron. When fishing, the little egret wades or stands completely still in shallow to fairly deep water almost to the top of its legs, and stabs suddenly, then throws its head back to swallow a fish.
HABITAT Coastal estuaries, mud flats, salt marshes and creeks; also feeds in nearby fields.
SIZE 55–63cm (22–25in)
EGGS 4–5, pale greenish blue
NEST Platform of sticks or reeds in a tree or bush.

FOOD Small fish, amphibians, aquatic insects.
SIMILAR TO Sometimes mistaken for a white swan at a long distance, but the slim, elegant, upright stance easily distinguishes the egret.
VARIATIONS In spring, birds trail a pair of long, fine plumes from the back of the neck and have many more on the breast and back.

61 Red-necked phalarope
Phalaropus lobatus

This is a rare wader, with short legs, a short tail and a short neck. It resembles a tiny, very elegant, buoyant gull when afloat. Unlike gulls, it has an exceptionally thin, almost needle-like, straight, entirely black beak. Adults in summer breeding plumage have a grey upper head, a white throat, a grey back and blackish wings with rows of contrasting buff lines; a bold chestnut-red flash curves down the side of the neck from just behind the eye to the throat. Unusually for birds, females are brighter than males.

HABITAT Late May–July: a few tens of pairs breed in Shetland, even fewer in the Western Isles and Ireland, on marshy pools and flooded peat cuttings. Migrants, mainly juveniles, are occasionally seen briefly on the east or south coast of Britain in autumn.
SIZE 18cm (7in)
EGGS 3–4, light brown with darker brown speckling
NEST On the ground, near water.
FOOD Marine invertebrates.
SIMILAR TO Grey phalarope, which has a slightly shorter, thicker beak and as a juvenile has fewer or no buff lines on the upperparts, and often grey shoulder patches.
VARIATIONS Winter adults are very pale, with a grey crown and upper-parts, white below, with a black, curving patch behind the eyes. Juveniles have a similar pattern but in blackish brown above, buff below, with prominent stripes on the back and often buff breast sides.

Role reversal
With most birds in which males and females are different, the male is the colourful one, as he has to compete for the female's attention; the female is usually drab so she is camouflaged while sitting on the nest. However, with a few birds, including phalaropes (above), it is the other way round – the female is brighter than the male, because he sits on the eggs. The female grey phalarope is especially brightly coloured – almost totally red, with brown wings and top of head and a white 'eye mask'. You'd be lucky to see them, because they nest mainly in the Arctic.

Fish

1 Shore clingfish
Lepadogaster lepadogaster
Also known as the Cornish sucker, this is a small, fairly common fish with a smooth, scale-less body, up to 10cm (4in) long, mottled yellow-brown, with a long, ribbon-like fin that runs lengthways round the rear half of the body incorporating the tail. It has a pair of blue spots behind the eyes and a wide 'suction cup' (which is actually the pelvic fins) on the 'chest', just below the gills.

HABITAT Summer: between the high- and low-tide marks, mostly on beaches in the south and south-west, attached firmly to a stone by its 'suction cup'. Winter: moves to deeper water.

2 Five-bearded rockling
Ciliata mustela
Related to the cod, this is a fairly common, long, slender fish, with a rather tubular body, up to 25cm (10in) long, ruddy brown on the top and sides and with paler undersides and fins. It has a short, sail-like fin immediately behind the head, and a long, ribbon-like dorsal fin running the full length of the body to the base of the tail, with a matching fin almost the same length along the underside. The face has 5 projecting barbels: 2 pairs on the 'nose' and a single one under the 'chin'. Counting the number of these barbels is the easy way to identify one rockling from another. The five-bearded rockling is the commonest species, but there are several others. The shore rockling (*Gaidropsarus mediterraneus*) is found in the same place as the five-bearded rockling, and looks virtually identical, except that the face has only 3 barbels (2 on the 'nose' and one under the 'chin').

HABITAT All round the coast, in rock pools or hollows in the seabed, round the pilings supporting jetties and piers.

3 Fifteen-spined stickleback
Spinachia spinachia
You might think the seaside is an unlikely place for sticklebacks, but this is a sea species. Easily recognized by anyone who's ever caught stickleback in freshwater ponds, it is a slender fish, to 15cm (6in) long, olive-green with yellowish sides and paler underneath, a long, narrow tail and a tiny, pike-like head, with a row of 14–16 short spines along the back, between the head and the dorsal fin.

HABITAT Lives in seaweeds around the low-water mark and also in rock pools.

4 Worm pipefish
Nerophis lumbriciformis
This is a most unlikely-looking fish, related to seahorses and found with difficulty as it's perfectly camouflaged. It is very slender and worm-like, to 15cm (6in) long, with a dark brown, dappled upper surface and cream-dappled underside. It has a small, eel-like head with a slightly upturned snout, and has only one fin, in the centre of the back.

HABITAT Lives among seaweed in rock pools.

5 Greater pipefish
Syngnathus acus
You can tell this fish is related to the seahorse by looking at its long, tubular snout and scaly body. The body is also elongated, slender and tubular (up to 45cm/17½in long) and patterned with irregular brownish bands, with a fin halfway down the centre of the back and a small, fan-like tail. Like the seahorse, the greater pipefish sometimes swims in an almost vertical position.

HABITAT Shallow water close to the shore, where the sea bottom is sandy or muddy, and in banks of eel grass or seaweed. Also in estuaries, particularly round the south and west coasts.

6

7

8 Lesser weever fish
Echiichthys vipera

The lesser weever is an unwelcome 'find' that ruins some people's seaside holidays in the British Isles. A small fish, it lies half-buried in sand in shallow water, where unwary swimmers often stand on it. The spiny dorsal fins are raised in defence; these carry a poisonous sting, which is very painful. It can reach up to 15cm (6in) long, has a rather bulldog-like expression – undershot jaw and large pop-eyes – and feeds on small fish, shrimps and invertebrates.

8

HABITAT All round the coast, in shallow water near the low-tide mark and a short distance offshore. It invariably chooses clean, sandy tourist beaches.

9 Common blenny
Lipophrys pholis

Often caught in shrimping nets, this is our best-known rock-pool fish (also known as the 'shanny'). It is very slimy and small (up to 15cm/6in long) and rather variable in colour, but it is usually an undistinguished, dull brown, red or green shade with blotchy markings. The head is short and

blunt, with a steeply sloping forehead and large eyes and lips but no 'eyebrows'. It has a ribbon-like, notched dorsal fin all along the back, from the gills to the tail.
HABITAT Found in rock pools and shallow water round rocky or sandy coasts, lurking among seaweed, particularly in winter.

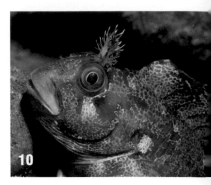

10

10 Tompot blenny
Parablennius gattorugine

This is a more unusual and harder-to-see blenny, up to 30cm (12in) long, with conspicuous, broad, dark, vertical, wavy-edged bands patterning a sandy-brown body. It has a continuous, unnotched dorsal fin along the back, from the head to the base of the tail fin, and a feathery 'tentacle' over each eye.
HABITAT Just off the beach below the low-tide mark and in shallowish water some distance from it, around the south and west coasts of England.

6 Corkwing wrasse
Crenilabrus melops

The corkwing is a fairly common, small and easily identified fish, up to 15cm (6in) long. Its coloration is rather variable – it can be mid-brown, greenish brown or reddish brown, but it always has a brown spot at the base of the tail (a good identification point). Males also have faint blue tracery on the fins and face, and the eye is partly outlined by a dark, curved mark.
HABITAT Shallow waters around rocky shores and deep rock pools that are uncovered only when the tide is low.

7 Ballan wrasse
Labrus bergylta

This is our commonest wrasse, and one of the few British representatives of a mainly tropical or subtropical family. It is a trout-shaped fish, up to 60cm (24in) long, seen in small groups or singly. Adults are a blotchy greenish brownish colour, paler underneath; the young are blotchy

green and well camouflaged among seaweed. A continuous, short, spiny, speckled fin runs from just behind the head to the base of the tail. It feeds on marine molluscs and invertebrates, which it crushes using a layer of knobbly teeth inside its throat.
HABITAT Often seen off rocky shores, particularly round the south-west of England. Young fish are often found in rock pools.

9

Identifying blennies

You can always recognize a blenny, even if you don't know precisely which species it is, by its pair of rather leg-like pelvic fins on the lower side, just below the gills. It uses these almost like legs, to work its way into crevices between rocks, so it can hide from predators – including small children with shrimping nets.

11 Butterfish
Pholis gunnellus

Also known as the gunnel, the butterfish is a common species that gets its name from being extremely slippery when handled. It is a rather ugly, tubular-shaped fish, up to 25cm (10in) long, in dirty cream irregularly blotched olive-brown to reddish brown, with a small head that is flattened from top to bottom. It has a continuous, ribbon-like fin that runs along the entire upperside of the body, with a similar one underneath from mid-way down the belly to the base of the tail fin. There is a line of white-edged black spots along the base of the dorsal fin, on each side. The butterfish is an important food source for many sea creatures, including commercial fish stocks.
HABITAT In rock pools and under stones between the low- and high-tide marks of rocky shores.

12 Lesser sand eel
Ammodytes tobianus

Despite its name, this is not an eel at all, but a very thin fish up to 15–20cm (6–8in) long, with large, silvery eyes and a long, narrow, knife-like, silvery body which is tinted green on top and yellowish underneath. It swims with an eel-like, wriggling motion in shallow water, usually in large shoals, or burrows in wet sand or shingle. Rarely seen by seaside visitors, sand eels are a vital link in the coastal food chain, being an important food source for seabirds such as puffins. Larger species of

sand eel live in deeper water and are food for commercially important fish, as well as for deep-sea birds, dolphins and other marine animals.
HABITAT All around sandy or shingly coasts, in the zone from just above to just below the low-tide mark.

13 Gobies

This group consists of several species of fairly common small fish seen in shoals, with short, blunt heads with large eyes and big lips, and mostly slender, rather stickleback-shaped bodies. They have 2 dorsal fins: the one closest to the head is short and sail-like; the other is rather rectangular in shape, with a matching anal fin on the underside of the fish. Under the 'chest' of gobies is a fan-shaped sucker, which they use to hold tight to stones to prevent themselves being washed away by strong tides and currents.

The black goby (*Gobius niger*, shown right) is a larger, stouter goby than most, up to 17cm (6¾in) long; it is not black but darker than the others, having a tan body with darker olive-brown mottles. The rock goby (*G. paganellus*) is a fairly common species, often found in rock pools, mostly round the southern half of the British Isles. It is up to 12cm (4¾in) long and solitary, unlike other gobies, which live in shoals. The colour is rather variable: various shades of lightish brown with darker mottles all over, with a paler band along the top of the dorsal fins. The two-spot goby (*Gobiusculus flavescens*) is unusually slim for a goby, up to 6cm (2½in) long, in mottled brown with a large black spot at the base of the tail fin; male fish also have a similar spot on either side of the body, just below the first dorsal fin.

The common goby (*Pomatoschistus microps*) is small, up to 6cm (2½in) long, buff-coloured and patterned with olive-brown blotches and a series of faint vertical bands. There is a row of regularly spaced, brownish spots along the mid-line each side, and a slightly larger, darker spot at the end of the row, by the base of the

tail fin. The undersides are slightly paler. The sand goby (*P. minutus*) is slim, pale and sand-coloured, up to 10cm (4in) long, patterned with a sprinkling of tiny, darker spots which appear to form indistinct, barred lines across the back.
HABITAT Shallow coastal waters and tidal rock pools, but also estuaries (even where the water is well diluted by river water and not very salty), creeks in salt marshes and brackish drainage ditches with access to the sea.

14 Flounder
Pleuronectes flesus

Also known as the fluke, this common flatfish – which is related to plaice – has dull grey-brown or greenish brown coloration mottled with large, darker markings and a faint scattering of dull orange, plaice-like spots. However, it is able to vary its surface colour to match the seabed for camouflage. The eyes are on the left of the face. Sharp spines along the base of the fins and a prickly scale just behind the centre of the head are good identification features. The flounder can reach up to 60cm (24in) long, although it is rarely over 20cm (8in), and it is a major food source for marine wildlife.
HABITAT Found offshore in deep water close to the coast as well as in estuaries.

15

15 Plaice
Pleuronectes platessa

The plaice is a well-known, common and very edible 'fish and chips' fish, often caught with a line if you go out sea-fishing from a boat when on holiday at the coast. It is a flatfish, up to 90cm (36in) long, with white undersides and dark grey-brown or greenish brown uppersides, patterned all over with conspicuous orange spots. The upper surface of the body can change colour to match its background, for camouflage. Both eyes are on the upperside of the strangely contorted face, always on the right; the mouth is twisted round at nearly 90 degrees to the flat body. Wide fins on either side of the body give it a rather rounded shape.
HABITAT Young plaice live close to the coast for several years, but adults live in deeper water with a sandy bottom and return to the shallows only for spawning in winter and early spring.

16 Dab
Limanda limanda

The dab is the one flatfish you are almost certain to catch if you go out sea-fishing in a boat. A sandy brown colour, it is a perfect match for the seabed, with distinctly rough skin on the upper surface and a short, blunt-ended tail. The most distinctive feature is the dorsal line, which, instead of running straight from head to tail, has a pronounced curve just behind the head, making it almost question-mark-shaped. The dab can grow as long as 30cm (12in), but it is usually about two-thirds that size.
HABITAT Close inshore, especially off the North Sea coast.

17 Basking shark
Cetorhinus maximus

The basking shark is one of the largest fish in the world and can reach up to 11m (36ft) long and 3 tonnes in weight. It is sometimes seen in summer, especially off the Cornish coast, often swimming slowly with its huge mouth wide open; despite its formidable appearance, it feeds by 'sieving' plankton out of the water through the 5 long slits each side of the 'neck'. The body is dark grey, with an easily identified shark shape, and the dorsal fin flops over to one side.
HABITAT In deep waters, mostly off the south-west coast but may be spotted off just about any coast.

17

16

Moveable body parts

All flatfish (including restaurant favourites such as brill, halibut, turbot and Dover sole) produce eggs that hatch into normally shaped baby fish that swim about in the upper layers of the water; it is not until they are older (about 2 months in the case of plaice) that the eyes start to move round to one side of the head, the mouth screws round to one side and the shape broadens out; they then take up residence on the seabed. The underside is always white or nearly so, since it does not need to provide a good match with the sea bottom as the upperside does.

Islands

Dotted all round our coastline are hundreds of small islands. Scotland is particularly well endowed, with about 790 of them if you include the very small ones. Although they are difficult to get to, they can be wonderful places to find wildlife, especially unusual kinds rarely seen on the mainland.

Except for birds and plants, which could reach land by air and spread by wind-borne seeds respectively, islands have largely kept much the same flora and fauna that existed at the end of the ice age, when the land was first cut off from the mainland. Those original animals and plants have been allowed to evolve without the usual competition, and they have sometimes developed into separate subspecies, which are found nowhere else and are generally bigger than their mainland counterparts. The best known of these is the Skomer vole, which is a subspecies of bank vole found only on the island of Skomer, off

Small islands in a coastal inlet on the island of Harris, Scotland.

the west coast of Pembrokeshire. There is also a blonde hedgehog that lives exclusively on the Channel Island of Alderney, and the Orkney vole – introduced to the islands by humans over 4000 years ago – is now an important food supply for birds of prey throughout Orkney.

On islands that have never been invaded by predators such as rats, feral cats or hedgehogs, the balance of power can be very different from that on the mainland, since all sorts of ground-nesting birds and other scarce creatures are left in peace and can thrive. Plants, too, have sometimes survived on islands when they died out on the mainland as a result of man's activities or grazing animals – for example, the only place the Lundy cabbage still grows in Britain is on Lundy island, off the coast of north Devon.

Far-flung offshore islands are great places to spot rarities, because they are often the first landfall for migrating birds blown off course by bad weather; the Isles of Scilly are extremely popular with 'twitchers' in spring and autumn. Islands are also particularly good places for seabirds to live – their rocky cliffs provide safe breeding grounds and the warm, shallow waters that surround them have a plentiful supply of small fish. This is why so many of our smaller offshore islands are now nature reserves, perfect for watching or studying wildlife, if you're prepared to make a special visit. But not all islands have been left alone by man. Those that were big enough, and close enough to the mainland, were just too tempting to use as secure sea-bound 'fields' for livestock, such as sheep, and so grazing has drastically altered their character. There are several ancient breeds of sheep that are very tough and can cope with extremely demanding conditions – for example, the Soay sheep, found in the St Kilda archipelago, off the north-western coast of Scotland, is still with us today. Some breeds even managed to survive by eating seaweed off the shore in winter when there wasn't much grass; the North Ronaldsay sheep, from the Orkney Isles, now eats little else but seaweed which, enthusiasts claim, gives the meat a unique flavour.

1 Common winkle
Littorina littorea

The well-known winkle, sold in fish shops and eaten by being twizzled out of its shell with a pin, is one of the commonest seaside snails. It is our largest winkle (3cm/1¼in), with a very dark grey, spiral shell marked with fine concentric ridges. You can tell an elderly winkle by its lack of ridges, as the shell eventually gets worn smooth. In a very sunny spot that's uncovered by water for long periods, winkle shells may bleach to a light brown-grey in the sun.
HABITAT All round the coast, in rock pools and on rocks, wooden pilings or breakwaters where there is plenty of seaweed that is partially uncovered at low tide.

2 Common limpet
Patella vulgata

The cone-shaped, 'coolie hat' shells of limpets are a familiar seaside sight. The shells measure up to 6cm (2½in) across, with ridges running up to the peak in the centre. Older specimens may have barnacles growing on their shells. Limpets are famous for clinging so tightly to rocks that they cannot be shifted. However, when covered by high tides the creature can unstick itself and move around, venturing about 1m (3ft) from its home base in search of food.
HABITAT All round the coast, on rocks, wooden pilings of piers, breakwaters and similar structures, where they are uncovered for up to half the day by low tides.

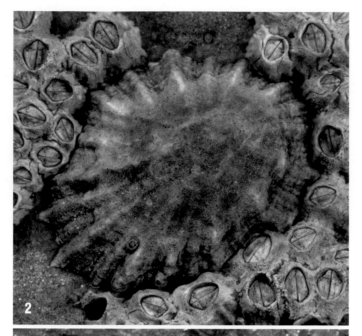

3 Slipper limpet
Crepidula fornicata

One of the most commonly seen shells washed up on the beach, this rather kidney-shaped shell (up to 4cm/1½in long) is wide at one end and pointed at the other. Slipper limpets are often stuck together in stacks, clinging to oyster or mussel shells or sometimes stones. Not a true limpet, this is an American species introduced accidentally. It is now considered a pest of oyster beds as it causes a build-up of silt that smothers them.
HABITAT Round much of our coast, from East Anglia to the Irish Sea, especially in estuaries close to oyster beds.

4 Common whelk
Buccinum undatum

This well-known whelk is the biggest of the shells commonly washed up on the beach – up to 12cm (4¾in) long, warm beige in colour, with a spiral shape patterned evenly all over with regular horizontal ridges. In the sea, empty whelk shells are often taken over by hermit crabs. Whelk egg cases are also washed up on shore: look for a spongy mass of large, off-white 'grains', which can be as big as a tennis ball. Whelks feed on carrion, which they locate by smell using a sensitive 'periscope' that they poke out of the shell just above their head.
HABITAT Rocky shores and rock pools, all round the coast.

have algae or small strands of seaweed growing from them. Hair-like threads protrude from between the shells when closed: these hairs are known as the 'beard' and are removed when preparing mussels for the pot.
HABITAT All round our coasts in tight-packed colonies on rocks or seaweed-encrusted timbers, such as the pilings for piers and jetties, where they are uncovered for part of the day at low tide. They are also farmed commercially in some areas, grown on ropes suspended in the water.

5 Painted top shell
Calliostoma zizyphinum
This is a striking sea snail with a very pretty and easily identified conical shell, up to 4cm (1½in). Almost perfectly triangular in cross-section, it has a pointed tip the shape of an old-fashioned spinning top, hence the common name. When alive, the creature has a very colourful shell in red, pink or orange with darker spots, but it is most commonly seen washed up, empty, on the shore when the shell is a more pearly pink and silvery white colour.
HABITAT Around the low-tide mark on rocky shores, grazing among seaweed, especially in the southern half of the British Isles.

6 Common cockle
Cerastoderma edule
A popular seaside delicacy, cockles live in large colonies, or cockle beds, a few inches below the surface in clean, damp sand or silty mud. The off-white or light beige, fan-shaped shells are marked with occasional darker bands and are lightly grooved from top to bottom. When washed up on the beach, cockle shells have often lost the hinge that usually joins the 2 half-shells together. An empty shell has a broad, grooved inner rim that distinguishes common

cockles from other kinds. Cockles feed by filtering food from the water column; lying close to the surface, they are easy prey for wading birds such as oystercatchers.
HABITAT Just above the low-tide mark, on sandy beaches and in mud flats in estuaries all round the coast, including the beautiful but treacherous Morecambe Bay.

7 Common mussel
Mytilus edulis
This is one of the commonest British shellfish, with shells that are roughly oval in shape (one side almost straight and the other curved) in black tinged with blue or brown, up to 10cm (4in) long. Mussel shells are often studded with clusters of barnacles, or may

are often washed up on beaches. Easily identified, the shells are large (up to 15cm/6in across), fan-shaped and buff-coloured, with heavy, reddish-tinged ridges arranged in a sunburst pattern. The lower half of the shell, which lies on the seabed, is paler and more bowl-shaped; the flatter shell lies on top and is hinged to enable the scallop to feed. Scallops are often fished for by scuba divers and their shells were once used to line paths in cottage gardens. **HABITAT** Around much of the British Isles, off sandy or shingly beaches below the low-tide mark.

10 Common razorshell
Ensis ensis
Rarely seen alive, these long, narrow, flattened shells, 15cm (6in) long, are commonly washed up on beaches. They are the same shape as the blade of an old-fashioned cut-throat razor, and roughly the colour of a horn-handled pocket knife, in shiny beige lightly ringed with brown. The live creature is an active burrower, moving to the top of its burrow to feed, and retreating rapidly to greater depths when disturbed.
HABITAT Just above the low-tide line in certain sandy bays and beaches all round the coast.

8 Common oyster
Ostrea edulis
Our native oyster is a well-known shellfish of fishmongers' slabs and restaurants, but it is most likely to be seen as an empty shell washed up on sandy to shingly beaches. It has 2 round, fairly flat, greyish shells, to 10cm (4in) across, with irregular and sometimes fluted ridges – these denote annual growth (it can live for 12 years). Farmed oysters are usually the Portuguese oyster (*Crassostrea gigas*), which has a much deeper shell with jagged edges, one half of which is more like a dish on to which the other half fits like a lid. Oysters feed on minute debris, which they filter out of the water.
HABITAT Glues on to stones on pebbly coasts just offshore from the low-tide line to a depth of 50m (164ft), usually in colonies known as oyster beds, particularly when they are farmed.

9 Great scallop
Pecten maximus
Scallops and their impressive shells are familiar sights at the fishmongers', and the empty shells

11 Thin tellin
Angulus tenuis
A fairly commonly found seashore shellfish with a slightly conical-shaped, bivalve shell, to 3cm (1¼in). The shell is patterned with concentric ridges in yellow, pink or red, giving it a slightly stripy appearance. When washed up on the beach, the shells are conspicuously thin, but the pair remain joined at the hinge.
HABITAT Lives in wet sand near the low-tide mark and for a short distance offshore.

Estuaries and mud flats

Estuaries are found where rivers reach the sea. They are where fresh water and tidal water meet, often in a network of creeks, and low tides uncover wide expanses of gently sloping mud flats and salt marshes, which are often surrounded by swampy grazing land.

The 'shores' of estuaries are made up of a mixture of sand, mud and silt washed down from the rivers, enriched with decaying plant remains. They provide a superb food supply for a range of creatures that form a complex food chain. At the bottom of the pecking order are microscopic mud-living creatures, then come various seashore worms (such as lugworms and the ragworms that fishermen dig up as bait) and shellfish such as cockles,

Estuaries are a great place to watch waders such as these dunlin. The largest numbers feed for two hours either side of high tide.

which in turn feed the sort of birds that probe into the mud to find their food, namely waders.

The whole process is fuelled by the tides, which bring new supplies of microscopic food and make huge changes to living conditions. Every 12 hours or so, the tides change the depth, temperature, salt levels and oxygen content of the water enormously. Only a few resilient plants have adapted to survive the salt, wind and fluctuating water levels of estuary life, but at least the slow-moving water means their roots aren't washed away (on exposed coasts, big waves make it impossible for shore plants to survive). However, conditions alter a lot as you move from beyond the high-tide mark closer to the water, and you find certain plants specialize in particular 'zones'.

Along the edge of mud flats, where the land gets flooded only at the very highest of high tides, live salt-marsh plants such as sea lavender and sea orache, which can't exist in seawater – they behave more like cacti, conserving rainwater using a thick, waxy outer layer to prevent excess water loss through their skin.

Next come species that don't mind regular light dunkings in seawater, followed by plants that remain underwater themselves for much of the time, such as marsh samphire. In shallow water, where the ground is rarely if ever uncovered even by very low tides, eel grass thrives; this is the main traditional food of Brent geese, which migrate to our south and east coast estuaries each autumn to escape the freezing conditions in their summer home in Siberia. Every winter we host about half the world's population of these magnificent birds; without the eel grass, we simply wouldn't see them.

14 Common starfish
Asterias rubens

The common starfish has 5 rubbery arms that radiate out from a small central circle in the familiar star shape, 5–30cm (2–12in) in diameter. They are usually a pale buff-orange colour, studded all over with small, off-white pimples that also form a row down the centre of each arm. Starfish feed on polychaetes and small crustaceans, which they pull open using the suckers on their arms.

HABITAT All round our coasts, on sandy or rocky shores and occasionally in deep rock pools, also for quite some distance below the low-water mark.

12 Beadlet sea anemone
Actinia equina

If you thought sea anemones lived only in warm, tropical seas, you're in for a surprise – several species inhabit British coastal waters, of which the beadlet anemone is the commonest. When the tide is out, beadlets look like blobs of deep plum-red jelly; however, when covered by water and feeding, they project a plume of hair-like tentacles that are the same colour as the jelly, and wave gently. There is a ring of blue warts, or 'beads', around the tentacle bases, hence their common name. Beadlets use their tentacles to sting neighbouring anemones, causing the defeated anemones to retreat – as a result, beadlets are quite widely spaced apart, the biggest and most aggressive individuals having the biggest space round them. They feed on small shrimps and baby fish.

HABITAT All round the coast, on rocks or timbers on rocky shores in shallow areas that are covered at low tide, and in deep rock pools.

13 Common jellyfish
Aurelia aurita

Whether washed up on the beach or spotted while swimming, jellyfish aren't our favourite find. However, unlike lion's mane jellyfish (*Cyanea capillata* and *C. lamarcki*), the common jellyfish (also known as the moon jellyfish) doesn't sting people. Often seen in large swarms, the translucent, bluish 'parasol' constantly pulsates to propel the creature gently through the water. Given a close view, you'll see 4 pinkish crescents that form a 4-leaved clover shape in the upper centre of the parasol. Jellyfish feed mostly on small planktonic animals, including other small jellyfish, arrow worms, fish eggs and fish larvae.

HABITAT Round the coast, especially sheltered bays, particularly from May to the end of August.

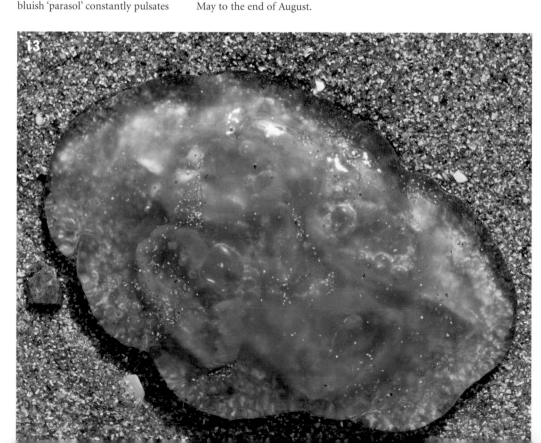

15 Common prawn
Palaemon serratus

This is Britain's largest prawn, served by the pint in seaside cafés. The live creature has a semi-transparent, grey-brown, scale-clad body, up to 7.5cm (3in) long (which turns the familiar reddish pink only when boiled), black, beady eyes on short stalks, a short tail and many short, bristle-like legs, the first pair of which have tiny pincers. The prawn is usually seen flitting between patches of seaweed in rock pools or walking around on the bottom. It scavenges on plant, fish and animal debris and also eats fish eggs.

HABITAT All round our coasts in shallowish water just offshore for most of the year, and in rock pools in spring.

16 Brown shrimp
Crangon crangon

It's difficult to believe that this creature, when cooked, is the pink looking shrimp of fishmongers' slabs. The semi-transparent, slightly laterally flattened, red-brown, fish-like shape (up to 5cm/2in long) flits quickly into patches of seaweed or sinks itself

into soft sand, where it spends much of its time. If you keep still for a while, you may get a good look at one hovering and see the whiskers and legs close up. It feeds on worms, young fish and small crustaceans.

HABITAT Common in sandy bays and muddy estuaries all round the coast.

17 Hermit crab
Pagurus bernhardus

Easily spotted on seaside holidays, the hermit crab is a soft-bodied crab that grows no shell of its own, so 'borrows' winkle, then whelk shells, moving up a size as its own body grows, eventually using a shell size of about 10cm (4in). It is often seen walking around the floor of rock pools; all you see are the reddish-brown-and-white head and legs poking out of the entrance hole of its borrowed shell – when disturbed, it retreats inside for safety. Seen in close-up, hermit crabs have 2 pairs of small legs used for walking and a pair of nippers at the front for feeding. The right nipper is larger than the left. It feeds by scavenging or grabbing passing small prey.

HABITAT Rock pools and rocky or sandy coasts all round the British Isles and some distance offshore.

18 Common shore crab
Carcinus maenas

Also known as the green shore crab, this is our commonest and most widely seen crab, with a small, brownish, reddish or greenish shell up to 10cm (4in) across. It has a single pair of nippers for feeding and 4 pairs of thin legs for walking, although you often see crabs with bits missing from the ends of their legs, or lacking a leg or two entirely. Lively, aggressive creatures, they are scavengers and will eat almost anything, so they do a good job clearing up dead seabirds and fish from the shore.

HABITAT Throughout the British Isles, common in rock pools and both above and below the low-tide mark of most beaches and estuaries. They hide beneath stones and scuttle between patches of seaweed.

19 Acorn barnacle
Semibalanus balanoides

Probably the most common of all our marine creatures, the acorn barnacle is a small, off-white, volcano-shaped crustacean (related to crabs and prawns), often living in dense colonies that build up to form a crusty layer over marine surfaces. When seen close up, each shell has 6 sides that form a hollow-topped 'crater', which has a lid inside made up of 4 tiny sections. Other barnacle species are identified by the different number or shape of the plates that make up their craters, for which you need a magnifying glass.

HABITAT All round the coast on rocks, timber structures, the bottoms of boats and indeed almost anything in seawater including the shells of mussels and oysters.

20 Sea slater
Ligia oceanica

This is a grey-green to black, woodlouse-like crustacean, up to 3cm (1¼in) long, with extended antennae that curve round from the head to the shoulders. It comes out only at night to feed, and scavenges on decaying shoreline debris in much the same manner as garden woodlice.

HABITAT Around the coast, in crevices between stones on rocky shores, close to the high-tide mark.

21 Common sandhopper
Talitrus saltator

The most common and abundant of all the sandhopper species, this is a tiny creature shaped rather like a freshwater shrimp, 1–3cm (⅜–1¼in) long, in greenish, yellowish or brownish shades. It shelters in the sand beneath seaweed flotsam but feeds downshore at low tide. Like all amphipods, the female *Talitrus* broods her eggs, which hatch as miniature adults. Sandhoppers are a good source of food for various shore-edge wading birds, for example turnstones.

HABITAT Among stones, especially near piles of seaweed on the shores of mainly stony or sandy beaches throughout the British Isles.

22 Lugworm
Arenicola marina

The lugworm casts commonly seen on soft beaches at low tide resemble large worm casts on your garden lawn; indeed, lugworms feed in the same way as garden worms, ingesting silty sand of a particular grade, digesting adhering bacteria and ejecting the rest. The creature itself is rarely seen, except by fishermen digging for bait; it is large, up to 20cm (8in) long, reddish and segmented, with small clumps of red, bristly gills along either side of its fatter mid-section, and a long, narrow tail. It lives permanently in the same U-shaped burrow, with a cast at one end and a blowhole at the other, so the casts and blowholes always appear in pairs. It is a popular food for wading birds with long beaks such as curlew, which can probe deeply.

HABITAT Sandy beaches and muddy estuaries all round the British Isles.

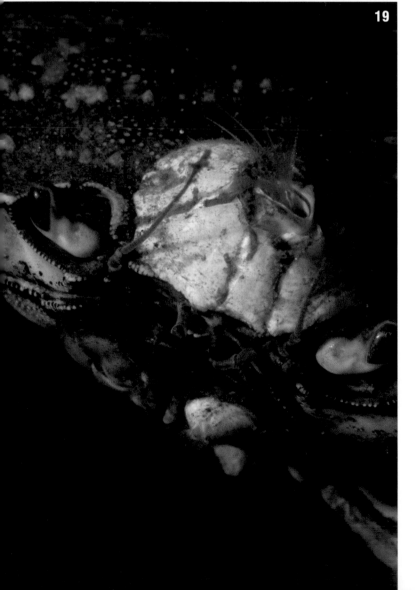

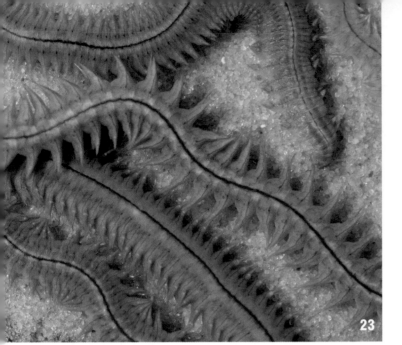

23

25 Kelp flies
Coelopa frigida and other species

Swarms of tiny flies around piles of rotting seaweed on the shore will most likely be one of the species of kelp fly, of which *Coelopa frigida* is the largest and commonest. It is a flattened black fly, about 6mm (¼in) long, with colourless transparent wings and brown legs. All kelp flies lay eggs in rotting seaweed, which their larvae eat, helping to break it down.

HABITAT Found in clouds round rotting seaweed, on seashores anywhere along the coast of the British Isles.

25

23 Ragworm
Nereis diversicolor

Popular with fishermen as bait, ragworms have flattened, greyish brown bodies that are made up of many segments and a fringe of tiny red-brown legs along each side, which ripple as they swim or scuttle through mud or wet sand. Ragworms are scavengers but they also grab live prey such as small shrimps.

HABITAT Muddy and sandy shores all round our coasts.

24 Shore wainscot moth
Mythimna litoralis

This is an unexciting, light buff-coloured, night-flying moth, whose caterpillar is more likely to be seen.

HABITAT Marram grass in sand dunes in most of the British Isles (adults seen June to September), but very rare in Scotland.

CATERPILLAR Cream to light yellow, with rows of black dots down the back. Feeds on marram grass. In hot weather it buries itself in the sand.

24

Beachcombing

The high-tide mark is known to biologists as the strand-line, because that's where all sorts of flotsam and jetsam, including piles of seaweed, plastic bottles and other litter are left stranded by the waves. Lower down the beach, at low tide, look for cuttlefish 'bones', mermaid's purses (ray and skate egg cases), whelk egg cases the size of tennis balls, and a range of sea shells including cockles, oysters, crabs, painted top shells, razorshells, scallops and tellins; also small crab shells that have been deposited on the beach. The action of waves against stones gradually grinds shells down to sand over many years, but tourists can often collect good specimens to take home.

On stony beaches, especially at the foot of cliffs along the Heritage Coast or the Isle of Wight after new rock falls, look for fossils – experts know precisely which stone to tap with a hammer to make it split open, revealing a creature inside. Ammonites are one of the commonest – spiral rams-horn-shaped fossils of creatures that lived in the warm tropical Jurassic seas 250–300 million years ago.

Mammals

1 Common porpoise
Phocoena phocoena

The common porpoise, also known as the harbour porpoise, is the smallest cetacean in our waters (1.4–1.7m/4½–5½ft, weighing up to 65kg/143lb), with a dark grey or dark charcoal back and uppersides, white undersides and a grey tail and flippers. It travels in small groups, although most sightings are of singles. Although it looks superficially like a dolphin, the common porpoise has a short, blunt head with no beak and a short, triangular dorsal fin (in the dolphin it is elongated and pointed). A relatively slow swimmer, it is easy to see but shows little of itself at the surface.
HABITAT Seen in coastal waters all round the British Isles, especially off the south-west coast of Wales.
FOOD Mainly fish.

2 Bottle-nosed dolphin
Tursiops truncatus

The bottle-nosed dolphin is one of the most commonly seen members of the whale family, and certainly the friendliest, often spotted 'planing' in the bow wave of boats, leaping playfully out of the water, or swimming with pilot whales or even human beings. Look for a long, muscular, streamlined, slate-grey body, 2.5–2.7m (8–9ft) long, with lighter undersides, a long, sickle-shaped dorsal fin and a conspicuous, distinct snout shaped like the neck of a bottle. This snout differentiates it from the otherwise very similar porpoise. Dolphins often occur in small groups, but whole schools of them may fish cooperatively when large shoals of fish are present – gulls also gather overhead, which is a good give-away if you are dolphin-watching. They communicate by a series of clicks and whistling sounds.

HABITAT Mostly off the south and south-west coasts as well as Scotland, in estuaries and close inshore, during the summer.
FOOD Fish, mainly herring.

3 Minke whale
Balaenoptera acutorostrata

The minke whale is an awesome sight. It has a large, typical whale-shaped body, up to 8.5m (28ft) long, with a very dark grey (almost black) back, a conspicuous light grey band across the flippers and a relatively small dorsal fin. Look for a very long mouth with a small eye almost at its end. Another useful identification feature is that a spouting minke produces a wide, inconspicuous blow rather than an upright jet of water, as is the case with many other whales. Like other similar whales, the minke feeds by taking in huge quantities of water via the mouth; it then filters out the fish and other small marine creatures using its baleen (comb-like plates that hang from the upper jaw), gulps down the food and forces the seawater out. A special whale-watching trip to see the minke is well worthwhile. Minkes seen off British waters are usually solitary but several may be seen during the migration season.
HABITAT Deep water well offshore; can be seen from cliff-tops off the north-west coast of Scotland and from the islands of Mull, Eigg and Rhum, from April to September.
FOOD Fish, krill and other small marine creatures.

OPPOSITE A group of grey seals basking on the coast.
OVERLEAF Bottle-nosed dolphins always look as if they enjoy life as they leap playfully out of the water.

4 Killer whale
Orcinus orca

It's incredible to think that the same aggresive predator you see in wildlife programmes killing seals on beaches on the other side of the world also turns up in British waters, but it is seen quite often. The killer whale (sometimes known as the orca) has a large, distinctive black-and-white body and often leaps playfully out of the water. Males are up to 9.5m (32ft) long, with a huge dorsal fin 1.8m (6ft) high; females are about 4m (12ft) smaller. Killer whales are not as aggressive as their name would suggest and aggression within the pod is rare. However, they have been known to attack boats and, since they attack seals, skin-divers (which a killer whale could mistake for a seal) tend to be wary. **HABITAT** May be seen all round our coasts, especially off west Scotland. **FOOD** Porpoises, dolphins, fish, seals, seabirds.

5 Grey seal
Halichoerus grypus

Colonies of grey seals (also known as Atlantic seals) are a breath-taking sight in the breeding season; larger than common seals, males can reach 2.5m (8ft) long, though females are a little smaller. Grey seals are noisy and quarrelsome in the breeding season and tend to be more wary of man than the common seal. The grey seal has a long face with a 'Roman nose', a flat head and often rolls of fat round the neck; the skin is dark grey with lighter greyish or brownish blotches, although the colour changes as the seal dries off. It feeds by pursuing large fish such as cod and salmon.

HABITAT In the breeding season (late autumn and early winter) seen particularly round the south-west of England, and all of Wales, Ireland and Scotland including the offshore islands, particularly the Farne Islands. The rest of the year it is seen either in coastal waters or out at sea.
FOOD Fish.

6

8 Old English goat
Capra hircus

An ancient breed, which evolved from goats first introduced from the Near East in the Stone Age, the old English goat isn't found anywhere else in the world. It is still found in free-living herds but it is now being diluted by genes from modern goats that have escaped or been released from captivity. Small, thickset and shaggy, its coloration is variable, ranging from off-white to grey-brown, with some piebald individuals. The males stand about 70cm (28in) at the shoulder and females are slightly smaller. Both sexes have rather flattened horns

6 Common seal
Phoca vitulina

The common seal, also known as the harbour seal, is often seen as a round head bobbing in the water. The pleasant, 'smiley' facial expression, short nose with nostrils that almost meet just above the mouth in a 'V' shape, and 'dished' face make it easy to tell from the long-nosed and more 'serious-looking' grey seal. The common seal often basks on mud and sand banks, with its body arched, keeping its head and tail off the ground (unlike the grey seal, which

just flops). The common seal is a greyish brown colour, mottled with darker spots, although the skin alters in colour when dry; males are up to about 1.8m (6ft) long, females are slightly smaller. It often swims singly, although it may bask in large numbers, and feeds by diving for flatfish on the seabed.
HABITAT Swims in sheltered bays, sea lochs and harbours or basks on sand banks, mostly off the Wash, the north-west coast of Scotland and all of Ireland.
FOOD Fish.

7 Soay sheep
Ovis aries

Our most ancient breed of sheep, Soay sheep are small, slender and dark brown with a white belly. Rams stand 50cm (20in) at the shoulder, but ewes are slightly smaller. Both sexes have horns but those of the ewe are slim and curve upwards and outwards on either side of the head, while those of the ram are thick and solid and curve round behind the ears and down towards the chin. Lambs have a lighter brown coat and no horns. Soay sheep are popular for conservation grazing on nature reserves, since unlike modern sheep they need little management, not even shearing, as their fleece moults naturally each June and their tiny feet do not cause soil erosion in sensitive habitats. They are also sometimes kept as lawn-mowing pets.
HABITAT St Kilda and other Scottish offshore islands, but also found in many coastal areas and inland, for example Cheddar Gorge.
FOOD Grass.

8

that sweep back from the top of the head; the horns of the males are larger. Kids are born in spring, at first hidden and solitary, but then females and kids gather in herds in summer; rutting takes place in autumn.
HABITAT Round some parts of the coast and in a few inland forests.
FOOD Mainly heather, gorse, scrub.

7

9 Ferret
Mustela furo

The ferrets in the wild in Britain are domestic ferrets that have escaped and turned feral. Look for a long, rather cylindrical animal, 36cm (14in) long with a bushy tail 12cm (4¾in) long, usually with

cream fur and pink eyes, nose and ears, though some have more polecat-like markings and are known as polecat ferrets – these have a brown body, buff face and a white nose and ear tips.
HABITAT Throughout the British Isles, but particularly on the Isle of Man, where there are no other large carnivores such as foxes for competition, so ferrets have become the dominant predator.
FOOD Rabbits, small rodents, frogs, insects.

10 Lesser white-toothed shrew
Crocidura suaveolens

Like other shrews, this locally common, small insectivore has a long, pointed nose and fairly short tail (body 6cm/2½in, tail 4cm/1½in); however, unlike other shrews (which have red-tipped teeth) it has all-white teeth. It produces a musky scent.
HABITAT Locally very common on the Isles of Scilly (where it is the only shrew present) and on Jersey and Sark, but not seen on the mainland.
FOOD Insects, snails.

11 Orkney vole
Microtus arvalis

Originally from the eastern Mediterranean, this vole was introduced to Orkney over 4000 years ago. Today it is so numerous on Orkney that it is responsible for supporting the unusually high density of birds of prey now found on the islands, making it a great favourite with bird-watchers. A plump, short-tailed, small-eared rodent, it is very similar in shape to a normal field vole but slightly bigger (body 11.5cm/4½in long; tail 5cm/2in) and darker in colour.
HABITAT Very common throughout Orkney, but not seen anywhere else in the British Isles (a different subspecies is found on Guernsey).
FOOD Grass, roots, bulbs.

12 Skomer vole
Clethrionomys glareolus skomerensis

Probably the best known of the various island races of rodents, the Skomer vole is a subspecies of the bank vole, with typical bank-vole shape and colouring – plump, with a moderately short tail and reddish brown fur. As is typical of island races, the Skomer vole is bigger than its mainland counterpart (body 11.5cm/4½in; tail 6cm/2½in long); it is also more thickset and almost twice the weight of the bank vole.
HABITAT Very common on the island of Skomer, off the Welsh coast, but it is not found anywhere else.
FOOD Seeds, nuts, berries, fungi.

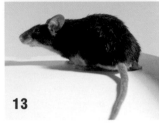

13 Black rat
Rattus rattus

Usually black but sometimes brown, this nocturnal creature has long whiskers and large pink ears that easily distinguish it from the brown rat. The body is 20cm (8in) long with a tail very slightly longer than the body (unlike the brown rat, whose tail is several centimetres shorter than the body). Originally a tropical species, the black rat is known to have been in Britain by Roman times and was responsible for introducing the plague – a deadly virus that was carried by rat fleas. Its numbers declined after the more resilient and more indiscriminate brown rat was introduced in the 1700s. The black rat is now rare in the British Isles.
HABITAT On a few offshore islands only (it was recently exterminated from Lundy).
FOOD Mainly vegetable matter.

Plants

1 Monterey pine
Pinus radiata

This is a reasonably common and attractive coastal conifer, up to 30m (100ft) tall, with a loose, slightly shaggy outline and a domed, bushy top when mature. The needles are very straight and grassy green, 10–16cm (4–6¼in) long, growing bunched together in groups of 3. The inconspicuous flowers appear in spring; male flowers are clusters of greenish yellow 'buds' at the base of new growth, and female flowers look like a cluster of 3–5 tiny red cones towards the tip of new growth. Mature cones are short and fat with a lopsided tip, and can hang on the tree for up to 30 years. The bark is brown with deep, craggy, horizontal fissures.

HABITAT Mostly southern England; being salt-tolerant it is often used as a windbreak.

2 Corsican pine
Pinus nigra laricio

This is a fairly common, tall, upright conifer, to 35m (115ft), with a straight trunk and a rather conical outline that tapers off to a pointed tip when mature. The branches are strongly horizontal and arranged in whorls, like the spokes of a wheel with the trunk as their spindle. The sage-green needles are unusually long, 12–18cm (4¾–7in), and often slightly twisted, growing in pairs. It flowers in spring; male flowers form the clusters of greenish yellow 'buds' at the base of new growth in spring, and female flowers look like tiny red dots at the very tips of the new growth. The cones seem very similar to those of Scots pine, but if you shake out the seeds from a ripe Corsican pine cone, you'll see they are twice the size. The bark is dark grey or brown, with shallow, horizontal fissures that are sometimes pink-tinted.

HABITAT All round the coast, including sand dunes. Also inland forestry plantations where soil is light, dry and sandy (such as the Brecklands of East Anglia).

3 Tamarisk
Tamarix gallica

Tamarisk is quite a common evergreen seaside shrub or small tree, with a loose, slightly untidy shape, to 3m (10ft). Its whippy branches are clad in small, scale-like leaves, giving the plant a feathery appearance. The flowers

are tiny, pink or white, borne in spikes at the ends of the twigs from July to September. It is one of the few big shrubs capable of growing in harsh, windy, salty seaside conditions, and the only one with feathery foliage.

HABITAT Planted all round the British coast, including windy headlands, right up to the beach and even on sand dunes.

4 Duke of Argyll's tea tree
Lycium barbarum

Although not native to Britain, this bushy-to-upright, spiny deciduous shrub, 2–3m (6½–10ft) high, has grown wild around the British coasts for hundreds of years, probably escaping from gardens before the beginning of the 19th century. It has narrow, pointed leaves, 5cm (2in) long – these are the food of the death's head hawkmoth caterpillar – and from June to October it bears pale lilac flowers, which are made up of 5 petals joined together at the base; these are followed in late summer to autumn by reddish orange or yellow, egg-shaped berries, 2cm (¾in) long. The berries are poisonous.
HABITAT Dry, sandy soil near the sea, often invading hedges or scrub, especially round the south coast of England.

5 Sea buckthorn
Hippophae rhamnoides

Most easily identified in autumn and winter, when it is covered with berries, sea buckthorn is a fairly common, prickly deciduous shrub, 1–2.5m (3–8ft) high, with needle-like leaves, 7.5cm (3in) long. In a

sheltered spot, it grows fairly upright to bushy, but in exposed areas it makes angular, wind-sculpted, craggy or even ground-hugging shapes. The flowers, borne from March to April, are tiny, inconspicuous and leaf-green; male and female flowers are produced on separate plants, so the oval, orange-yellow berries are produced only where there is a mixed group.
HABITAT All round the coast, including very windswept sites right down to the beach, but only in open, sunny sites.

6 Channel wrack
Pelvetia canaliculata

Also known as channelled wrack, this is a very common, deep green seaweed that grows in dense, mistletoe-like clusters. It has narrow, ribbon-like fronds, up to 15cm (6in) long; the slightly elongated-to-bulbous frond tips are the reproductive bodies (there are no air bladders). It spends much of the day exposed to the air, when the edges of the fronds roll inwards to reduce moisture loss, creating the 'channel' that gives this plant its name. Channel wrack may turn blackish during long exposure to hot sun, but revives at the next high tide.
HABITAT High up on the shore all round the coastline, including Scottish offshore islands, attached to rocks and stones; also in estuaries and creeks.

7 Spiral wrack
Fucus spiralis

Uncovered for half the day or more, this commonly seen, deep khaki-green seaweed grows in loose clusters, with fronds 30–40cm (12–16in) long, sometimes slightly twisted (but hardly noticeable enough to justify the common name), with no air bladders. The tips of the fronds are often enlarged and are sometimes heart-shaped.

HABITAT All round the British Isles' coastline on the upper and middle shore, attached to rocks or stones, or growing on jetties and pilings of piers.

8 Bladder wrack
Fucus vesiculosus

Easily identified by its conspicuous, pea-sized bladders, usually arranged in pairs, this is a very common, brownish seaweed with narrow, branching fronds, up to 90cm (36in) long. It is uncovered for roughly half the day, and at low tide it dries out to a dark, green-tinged black.

HABITAT All round the coast, often growing on rocks uncovered at low tide, including those in creeks and estuaries.

9 Kelp
Laminaria species

This is a group of fairly common seaweeds with long, brown, rubbery, ribbon-like fronds, 1–2m (3–6½ft) long, that grow in large underwater 'forests'. Each branching plant has a long, straight, slippery, bootlace-like stem at the base, attaching the bunch of fronds to a holdfast, which wraps itself round rocks and pebbles on the sea floor for anchorage. Most species are very similar, but one stands out as different – the sea belt (*Laminaria saccharina*), which produces a single, long, stemless leaf like a wide, rubbery brown ribbon with a wavy edge. It is rarely (if ever) uncovered by low tides.

HABITAT Just offshore all round the coast.

Seaweeds and their uses

As a general rule, the darker the colour of seaweed, the deeper it tends to grow. Green seaweeds are found on the shoreline, in shallow rock pools and in shallow water, where they may be uncovered by the tide for part of the time; red seaweeds grow in slightly deeper water, including rock pools; brown seaweeds live in deeper water still, where they are rarely (if ever) uncovered by low tides.

Several seaweeds are edible. Laver (*Porphyra umbilicalis*) is the Welsh delicacy laverbread, and it's the same plant that the Japanese dry in sheets to roll round their sushi. It has large, soft, delicate, lettuce-like leaves and is green when young, becoming purple when older – it turns black when it dries out at low tide. Types of kelp (*Laminaria* species) are harvested in much of the world to provide alginates used in the manufacture of ice cream and cosmetics, and for the iodine they contain. Carragheen (*Chondrus crispus*) is another edible seaweed, also known as Irish moss; in Mrs Beeton's day, it was used to make milk 'set' in the preparation of a nutritious (and almost certainly revolting) blancmange fed to invalids.

In the photograph above, taken in Northumberland in autumn, redshank and turnstone are seen feeding on invertebrates that they find among the seaweed as the tide comes in.

10 Eel grass
Zostera marina

Despite the name, this is not a grass, or even a seaweed, but a common flowering plant that is pollinated in water. It has narrow, ribbon-like strands, up to 1m (3ft) long and 5mm (³⁄₁₆ in) wide, that grow from creeping rhizomes in the mud and form dense thickets. It is the main food plant of Brent geese, which spend the winter on Britain's coasts.

HABITAT Salt marshes, extending from the tidal mud flats down to the low-tide mark, all round the coast.

11 Scurvy grass
Cochlearia officinalis

The thick, succulent, heart-shaped leaves of this slightly unusual plant are rich in vitamin C and were once eaten by sailors to prevent scurvy. Despite its name, it is not a grass but a loose, rosette-shaped flowering plant, 10–50cm (4–20in) high, related to wild cabbage. The faintly scented flowers appear towards the tips of short spikes from May or June to August, and are followed by round seedpods.

HABITAT Drier areas within salt marshes, and also pockets of soil on cliff ledges.

12 Sea lavender
Limonium vulgare

This fairly common, low-growing, semi-woody perennial plant, 12cm (4¾in) high, has loose rosettes of glaucous, succulent foliage that spreads to make ground-hugging mats. It flowers from July to September/October, producing branching spikes tipped with tiny, lavender-coloured 'buds', and looks very similar to the closely related statice, grown by gardeners for flower arranging.

HABITAT Along the high-tide line of salt marshes.

13 Sea aster
Aster tripolium

One of our showiest coastal plants, the sea aster is a short perennial, 15–45cm (6–17½in) high, with loose spikes of small, pale lavender, daisy flowers with yellow centres from July to October. It resembles a short, squat Michaelmas daisy growing in large clumps, or sometimes covering the ground with mats of long, narrow foliage.

HABITAT Mainly around the high-tide line of salt marshes, often growing with sea purslane, but also sometimes on cliffs and rocks.

14 Marsh samphire
Salicornia europaea

Also known as glasswort, and locally common on some coasts, samphire is the delicacy occasionally sold in fish shops and restaurants. Look for tussocks of succulent, branching, short-jointed green stems, 7.5–30cm (3–12in) tall, looking rather like tiny Christmas trees arising from bare mud at low tide. The old stems turn reddish brown later in the season, then plants die down for the winter. It has inconspicuous flowers from August to October.

HABITAT From spring to autumn, on some salt marshes round the south and east coasts of England, growing in the muddy lower regions that are covered by seawater for part of the day.

15 Sea purslane
Atriplex portulacoides

A common feature of salt marshes and creeks, this rather unexciting plant is identified by its large, low, sprawling, silvery green mats (15–60cm/6–24in high) made up of

14

densely packed, elliptical to paddle-shaped leaves, roughly 2–3cm (¾–1¼in) long. The spikes of yellow flowers, which are borne from July to September, are not especially showy.

HABITAT Higher ground round the edges of salt marshes and creeks, and along the high-tide marks round coasts, especially of southern England and the western side of Scotland.

16

16 Sea beet
Beta vulgaris subsp. *maritima*

This is a common perennial that looks like a large, tough, glossy-leaved version of garden spinach that's run to seed (it is a close cousin). It forms a rosette of large, almost triangular lower leaves, 30–90cm (12–36in) tall, through the centre of which appears a tall central spike with inconspicuous greenish yellow flowers from June to October.

HABITAT Salt marshes, shingle, pebbly or rocky beaches and cliffs all round the British Isles' coast from spring to autumn.

15

17 Thrift

Armeria maritima

This attractive and fairly common coastal plant, with narrow, grassy leaves, forms short evergreen tussocks or larger clumps, approximately 15cm (6in) high. Plants are covered with pink and very occasionally white flowers from April to August.

HABITAT Mostly grassy cliffs and rocks; occasionally on raised ground above the high-tide mark of stony shores.

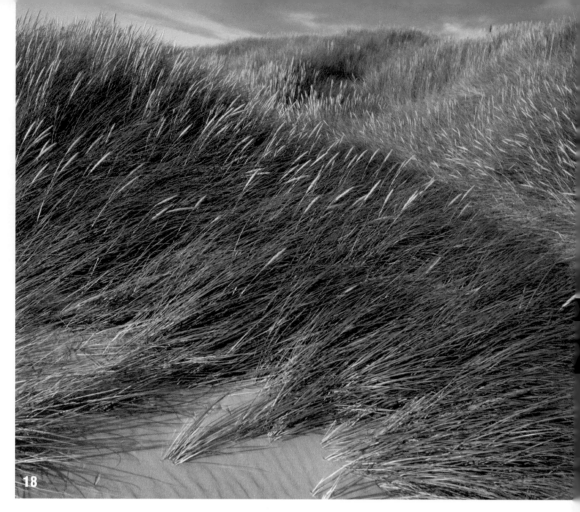

18 Marram grass

Ammophila arenaria

Probably our commonest coastal grass, this is often deliberately planted to stabilize sand dunes. It makes tall, coarse, stiff, upright evergreen tussocks, 60–120cm (2–4ft) high, and spreads by underground runners, in a similar way to couch grass. The roots, which hold the sand in place, form a dense network several centimetres underground; they are often visible at the edge of areas where erosion has set in. It has unexciting cream plumes of typical grass-like flowers from June to August.

HABITAT Sand dunes, all round the British Isles' coast.

19 Sea holly

Eryngium maritimum

Resembling a rugged version of the cultivated sea hollies that grow in gardens, this is a fairly uncommon but easily recognized coastal perennial, 30–60cm (12–24in) high, with tough, steely blue, prickly, holly-like leaves. When it first appears above ground in spring it forms a shaggy rosette, which develops over the summer into an untidy, tight-packed, bushy plant with metallic silvery blue, starburst-shaped flowers from July to August.

HABITAT Found on sandy, shingle or pebble beaches all round the coast.

OPPOSITE Thrift makes a colourful covering to cliff-tops on rocky coasts, and the evergreen tufts knit together, making an all-year-round covering that reduces soil erosion.

21 Sea kale
Crambe maritima
This is a handsome, solid, cabbage-like perennial plant, 30–60cm (12–24in) tall and the same across, with rather wavy-edged, thick, waxy, silvery blue-grey leaves, and stalks of small, crowded white flowers from June to August. The flowers resemble those of run-to-seed garden cabbage.
HABITAT From spring to autumn, on stony or shingly shores, sometimes cliffs and rocks, all round the coast except northern Scotland.

22 Sea campion
Silene maritima
The sea campion is a fairly common small perennial plant, 7.5–20cm (3–8in) high. It forms rather straggly clumps, with pairs of oval green leaves spaced out along the stems. The attractive white flowers appear between June and August and have a pronounced grey 'bladder' at the base of their petals.
HABITAT Shingle and stony beaches, rocks and cliffs, between spring and autumn.

20 Sea spurge
Euphorbia paralias
Short and bushy, this fairly uncommon perennial, 7.5–20cm (3–8in) high, has unbranched upright stems clad in delicate foliage. From June to September it is topped with small, lime-to-apple-green flowerheads made up of cup-shaped green bracts encircling small, inconspicuous, yellowish flowers, which are easily recognized by anyone who grows *Euphorbia* in the garden.
HABITAT On sand dunes round the coasts of southern England, Norfolk, Ireland and the Channel Islands from spring to late autumn.

23 Tree mallow
Lavatera arborea

Striking and rather upright, this biennial has a single 'trunk' or several tall, straight, upright stems, 90–120cm (3–4ft) high, growing up from the base of the plant. The stem or stems are clad in large, tough, thick, almost rounded, grey-green leaves with a slightly felty texture, and spikes of pink flowers appear from July to September. The tree mallow is similar to the mallows that grow in the garden, but it is smaller and more ragged.
HABITAT Stony or rocky shores and coastal wasteland, mostly along the south and west coasts of England.

24 Hottentot fig
Carpobrotus edulis

The Hottentot fig is a creeping evergreen succulent, 15–90cm (6–36in) high, which eventually forms large mats several metres wide. The leaves are finger-like, and from May to August the plant carries large, yellow or magenta-pink flowers, which are 5–7.5cm (2–3in) across and open only in direct sunlight; they are very similar to the Livingstone daisies that are grown in gardens as summer annuals. In very warm, sunny spots, flowers are often followed by a fleshy fruit, originally eaten by the Hottentot tribe of South Africa.
HABITAT A South African 'escapee', now locally common on sandy banks, dunes and wasteland along the coasts of Devon, Cornwall, the Isles of Scilly and parts of Ireland.

25 Wild cabbage
Brassica oleracea

A rather unexciting wildflower, this is of interest as it is the ancestor of today's cabbages, kales and other greens. It is a thickset plant, up to 60cm (24in) high, with typically grey-green, cabbage-like leaves at the base, but instead of forming a heart-like cultivated cabbage it runs to seed, producing a tall, charlock-like spike of yellow flowers on an upright stem.
HABITAT Now grows only on sea cliffs round parts of southern England (especially the Dover area), Wales and Yorkshire.

26 Yellow horned poppy
Glaucium flavum

This is a striking, slightly unusual annual or perennial seashore plant, forming a loose, untidy mound, 30–75cm (12–30in) high, of ferny, glaucous green foliage. From June to September it bears large, yellow, typical poppy flowers, up to 7.5cm (3in) across, with crumpled petals. The long, slender, often slightly curved seedpods, up to 30cm (12in) long, give the plant its 'horned' name, and both the flowers and the seedpods can be seen on the plant at the same time. All parts of the yellow horned poppy are poisonous.

HABITAT Stony and shingle banks on the upper shores of beaches round the British Isles' coast, but absent in northern Scotland.

27 Sea bindweed
Calystegia soldanella

This is a relatively unusual, sprawling seaside perennial that grows completely prostrate, creeping out over the ground for 45–60cm (17½–24in). The stems are sparsely clad with small, neat, waxy-textured, kidney-shaped leaves in mid-green to deep green. The flowers, which are dotted singly along the stems from June to August, are circular and striped pink and white with a yellow eye in the centre; they are up to 5cm (2in) across.

HABITAT Sand dunes or shingle coasts of England and Wales.

28 Sea sandwort
Honckenya peploides

Although unremarkable to look at, this is an invaluable coastal plant, as it is one of the first to colonize sand dunes, thus helping to stabilize this fragile ecosystem. The closely packed leaves form a low, bright green mat, about 5cm (2in) high, spreading to 30–90cm (12–36in). From May to September, small, fairly insignificant, single, pale yellowish green, star-shaped flowers are tucked in between the leaves.

HABITAT Sand dunes, shingle and stony banks and wasteland at the top of sandy beaches.

29 Sea rocket
Cakile maritima

This is a common, low-spreading, mat-shaped plant that looks rather like an untidy patch of pale green seaweed, with weak, floppy stems and much-reduced glaucous foliage. From June to August it has small clusters of smallish pink, lilac or white flowers at the tips of the stems. Although not particularly special, it is one of the few plants

that grows in the part of the beach that is notorious for accumulating all the litter, plastic bottles and other rubbish left stranded by high tides. **HABITAT** Along the high-tide mark, growing at the top of sandy and shingle beaches.

30 Wild carrot
Daucus carota

The ancestor of cultivated carrots, the wild carrot has a small, off-white taproot that bears little similarity to the vegetable we know today, although the carroty scent is distinctive and familiar. It is a slightly unusual, cow-parsley-like perennial, making a clump of ferny foliage, with tall, upright stems 75–90cm (30–36in) high. Between June and August, the clump is topped with dense, white, slightly domed heads of flowers (up to 7.5cm/3in across) that resemble cow parsley flowerheads but are more tightly packed, and with a conspicuous, long, shaggy green frill at the base of each flower. When the wild carrot has finished flowering, the seedheads close up to form a tight-packed ball, making plants easy to identify from some distance away. **HABITAT** Well drained, sandy or chalky soil near the sea, in wasteland and fields near the coast but also further inland.

31 Rock samphire
Crithmum maritimum

This is an unusual, bushy succulent, 15–30cm (6–12in) high, with branching, ribbed, tubular stems and long, narrow, grey-green leaves and umbels of pale greenish yellow flowers similar to those of fennel from June to August. **HABITAT** Rocks, cliffs and shingle in southern and western British Isles.

Also found on coasts or islands

Carrion crow (see p.304)
Irish hare (see p.199)
Jackdaw (see p.304)
Kestrel (see p.298)
Lapwing (see p.190)
Mountain hare (see p.147)
Peregrine falcon (see p.134)
Pygmy shrew (see p.147)
Short-eared owl (see p.136)
Skylark (see p.191)
Starling (see p.304)
Wren (see p.301)

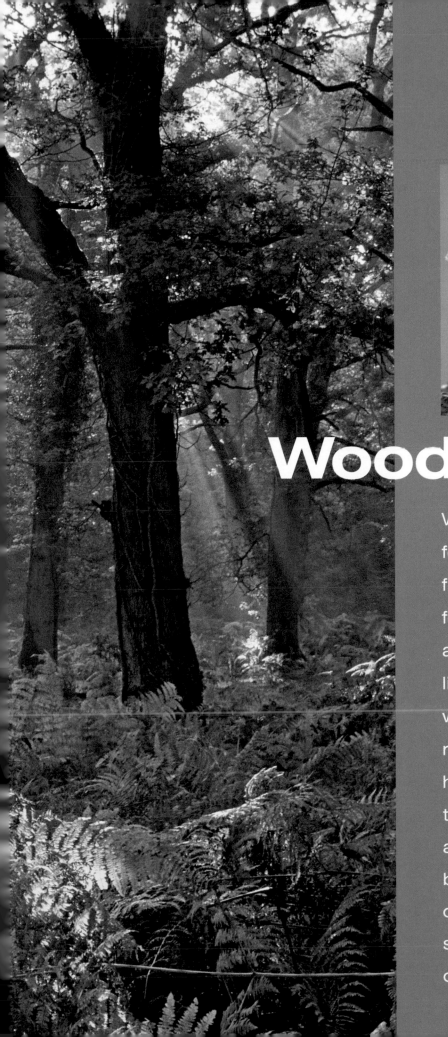

Woodland

Woodland is a high-rise hotel for wildlife, providing five-star facilities right the way up the food chain. The basement is alive with 'creepy-crawlies' living in leaf litter and rotting wood. Undergrowth full of roots, shoots and fallen nuts houses anything from rodents to foraging wild-boar families, and trees offer bed-and-breakfast to a variety of creatures that enjoy the security of height and dense, leafy cover.

Arctic landscape to wildwoods

After the last ice age ended and our climate began to warm up, roughly 10,000 years ago, retreating glaciers left bare ground, known as tundra, in their wake. At first all that grew was arctic scrub, but trees slowly colonized the warming land. Britain was joined to mainland Europe until around 8000 years ago, when the melting ice refilled the English Channel and cut us off from the Continent.

Trees first started growing in the south of Britain and slowly seeded themselves northwards as the ice retreated and the land thawed out, allowing growing conditions to improve. It happened in much the same way as it does if you leave your garden untended for years. Some species arrived early, and those with the ability to take over bare ground quickly filled the space, making it hard for later arrivals to elbow themselves in, so these dominant species took over.

The first colonizers were birch, pine, hazel, aspen (*Populus tremula*, the one with the famous quivering leaves) and sallow (various species of willows), followed by alder and oak. Next came elms and lime – not the lime you see growing in parks and planted as street trees today, but the small-leaved lime *Tilia cordata*, which is now quite uncommon as a wild woodland tree. Holly, ash and hornbeam came later,

when the ground was already fairly well shaded by earlier arrivals, so they had a struggle finding places where there was enough light for them. Beech came later still.

Over time, a great proportion of Britain was covered by a dense layer of huge, tall trees. These were the wildwoods. They weren't like a modern forest, which is usually made up almost entirely of one sort of tree. The wildwoods contained a mixture of species, but the precise make-up varied all round the country, since some species did better in certain areas than others, all depending on how the soil, rainfall and temperatures suited them. Scotland ended up with mostly pines and birches, while oaks thrived in England. As old trees died, they were regenerated by self-sown seedlings growing up from the forest floor. These woods were the dominant feature of Britain's landscape for thousands of years.

There's a popular belief that the wildwoods persisted into medieval times and that our original oak forests were cleared to provide timber for Tudor warships, but that's just not true. The oaks used by Tudor ship-builders came from managed forests that grew up much later. The wildwoods had been heavily managed long before that by early man. Evidence suggests that areas of ground, kept open by grazing animals, may also have been a vital part of wildwoods.

Enter man, the farmer

The first wave of human settlers to colonize Britain after the last ice age didn't make much impact on the forests – they were hunter-gatherers, who moved around looking for food where they could find it. However, around 4000 BC new arrivals brought with them the basics of a brand-new cottage industry – farming – which had already been developed in the Near East. It was a huge advance. At last we could settle down in one place, keep livestock and grow food crops, which meant that it was worth building proper houses instead of temporary huts.

You can see the immediate problem. Agriculture emerged in countries whose natural landscape was dominated by wide, open plains – vast areas on which field crops could easily be superimposed. But Britain was covered in enormous trees, so our ancestors had to chop them down in order to farm the land. In the areas of densest population, such as the Brecklands of East Anglia, the chalk downs of southern England and the Somerset Levels, the wildwoods were replaced by open countryside within 2000 years. River valleys were also popular places for farmers to settle, because the soil was rich and silty and water was in plentiful supply. These areas were quickly cleared too.

It has been estimated that by the Iron Age, around 500 BC, half the country had already been cleared of wildwood, and pollen records show that a lot of plants typical of open countryside were becoming quite widespread. We don't know for sure when the very last patch of wildwood was cleared, but it was almost certainly way back in prehistory – which tempers the righteous indignation you might feel at all this desecration of the countryside with a certain admiration for an ancestor equipped only with primitive hand tools.

But Iron-Age Britain wasn't a total patchwork of fields. There were woods right enough, but these were secondary woodlands that had regrown naturally on previously cleared land, from fallen seeds, tree stumps or underground roots (a lot of our British native trees are very good at regenerating themselves in this way). Birds and animals would have had a hand in redistributing tree seeds too.

PREVIOUS PAGES Oak woodland in autumn (main picture), and blood foot fungus on a fallen tree (small picture).
BELOW LEFT A deciduous forest of beech trees in spring.
BELOW CENTRE A carpet of bluebells is a good indicator of undisturbed ancient woodland. They grow and flower in spring, before the leaf canopy makes conditions too dark.
BELOW RIGHT An oak tree in the Lake District. Oaks are among our most ancient trees, and their shape plays a key part in the British landscape.

These self-grown woods were valuable resources that were managed over many centuries – they were the supermarkets and DIY centres of Britain, well into medieval times. Woodlands provided a fair bit of food – nuts and woodland fruit – and meat; pigs were turned out in the woods in the autumn to fatten up on acorns ready for the seasonal slaughter. Woods were also the source of fuel – people collected firewood for cooking and heating. Suitable tree species, such as hazel, were also 'coppiced' – cut hard back regularly – to produce long, straight poles for fencing and building materials (see page 117). But dotted in with coppiced hazels were a few good timber species, such as oak, which would be left to grow up to a good size before being cut and sawn up into planks and beams for house-building. It was all done by hand, with one man standing in a saw-pit with a very long saw, which was controlled by his mate at the other end, above ground. No hardwood timber was wasted; when buildings were taken down, the old beams and planks would be carefully reused.

Medieval era to the twentieth century

By the time Britain had been invaded by the Normans, woodland covered one-fifth of the country. We know because it's all in the Domesday Book, compiled in 1086 by order of William the Conqueror, who wanted to keep tabs on who owned what in his new territory in order to tax them. William and his Norman noblemen were very keen on hunting – they introduced fallow deer to this country and set aside large areas of suitable land for hunting parks, which were called 'forests'. But don't imagine areas of densely planted trees, like you see in today's forests – the word originally meant a place for hunting deer, regardless of the landscape. Think of the much more open terrain of the New Forest in Hampshire, which was one of those set up by William. It hasn't changed much since.

The area of land covered by woodlands increased as a result of the Black Death, which started in 1349 and came back in several waves over the next 300 years. As it killed off a third of the population, most of whom were farm workers, landowners had to find a new crop that didn't need as much labour as field crops – so they settled on sheep, and a lot of arable fields were put down to grazing. When the sheep were taken out of the fields, uncultivated ground slowly returned

to woodland, all on its own, since stray seedlings were no longer being grazed off. The only places this didn't happen were where the soil was too wet or too dry for trees to do well, such as the Fens of East Anglia and the Brecklands of Norfolk.

By Elizabethan times, the weather took a turn for the worse and Britain suffered a 'mini ice age'. It was so cold that the river Thames regularly froze over and 'frost fairs' were held on the ice. By now a lot of people were living in towns, so they couldn't just help themselves to free firewood from the countryside; they had to buy it from vendors and, because of the cold, the high demand pushed prices up enormously. Not only that, they also had to buy their bread from bakers, whose ovens were fuelled by bundles of straight sticks – faggots – that had to be produced in just the right shape and size to fit. Woodlands had become valuable assets.

The Industrial Revolution changed daily life enormously in eighteenth-century Britain, but, far from vanishing, woodlands became more important. Industry needed charcoal to provide the high temperatures needed for iron- and glass-making furnaces, and when coal mining began, there was a huge demand for wooden pit props. Timber was also needed for ship-building – particularly at the time of the Napoleonic wars and, later, for the tea clippers that made high-speed deliveries between London and the colonies.

By the nineteenth century, coal had taken over as our chief industrial fuel and building materials were becoming more sophisticated. There was now little demand for wooden poles, so many areas of woodland that had previously been coppiced were left to go wild. However, the First World War soon changed that state of affairs. Suddenly the country needed to be self-sufficient, so coal production was stepped up to power factories and woodlands were back in pit-prop production. Timber was also needed for shoring up military trenches and for general building works. Indeed, half a million acres of woodland was cut down for the war effort.

Seeing supplies of wood vanishing so quickly, the government set up the Forestry Commission to replenish supplies. Native timber trees, such as oaks, were too slow-growing for commercial production; quick results were essential, so the Forestry Commission planted conifers, mostly North American species such as lodgepole pine, Douglas fir and Sitka spruce – the latter was ready to cut in just 40 years, a third of the time it took to grow usable oak.

Conifers also had the great advantage of doing well on poor soil in cold areas at high altitude, so they were planted in huge numbers on northern moorlands and in the Scottish highlands – areas which were of little use for agriculture. And while it's true that conifers don't yield high-quality timber, it was these cheap and cheerful softwoods that were needed in post-war Britain for making prefab buildings, window frames, telegraph poles and railway sleepers, among other things.

Wildlife woods

Modern woodlands are often managed more for wildlife than for timber production. If you go down to the woods today, you'll often find a wealth of spring flowers, such as primroses, violets, bluebells and wood anemones, which pop up and flower while the trees are bare. Once the trees come into full leaf, the regular 'dark spell' each summer is enough to keep nuisance weeds like invasive grasses and nettles under control naturally. You may see a good range of fungi growing on fallen logs and in the rich leafmould, and round the edges of woods, or in wide 'rides' through the middle, the extra light makes it possible for a good many countryside wildflowers

and several butterflies to thrive, so there's a fair food supply for a range of birds and animals as well.

Where ancient woodlands have been lost, the memory often still lingers in old place names. The Anglo-Saxons had almost as many different words for woods as the Eskimos do for snow – in both cases referring to different types – so look out for places ending in 'holt', 'grove', 'shaw' or 'hanger'. Copse is short for coppice, which they called a 'hag' in the north of Britain, and a 'spinney' was a wood full of prickly trees such as hawthorn or blackthorn, from the Latin *spina*, meaning a thorn. Viking or Saxon woodland place names ended in 'land', or began with 'lound' or 'lownde'. So keep your eyes peeled whenever you are out in the car with a map. Ancient woodlands have left their legacies, even if many of them are now covered by concrete.

Today 'commoners' are still allowed to graze livestock, including pigs, in the New Forest in Hampshire. They rootle for acorns, beech mast, worms and insects.

Birds

1 Sparrowhawk
Accipiter nisus

This increasingly common bird has a streamlined bird-of-prey shape. The male sparrowhawk has a rich blue-grey head, back, wings and tail, with a strongly barred, orange-brown breast and underparts, orange eyes, orange 'cheeks' and yellow feet.

Sparrohawks have a strident 'kik-kik-kik' call. When cruising, they have a characteristic 'flap, flap, glide' flying style typical of a hawk.

Hunting sparrowhawks are very agile and chase small songbirds, negotiating obstacles at high speed. Female sparrowhawks, which are considerably larger than males (up to 25 per cent in some cases), can tackle birds up to the size of wood-pigeons. If you find a heap of soft grey dove feathers on the lawn – with no trace of a carcass – suspect a sparrowhawk strike rather than a cat. Urban sparrowhawks have learned to perch up on roofs or tall trees looking out for bird tables in use. In areas known to have resident sparrowhawks, songbirds are increasingly wary at bird tables, with very good reason.

HABITAT Woodland and well-wooded farmland, but increasingly makes lightning appearances in domestic gardens.
SIZE Male 30cm (12in); female 38cm (15in)
EGGS 4–5, white
NEST Flat arrangement of sticks high up in trees, where a strong branch joins the trunk.
FOOD Males take small birds, such as sparrows, finches and tits, while the bigger females take larger prey, including blackbirds, starlings and also collared doves.
SIMILAR TO Kestrel (but the kestrel has a different hunting technique, hovering, then descending on prey), other birds of prey (which prefer more open territory) and cuckoo (which has very pointed wings, while sparrowhawks' wings are broader with rounded tips).
VARIATIONS Female is grey-brown with brownish grey bars on the underparts (which appear light buff from a distance) and a more strongly barred tail in light and dark grey-brown (the male's blue-grey tail is more subtly barred darker grey); the eyes are yellow, not orange. The juvenile has a warm brown back and bars.

2 Goshawk
Accipiter gentilis

This is a rare and secretive, sparrowhawk-like bird of prey, much used in falconry. The male goshawk is about one-third larger than the female sparrowhawk, while the female goshawk is much bigger, nearly as big as a buzzard. Both sexes have grey upperparts, bluer in the male, browner in the female, with whitish, grey-barred underparts and yellow legs; if

given a good view of a perching bird, you may see the broad white stripe above the dark orange eyes.
HABITAT In scattered locations throughout the British Isles, but not Ireland, in forests or very dense woodland with open countryside, which it hunts over, nearby.
SIZE Male 50cm (20in), wingspan 90cm (36in); female 60cm (24in), wingspan 1.2m (4ft)
EGGS 3–4, pale blue
NEST Large construction of sticks in the fork of a fair-sized tree.
FOOD Squirrels, rabbits, hares, pigeons, other birds up to the size of large grouse or pheasants.
SIMILAR TO Sparrowhawk, which has less prominent white 'eyebrows' and is much smaller. Look for a round end to the tail in the goshawk (it is squared in the sparrowhawk) and in flight, a much bulkier, deeper-chested body and slower wing-beats.

3 Tawny owl
Strix aluco

The tawny owl is our most widespread and numerous owl. It is more often heard than seen, since it roosts by day and hunts at night – this is the species that

makes the well-known nocturnal hoots. It roosts in trees (often in hollows, or close up against the trunk, or among ivy) with an upright stance, but is hard to spot – look for a chestnut owl with a buff breast and underparts patterned with brown streaks and chevron shapes (a hand-knitted-toy effect), with a large, round, bright buff face and distinctive, big black eyes from which fine facial feathers radiate. This 'facial disc' (for focusing sound) is surrounded by a ring of darker feathers.
HABITAT Woodland, parkland and woodland gardens throughout the British Isles but not Ireland.
SIZE 38cm (15in)
EGGS 2–5, white
NEST In a hole in a tree, or in special owl nestboxes.
FOOD Mainly small rodents, also small birds and insects.
SIMILAR TO Other owls look similar in flight but the tawny flies only at night. The barn owl is much paler than the tawny.
VARIATIONS Juveniles are fluffy and downy, often grouped on tree branches during the day.

4

4 Long-eared owl
Asio otus

The long-eared owl is almost the size of a tawny owl but it has longer wings and a less stumpy shape. Also, the long-eared owl is far less vocal, although displaying males may clap their wings together overhead while flying. It is fairly common in Ireland but uncommon in Britain and is hard to see as it is usually strictly nocturnal. By day, roosting birds (sometimes in a group) perch with an upright stance on branches tucked close in to tree trunks; this is when you can see the streaky warm brown coloration and rounded, flattish face with large orange eyes. The long 'ears' are actually feathery tufts and stand up on end only if the bird is alarmed, so don't rely on them for identification.

5

HABITAT Mainly conifer plantations, but also woods and thickets; hunts at night over open countryside such as fields and coastal marshes.
SIZE 36cm (14in)
EGGS 3–5, white
NEST Usually takes over old nests of other birds or even squirrels' dreys.
FOOD Mainly voles but also other rodents and small birds.

5 Green woodpecker
Picus viridis

Also known as the yaffle, this is our largest woodpecker (town-pigeon sized), more often heard than seen, in bright green with a conspicuous red top to the head and back of neck, a dagger-like beak, a bright yellow rump and pale greyish green underparts and a long, lean, streamlined shape. In flight, it is recognized by its dart-like shape that heads determinedly in a straight line of successive swoops, often accompanied by a loud, raucous call. In a tree, birds usually cling to an upright branch or to the trunk of the tree with their beak pointing upwards at about 45 degrees to the horizontal. Perching birds often produce the characteristic 'yaffle' call – a rapid series of high-pitched, ringing, laughing sounds – that gives this woodpecker its old country name.
HABITAT In open woodland, well-wooded farmland, parkland, heaths and gardens, especially where ants nest in the lawn. Increasingly frequent throughout England and eastern Scotland.
SIZE 32cm (13in)
EGGS 4–6, white
NEST Cavity about 30cm (12in) deep, which it excavates in a tree trunk, with a modest 6cm (2½in) diameter entrance hole.
FOOD Mainly ants and their eggs, larvae and pupae.
VARIATIONS Juvenile is similar to the adult but heavily spotted whitish above and strongly streaked and barred below.

6 Great spotted woodpecker
Dendrocopos major

Our most numerous woodpecker, this is the size of a blackbird with a black-and-white-patterned body, white underparts and a red rear end and nape. If you hear 'drumming' on a tree, it's almost certainly a great or lesser spotted woodpecker performing its territorial display.
HABITAT Woodland, wooded farmland and gardens throughout the British Isles but not Ireland.
SIZE 23cm (9in)
EGGS 4–6, white
NEST Cavity in a rotting tree with a 5cm (2in) entrance hole.
FOOD Insects in summer; seeds and nuts in winter.
SIMILAR TO Lesser spotted woodpecker, but the latter is smaller and rarer and lacks the red rear end.
VARIATIONS Females lack the red nape; juveniles have duller white areas of plumage and an almost all-red crown.

6

7 Lesser spotted woodpecker
Dendrocopos minor

This is our smallest, most elusive and least common woodpecker, looking rather like a great spotted woodpecker but very tiny – only sparrow-sized – with narrow black-and-white bars on the wings and back. The underparts are buffish white with a few fine, dark streaks on the flanks. The male has a bright red cap. It spends most of its time high up in trees, fluttering about, or creeping along the outer branches looking for insects. Its drumming is longer and softer but more rattling than that of the great spotted woodpecker. Its call is a high-pitched 'pee, pee, pee'.

HABITAT Mostly deciduous woods, sometimes orchards, parks or gardens, throughout England, except the north-east.
SIZE 14cm (5½in)
EGGS 4–6, white
NEST Well hidden, in a hole bored in a tree trunk.
FOOD Mainly insects; some fruit in autumn.
SIMILAR TO Great spotted woodpecker, which is bigger, has a red rear end and is more assertive.
VARIATIONS Female lacks the red cap and has a dirty white crown. Juvenile has some red in the crown and duller, streakier underparts.

8 Nightingale
Luscinia megarhynchos

The nightingale is an uncommon summer visitor and is secretive and hard to see; you are more likely to hear its song, in the peak of the breeding season, from April to early June. Look for a large, robin-like bird but without the red breast – it has a warm brown crown, 'cheeks', back and wings and a slightly brighter chestnut tail, with a pale grey-buff breast and underparts. The nightingale is said to have the best song of any British bird and, contrary to popular belief, it sings day *and* night. However, if you think you hear a nightingale singing in town, it's almost certainly a robin (especially in Berkeley Square!).

HABITAT Summer: among brambles and dense undergrowth of woodland edges and untidy hedgerows, often near fresh water. Found roughly south-east of a line from the Humber through the Severn estuary to the Devon coast; most abundant in East Anglia and Kent.
SIZE 16cm (6¼in)
EGGS 4–5, blue-green with darker speckles
NEST Bulky cup of grass and leaves near the ground.
FOOD Woodland-floor insects and larvae; berries in autumn.
VARIATIONS Juvenile is speckly brown with a chestnut tail.

9 Redstart
Phoenicurus phoenicurus

The male redstart is one of our most striking summer visitors, with a vivid orange-red breast, a blue-grey crown and back, dark brown-grey wings, an orange-red tail with a central dark streak and a black, wedge-shaped face and throat.

HABITAT April–September: deciduous woods, old parkland with large mature trees, sometimes hilly countryside with scattered trees, throughout most of the British Isles except central England, most of East Anglia and Ireland.
SIZE 14cm (5½in)
EGGS 5–7, light blue
NEST In a hole in a tree or wall; often uses open-fronted nestboxes.
FOOD Insects and other invertebrates; fruit in autumn.
SIMILAR TO Robin, but slimmer. Look for the black, wedge-shaped face and the red tail of the redstart (red finish may be more accurate!).

10 Mistle thrush
Turdus viscivorus

Britain's largest thrush, the mistle thrush looks like a larger, longer and greyer version of the more commonly seen, browner song thrush. The mistle thrush has a grey-brown back, wings and tail, and a pale breast and underparts heavily speckled with darker brown. It is normally seen as a long, spindle-shaped silhouette against the sky, and flies high, unlike the song thrush, which typically makes a low-level dash for cover. In flight, the large patches on the underside of the mistle thrush's wings flash white. The call, which is often heard in stormy weather, sounds like a sudden, very loud football rattle.
HABITAT Open woodland, parks, large gardens and wooded farmland.
SIZE 27cm (11in)
EGGS 3–5, pale blue-green, rufous-spotted
NEST Cup of roots and grass in the crook of a tree branch.
FOOD Insects, earthworms, slugs, berries, fruit.
SIMILAR TO Song thrush, which is smaller and more compact, and more likely to be found in gardens.

11 Garden warbler
Sylvia borin

The ultimate 'little brown job', this unexciting-looking summer visitor is slightly smaller and more streamlined in shape than a house sparrow. Medium brown in colour, with a paler dull buff breast and underparts and dark eyes, it is often identified more by a process of elimination than by any positive characteristic features. Despite its name, the garden warbler is not often seen in gardens, although it does occur in some large, mature, undeveloped rural ones.
HABITAT April–October: in woodland, especially in coppiced woods, overgrown hedgerows, thickets and scrub throughout England and southern Scotland. Winter: Africa.
SIZE 14cm (5½in)
EGGS 4–5, pale buff or off-white with darker spots
NEST Cup-shaped, built of grass, moss and twigs, located low down in scrub.
FOOD Insects, berries and other fruit in autumn.
SIMILAR TO Chiffchaff and willow warbler are similar, but both are smaller and generally more greenish tinged.

12 Blackcap
Sylvia atricapilla

The easiest of the warblers to recognize, the blackcap is smaller and greyer than the garden warbler, especially on the 'cheeks' and underparts. The male has a conspicuous, long, narrow, horizontal black cap over the upper half of the head. Although it is chiefly a summer visitor, a small but increasing number now stays in the British Isles over winter.
HABITAT In woodland and parkland with mature trees, copses, scrub and in gardens, throughout most of the British Isles. Wintering birds visit bird tables.
SIZE 13cm (5in)
EGGS 5, pale buff with darker spots
NEST Grassy nest low in bushes or clumps of bramble.
FOOD Insects, berries.
SIMILAR TO The male blackcap might be mistaken for a marsh or willow tit at first, but tits are rounder and dumpier with a bigger head and larger black cap.
VARIATIONS Females and juveniles have a chestnut-brown cap.

13 Wood warbler
Phylloscopus sibilatrix

A rather scarce (though it can be locally common) summer visitor, this is the largest and sturdiest of the 3 British 'leaf warblers'. It has rich yellow-green upperparts, a bright lemon-yellow lower face and throat and white breast, belly and underside of tail. Unlike the willow warbler and the chiffchaff, it has strongly patterned wings. In spring, listen for the shivering, trilling song: the bird vibrates so much that you wonder how it hangs on to its perch.

HABITAT Late April–August: in most of the British Isles, with only a few in East Anglia and Ireland, in dense mature woodland (especially oak or beech) where the ground is relatively free of vegetation. Winter: Africa.

SIZE 12cm (4¾in)

EGGS 5–7, white with brown speckles

NEST Dome of grass and leaves on the ground.

FOOD Insects.

SIMILAR TO Willow warbler and chiffchaff, which are both smaller with shorter wings and longer tails. They also have different songs and calls.

14 Willow warbler
Phylloscopus trochilus

About the size of a blue tit, this warbler has a light-olive-green-to-brown back and wings, a pale greenish yellow breast and underparts, a greenish brown head with paler chin and a pale eye-stripe. It is very active, foraging inside bushes looking for insects and darting out to catch flies. The flight is weak and fluttering, and the call is a slightly plaintive, 2-syllabled 'hoo-eet?'

HABITAT April–September: in upland woodland edges, scrub and gardens, especially in April or September while migrating.

SIZE 11cm (4¼in)

EGGS 5–8, white with darker spots

NEST Domed nest of leaves, moss and lichens on the ground.

FOOD Insects, especially aphids, caterpillars, grubs and spiders; berries in autumn.

SIMILAR TO Wood warbler and the chiffchaff, but the willow warbler is very slightly longer and leaner with paler legs. Listen for the song. The willow warbler's has a series of descending notes ending in a flourish, while the chiffchaff's is a repetitious 'chiff-chaff'.

15 Chiffchaff
Phylloscopus collybita

This is generally browner than the willow warbler but similar in appearance, with its brownish olive-green colouring, pale greenish yellow breast and underparts and a pale eye-stripe. It is distinguished by its song – a monotonous, 2-note 'chiff-chaff'. Normally a spring-to-autumn visitor, this warbler is often spotted in willow trees near water.

HABITAT March–October: throughout the British Isles, except for the northern half of Scotland. Small but increasing numbers spend the winter in mild southern areas of Britain, especially near water and farms with manure heaps, where a constant supply of small flies and grubs is assured. Winter: mostly the Mediterranean.

SIZE 11cm (4¼in)

EGGS 4–6, white with sparse darker spots

NEST On the ground.

FOOD Insects, especially aphids, caterpillars and grubs.

SIMILAR TO Willow warbler, which has a slightly longer, leaner shape and longer wings. Listen for the song and check the season.

16 Goldcrest
Regulus regulus

Europe's smallest bird, the goldcrest is tiny, round and dumpy, with a dark greenish brown back, blackish wings with white edges, a short, mid-brown tail and an off-white breast and underparts. The head is black on top with a yellow line down the middle, which in the male is bright golden-orange in the centre. When the crest is raised it resembles a crown. Goldcrests are very active, constantly darting around in trees; in flight, they look almost like oversized bumblebees. The call is a

thin, reedy, extremely high-pitched 'see-see-see' and the rhythmic song also has very high notes.

HABITAT Conifer plantations and coniferous woodland, but sometimes in mixed woodland; more widespread in winter.

SIZE 9cm (3½in)

EGGS 7–8, white with fine red-brown spots

NEST Very small, neat cup, made of moss and cobwebs suspended under the end of a conifer branch.

FOOD Small insects, spiders.

SIMILAR TO Firecrest, except the latter has orange-bronze shoulder patches and a strongly patterned, striped head. Also resembles the wren in terms of size and energy but not plumage.

VARIATIONS The female has a yellower crown patch; juveniles look similar to adults but without the black and yellow on the head.

OPPOSITE Long-eared owl disturbed in its daytime roost.

17 Firecrest
Regulus ignicapillus

The firecrest is a very scarce woodland bird that is fractionally bigger than Britain's smallest bird, the more frequently seen goldcrest. Similar to but brighter than the goldcrest, the firecrest has a bronzy patch just in front of the shoulders, a touch of black on the wings and tail and whiter underparts. The head is striped white, black and orange, with a second black stripe running through each eye. The centre of the male's crown, when erected, is even brighter than that of the goldcrest.
HABITAT Deciduous woodland and scrub with some evergreens; often in Norway spruce plantations. Most breed south of London or round the East Anglian coast.
SIZE 9cm (3½in)
EGGS 7–10, very pale buff, speckled brown
NEST Similar to goldcrest's but almost spherical.
FOOD Small insects, spiders.
SIMILAR TO Goldcrest, but the goldcrest is duller greenish brown above, with one black stripe each side of the head and a yellow stripe down the centre and, importantly, no white on the head.
VARIATIONS Female has a yellow rather than mainly orange crown. The juvenile is similar to a juvenile goldcrest but has dark eye-stripes and pale 'eyebrows', like a shadow of the adult's head pattern.

18 Pied flycatcher
Ficedula hypoleuca

This is a small, almost robin-sized summer visitor with a white chin and underparts that contrast cleanly with the black head, back and tail, and black-and-white wings. It feeds by catching insects in mid-air, then returning to a landing point, but it can also be seen searching inside bushes for caterpillars and other prey.
HABITAT April–early October: locally common in sessile oak woods and also in uplands, among birch. Most are seen in Wales; also occurs in western and northern England and southern and west-central Scotland, but not Ireland. Winter: Africa.
SIZE 13cm (5in)
EGGS 6–7, light blue
NEST In a hole in a tree; readily uses nestboxes.
FOOD Insects, fruit, seeds.
VARIATIONS Females have mid-brown coloration in place of the breeding male's black. Juveniles appear similar to females, but with pale mottling above and brown speckles below.

19 Long-tailed tit
Aegithalos caudatus

Although this is not a true tit, it looks and behaves like one and mixes with tits. It is a tiny, dumpy bird with an almost ball-shaped body, a very long tail and distinctive pink-white-and-black coloration. It has increased in recent years. It is sociable and often seen in family groups, hurrying between trees with a weak, undulating flight, making soft, high-pitched, almost wheezing 'see-see-see' calls.
HABITAT Deciduous woodland edges, thickets, hedgerows and gardens throughout the British Isles.
SIZE 14cm (5½in), over half of which is the tail
EGGS 6–12, white with small reddish spots
NEST A remarkable, purse-shaped structure made of moss and lichen held together with cobwebs. The entrance hole is high up and the nest is lodged among spiky gorse or blackthorn for protection.
FOOD Insects and spiders; increasingly feeds in gardens from peanut-holders and fat-balls.
VARIATIONS Juveniles lack the pinkish coloration.

20 Marsh tit, Willow tit
Parus palustris, P. montanus

These 2 species, more than any other pair of British birds, are virtually identical in appearance but are found in slightly different habitats (although some overlap does occur). Both are short, chunky, blue-tit-sized tits with a black cap and white lower face, grey-brown back, wings and tail, and a pale buff breast and underparts. The best way to tell them apart is to listen to their songs and calls. The marsh tit's call is like a sharp sneeze, 'pi-chu', and the song is a repetitive 'chip-chip-chip'. The call of the willow tit (shown below) is a repetitive nasal 'chair-chair-chair', but it also has a harsh 'tchay' call that is unique to it, and a rarely heard, sweet, clear 'sue-sue-sue' song.

HABITAT Both are resident in England and Wales, although populations are scattered and declining. Marsh tits also occur in southern Scotland; neither occurs in Ireland. Despite its name, the marsh tit prefers drier habitats in deciduous woodland with plenty of undergrowth and scrub, also thickets; the willow tit prefers damp conifer woods and alder, although some occur in other types of woodland and thickets, particularly on damper ground.

SIZE 11.5cm (4½in)

EGGS 6–10, white with reddish spots

NEST Hole in a tree.

FOOD Insects, seeds, fruit.

SIMILAR TO Coal tit, which is found in the same habitats, but has a bold white nape patch and 2 white wing-bars that marsh and willow tits lack.

21 Crested tit
Parus cristatus

This is an easily identified but scarce and extremely localized species. It has brown upperparts, pale peachy-buff underparts and a striking black-and-white head. Look for a black collar, a black-and-white ring outlining the face, and a jaunty, pointed black-and-white crest on top of the head.

Birds cling to tree bark to feed. The call is a soft purring sound.

HABITAT In Britain, found only in the conifer forests of northern Scotland, particularly the old Caledonian pine forests – look in areas with lots of dead wood and listen for the distinctive call. It may also be seen in younger trees in surrounding moorland.

SIZE 11.5cm (4½in)

EGGS 4–6, white with reddish freckles

NEST In a hole in a dead tree stump or post.

FOOD Small insects, spiders, seeds.

22 Coal tit
Parus ater

Very small and acrobatic, this tit has a slightly outsized head and a short tail. The head is black and white and has a white blaze down the neck, the wings and tail are dark grey and the underparts are a warm, orangey-buff colour.

HABITAT Mainly conifer woods and plantations, sometimes mixed and deciduous woodlands, especially in northern and western Britain.

SIZE 11cm (4¼in)

EGGS 7–10, white with small reddish spots

NEST In a hole in a tree or in the ground and in hollows among tree roots.

FOOD Insects, spiders, seeds.

SIMILAR TO Marsh and willow tits, but the coal tit has white 'cheeks' and a white blaze down the back of the neck. The other distinguishing feature is the 2 small white bars on each closed wing.

VARIATIONS Juveniles are similar but the underparts and nape stripe are warm egg-yolk yellow rather than orangey-buff and white respectively.

23

24 Brambling
Fringilla montifringilla

This is a winter visitor, easily mistaken for its close relative the chaffinch, except the coloration differs. In autumn and winter, the male brambling has a warm, buff-orange breast and white belly, a charcoal-and-buff-laced back, orange-buff bars on the wings, and a charcoal-and-buff head. There is a very conspicuous white rump patch, which is easily seen in flight. The brambling is usually spotted in small flocks, often with chaffinches.
HABITAT Mid-September–April: mostly in beech woods but also farmland, parks and gardens throughout the British Isles. Summer: north-east Europe.
SIZE 14cm (5½in)
EGGS 5–7, greenish to brownish with dark brown spots
NEST Untidy cup of grass, lichen and bark, in the fork of a tree or bush.
FOOD Seeds and especially beech mast in winter.
SIMILAR TO Chaffinch, which looks rosier pink and lacks the white belly and white rump patch of the brambling, but has conspicuous white wing-bars, which in the brambling are orange-buff.
VARIATIONS Female has same patterns as the male but is duller.

25 Siskin
Carduelis spinus

At first glance, this small finch looks mostly green and black. A close-up view shows a greenish buff head, body and tail, with a blackish crown, and black-and-

green wings barred with bright yellow. Small groups work their way restlessly through dense twigs looking for food before flying on.
HABITAT Summer: in conifer woods and plantations. Winter: often found in wettish farmland in woodland edges and overgrown hedgerows containing alders; increasingly common in gardens.
SIZE 12cm (4¾in)
EGGS 4, deepish blue with lighter spots

25

NEST In conifer woods and plantations, mostly in Scotland.
FOOD Larch seeds and conifer cones; alder and birch seeds in winter.
SIMILAR TO Goldfinch, but siskin lacks the red and gold on the head. Also similar to the greenfinch, which is distinctly larger and more assertive, with plainer green coloration and a much bigger beak. The greenfinch lacks black on the wings and has a narrow yellow stripe along the edge of

23 Nuthatch
Sitta europaea

The nuthatch is a pert, active, colourful bird with a bright blue-grey head, back and wings, white 'cheeks', bright buff-orange underparts and a bold black stripe through the eyes back to the shoulders. It scuttles quickly up trees and, unlike the treecreeper and woodpecker, it can also shuffle down tree bark head-first, by hanging on with its toes.
HABITAT Woodland, parks and woodland gardens, mainly in the southern half of England and Wales but now colonizing northern England and, more recently, southern Scotland.
SIZE 14cm (5½in)
EGGS 6–8, white with reddish brown spots
NEST In a hole in a tree, sometimes

in nestboxes. Nuthatches are expert plasterers. They collect mud to seal gaps and to reinforce the edges of either a natural hole or the entrance to an old nest-hole made by another bird, reducing the size so that predators cannot get in.
FOOD Insects, nuts, seeds.

24

27 Crossbill
Loxia curvirostra

This is a remarkable, striking, parrot-like finch. The mature males are brick-red with dark brown wings and tail. Given a good view, you can see the curious, twisted beak – the mandibles of this and other crossbill species are uniquely curved and cross over each other, and are able to prise open pine cones and extract seeds. Look for the distinctive, parrot-like shape and behaviour – acrobatic climbing action, raucous calls when disturbed and messy feeding habits, dropping pine needles and bits of fir cone out of the trees. The crossbill is present all year but larger numbers visit in winter.

HABITAT Widespread but scattered throughout Britain and Ireland, in conifer forests of spruce and larch.

SIZE 16cm (6¼in)

EGGS 3–4, off-white, spotted and streaked purple-red or black

NEST Cup of grass, moss, lichen and bark, typically high in a tree.

FOOD Conifer seeds.

VARIATIONS Female is a yellowish green with brown wings and tail; juvenile is a very streaky brown with a slight greenish tinge and brown wings and tail.

each wing, while the siskin has 2 much bolder yellow bars across the centre of each wing.

VARIATIONS Female lacks the male's black head; the juvenile is like a more buff-coloured female.

26 Lesser redpoll
Carduelis cabaret

The redpoll is a very small linnet-like finch. In spring, the male in breeding plumage has a red blob above the beak, a black chin and a pink-tinged breast with white, speckled underparts and brown, streaky upperparts. In autumn, the plumage becomes browner and darker, and the red on the forehead and breast are obscured. The birds are seen mostly near the tops of trees, feeding acrobatically, and are often in flocks with siskins in winter. They have a bouncing, chaffinch-like flight and their call is a tinny twittering when in flight.

HABITAT Mainly upland birch woods and young conifer plantations, although now more widespread, particularly where there are alder and hawthorn thickets; might be seen in woods, mature parks, heaths and scrub.

SIZE 11.5cm (4½in)

EGGS 4–5, pale blue spotted with brown

NEST Untidy cup of grass and moss, high in a bush or a tree.

FOOD Seeds, especially alder and birch in winter; grass, wildflower seeds and insects in autumn.

SIMILAR TO Linnet, which lacks the redpoll's black chin and feeds on the ground rather than in trees.

VARIATIONS Females and juveniles lack the red forehead and pink breast of males.

28 Hawfinch
Coccothraustes coccothraustes

This very large, striking and colourful finch has secretive habits. It has a large head, thick 'bull' neck and a very strong, massive beak. A flying bird has black-and-white-patterned wings and an apricot-coloured body. In close-up, you may see the sandy brown head with a grey patch at the back and the orange-buff 'cheeks'. The back is sandy brown, the breast warm buff, and the wing-tips are bluish black with strangely notched feathers. The hawfinch is seen in small groups, high in the tops of trees, but it sometimes feeds or

drinks on the ground.

HABITAT Breeds locally throughout England, with only a few in Scotland and Wales but not Ireland. Found in mixed woodland with hornbeam and, in autumn, in hedgerows and areas of orchard with cherries.

SIZE 18cm (7in)

EGGS 4–6, grey-green, streaked and spotted black and brown

NEST In fruit trees.

FOOD Large seeds, pips, hornbeam seeds, beech nuts, fruit stones.

VARIATIONS Female is like a duller-coloured version of the male; juvenile is duller brown-grey and speckly with dark wings and tail.

29 Bullfinch
Pyrrhula pyrrhula

This beautiful bird of woodland undergrowth, hedges and orchards is now, sadly, much scarcer than it was 25 years ago. It is very plump-bodied, with soft plumage and a 'bull' neck, and the male has a glossy black cap, rose-pink 'cheeks' and breast, and a black tail and wings with a single white wing-bar. The beak is short, black and triangular. Birds rarely fly far from the cover of trees or undergrowth, but in flight look for the rose-pink breast, the single white flash on the wings and a white rump that contrasts with the black tail and slate-grey upperparts.
HABITAT Most abundant in southern England, but occurs virtually all over the British Isles.
SIZE 14.5cm (5¾in)
EGGS 4–5, greenish blue with purple-brown spots at the larger end
NEST Loose, flimsy cup of small twigs in dense bushes and hedges.
FOOD Buds (especially of fruit trees), seeds, fruit.
SIMILAR TO Superficially similar to the chaffinch but with a pinker breast and black cap.
VARIATIONS Female has the male's markings but a pinkish grey face and breast and 2 white wing-bars. The juvenile lacks the black cap and could be mistaken for a male chaffinch outside the breeding season, except the chaffinch has a paler head and longer, less stout beak.

30 Capercaillie
Tetrao urogallus

The capercaillie is a very elusive grouse, mostly black with a bushy black 'beard', red markings above the eyes and brown wings. It may be seen creeping around on the ground or perching on branches in trees – when disturbed, it crashes noisily out of the foliage. The male is turkey-sized, and flying birds look huge and dark, with white 'armpits' and underside of the tail. Males display alone or in small groups, by fanning the tail upwards and outwards and throwing their head back to call. They can be aggressive towards other birds, animals, people and even vehicles. The call is unique and sounds like someone popping a champagne cork, pouring the contents, then throwing the 'empty' into the loch afterwards – varied sequences of 'pelip – plip, plip – kersposh'.
HABITAT Mostly found in ancient Caledonian native Scots pine forest; some in a few other well-managed mature forests where pine regenerates naturally and there is varied ground cover to provide food. Since 1970, its population has declined and it is now in grave danger.
SIZE 60–87cm (26–34in)
EGGS 6–10, beige with brown speckles
NEST Shallow scrape on the ground among trees, lined with grass and pine needles.
FOOD Pine buds, young cones and needles, juniper berries, bilberry.
SIMILAR TO Female resembles a black or red grouse, but the capercaillie female is much bigger and has a fanned tail and a reddish orange breast patch.
VARIATIONS Females and juveniles are warm beige, densely patterned with brown bars, with a reddish orange breast, reddish orange beneath the eyes and on the neck, paler blackish-and-orange-barred underparts and a wide, fanned tail.

31 Treecreeper
Certhia familiaris

This is a small, furtive, almost mouse-like brown-and-white bird, almost identical in colour to the tree trunks it clings to, with a streaky brown-and-tan head, back and wings, plain brown tail and silvery white breast and underparts. The brown crown is flecked with white and it has a streaky brown eye-stripe. The treecreeper is easily recognized by its behaviour – creeping *up* (never down) tree trunks, with a fast, jerky, shuffling, mouse-like action, working its way round in a spiral, poking its thin, down-curved beak into crevices to find food, before flying to the base of another tree to start again.
HABITAT Mature woodland, parkland and wooded gardens.
SIZE 12.5cm (5in)
EGGS 5–6, white with reddish spots
NEST Neat cup of grass, moss, cobwebs, hair and feathers, behind loose, craggy bark and crevices in trees, among ivy or other climber or in a hole in a building.
FOOD Insects; seeds in winter.

32 Woodcock
Scolopax rusticola

The woodcock is a superbly camouflaged wader with a chunky, rich dark brown, brindle-patterned body with bold brown-and-tan bars on the head and a very long beak. It is mainly nocturnal and usually hunkered down during the day in the undergrowth; if you get very close, it suddenly rockets up with loud, whirring, broad wings. It is easiest to see in spring, when males display at dawn and dusk by flying round and round a small area at the edge of woodland, at roughly tree-top height, making a frog-like croaking noise followed by a shrill, thin, sneezing sound.

HABITAT Deciduous woodland and young conifer plantations with boggy patches or damp ditches. Present all year round but larger numbers in autumn and winter.
SIZE 34cm (13½in)
EGGS 3–5, brown and blotchy
NEST Scrape on the ground, well-camouflaged among bracken.
FOOD Worms, soil grubs, insects.
SIMILAR TO Large snipe, but snipe have cream stripes on the head, back and wings, and narrower wings. Also, snipe inhabit wetlands, not woodland.

Count the coos
To tell one from another by sound in a rural situation count the 'coos' – 5 coos in a phrase tells you it is a woodpigeon, 3 indicates a collared dove and 2 is a stock dove.

33 Stock dove
Columba oenas

The stock dove is a widespread, rich blue-grey pigeon with a breast tinged rosy pink and a large, iridescent green-and-purple patch on the nape of the neck. The wings' trailing edges and tips and the tail tip are black, and there are 2 very small black flashes on each wing. Birds are mostly solitary or in small groups rather than large flocks. The call is a deep, gruff, rhythmic 2-note 'ooo-oo'.

HABITAT Farmland and parkland with large old trees, cliffs, quarries and old buildings, throughout the British Isles except northern Scotland and northern Ireland.
SIZE 32cm (13in)
EGGS 2, white
NEST In holes in trees, on cliffs, quarries or ledges on buildings.
FOOD Seeds, foliage, flowers.
SIMILAR TO Woodpigeon, but the stock dove is smaller, lacks the white neck band and looks blue-grey from a distance (the wood-pigeon looks grey). Unlike the woodpigeon, the stock dove does not appear in very large flocks. May also be confused with a feral pigeon, but this has small red eyes, a dull grey beak and a darker grey head, wing-tips and tail, and 2 wide black bars (rather than small black flashes) across the upper wings.

34 Jay
Garrulus glandarius

This is a colourful and widespread but secretive, dove-sized crow, often mistaken for an escaped exotic bird. It is easily recognized in flight as a flash of pink with a blue streak and a prominent white rump and black tail pattern. A perched bird is overall salmon-pink with large, beady eyes, a black beak and 'moustache', black streaks on top of the off-white head and a white throat. There is a black-barred, bright blue patch at the bend of each wing, in front of a white bar and white-edged, black wing-tips, and the tail is black. Jays are the squirrels of the bird world, hiding acorns in the ground for winter stores; a good many of these are never found and grow into new oak trees, helping the recolonization of oak woods.

HABITAT Woodland, especially oak woods throughout the British Isles; uncommon in northern Scotland and western Ireland.
SIZE 34cm (13in)
EGGS 4–5, blue
NEST Very well hidden, located low down in bushes.
FOOD Varied but mainly acorns.
VARIATIONS The juvenile's tail is short and stumpy, and the black head markings are streaky at first.

1 Speckled wood
Pararge aegeria

Also known as the wood argus, this common and widespread, medium-sized butterfly (4.5cm/1¾in wingspan) is dull earth-brown with a row of pale creamy-buff blotches running along the edges of the wings. There is one large eyespot on the front of each forewing, and 3 or 4 smaller ones along the edge of the rear

wings. Adults feed mostly on honeydew from insects.
HABITAT Woodland glades, rides and clearings, also woodland edges and large, overgrown hedgerows and wooded gardens. They usually fly in sunny patches, often alongside a path. Throughout Ireland, Wales and England, and increasing in Scotland from the north-west to the Moray Firth, from March to mid-October.
CATERPILLAR Grassy green with faint yellow stripes running from head to tail. Present at any time of year, feeding on cocksfoot, couch and other grasses.

2 Silver-washed fritillary
Argynnis paphia

Our biggest fritillary, this large orange butterfly (7cm/2¾in wingspan) is wonderful to see in flight. It is strikingly patterned, with 2 rows of evenly spaced, dark brown spots round the edges of the wings, chevrons along the edges and streaks closer to the body. The rear wings have slightly scalloped edges. The underside of each rear wing is 'washed' with silver, hence the name. Adults feed on brambles and thistle flowers.
HABITAT Woodland clearings, woodland rides and round the edges of oak woods, in south and south-west England, Ireland and Wales in July and August.
CATERPILLAR Spiky, grey-brown with a double yellow stripe from the head to the tail; present any time except May to July, feeding on violets.

3 Purple emperor
Apatura iris

The purple emperor is the most spectacular butterfly of oak woods. Today it is rare, but it is worth watching out for. The males have large, iridescent purple wings (they look dark brown until the sun catches them – usually one at a time), with scattered white spots and an orange eyespot at the base of the rear wings (wingspan 7.5cm/3in). Purple emperors are seen mostly flying along tracks or paths in oak woods in the mornings, then in the afternoons up in the canopy at tree-top height. The females are seen less often; they have similar markings to the male but the background colour is a warm dark brown rather than purple. Adults feed on honeydew and tree sap but also gather moisture and nutrients from dung and rotting animal remains.

HABITAT Found only in central southern England, mainly Surrey, Sussex and Hampshire, including areas of the New Forest, in July and August.
CATERPILLAR Green, with faint red horizontal stripes, and slug-shaped – pointed at each end – with 'horns' at the front; feeds on sallow leaves.

4 White admiral
Limenitis camilla

This is an unusual, large, striking, black-and-white butterfly (6cm/2½in wingspan). The dark grey-brown wings look almost black, with a row of white 'blocky' shapes running in a rough stripe through the centre of both wings. Adults feed on bramble nectar.

HABITAT Woodland, particularly overgrown coppice, where there is wild honeysuckle; only in southern England, in June and July.
CATERPILLAR Green with curious red bristly tufts on the back of each segment, a red bristly head and a reddish line along the base of the centre section of the body; feeds on honeysuckle.

5

7

8

5 Purple hairstreak
Neozephyrus quercus

Rarely seen, this is an unusual, medium-sized butterfly (3cm/1¼in wingspan) that spends all its time high up in the canopy of oak woods, only occasionally visiting lower leaves to bask in hot, sunny weather. The males have iridescent purple wings with black edges and a black body; females are entirely dark grey to black, except for 2 iridescent purple flashes on each forewing. Both sexes have pointed protrusions near the inner corners of the rear wings. Adults feed on honeydew shed by oak aphids.

HABITAT Mostly in central and southern England in July and August, with a few scattered pockets further north including Wales, Scotland and Ireland.
CATERPILLAR Brown-grey, flattened and grub-like, feeding on oak buds and young leaves from April to June; it is easily dislodged and falls off if leaves are disturbed.

6 Winter moth
Operophtera brumata

This is a common species, whose caterpillars often strip trees so badly in spring that they look as they do winter. The female moths are wingless and look like grey-brown lice or scales with legs clinging to the bark – they climb up the trunks during the winter, from chrysalises that hatch in the ground in October. Males have dull, mottled-buff-and-brown wings, 2.5cm (1in) across.

In the past, gardeners used to put grease bands round tree trunks in autumn in order to trap female winter moths crawling up the trunks. This helped to protect the trees from early defoliation, which reduces the crop of fruit. Winter moth caterpillar damage also leaves characteristic, round, brownish buff scars with a small crater in the centre of the fruit, particularly on apples, although they can still be eaten as there is no maggot inside (it is the codling moth that is responsible for the maggots often found inside the core of apples). Although it's no longer such a routine garden precaution nowadays, grease bands or crop-protection glues are available for organic control of winter moth.

HABITAT Gardens, orchards, hedgerows and oak woods from October to January.
CATERPILLAR Small and green; feeds mainly on foliage but also flowers and, to some extent, small, developing fruit.

7 Green oak tortrix moth
Tortrix viridana

Also known as the green oak-roller moth, this common, night-flying moth of oak woods has small, silvery-frosted, leaf-green wings, 2cm (¾in) across, with a small white fringe along the edge, when seen at rest on foliage. Because of the poisonous tannins in oak leaves, the green oak tortrix moth and other species that feed on oak leaves mostly complete feeding and pupate by June, when the tannins are less strong. Sometimes caterpillars can still be found on the leaves later, but the high level of tannins means that their development is slow.

HABITAT Hiding among oak leaves by day and flying at night, from June to August.
CATERPILLAR Cream, up to 1.5cm (⅝in) long, with a red-brown head and small spots dotted evenly over the body. Feeds exclusively on oak. For protection, the caterpillars live inside rolled-up tubes of leaves that they fix in position with silk; they are sometimes seen dangling from their leafy tubes on the ends of short threads – a result of disturbance from wind or mechanical interference.

8 Hornet
Vespa crabro

An enormous, bright-yellow-and-brown wasp, 3–5cm (1¼–2in) long, the hornet is the biggest wasp in Europe but is uncommon (though increasing) in the British Isles. It makes a very loud, buzzing sound, but despite the frightening appearance it is very unlikely to sting. Hornets live in small colonies of no more than 100–200 individuals in a hollow tree, in a nest constructed of 'paper' made by chewing up rotten wood. Most adults die at the end of summer, leaving only a few mated queens to survive the winter. The larvae are fed on insects such as aphids and small caterpillars.

HABITAT Now quite widespread in central and southern England in old woodland with plenty of rotting wood, from April or May to October.

6

9

11

12

9 Oak galls

Oak apples and many other strange growths on oak trees are galls that form the 'nurseries' of various species of tiny gall wasps – unexciting, fly-like insects that you'd never notice, which cause the tree to produce a gall, which may contain just one larva or a large number, depending on the species. You can identify the different species by the 'nursery' they leave behind, not the fly. The best known is the oak marble gall (*Andricus kollari*) which, as the name suggests, is the size of a small marble and grows at the tip of oak stems where it hardens and dries out, so it looks like wood and lasts through the winter – only one gall wasp lives inside each 'marble'. The true oak apple gall (*Biorhiza pallida*) is larger (about 4cm/1½in across) and can contain several dozen larvae, in separate cells inside, but these galls are seen only in the summer. Oak cherry galls (*Cynips quercusfolii*) look like greenish cherries (2cm/¾in) found underneath the oak leaves in autumn. The knopper gall (*Andricus quercuscalicis*) produces strange, green or greenish brown, knobbly growths that grow out of acorns and acorn cups. Spangle galls (shown above) have tiny, round, flattish, pustule-like galls, growing in clusters rather like limpets on the back of oak leaves. The common spangle gall

(*Neuroterus quercusbaccarum*) has light green galls, each with a dull red-brown edge and centre. Galls of the silk button spangle gall (*Neuroterus numismalis*) have pink edges and a cream centre.

HABITAT Oak woods throughout the British Isles.

10 Southern wood ant
Formica rufa

Britain's largest ant, this is a two-tone insect, approximately 0.5–1cm (¼–⅜in) long, with a light sandy brown head and thorax and a dark brown abdomen. Its nest is located inside a large mound of leaf litter, from which columns of ants can be seen scurrying back and forth, carrying food for the ant larvae on the return trip – several ants will join forces to carry a big caterpillar. Wood ants feed on a variety of moth caterpillars and

other insect pests that harm timber trees, so foresters tend to leave ants to get on with the job. The ants kill their prey by biting them and spraying them with formic acid squirted from their rear ends. They don't hesitate to use this weapon for defence if disturbed, so watch where you picnic.

HABITAT Woodland and wooded heaths throughout southern England, and occasionally in the Midlands and northern England, but not Scotland or Ireland.

11 Stag beetle
Lucanus cervus

This is our largest and most easily identified beetle. The males are bigger (up to 5cm/2in long) and they have a pair of strong 'antlers' at the front, used for fighting rival males. The head and thorax are black, the 'antlers' and the wing-cases deep chestnut-brown. Apart from being smaller, the females are identical but lack the antlers. Adults may live as little as a month and don't feed at all; larvae take 3–7 years to mature.

HABITAT Predominantly found in woodland or gardens in the south-east of England, between June and August.

LARVA Fat, white, curved grub with a small brownish head, living in rotting logs.

12 Click beetles
Ampedus cinnabarinus and other species

This is a whole family of elongated, bullet-shaped beetles, so-named because they 'click' loudly. This happens when they land upside-down and use the 'peg' on their back to flick themselves upright. (They sometimes have to make several attempts.) *Ampedus cinnabarinus* (shown above) is a local woodland species, 1cm/⅜in long, bright red with a black head and thorax, whose larvae feed on other beetle larvae under rotten tree bark. The larvae of several well-known garden and farmland click beetles are more familiar as wireworms. These are notorious pests that eat the roots of grasses, agricultural crops and garden plants, though they also feed on decaying wood or other organic matter in the ground.

HABITAT Woodland, agricultural land and gardens.

LARVA Long, thin, many-segmented, glossy chestnut-brown or yellowish grub.

10

LARVA Develops inside acorns in summer and chews its way out in late summer or autumn, leaving a characteristic small, round hole.

15 Oak aphid
Phylloxera quercus
This common aphid, which is quite different from the garden greenfly, is found in oak woods on the undersides of leaves. Only wingless females are seen in spring; the winged form appears in summer. Wingless females are cream to yellow, with pear-shaped bodies and very short legs; their eggs may be seen on the foliage around them. The winged form has a light brown head and a longer body with a black neck and clear wings. Both are smaller than 3mm (⅛in) long.
HABITAT Oak woods.

16 Oak bush-cricket
Meconema thallasinum
This is a small, leaf-green cricket, 1.5cm (⅝in) long, with faint yellowish marks on its back and a very long pair of curving green antennae at the front of the head. It is most easily identified by its size and location – usually on oak leaves – but it takes a bit of seeing as it is perfectly camouflaged.
HABITAT Mainly on oak trees throughout England and Wales.

13 Violet ground beetle
Carabus violaceus
This is a fairly large, non-flying black beetle, up to 3cm (1¼in) long, with a distinct, iridescent purplish sheen. It has shield-shaped wing-cases and rather square 'shoulders' with flattened edges, long legs, and a pair of long antennae at the front of the head. Both adults and larvae feed on other insects; in gardens they are regarded as beneficial insects.
HABITAT Once common in gardens but now mainly found on woodland floors in leaf litter and under stones and logs, from June to August.
LARVA Brown, caterpillar-like grub in leaf litter, but with legs only at the front end, just behind the head.

14 Acorn weevil
Curculio villosus
This is a small, rounded, grey-black beetle, 4mm (⅛in) long. The curved snout has a pair of fine, thread-like antennae, like a tuning fork, growing out about halfway along. Its jaws are at the end of the snout; after chewing a deep drill-hole into an acorn, it turns round and lays an egg inside.
HABITAT Oak woods.

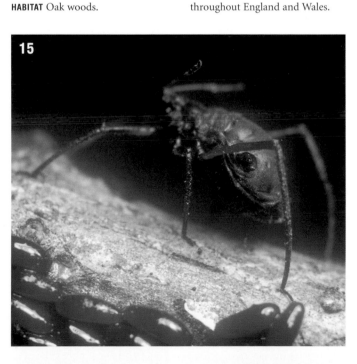

17 Fungus gnat
Sciara thomae
Also known as the sciarid fly or midge, these tiny flies mass together to form black, hovering clouds. *Sciara thomae* is one of the commonest of a number of very similar species that behave in the same way and are collectively called fungus gnats. They are short-lived and don't bite. The larvae live on decomposing plant remains. Both adults and larvae are a valuable food source for insectivorous woodland songbirds, including wrens. The winter gnat, another common species, behaves similarly and is most prevalent in winter, thus ensuring a year-round food supply. (Don't confuse harmless fungus gnats with the gnats and mosquitoes that breed in water and *do* bite.)
HABITAT Clearings in moist woods where there is plenty of decaying vegetation; also in gardens round compost heaps, in spring, summer and early autumn.

18 Black snake millipede
Tachypodoiulus niger

Our commonest millipede, this widespread though little-seen creature, up to 3cm (1¼in) long, is black, shiny and tubular, and made up of many short segments. It moves with a slow, rippling motion. If you were to count the legs, you'd find 96 pairs in total. Unusually for millipedes, most of which feed on the ground, this species will also climb up trees and bushes to find food. If alarmed, it curls up into a flat coil. The black snake millipede is generally seen only from spring to autumn, as it hides away during the winter months. It feeds on plant matter, both living and dead.

HABITAT In leaf litter on the woodland floor and in hedgerows and gardens.

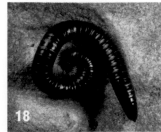

19 Common centipede
Lithobius forficatus

Our commonest centipede, this warm brown, rather shiny, flattened creature, up to 3cm (1¼in) long, is made up of a series of segments, with a row of bristling legs visible along both sides of its body. This species runs in a straight line, unlike other centipedes, which move in a series of S-shaped curves, from side to side. It comes out only at night and hides by day under logs and in other damp places. The common centipede feeds on a wide variety of small, ground-living insects including young woodlice.

HABITAT Woodland floors, hedgerows and gardens.

20 Smooth woodlouse
Oniscus asellus

This is a very common and widespread, oval, flattish, grey-brown creature, 1–1.5cm (⅜–⅝in) long, made up of a number of overlapping plates; the paler edges distinguish the smooth woodlouse from other similar species. The woodlouse is sometimes confused with the familiar, deep slate-grey, armadillo-like pillbug (*Armadillidium vulgare*), which

often comes indoors and can roll itself into a tight ball.

If you've ever spotted some passing similarity between woodlice and the very much bigger fossilized trilobites, you are probably right – it's very likely that they have the same common ancestor. Today's woodlice evolved from sea creatures and are crustaceans, so are therefore related to lobsters. Even today, most species of woodlouse cannot live for long if they dry out, which is why they hide under logs and stones by day and come out to feed at night. They eat dead plant matter, although it is not unknown for them to nibble seedlings in the greenhouse. Also, they move into potato tubers underground, usually when slugs have initiated the first damage. Although they are not our most glamorous creatures, woodlice are invaluable for recycling dead plant remains back into the ground.

HABITAT Damp places in woodland and hedgerows, under logs, even in compost heaps.

Mammals

1 Wild boar
Sus scrofa

This is a large, solid, fast-moving and surprisingly agile pig. It is covered with shaggy, dark brown bristles, has a long, strong, blunt snout and small, reddish eyes. Not to be trifled with, a big adult male can measure 1.8m (6ft) in length, stand up to 1m (3ft) high at the shoulder, with tusks up to 30cm (12in) long, and weighs about 100kg (220lb). Wild boar are normally shy and reclusive, living in family groups (the young piglets are brown-and-yellow-striped for camouflage), but adults can be aggressive, especially if cornered or if a female has young to defend.

Wild boar were once common throughout the British Isles until they were hunted to extinction, but they are now re-establishing themselves from animals that have escaped from farms. However, it's

unlikely that wild boar in Britain are pure-bred, since they originate from animals that were hybridized with domestic pigs for greater productivity. The result looks like wild boar, but should more accurately be called a feral pig.

HABITAT Mostly south and east England, found only in dense, remote woodland surrounded by farmland and hedgerows.

FOOD Roots, bulbs (especially bluebells), nuts, berries, fruit, carrion, birds' eggs, small rodents; also raids fields to eat crops.

2 Badger
Meles meles

The reclusive, nocturnal badger lives in family groups in large underground setts. A shaggy animal, 1m (3ft) long, the badger is easily identified by its black-and-white-striped face and dark grey body flecked with banded-black-and-white bristles. It uses its strong snout to root for food. Badger setts are large earthworks below ground, often used continuously by many

black and divided in two by a longish tail with a black stripe down the middle. They are found in herds, which can often be quite large. In autumn, bucks make loud, groaning sounds as part of their rutting display.

HABITAT Found in the southern half of England, but rarer in Scotland and not found very far north. They live in open woodland but graze on nearby farmland. Mostly seen in parkland at stately homes with plenty of grazing and trees; now also farmed for venison.

FOOD Grass, but may strip tree bark and eat small tree seedlings in winter.

generations of badgers over a hundred years or so. They consist of 20–30 entrance holes, each roughly 30cm (12in) in diameter, with an interconnecting series of tunnels linking chambers together. The bedding inside the chambers is changed regularly, and you can often tell an inhabited badger sett by the piles of fresh soil from new excavations, or old grass and vegetation that have been cleared out as part of the routine 'housekeeping'. Look, too, for long, stiff, banded-black-and-white hairs mixed in with the refuse, or strands snagged on barbed-wire fences in the area. If you want to watch badgers, take up your position before sunset, when they start coming out of their setts, and keep very quiet – the animals show up well on a moonlit night.

HABITAT Secluded woods close to farmland throughout the British Isles, but especially common in south-west England.

FOOD Mainly worms, also insects, small mammals, roots, fruit.

3 Fallow deer
Dama dama
Introduced by the Normans for sport in the 11th century, fallow deer are our prettiest deer, and the second largest (after the red deer), with the male standing 90cm (36in) at the shoulder and the female 80cm (31in). The fallow is usually reddish brown, evenly

dappled with spots, varying in colour from pure white to black. In winter, the coat is darker with fewer spots. The antlers of the bucks form broad, flattened shapes quite unlike the branching or spiky headgear of other deer. Fallow deer are easily distinguished from the rear by the heart-shaped white rump patch, which is outlined in

4 Roe deer
Capreolus capreolus
One of our 2 native species (the other being red deer), the roe is a medium-sized, unspotted, mid-

brown deer with a black muzzle (the quick, easy identification feature). It stands 65cm (26in) at the shoulder and has a plain white rump patch and short, upright antlers with several branches at the top. Unlike fallow or red deer, it is usually found singly or in small groups rather than large herds.

HABITAT Found mainly in forestry plantations, particularly newly cultivated ones, especially in Scotland, northern England and south and south-west England.

FOOD A browser rather than a grazer, it lives mostly on leaves and young shoots of trees and shrubs.

5

Male and female deer

Male and female deer are not always referred to as stags or does; terminology varies according to species. The males and females of the red deer and sika are known as stags and hinds respectively, while those of the fallow deer, Reeves' muntjac and roe deer are referred to as bucks and does.

Male deer grow new antlers every year, timed to reach full size before the start of the breeding season, when they are used for impressing females and for fighting rival males. They are shed later in the season at a time that varies for each species. New antlers start regrowing as soon as the old ones are cast off and take 120 days to grow, irrespective of size and species. Any deer will spend some part of the year with a bare head – males can then be distinguished from females by their larger size. While new antlers are growing they are covered with soft 'velvet', which male deer rub off on slender, young tree trunks and branches – the effect of this 'fraying' can be devastating in young plantations.

6

5 Sika
Cervus nippon

Originally from Japan, the sika was introduced deliberately to the British Isles and now lives wild in some areas; it often cross-breeds with red deer, diluting the wild stocks by hybridization. The sika is slightly smaller and less spotted than the fallow deer, standing 65–85cm (26–33in) at the shoulder; in winter, the brown coat of the sika turns darker and the spots often disappear. Seen from the rear, the splodge-shaped white rump patch is edged with black, and the short white tail sometimes has a stripe down it. The antlers are upright and spiky – the quick way to distinguish sika from fallow deer.
HABITAT A few isolated pockets all round the country where there is open woodland or heath, including the New Forest, the Lake District and much of Scotland. It is spreading rapidly in all areas.
FOOD Grass, young shoots of trees and shrubs; may strip tree bark.

PREVIOUS PAGES In the rutting season in autumn, male fallow deer challenge one another, mostly pushing and shoving, followed by a chasing-off.

6 Reeves' muntjac
Muntiacus reevesi

This is a South-east Asian species, deliberately released almost 100 years ago and now living wild throughout much of southern England, with odd populations in the north. A small, slightly hump-backed deer, about the size of a Labrador dog (50cm/20in at the shoulder), it is warm brown in colour, with no spots, although some white markings may be seen on the chin or neck. When the deer is alarmed, it raises its brown tail vertically, showing a white, flared-up rump patch (the patch is otherwise hidden). Look for the large, dark, comma-shaped glandular pits below the eyes; no other British deer has these. The antlers are short, usually straight spikes; the bucks also have long eye-teeth protruding from the jaw, used for defence. Another name for the muntjac is the barking deer, as it does indeed make a barking sound. However, don't rely on this as an identification feature.
HABITAT South, east and central England, in woods and farmland.
FOOD Grass, brambles, scrub, young tree and shrub shoots; may strip tree bark in winter.

7 Pine marten
Martes martes

This rare, agile and secretive creature looks like a cross between a giant weasel and a cat. It has a long, slender, rich brown body (75cm/30in nose to tail) with a buff 'bib' and ears, a long, fluffy tail and a sharp-pointed face with an alert, intelligent expression.
HABITAT Found only in a few scattered locations in wild woods and pine forests. They are common in the northern half of Scotland, pockets of England and possibly Wales and Ireland.
FOOD Hunts squirrels in trees but mostly feeds on the ground on rodents, small birds, eggs, large insects, carrion and berries.

8 Scottish wildcat
Felis sylvestris grampia

This scarce, secretive, rarely seen predator of the Scottish Highlands is our only remaining native wildcat, now increasingly under threat from cross-breeding with feral cats and domestic moggies, which dilute its genes. It looks like a large, thickset, chunky tabby and is hard to tell apart from the domestic cat. The fur is thick, grey-brown or faintly ginger-tinged and patterned with darker stripes – not the blotches of a real tabby. The male wildcat is 1.2m (4ft) long from nose to tail, but in winter it looks bigger owing to its extra-thick winter fur coat. The tail, which is heavily patterned with black rings, is thick and tubular in shape with a rounded tip. Wildcats are really animals of lowland woods, but they were long since exterminated in those places by farmers out to protect their livestock, so they are now confined to moorlands and high-altitude forests where there is less food, but less persecution. They are nearly extinct and most of the remaining wildcats are hybrids with domestic cats.
HABITAT Found in high forests and on moors in Scotland, well away from human habitation.
FOOD Mostly rabbits and small rodents, but also birds, fish or amphibians if all else fails.

9 Grey squirrel
Sciurus carolinensis

A widespread and common, small, active, acrobatic, fluffy grey rodent (48cm/19in long) with white underparts and a long, bushy tail normally carried in a graceful curve over the back. Non-native, it was originally introduced from America by the Victorians to decorate country parks but has now taken over from our own red squirrel in all but a few areas. The grey squirrel can become quite tame in parks and gardens, and it is often seen scurrying up tree trunks, leaping from tree to tree, or gathering and burying nuts in the ground in autumn for winter stores. It nests either in holes in trees or in dreys, which are large balls of twigs and leaves lodged high up in the crooks of trees. Contrary to popular belief, squirrels do not hibernate, though they are certainly seen out and about less in bad weather. On mild days, they can often be observed looking for food or digging up stored nuts right through the winter. Not all stored nuts will be found, leaving plenty to regenerate woodlands – or, as often happens, to appear in garden borders as uninvited tree seedlings.
HABITAT Woodland, overgrown hedgerows, parkland, orchards and gardens, and frequently found in urban situations.
FOOD Nuts, seeds, beech mast, young shoots, buds, birds' eggs, young nestlings, garden bulbs, peanuts put out for the birds.

10 Red squirrel
Sciurus vulgaris

Our native squirrel is common in Scotland and is easily identified as a smaller (40cm/16in long), reddish version of the better-known grey squirrel. It is a quite dark, blackish red colour and has long red ear-tufts in winter, white underparts and a slightly paler tail. It is a far fussier feeder than the more adaptable grey squirrel.
HABITAT Rarely seen in much of the British Isles, and now mostly

found in conifer forests (particularly pine) in Scotland, Wales, Ireland and the north of England, or in mixed woodland where the more successful grey squirrel has not spread, such as Brownsea Island off the Dorset coast. Also found on the Isle of Wight, where the grey squirrel is absent.
FOOD Almost exclusively conifer seeds, shoots and buds, although may sometimes feed on nuts, including acorns and peanuts.

13 Common dormouse
Muscardinus avellanarius
Also known as the hazel dormouse, our native dormouse – which is now rare – is a hamster-like rodent (body 7.5cm/3in; tail 6cm/2½in) with bags of '*aaahhh*' factor. It has large black eyes and a rich warm-brown coat with white underparts, but unlike the hamster it has a long, furry tail, often with a slight tuft at the tip. Not often seen, being nocturnal, the dormouse climbs about inside bushes to feed and rarely feeds on the ground. It nests in a 15cm (6in) ball of bark strips woven into twigs, located in a tree or a bush for safety, or inside a custom-made dormouse box (you need a special licence to handle dormice, so don't look inside). In winter, the dormouse hibernates, building a winter nest at ground level or below the ground.
HABITAT Undisturbed hazel woods and coppices well away from human habitation, almost entirely in south and south-west England.
FOOD Nuts, especially hazel, insects, pollen, fruit.

11 Bank vole
Clethrionomys glareolus
Britain's tiniest vole, 9cm (3½in) long with a 4–6cm (1½–2½in) tail, the bank vole has rich red-brown upperparts and is paler grey or buff below. It has the small, plump body shape typical of a vole, with a short face, blunt nose, small ears and shortish tail (shorter than that of a mouse). It is often seen scrambling among shrubs, during the day or at night, and is frequently confused with the field vole, which has a grey-brown coat, rather than reddish, and much smaller ears.
HABITAT Throughout lowland areas in the British Isles; introduced to Ireland. Found in woodland and (unlike the field vole) also lives in scrub and hedgerows.
FOOD Seeds, berries, nuts, vegetation including buds and some insects.

12 Yellow-necked mouse
Apodemus flavicollis
If given a good view of this nocturnal mouse, you will see its distinguishing feature – an irregular yellow collar round the shoulder and neck. Its head and back are a more vivid orange-brown than the wood mouse's, the flanks are tinged almost orange and the underparts are white. Relatively large, it is 10cm (4in) long and the tail is slightly longer. The yellow-necked mouse is less often seen than the wood mouse or house mouse.
HABITAT Mostly in south-east England and round the Welsh borders, usually in woodland but also fields and hedgerows. In populated areas, it may come into gardens, outbuildings or houses.
FOOD Berries, fruit, seeds, nuts, insects, snails.

A delicacy for the table
The edible dormouse (*Glis glis*), which was introduced to Britain by Walter Rothschild at Tring Park in 1902, is a completely different species from the common dormouse. Found only in the Chilterns, the edible dormouse is more likely to be seen in that area than our native species, since it often goes into houses. It is grey with white underparts, has a long body (15cm/6in) and a fat, bushy tail that is almost the same length as the body. It is nocturnal and hibernates in winter. The edible dormouse used to be considered a delicacy by the Romans, who served it roasted and stuffed.

OPPOSITE The Scottish wildcat looks similar to the domestic tabby but is rarely seen as it is secretive and under threat from extinction.

14 Noctule bat
Nyctalus noctula

The noctule bat is relatively big for a bat, with a wingspan of 35cm (14in). It is often out shortly before dusk on summer evenings, when it flies high and swoops down to take large insects, such as moths, in mid-air.

HABITAT Mainly in England and Wales, in mature deciduous woodland and parkland. Roosts in colonies in tree holes, and spends the winter hibernating in trees or undisturbed outbuildings – it is not commonly found in house lofts.

15 Brown long-eared bat
Plecotus auritus

This is a fairly common, medium-sized, light brown bat (body 4.5cm/1¾in long, wingspan 25cm/10in) with enormous, pointed, oval ears, 3cm (1¼in) long, and rather broad wings. An extremely agile flier, it twists and weaves through branches or other obstructions, unlike other bats, which tend to fly in wide open spaces.

HABITAT Throughout the British Isles, including the far north. Seen at dusk from April to November foraging along woodland edges and rides. Roosts colonially in lofts or woodland edges.

Watching bats

Bats are incredibly difficult to identify as they are very fast-moving in flight and appear only from dusk onwards through the night, which means it's impossible to get a good look at them. Though they are out and about from spring to autumn, the best time to watch them is on warm, still summer evenings around dusk. You can't handle or disturb bats without a special licence, and that includes their roosts, so leave identification to an expert. Some wildlife reserves, stately homes and gardens hold occasional evening 'bat walks' in summer; electronic bat detectors are available that allow you to eavesdrop on bats' calls, and by slowing them down and lowering the pitch they enable experts to identify the various species of bat by sound. (The tiny lesser horseshoe bat makes the highest-frequency sounds of any bat in the British Isles.) Otherwise, just enjoy watching the aerial acrobatics of bats hunting moths and other night-flying insects without worrying about putting a name to them.

All bats are reasonably endangered these days, owing largely to loss of habitat; timber treatments, home improvements and modern building techniques all contribute by making lofts inaccessible. Among the rarest bats are Bechstein's bat, the grey long-eared bat, the barbastelle and the lesser horseshoe bat.

16

16 Lesser horseshoe bat
Rhinolophus hipposideros
A classic woodland species, this is one of our tiniest and rarest bats, with a body smaller than most people's thumb. Males are 4cm (1½in) long with 25cm (10in) wingspan; females are slightly smaller. It has a characteristic horseshoe-shaped flap of skin on the front of the face, which directs and receives the high-pitched echolocating sounds used when hunting. Broad, rounded wings and slow flight also help to identify horseshoe bats. The greater horseshoe bat is similar but half as big again. (Unlike other species of bat, horseshoes have no 'tail' – the skin is fairly straight between the legs.)
HABITAT South-west England, Wales and the west coast of Ireland. It roosts in trees singly or in small groups, upside-down with wings wrapped around the body like a cloak, and hibernates in cellars or tunnels in winter, never in crevices.

17 Whiskered bat
Myotis mystacinus
The whiskered bat is a small, fragile-looking woodland bat (body 4cm/1½in long, wingspan 23cm/9in), with narrow, pointed wings and an unusually furry face, though no whiskers. Although it is out and about at dusk on summer evenings, it is very difficult to recognize and is seldom seen; look for the weak, fluttering flight and its habit of covering the same ground several times before moving on when hunting.
HABITAT Throughout England, Wales and southern Scotland. Hunts along hedgerows and buildings, often singly or in small groups, roosts in trees and buildings and hibernates in caves, crevices in buildings or cliffs in winter.

18 Bechstein's bat
Myotis bechsteini
This is a medium-sized bat (body 4.5cm/1½in, wingspan 30cm/12in) with a pinkish nose and very elongated ears, 2.5cm (1in) long. One of our least common mammals, it has been sighted only a few times.
HABITAT Mostly in Dorset. Roosts in trees, but also thought to use attics and bat nesting boxes; hibernates in particular limestone mines.

19 Leisler's bat
Nyctalus leisleri
This is a rare woodland creature with a medium-sized body (6cm/2½in, wingspan 30cm/12in), a slightly squashed, pug-like face and overall warm brown fur with a bronze sheen.

19

20

HABITAT In isolated pockets in central England and at a very few locations in Ireland. Lives only in trees, where it both roosts and hibernates.

20 Barbastelle
Barbastella barbastellus
An uncommon, shy and rarely seen, medium-sized bat with a squashed, pug-like face and very large, triangular ears with a broad, reinforcing fold along the inner edges that meets between the eyes. The fur and wings are dark with a pale grey, frosted appearance.
HABITAT Only in the southern half of England and Wales, in open woodland, but it often hunts over rivers with well-wooded sides.

17

18

Plants

1 Sessile oak
Quercus petraea

The sessile oak grows up to 40m (130ft) high and has deeply fissured bark. It is very similar to the English oak but has a more untidy habit. To distinguish between the 2 species, look at the leaves and the acorns: if the leaves lack 'earlobes' at the base and the acorns attach straight to the stems without stalks, you know you are looking at the sessile oak.

HABITAT Woodland, farmland and hedgerows.

2 English oak
Quercus robur

Also known as the pedunculate oak, this is a neat, cone-shaped tree, up to 35m (115ft) high, whose lower branches stand out horizontally from the trunk, forming a tidy, flat base to the domed shape created by the upper branches. As in the sessile oak, the bark is deeply fissured. However, the leaves of the English oak (shown below) have 'earlobes' at the base, close to where they join the stem, and the acorns are attached to the tree by stalks 2.5cm (1in) or more long.

HABITAT Woodland, parkland and growing up through hedgerows.

Oaks and their uses

Oak is probably our best-known timber tree, used for house-building, ship-building and furniture-making throughout medieval history. What's not generally realized is that our traditional native oak tree is in fact 2 species rather than one. The sessile oak is the standard native oak tree of the north and western regions of the British Isles, as it prefers the more acid soil and higher rainfall present in those areas. The English oak, which is also known as the pedunculate oak, is found particularly in the drier and more alkaline southern and eastern regions, where conditions are more to its liking. But the division is not totally clear-cut, and both species can often be found growing together over much of the country. (They also hybridize, making identification difficult.) To tell the two apart, look at the leaves – do they have 'earlobes' or not? And see if the acorns grow on stalks or not.

Oak trees house a huge range of insect life, and the caterpillars of a great many different moth and butterfly species feed on oak leaves. However, oak leaves produce tannin, which becomes more concentrated as the growing season progresses, so that by mid- to late June the leaves are unpalatable to all but a very few species. This means that caterpillars that rely on oak need to complete their feeding cycle early in the season. Besides acting as a natural insecticide, tannin preserves the leaves, making oak leaves very slow to decay after they've fallen in autumn – if you make leafmould, oak leaves need to be set aside to rot separately as they take 2 years to break down. The preservative effects of tannin have also been useful to man: in medieval times, the tannin from oak leaves was used for processing leather.

3 Sweet chestnut
Castanea sativa
This is a striking and easily identified, non-native tree, reaching 30m (100ft) tall, with characteristic, deeply fissured bark forming long, deep bands that spiral up the tree. The leaves are long and narrow with jagged edges; spiky green clusters of fruit contain the nuts, which ripen in autumn – the husks split open when the clusters hit the ground. In the British Isles, sweet chestnuts are small and the crop is unreliable; the big, fat chestnuts you buy at Christmas are grown in much warmer climates in southern Europe or California.
HABITAT Parkland and country estates. Also found in plantations that were originally coppiced to produce chestnut palings for fencing and where the trees have long been left to grow back into dense, shady woods.

4 Beech
Fagus sylvatica
A large, spreading, woodland tree, beech grows up to 40m (130ft) tall and has characteristic, smooth, light grey bark and oval leaves, approximately 5cm (2in) long, which turn rich coppery shades in autumn before falling. The small, triangular nuts are packed inside small, bristly husks, known as 'beech mast', that peel back from the tip when they ripen and fall to the ground. Seedlings of the same species of beech are grown in rows in the garden for hedging, but regular hedge-clipping makes them stay small. Beech trees cast very deep shade, so little grows in beech woods in summer, although several species of toadstools thrive on the deep layer of leaf litter that builds up underneath in autumn and they are a good place to go fungus-spotting.
HABITAT Particularly on chalklands of southern England, but was once widely planted as a parkland species throughout the British Isles.

5 Hornbeam
Carpinus betulus
The hornbeam is an attractive tree with a rounded shape, to 30m (100ft) high. The beech-like leaves have pairs of evenly spaced veins arranged in a fishbone pattern, but they are smaller than beech leaves and non-glossy. In spring dangling green catkins appear, followed by bunches of bracts resembling green 'keys' housing small nuts. Hornbeam is native only to the south-east quarter of England, but it was once used for timber and is much grown as a garden hedging plant throughout the British Isles.
HABITAT Woods and parkland.

6 Bramble
Rubus fruticosus
Also known as the blackberry, this is a very widespread, invasive and much maligned, fruiting scrambler with sinuous stems bearing backward-facing hooks that enable them to scramble through bushes, hedgerows and small trees or form their own impenetrable thickets. The usually 5-lobed leaves have prickly backs, and the white-to-pale-pink flowers, carried from June to August, are followed by edible berries that turn from green to mauve to black as they ripen. (If you are indulging in the favourite countryside pastime of blackberrying, pick from bushes well away from heavy traffic.)

Brambles spread quickly from seed dropped by birds, and also because when stems arch over they take root where they touch the ground and start up a new plant. It's not long before a single bush turns into a thicket. Bramble thickets provide safe places for foxes, rabbits and a wide range of rodents to excavate their holes. Brambles are also very successful at taking over hedgerows, turning them into impenetrable fortresses that feed and shelter a variety of wildlife. The fruit provides food for all sorts of birds but is also eaten by rodents, foxes and badgers, and the foliage feeds several species of caterpillars – in addition, the nectar of the flowers is a regular favourite with a large range of hedgerow and garden butterflies. While we tend to think of 'brambles' as being all the same kind, there are actually many similar species.
HABITAT Woodland, hedgerows, fields and wasteland.

7 Lodgepole pine
Pinus contorta

This North American conifer from the Pacific coast is known for its rugged disposition and naturally straight trunk. It grows up to 25m (80ft) high with a flame-shaped outline, and resembles the Scots pine. However, the lodgepole pine has mid-green leaves and brown bark, while the leaves of the Scots pine have a bluish tinge and the bark is tinged orange. Older lodgepole pines have a square pattern of fissures. Look for short (5cm/2in), slightly twisted needles in pairs, and small, pointed cones in clusters (very much like those of Scots pine, except that each scale of the cone bears a prickle at the tip). Male flowers are cream, held in clusters at the base of new growth; female flowers are small and pinkish, present at the tips of new growth. The male and female flowers, borne from late spring to early summer, are carried in

separate clusters on the young shoots. The lodgepole pine is so named because Native Americans traditionally cut these young pine trees to make the straight poles that supported structures such as wigwams or lodges.
HABITAT Widely grown in forestry plantations throughout north-west Britain.

8 Norway spruce
Picea abies

The Norway spruce is a forestry plantation favourite. It begins life as the easily recognized Christmas tree – with a pointed, conical shape and horizontal tiers of branches – and develops bare, straight trunks with occasional dead stubs of branches, with interlocking 'Christmas tree' tops higher up, as it matures. It eventually reaches 40m (130ft) high. The pale brown bark is lightly 'crazed' and pimpled, and it doesn't crack into fissures like pine bark does. The needles are single, each with a short, woody 'peg' at the base. Cream male flowers or pinkish female flowers are clustered at the tips of young shoots in May. The cones of this spruce are brown, borne in clusters, and elongated in shape, not at all like pine cones; they always hang downwards.
HABITAT Grown on an enormous scale in northern Britain in places such as the Kielder Forest of Northumberland, but also cultivated in smaller plantations throughout Britain for cutting at an early stage as our traditional Christmas tree.

9 Sitka spruce
Picea sitchensis

This is the most numerous forestry conifer in Britain, and is very fast-growing – it can put on 1m (3ft) a year. It is a conical tree, to 45m (148ft) high, with greyish bark that flakes into irregular, rounded 'platelets', and slate-blue-to-grey-green foliage. The needles are single and very sharp-tipped, each attached to a branch by a short 'peg'. The cones are long and brown, with large, loose, slightly shaggy-looking, blunt-tipped scales, and carried singly, always hanging downwards. Flowers

appear near the top of the tree in late spring, loosely clustered at the tips of new growth: the male flowers are cream, and female flowers are green, tipped with dullish red.
HABITAT Originally from the Pacific coast of the USA, now very widely planted throughout northern and western Britain, in areas where rainfall is high.

10 Douglas fir
Pseudotsuga menziesii

This is the tallest timber tree grown in Britain, to 55m (180ft), though it reaches 100m (330ft) in its homeland on the Pacific north-west coast of the USA. A tall, conical conifer with gracefully downward-arching branches, it has short, single needles, each with 2 white, length-ways stripes beneath. It flowers in spring: the female flowers are red tassels held singly at the tips of young shoots; the male flowers are cream and clustered near the tips of the shoots. The cones are light reddish brown and shaggy-looking, hanging down singly underneath the branches; look for the scales, which are 1cm (⅜in) wide and about half as long, with a whiskery, 3-pronged 'tongue' at the tip.
HABITAT Grows in the main forestry areas of north-west Britain.

Forestry plantations

Commercial forestry plantations are relatively new to our landscape, having arrived in quantity only since the First and Second World Wars. Unlike woods that sprang up naturally over centuries and contain a wide mixture of species, a forestry plantation is more like an agricultural crop – large areas are planted with the same species, grown close together in rows to make the best use of the land, and all are harvested at the same time, then replanted. It's a classic mono-crop, only instead of wheat or sugar beet, they grow lodgepole pine, Sitka spruce or Douglas fir. It's not unusual to see plantations of poplars grown for making matchsticks, or young Norway spruce, which will be cut and sold for Christmas trees.

One of our largest forestry plantations is Kielder Forest in Northumberland, where the native red squirrel still survives and feeds almost exclusively on conifer seeds, shoots and buds.

All these acres of the same type of tree mean that forestry plantations are not nearly as much of an attraction for wildlife as our native mixed woods. 'Farmed' conifers are all planted at the same time, so there is no mixture of young and old specimens to provide a range of habitats for wildlife; and they are kept clean and tidy, so they don't have the holes that all sorts of animals like to live in; also, there are no dead branches or rotting logs to feed and house the insects that are the natural food for a lot of our normal woodland wildlife. In addition, once new forestry plantations grow big enough for the trees to cast total shade beneath, they act like a giant, living mulch that smothers out everything underneath. Without weeds and wildflowers, we lose most of the insects and the woodland songbirds that live on them. Forestry plantations also displaced the natural habitat of a lot of moorland birds, and their numbers continued to dwindle along with their habitat.

But it's not entirely bad news, and there are a few species that like conifer forests – crossbills, which feed on conifer seeds, and red squirrels in particular. For some reason the grey squirrels (which the Victorians introduced as a novelty) didn't find conifer forests as good a habitat as other woodland, so even now the native reds still survive in some of our biggest forestry plantations, like Kielder Forest in Northumberland. You may also find some wildflowers in clearings and rides – long, straight tracks through blocks of forestry land – where the light gets in. Some forests have fair populations of interesting fungi (for instance Thetford Forest in Norfolk) and several forestry plantations in Scotland are managed to encourage rare birds such as capercaillie. Rare wildlife, for example the pine marten and Scottish wildcat, will also hide up in forestry land, largely because of the dense cover mature forestry provides, while their original habitats are in decline.

11 Japanese larch
Larix kaempferi

This is a common and widely grown forestry tree, to 30m (100ft) high, with an open, conical shape; it is easily recognized, since unlike other common conifers it sheds its needles in winter and in spring new growth is very bright, pale green; in autumn, the needles turn golden-yellow before falling. It flowers on bare twigs in spring, with male and female flowers dotted evenly along the same twigs: the males are yellow, short and tassel-like, hanging down; the females are tight, rounded, orangey clusters, facing upwards. The cones are brown when ripe, squat with scales curving out slightly at the tip, and look a bit like candle-holders, upright on the branches. Other larches include the hybrid larch (*Larix × eurolepis*), a cross between the European larch and the Japanese larch, which is now also very widely grown for forestry. The European larch (*Larix decidua*) used to be the main larch grown, but over the last 50 years it has been replaced by the Japanese and hybrid larches.
HABITAT Throughout the British Isles, often planted on recently cleared coppice or woodland.

12 Hybrid poplars
Populus nigra hybrids

Various fast-growing commercial hybrids of our native black poplar are grown for timber and for making matches and matchboxes (even clogs, in Holland). Quickly reaching 30m (100ft) high, the hybrid poplar has a straight, upright trunk and rounded top, with grey-brown bark that has long, almost vertical fissures. The leaves are mid-green, slightly glossy, 5cm (2in) long, and almost triangular with pointed tips. In March the tree bears dangling catkins; the female catkins are short and green, those of males are long and reddish chestnut, carried on separate trees. Female catkins are followed by strings of white fluffy seeds that are shed in June.
HABITAT In plantations, but also for screening industrial estates or making roadside windbreaks.

13 Wild cherry
Prunus avium

The wild cherry is an attractive, potentially large tree, reaching 10–12m (33–40ft), with white cherry blossom on bare branches in April. It has a shiny, mahogany-brown trunk and typical cherry leaves – 10cm (4in) long, oval and slightly toothed round the edges, with herringbone ribs. The white, 5-petalled flowers grow in clusters on short spurs before the tree comes into leaf; they are followed in late summer by bunches of dangling, yellow-orange fruit that resembles small, stunted, cultivated cherries. (This tree is thought to be an ancestor of today's edible cherries.) The leaves turn orange-red in autumn.
HABITAT Mostly woods, but also hedgerows or the corners of fields, mainly on dry loam soil over chalk in the south of England.

14 Small-leaved lime
Tilia cordata

Elegant and round-topped, this native tree was one of our original coppice trees, although it is rarely grown that way now. It reaches 22m (72ft) and has an upright trunk that sometimes forks halfway up, with branches that arch downwards. The bark is smooth and grey; older trees have shallow, squarish cracks. The mid-green, heart-shaped leaves are 6–8cm (2½–3¼in) wide and the same length, arranged alternately along the stems. It flowers in July, with small clusters of tiny, fragrant, yellowish green flowers, about 4cm (1½in) across, on short stems, each bearing a yellowish green bract. The flowers are followed by small, smooth, round green berries that resemble tiny peas; the berries eventually drop from the trees still attached to their stem and bract, which acts as a wing.
HABITAT Occurs wild mostly in limestone regions and is much planted in ornamental parks and avenues leading up to stately homes – there are still some very old limes at Hampton Court.

OPPOSITE A beautiful carpet of naturalized wild snowdrops covers this woodland floor in spring.

15 Primrose
Primula vulgaris

A well-known and common woodland flower, the primrose blooms in March and April. It is a small, rosette-shaped perennial, 15cm (6in) high, with long, oval leaves that have smooth upper surfaces but slightly hairy undersides. The flower stems are hairy and each one bears a single, pale yellow, wide-open flower with 5 petals, each of which has a notch in the centre, above a long, tubular, slightly hairy green calyx.

HABITAT Damp, shady hedgerows, woodland clearings and also woodland edges.

16 Wood anemone
Anemone nemorosa

The wood anemone is a charming, delicate, perennial spring flower found in large groups carpeting the ground. It is an indicator of ancient woodland. The 10–15cm (4–6in) flowering stems have a frill of 3 deeply divided leaves roughly halfway up, and are topped by a single, upward-facing, 6–7-petalled, white or palest pink-tinged flower, approximately 2cm (¾in) across. These appear from March to May, but close in dull weather, and are followed by the main foliage, which grows directly up from spreading rhizomes underground.

HABITAT Clearings and coppices with a light canopy of leaves.

17 Dog's mercury
Mercurialis perennis

This is the sort of inconspicuous 'little green job' that is invariably overlooked compared to the more eye-catching flowers usually growing nearby. It is an upright, clump-forming (poisonous) perennial, 30cm (12in) tall, with straight stems that are clad in evenly spaced pairs of dark green, oval leaves (about 6cm/2½in long) with toothed edges. The stems are topped by sprays of airy green blobs of flower from February to April.

HABITAT Woodland, sometimes in fairly deep shade.

18 Wild daffodil
Narcissus pseudonarcissus

Our scarce, native narcissus, which grows to 30cm (12in) high, flowers from February to April. The slightly nodding flowers have a ring of pale yellow outer petals that surround a slightly deeper yellow trumpet. Like garden daffodils, our native 'Lent lily' (as the wild daffodil is also known) grows from a bulb and the foliage dies down 2 months after flowering, leaving nothing visible for the rest of the year.

If you see colonies of larger daffodils, especially when they look mixed instead of all absolutely identical, they may well be cultivated daffodils that have escaped into the wild, which happens commonly when people fly-tip garden rubbish in the countryside. There can also be hybrids produced when cultivated daffodils are grown close enough to wild ones for cross-pollination to take place. Wordsworth's famous poem that describes the 'host of golden daffodils' on the banks of Lake Ullswater referred to the true

wild daffodil, but this may now be threatened owing to misguided planting in the area. It is a matter of some concern to botanists.
HABITAT Widespread in certain areas, for example the Welsh borders. Usually occurs in large colonies where it is present.

19 Wild snowdrop
Galanthus nivalis

Wild snowdrops are short, bulbous plants, 10cm (4in) high, making clumps of upright, strap-shaped leaves, often spreading to cover the ground in carpets. The flowers, which appear from February to March, have 3 white outer petals surrounding a central cup formed of 3 green-tipped sepals. The whole plant dies down around July. Experts are uncertain whether snowdrops are truly British natives, but if not they have naturalized themselves well in some places. Gloucestershire has particularly stunning snowdrop woods in spring.
HABITAT Scattered locations in all but the north of Scotland, especially in damp woodland and shady stream banks.

20 Lesser celandine
Ranunculus ficaria

Although lesser celandine is often unwelcome in gardens because of its vigorous spreading habit, the cheery yellow, buttercup-like flowers are a grand sight in the countryside in spring, from March to May. The plants grow from tiny, shallow tubers, making small clumps, 15cm (6in) high and the same across, that spread to form a continuous carpet. The leaves are thick, glossy, deep green and heart-shaped and the flowers, 1cm (⅜in) across, are shining yellow, with one at the end of each flower stem in much the same way as lawn daisies. The foliage dies down shortly after the last flowers are over.
HABITAT Damp, shady places in woods, ditches and wasteland.

23 Ground ivy
Glechoma hederacea

Ground ivy is a common semi-evergreen perennial that keeps its leaves in all but the coldest winter, with creeping stems that root as they run, spreading to 30cm (12in), and bearing small, slightly wrinkled, kidney-shaped leaves. The short, erect flower stems carry both small leaves and whorls of small, pale mauve flowers that all grow on the same side of the stem, from March to May or June.
HABITAT Woods and wasteland.

24 Wood sage
Teucrium scorodonia

This is an unspectacular perennial 'filler flower' of woodland, forming loose, untidy, fairly upright clumps, 20cm (8in) high and 40cm (16in) wide, depending on how successfully the clump has spread. It has reasonably thick, heavily textured, almost triangular leaves, which have a hop-like fragrance if crushed. From July to September, airy, upright spikes of greenish dead-nettle-like flowers with protruding brown anthers are held above the plant.
HABITAT Dryish woodland and undisturbed hedgerows on acid soils.

21 Bluebell
Hyacinthoides non-scriptus

The evocative flowers of spring woodland, bluebells carpet the ground beneath deciduous trees shortly before they come into leaf. Each plant forms a cluster of long, narrow, succulent leaves that grow from a bulb deep underground (often 30cm/12in or more down). Nodding heads of tubular blue flowers open in April and May and can continue until early June. In Scotland, the name 'bluebell' is used for *Campanula rotundifolia* – the plant we know as harebell south of the border.

A large, dense carpet of bluebells takes a long time to build up, so it is a natural indicator of ancient woodland that has existed for hundreds of years or more. (Most bluebell woods were once coppiced hazel and hornbeam woods, which have long since been abandoned and left to regrow naturally.) After the flowers are over, the dense bluebell foliage slowly dies down over the next couple of months – acting as a deep living mulch – at the same time as the trees come into full leaf overhead. The combined effect is to shade out any other plants, so little else grows in competition with bluebells once they have established a good ground-covering layer. Keep to the paths in bluebell woods, because treading on the plants' leaves damages them and prevents nutrients returning to the bluebell bulbs during the long dying-down season. Too much of this eventually kills off the clumps.
HABITAT Woodland.

22 Wood violet
Viola riviniana

This small, neat perennial plant, 10cm (4in) high and wide, has heart-shaped leaves, 4–5cm (1½–2in) long, and unscented, blue-violet flowers with 5 petals, from April to June. You can tell it apart from the very similar sweet violet (*Viola odorata*) as flowers of the latter open earlier, between January and April, and are scented.
HABITAT Moist woodland and hedgerows throughout the southern half of the British Isles.

Coppices

There is a very long history of coppicing woodland in the British Isles; indeed, there are indications that man used this technique as long as 4000 years ago. Native trees, such as the hazel, hornbeam and small-leaved lime, as well as the sweet chestnut (which was brought to Britain by the Romans), were the chief species that were grown in this way. The principle is very simple: regularly cutting established trees of suitable species down almost to ground-level causes them to form 'stools' – another name for the rootstock – from which long, straight stems grow out strongly. After a few years, these are big

Sweet chestnut was introduced into the British Isles by the Romans, as its long, straight stems are ideal for coppicing. The background image shows a framework of coppiced hazel poles being used to make furniture.

enough to cut as poles. In medieval times, hazels were cut every three or four years, and the poles would be split and woven into hurdles to make the wattle-and-daub panels that formed the walls of timber-framed houses; thinner sticks were tied into bundles (faggots) and were used for fuelling bakers' ovens. Coppicing experienced a mini-boom at the start of the Industrial Revolution for providing charcoal for furnaces, and more recently for making split chestnut poles for fence posts and paling fences.

Coppicing largely died out when demand for straight poles ceased, but it has started up again on a small scale as a woodland-management method, with small sections of woodland being coppiced in rotation every 12–15 years. As all things natural came back into fashion, woodland products once again had a market – for making fashionable hurdles for fencing, walking sticks, trugs and baskets.

Coppicing is also fantastic for wildlife. By opening up gaps in the tree canopy to let light in, it gives woodland flowers such as primroses the chance to recolonize previously dark areas, and wild orchids that have remained dormant underground for years are often triggered back into flowering within a couple of years of coppicing. As the canopy of trees slowly grows back, the increasing shade prevents invasive species such as grasses from overwhelming them. The regular cycle of shade, plus the shortage of phosphates common to most ancient woodland (owing to wood being harvested over centuries without fertilizers ever being used), also acts as a natural control for fast-growing species such as elder trees, so instead of slowly returning to scrub, coppiced woodland tends to have quite a good population of interesting plants and their related animals (the hazel dormouse and the nightingale, in particular, have benefited).

The remarkable thing about coppicing is the way it regenerates the tree: a coppiced stool lives many times longer than the same species left to grow normally with a single trunk. Instead of perhaps 60–100 years, coppiced trees live for hundreds of years, and many ancient coppices are still around today – bluebell woods are often old overgrown coppices, and dense carpets of bluebells growing alongside wood anemones are an indicator of an ancient wood.

27 Bugle

Ajuga reptans

This is a spreading perennial with a basal rosette of slightly wrinkled, long, oval leaves, sometimes tinged purple. Upright stems, 15–25cm (6–10in) high, bear pairs of pale blue, tubular, lipped flowers in the axils of the opposite leaves from May to July. Later in the season, creeping stems spread out from the main plant and take root, so the plant gradually spreads to form a circular, ground-covering mat, often growing through other plants.
HABITAT Woodland, in all but the far north of the British Isles.

28 Foxglove

Digitalis purpurea

The foxglove is a common, familiar and much-loved wildflower. It is an upright biennial or short-lived perennial, 1–2m (3–6½ft) high, growing from a basal rosette of large, pointed, slightly felty, light green leaves, up to 30cm (12in) long. From June to August it bears tall spikes of large, mauve, white or purple and often heavily spotted, thimble-shaped flowers. All parts of the plant are poisonous. However, the foxglove

was cultivated as a medicinal plant in parts of Europe before the First World War; it is the source of the heart drug digitalin.
HABITAT Woodland clearings, coppices, woodland edges, hedgerows and also more open situations.

25 Red campion

Silene dioica

Red campion is an abundant and colourful perennial wildflower, forming rather upright, bushy clumps, 30–60cm (12–24in) tall and almost as wide. It has paired oval leaves arranged evenly along the flower stems which, from May to June, are topped with a loose, airy spray of bloom made up of a ring of 5 deeply divided petals growing out of a bell-shaped calyx.
HABITAT Woodland clearings, hedgerows and woodland edges.

26 Wood spurge

Euphorbia amygdaloides

Wood spurge is an unusual perennial wildflower, but a subspecies of this plant will be familiar to gardeners. It makes upright clumps of stems 75cm (30in) high, clad in whorls of narrow, dark green leaves, topped from March to May with airy, open heads of tiny yellow flowers cupped inside small, yellowish green, bowl-shaped bracts on long, thin stalks.
HABITAT Woodland.

29 Ramsons
Allium ursinum

A relative of culinary garlic, this is a pungent, widespread, clump-forming perennial that spreads to form complete carpets of lily-of-the-valley-like foliage. The leaves, up to 15cm (6in) long and 5cm (2in) wide, smell very strongly of garlic if bruised and can be chopped up and used instead of garlic for cooking. Ramsons has domed, airy heads of small white flowers from April to June.
HABITAT Woodland, often bluebell woods, including quite heavy shade, in all but the northernmost parts of the British Isles.

30 Yellow archangel
Lamiastrum galeobdolon

This is a short, semi-evergreen, clump-forming perennial with upright stems, 20–30cm (8–12in) high, growing from a network of creeping stolons. The stems bear small, oval leaves with jagged edges similar to those of the dead-nettle, which are sometimes faintly patterned with white or silvery patches, with clusters of small, hooded, yellow, dead-nettle-like flowers found tucked into the leaf joints in May and June.
HABITAT Woodland and shady hedgerows, mainly in England and Wales.

31 Herb Robert
Geranium robertianum

This is a fairly common annual wildflower flowering from May to September. It makes a loose clump, very similar to those of cultivated hardy geraniums, made up of deeply toothed, slightly hairy leaflets, which are arranged roughly in the shape of a hand, at the end of long, reddish, hairy stems. The foliage smells acrid when bruised. The small, solitary, 5-petalled pink flowers appear on short, branching, thread-like stems above the foliage, and are followed by characteristic stork's-bill fruit from which the ripe seeds split off. Both the flowers and the fruit appear on the same plant throughout the summer. The lower leaves start turning red in a dry summer, and as autumn progresses most of the plant takes on reddish autumn tints before dying back.
HABITAT Hedgerows, woodland edges and wasteland, also occasionally in shady corners in country gardens.

32 Giant bellflower
Campanula latifolia

An 'occasional' flower rather than a regular find, this is a perennial with tall, slim flower spikes (1–1.2m/3–4ft high) bearing long, pointed, spearmint-shaped leaves with slightly jagged edges spaced alternately up the stem. In July and August it bears pale blue, bell-shaped, jagged-edged flowers, which resemble pixie hats and decrease in size towards the tip of the spike.
HABITAT Woodland and shady hedgerows, almost everywhere south of the Scottish border.

Origins of garden varieties

For many centuries, country folk spotted unusual forms of common countryside plants – often 'freaks' (or as scientists would say, mutations) with unusual colours, double flowers or patterned leaves – which they dug up and took home to grow in their gardens. Very often, these oddities would not have survived in the wild, since they usually grow less vigorously than the standard species. But they were cultivated, clumps were divided up and passed around among families and friends, eventually becoming what we know of today as cottage-garden plants. Quite a few old favourites have reached us in this way: cultivated varieties of celandines, several of the bellflowers, including *Campanula trachelium* (intriguingly known as 'bats in the belfry'), *Campanula latifolia*, *Campanula glomerata*, several hardy cranesbills such as *Geranium pratense*, bugle, yellow archangel and double forms of both lady's smock (*Cardamine pratensis*) and red campion. If you see these perennials for sale in a nursery you know straight away that these are not the original wild plants, since they carry an English cultivar name after the basic Latin name.

33

33 Wild strawberry
Fragaria vesca

With its 3-lobed leaves, this ground-covering perennial is very similar to the cultivated strawberry but is smaller and more delicate. It grows in small, loose clumps (approximately 10cm/4in high and the same across) that spread by weak runners. The flower stems are topped by a cluster of small, 5-petalled white flowers in late spring, after which tiny, sweet wild strawberries ripen to a deep red in summer; the fruit is appreciated by a great deal of British wildlife from mice and birds to foxes.
HABITAT Woodland and hedgerows.

34 Early purple orchid
Orchis mascula

The early purple orchid is a beautiful woodland flower, 45cm (17½in) high, seen from April to July. It forms a loose, rather upright rosette of lance-shaped leaves with dark spots, and upright spikes of pale purple flowers, each consisting of 3 small, slightly twisted upper petals above a 'lip', which makes a landing platform for pollinating insects.
HABITAT Throughout the British Isles, but especially on chalky soils in the southern half of the country, often growing in bluebell woods and with dog's mercury as it enjoys undisturbed, long-established ancient woodland.

35 Bird's-nest orchid
Neottia nidus-avis

This is an extraordinary-looking wild orchid, with no leaves or any green parts at all, which appears briefly above ground in June and July to flower before dying down for the rest of the year. Look for a

35

single, upright, ochre-to-yellowish-brown stem, 30cm (12in) tall, bearing a few small scales, topped with a spike of strange flowers of the same colour with droopy petals. It grows in bare ground, often in very deep shade where not much else survives.

Having no chlorophyll, the bird's-nest orchid derives its nutrients from rotting leaves via its special relationship with a microscopic fungus that lives in the soil round the untidy mass of thick roots that give the plant its name. You might just about be

able to see a few roots at the base of the plant, otherwise trust me – the 'bird's nest' is underground; don't dig up or disturb it.
HABITAT Grows locally in woodland, particularly beech woods, on chalky soil; mostly in the south of England, although it can occur in other areas with chalky soil, except the far north.

36 Yellow pimpernel
Lysimachia nemorum

Very similar to the creeping Jenny grown in gardens (which is a relative), this low, sprawling

36

perennial (5–10cm/2–4in high, approximately 30cm/12in across) has prostrate stems with pairs of elliptical leaves and flowers from May to September. The 5-petalled flowers, which are borne on short, slender, thread-like stems from the leaf joints, are yellow and small, approximately 1cm (⅜in) across.
HABITAT Damp, dappled shade in woodland and hedge-bottoms.

34

37 Wood sorrel
Oxalis acetosella

This dainty, little, shamrock-like perennial can create large carpets on the woodland floor. Each plant is a spreading clump, 15cm (6in) high, with clover-like leaves that fold down at night so it looks as if the plant is asleep. Fragile white flowers are carried on stems up to 15cm (6in) tall in May and June. The wood sorrel is no relation to the true sorrel, but it is named after it because it has a similar, sharp taste.
HABITAT Deciduous woods.

38 Moschatel
Adoxa mochatellina

This is a tiny and easily overlooked curiosity that flowers in April and May. However, it is most easily detected by its musky scent, which is strongest on damp evenings. Look for a small, upright, tuft-shaped perennial with rather celery-like leaves on short, semi-succulent, upright stems up to 10cm (4in) high, with small clusters of 5 tiny, yellow-green flowers arranged in tight-packed globes standing out slightly above the foliage. It was said to be the

symbol of Christian watchfulness, with the 5 flowers facing north, south, east, west and up to heaven.
HABITAT Locally common in woodland and hedge-bottoms.

39 Jew's ear
Auricularia auricula-judae

Also known as jelly ear, this is a curious but common, bracket-type fungus, shaped very much like a human ear, with a rubbery, jelly-like texture and a glossy surface. Overall, it is plain rich chestnut, sandy brown or grey-brown in colour with no zoning or pattern of any kind, growing in spreading clusters on vertical branches or untidily stacked up a horizontal branch or tree trunk. It is edible when young and at its most jelly-like, before it starts drying out and darkening in colour, but be very certain of your identification.
HABITAT Woodland or shady hedgerows, usually on elder but sometimes other deciduous trees (both living and dead) including fallen logs, sometimes in quite large clusters. Found growing all year round.

40 King Alfred's cakes
Daldinia concentrica

Also known as cramp balls, these strange-looking, rounded black eruptions bubble up on dead trees, particularly ash. The irregularly shaped, hard, rounded 'bubbles' (2–7cm/¾–2¾in across) are initially a maroon-brown colour but soon turn black. If they are removed from the tree, you can see concentric circles inside the dark brown-black interior (rather like beetroot). The texture is charcoal-like, resembling a lump of carbon that you find in the oven after a casserole has boiled over and burnt. This fungus takes its name from the famous incident when King Alfred was left in charge of the cakes while a cottager popped out, only to come back and find the charred remains, the King's mind

having been occupied with higher things. In ancient times, the dry fungus was carried in people's pockets in the belief that it prevented cramp, hence its alternative common name. There is no evidence to substantiate this, and it seems unlikely. But then, if you suffer from cramp…
HABITAT Widespread in woods and hedgerows, on the trunk or larger branches of dead hardwood trees and fallen trunks, but especially common in the north. Present all year round.

41 Honey fungus
Armillaria mellea

Honey fungus forms tufts of attractive, honey-coloured toadstools, but these are difficult to identify positively as they are rather variable. The toadstools grow in groups joined together at the base, with flattened, dome-shaped caps (3–5cm/1¼–2in wide) whose tops have rings of loose brown scales round a darker centre. The stalks are slightly tapering with a 'ring' a short distance below the cap; the gills on the underside of the cap are white. To help identification, lay a cap on a piece of dark-coloured paper overnight and check that the resulting spore-print is white. Black 'bootlaces' (known scientifically as rhizomorphs) are found underneath the bark and in the ground; these are characteristic of honey fungus, and help the fungus spread between trees.

HABITAT Widespread in woodland and parkland in late summer and autumn, and now also common in woodland gardens, on tree stumps or fallen logs of many species of broadleaved trees, especially beech and oak.

42 Stinkhorn
Phallus impudicus

Also known as devil's prick, this is really a rather rude-looking fungus, up to 20cm (8in) high, that starts as a curious white, egg-like 'body' the size of a hen's egg and later 'hatches' into a thick, tapering, spongy-textured white stalk, topped by a slimy, dark brown, thimble-shaped cap that emits a ghastly stench. It grows in colonies, which can be detected by smell from some distance away.

HABITAT Conifer and mixed broadleaved woods with light, sandy or loam soil, in summer and autumn.

43 Fly agaric
Amanita muscaria

Probably the best-known and most distinctive of all fungi, this is the classic red-and-white-spotted toadstool of illustrated fairy stories. It is a medium-sized toadstool, up to 15cm (6in) high, with caps up to 15cm (6in) wide, in bright scarlet-red dotted with irregular, small white patches (the remains of the thin membrane of the emerging toadstool pushes up through as it appears out of the soil). The gills on the underside of the cap are white and very closely spaced; the stem has a ring just under the cap and a swelling at the base, at or just below soil-level. (The presence of this swelling, plus a ring round the stem, is an important identifying characteristic of the whole *Amanita* genus). This fungus is highly poisonous.

HABITAT Widespread, always grows in association with birch trees, in late summer and autumn.

44 Birch polypore
Piptoporus betulinus

Also known as razor-strop fungus, this is a very common and widespread bracket fungus with chunky, thickset, kidney-to-fan-shaped brackets, up to about 20cm (8in) across and 2–3cm (¾–1¼in) thick, with a narrow, almost tubular attachment to the tree trunk. It occurs in groups, often arranged in tiers when growing on a vertical trunk. The upper surface is hard, very smooth, warm fawn-brown turning to grey-brown on older specimens, with a rounded edge; the underside is white and spongy-looking.

Few fungi have common names, and those that do usually have

44

46

46 Penny bun
Boletus edulis

Also known as cep or porcini, this is one of the most sought-after edible toadstools and one of the main ingredients of packs of mixed dried wild fungi sold in the shops. It is a medium-to-large toadstool, 8–20cm (3¼–8in) wide and as high, with a dome-shaped, warm brown cap and plump, barely off-white stem covered with a network of very fine, raised, thread-like veins. The underside of the cap consists of pores instead of gills (as in all *Boletus* toadstools). A young *Boletus edulis* has a white underside, which turns olive-brown in older specimens. If the fungus is cut in half, the flesh is white and remains white, while some other species of *Boletus* 'stain' shortly after exposure to air. Be very certain of your identification if picking for the table, and choose only young, fresh, undamaged specimens – leave the rest in the ground so they can shed their spores.

HABITAT Woodland of all sorts, in summer and autumn.

them because they are either extremely common or else useful to man. The birch polypore was once used for sharpening old-fashioned, cut-throat razors, hence the common name of razor-strop fungus, but it was also used as a convenient and portable source of tinder for lighting fires.

HABITAT On living, dead and fallen birch tree trunks, all year round.

45 Earthball
Scleroderma citrinum

The earthball is a common and widespread, puffball-like, toxic fungus. Look for a round, oval or vaguely potato-shaped fungus, up to 15cm (6in) across, growing in colonies containing a mixture of isolated individuals and groups. The outer surface is off-white, covered in yellowish scales that give a slightly scabby appearance; if the fungus is cut in half with a pocket knife, the interior – even of a young specimen – is black. (This black colour helps identification and tells you it's not an edible puffball, which has a white interior.) The flesh smells faintly of warm rubber. Old specimens look as if they've exploded.

HABITAT Any woods (including conifer forests) where there is acid soil. They are found growing in deep leaf litter or amongst decomposed pine needles, usually in quite dense shade where there is little or no nearby vegetation, from late summer to late autumn.

45

Also found in woodland

Blackbird (see p.302)
Carrion crow (see p.304)
Chaffinch (see p.305)
Common spotted orchid (see p.180)
Dunnock (see p.301)
Hart's tongue fern (see p.183)
Mole (see p.202)
Native ponies (see p.147)
Orange tip (see p.195)
Peacock (see p.306)
Polecat (see p.203)
Robin (see p.301)
Shrews (see pp.147, 279)
Song thrush (see p.302)
Stoat (see p.278)
Tits (see pp.302, 304)
Weasel (see p.278)
Wood mouse (see p.315)
Woodpigeon (see p.190)
Wren (see p.301)

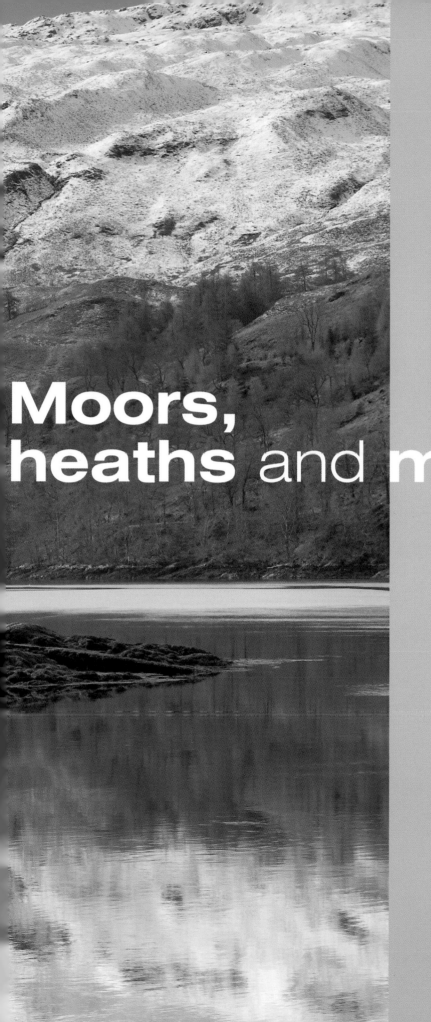

Moors,
heaths and mountains

Moors, heaths and mountains make up our most rugged and often remote scenery today. The most impressive range is the Grampians, which contains Britain's loftiest peaks (including Ben Nevis) and its deepest lake (Loch Ness). Mountains and moorland are among our oldest landscapes – their creation began about three billion years ago – while heathlands are the result of early man's agriculture.

The origins of rocks

Way back, near the start of geological history, massive continents collided, forcing rock upwards under enormous pressure and causing huge bends and folds in the earth's crust. These folds became giant mountain ranges and valleys. The remains of these underpin our islands today, but they are visible only in the north of Scotland, where you can still find our very oldest rocks – gneiss.

Britain wasn't always the shape we are familiar with today. It started out in two pieces that were attached to different continents half a world apart. These floated on a sea of molten rock, which met and stuck together some 400 million years ago. Volcanoes erupted, underwater ones forming parts of Wales, and where molten lava remained trapped underground it slowly cooled and turned to granite, as happened with much of Cornwall and Devon.

Now, rock might seem pretty solid, but if you leave it exposed to the elements for long enough – and we are talking millions of years here – it shrinks. The original mountains of Scotland were once about 7600m (22,000ft) high, roughly the same height as the Himalayas are today (the summit of their biggest peak, Mount Everest, is 8840m/29,000ft), but now there are only ten peaks in Britain over 1220m (4000ft) and

all of them are in Scotland. When the softer bits of granite in Devon and Cornwall shrank, we were left with Bodmin Moor, Land's End and the Scilly Isles.

Well, perhaps 'shrink' isn't quite the right word to describe what happens to rock. It's more accurate to say it weathers away – and it's all due to water. Water finds its way into every little crevice in even the hardest rock, then freezes in cold weather; since ice expands, if it repeatedly freezes and thaws over a very long time it chisels away at weak points in the rock. With porous rocks, such as sandstone and chalk, water soaks in, and when it freezes it expands so the rocks eventually shatter, in much the same way as clay flowerpots you leave outside in your garden in winter. Broken bits of rock then roll down the mountainside, crushing and smashing other rocks on the way down, until they reach the bottom where they pile up, leaving us with screes. It still happens today.

Meanwhile, rain landing on ancient mountains ran into rivulets that formed streams, rivers and waterfalls on their route downhill, and gradually wore away the softest parts of 'soft' rocks, such as limestone or sandstone, forming gullies and ravines. These grew steadily deeper because of all the tiny pieces of shattered rock carried along with the rushing water:

as the rock fragments rattled round in the ravine beds, the rough edges gradually wore off to make pebbles, which hammered away at the stream bed and eventually broke up again. That sort of pounding, over several hundred million years, has greatly reduced the size of the mountains.

A lot of mountain rubble fetched up in the sea or big lakes or rivers, where it was gradually compressed by the weight of new material being piled up on top of it, and turned into another kind of rock – old red sandstone – in the Devonian era (408–362 million years ago). We know it was formed underwater as it contains fossilized fish, but it now turns up in Orkney, the Black Mountains and the Brecon Beacons of Wales. Gritstone, which forms the Pennines and much of the scenery in Yorkshire, is also made of geological junk that's been pressed down hard underwater – usually along the banks of gigantic ancient rivers, around 325 million years ago.

The emergence of the landscape

Another element that gave us the landscapes we know today was ice. During the last ice age in Britain (the most recent ending about 10,000 years ago) ice built up over most of the country (except for land south of London and Bristol), forming a sheet up to 2.5km (1½ miles) thick in places. With new snow being added at the northern end, and some slight melting occurring at the thinnest end, in the south, the sheer weight made this giant glacier creep slowly forwards. As it moved, it picked up lots of loose rocks, which embedded themselves in the base and then ground away at the land underneath it, just like giant sandpaper, digging out the softer areas and small stones, large numbers of which were all swept along with the ice. When the ice eventually melted the stones were dropped – often hundreds of miles from their 'rightful place' – along with lots of soil, sand, grit and other ground-up rock debris.

Suddenly a new landscape was revealed. Well, when I say suddenly, it was sudden in geological terms. It probably took a couple of thousand years for the ice-age glaciers to melt entirely, but the results were amazing – the work of nature's

PREVIOUS PAGES The remote Eilean Donan Castle on the west coast of the Scottish Highlands (main picture), and the golden eagle (small picture).
BELOW LEFT Although not as high as alpine mountains, Ben Nevis has a more northerly latitude and the climate is similar to that of Arctic regions.

BELOW CENTRE Loch Ness – the deepest freshwater loch in the Scottish Highlands.
BELOW RIGHT The Isles of Scilly, off the Cornish coast, are part of the great granite mass that formed at the same time as Dartmoor, Bodmin Moor and Land's End.

very own Capability Brown. The moving ice had softened the entire shape of the ground, rounding off the points of mountains, grinding the rough edges off ravines and smoothing riverbeds into gently curving shapes. It had moulded the scenery of famous beauty spots such as the Lake District, Snowdonia, the Yorkshire Dales and the Cairngorms, hollowing out Scottish tarns and lochs, which then filled with the meltwater from the retreating ice.

The ice-age glaciers did us another very good turn, because the rock dust that was created when they crushed and ground up softer rocks became soil. Most of the stuff we take so much for granted today came from glacial action, and it was the very first step in the evolutionary process that has left us with the wealth of wildlife we have today.

As the ice melted and withdrew, slowly unveiling a newly sculpted landscape from south to north, the first plants to appear in the bare ground were tundra plants. These were tolerant of extreme cold and desperately harsh conditions, the sort you still find in Arctic regions today. Lichens came first – very primitive organisms that are half fungus and half alga, which can grow on bare rock. The primary colonizers paved the way for 'proper' plants, such as bog myrtle, crowberry, dwarf birch and small, bushy arctic willows. Today, these willows survive in Britain only in places where they were 'stranded' in the last outposts of 'arctic' conditions – on remote mountain tops in the Cairngorms and Snowdonia, and on cold northern moorlands at high altitude.

Mountains

From a wildlife point of view, the great thing about mountains is that they are remote and inaccessible, which makes them ideal homes for the larger carnivores such as pine martens, Scottish wildcats and golden eagles that were traditionally persecuted by livestock farmers and gamekeepers. Cold, high-altitude areas are also the last outposts of arctic creatures such as ptarmigans and mountain hares, which were 'cut off' when the ice retreated at the end of the ice age.

But mountain scenery is not all snowcaps and rugged rocks. Even on top of a mountain range such as the Pennines, you can find pockets of moorland habitat, where centuries of plant debris, trapped in a basin of non-porous rock filled with water, have decomposed to form peat. This creates a specialized habitat for particular plants and the insects and birds associated with them. And if the rock that makes up most of the mountain is limestone, as in parts of Yorkshire, rock-lined pockets of peat will give acid conditions that generate a very different type of flora and fauna indeed, so you can find quite strongly contrasting habitats within a short distance of each other.

Peat moors

Peat is the great defining characteristic of moorland. There is often a thin layer of very black soil over a layer of pure peat, which may be many feet deep, above a base of very poor, clay-like soil, which helps to keep the water in. This means that the ground is usually wet to boggy in winter and rarely entirely dry, even in summer. The soil pH is nearly always acid, although when 'islands' of shallow moorland peat form in pockets of limestone the soil may be neutral.

Moorlands formed after the wild woodland was first cleared from places like Dartmoor, the Peak District, the Brecon Beacons and the North York Moors in Mezolithic times, to use for agriculture. However, instead of secondary woodland regenerating later – as happened over much of the country – the land remained treeless, owing to severe soil erosion. The naturally high rainfall in these very steep, exposed areas meant that much of the soil was washed away into rivers, where it ended up creating fertile silt in the valleys, leaving behind bare moors where only nature's survivors such as sphagnum moss or sedges could grow.

Where these grew, there was a natural turnover as plants died and were replaced by younger ones, and their remains slowly built up over thousands of years to form peat. Why didn't they just rot down to humus as usual? Well, in boggy conditions plant remains cannot decompose completely, as they do in your compost heap, since there is no oxygen for the beneficial bacteria to work, so instead of aerobic decomposition, you get anaerobic conditions, which means plant remains only partly decompose – making peat. In a few places, peat is still being laid down, but in the main it's a vanishing resource, especially in places like Yorkshire and the Somerset Levels, where for many years it was dug up and sold – gardeners, take note: to protect this diminishing resource, try to use environmentally friendly, peat-free potting composts instead!

Heather moors

The plant you are most likely to notice straight away on many moors is heather. It grows in huge carpets of pink or purple – it's a classic survivor in conditions that never dry out completely, with full sun, and it can cope with any amount of wind and exposure because of its much-reduced leaves that lie flattened close to the wiry stems.

Traditionally, heather provided valuable grazing for sheep, and it still does to some extent. But as hunting and shooting became fashionable, first with Victorian and then Edwardian gents, the moors (especially in the Scottish Highlands) were developed for the far more profitable crops – red deer and grouse. And it is that management that has created the landscape we see there today.

From the early nineteenth century, moorlands were managed by regularly burning off parts of the heather in rotation, so that there were always several areas of different ages. Young heather has plenty of the soft, tender, new shoots that grouse and sheep feed on; as the plants age they grow taller and bushier, providing cover for nesting birds. However, since the soft tips are needed for feeding, areas of young heather have to be close to the breeding grounds. By the time heather reaches 10 to 12 years old it is too bare and woody to provide much cover or useful food, so it is burnt off to encourage it to regenerate. Burning also helps to limit the spread of bracken over moorland. Nowadays, managed moors provide superb summer breeding grounds for several waders such as golden plover, dunlin, snipe and curlew, which spend their winters in the lowlands and on the coast.

Herdwick sheep are the native breed of the Lake District, Cumbria. They live on England's highest mountains and are the most hardy of all Britain's breeds of hill sheep.

1 Red kite
Milvus milvus

The red kite is distinctly bigger than a buzzard, with a body that is longer, leaner and more graceful, with longer wings. In flight, the red coloration shows up well, as does the deeply forked tail. The upperparts are reddish brown with a fox-red tail and dark wing-tips; seen from below, the body and 'armpits' are red, with large white patches towards the tips of the wings, ending in long, 'fingered' black feathers. The tail (pale buff below) turns in flight like a rudder.

HABITAT Breeds in wooded, hilly countryside; hunts more widely, especially in winter. The small native population in central Wales is increasing, as are those introduced to central, northern and north-eastern England and parts of Scotland.

SIZE 60–66cm (24–26in), wingspan 1.4–1.6m (4½–5ft)

EGGS 2–3, off-white and blotchy

NEST Pile of sticks, often decorated with rags, plastic bags and other items in a tall tree, particularly oak.

FOOD Mainly carrion but also rodents, rabbits and small birds.

OPPOSITE Red kites are an increasingly common sight over parts of Britain and it's thought they may become as widespread as buzzards in the future.

2 Hen harrier
Circus cyaneus

The hen harrier is a graceful, medium-to-large bird of prey, which is slightly smaller and much slighter than a buzzard. The male is light grey and white, with long, blunt-ended wings with large black wing-tips divided into 5 'fingers' when in flight. It hunts by gliding low over the ground and pounces on small mammals or birds. The name hen harrier came about when it was more common and known to attack domestic fowl. It is still Britain's most persecuted bird of prey by gamekeepers.

HABITAT Summer: mainly northern heather moors. Winter: as summer, but also farmland and marshland over most of the British Isles, except the heart of England.

SIZE 44–52cm (17–20in), wingspan 1–1.1m (3–3½ft)

EGGS 4–5, off-white

NEST On the ground, in heather and in young conifer plantations.

FOOD Rodents, small birds.

VARIATIONS Females and juveniles are mottled brown with bars across the tail and dark brown and buff bars at the wing-tips.

3 Buzzard
Buteo buteo

This brown bird of prey is quite a bit larger than a crow, and is often seen soaring in circles with slightly upswept wings making a distinct 'V' shape. The underwings and underside of the tail are dotted or barred with white (though the amount and depth of colour is variable), and the 'fingered' wing-tips are dark brown. Buzzards commonly perch on top of posts, which gives us a better view of them – a slightly scruffy, mottled-brown figure with a short, hooked beak and yellow feet. Once almost persecuted to extinction in Britain, buzzards are now the commonest birds of prey in the north and west of Britain, and are steadily extending their range – they have already reached Hampshire and even Norfolk. They can be seen over farmland and rolling country-side where there are plenty of trees and rabbits. In areas with the densest populations of buzzards, such as Scotland, the Lake District and parts of the West Country, they occur in large groups, but elsewhere they are seen mostly singly or in pairs, even though in my part of Hampshire I have seen up to 10 in the sky at any one time.

HABITAT Wild, rugged countryside, with woods or cliffs for nesting, also in farmland with plenty of trees.

SIZE 52–57cm (20–22in), wingspan 1.1–1.3m (3½–4ft)

EGGS 2–3, off-white with brownish blotches

NEST Large stick nest, lined with bracken and moss, hidden well up in the canopy of dense trees.

FOOD Rabbits, voles, carrion.

4 Golden eagle
Aquila chrysaetos

The golden eagle is the largest bird of prey you are likely to see inland in Scotland. Only the white-tailed eagle is larger, and that is an easily identified coastal bird. Scarce in Britain, the golden eagle is restricted almost entirely to Scotland. This massive and majestic brown bird is most often seen in flight, with its long, wide wings 'fingered' at the tips. It soars like a buzzard, circling with slightly upswept wings, but the golden eagle is twice the size and the trailing edges of its much longer wings show more of a 'bulge'. In normal flight, the wing-beats are low, slow and deliberate. The golden eagle hunts by flying low, parallel to the ground, to frighten small animals into running, then

pounces on them. A good view of a perched bird shows feathery 'trousers' running right down to the feet, a big, powerful, strongly hooked grey-and-black beak and goldish buff feathers on the back of the head and neck. The absence of any markings on the underside makes it easy to tell an adult golden eagle from other birds of prey, although juveniles are harder to identify – size is the big giveaway.

HABITAT Mostly northern and western Scotland, in areas without extensive, dense, coniferous forest plantations.

SIZE 75–88cm (30–35in), wingspan 1.9–2.2m (6¼–7ft)

EGGS 1–3, off-white

NEST Huge eyrie built of sticks on a crag or cliff ledge or in a tall tree.

FOOD Rabbits, mountain hares, crows, grouse and other birds, sometimes carrion (especially dead sheep and deer).

VARIATIONS Juveniles are the same shape and size as adults but with white patches on the undersides of the wings and tail – these leave a dark band along the tip of the tail and are easily seen in flight.

About birds of prey

Birds of prey, or raptors, have had a very rough time of it for centuries. They were persecuted by gamekeepers and farmers, who worried they might take young game birds or lambs. More recently, numbers have dwindled owing to the build-up of pesticides in insects and songbirds, finally becoming so concentrated in birds of prey (the top of the food chain) that in many cases their eggs did not hatch or adult birds were poisoned by the accumulated toxins. Many species were close to extinction in Britain, but a few that did vanish have either reappeared by themselves (such as the osprey) or have been successfully reintroduced (red kite and white-tailed eagle) so that numbers have been steadily increasing; some kinds are quite a familiar sight once again, especially buzzards, kestrels and sparrowhawks. Today, rare birds of prey do a lot of good for the tourist industry by attracting visitors – particularly the ospreys at Loch Garten, Rutland Water and Snowdonia, white-tailed eagles round parts of the Scottish coast and islands such as Mull, and red kites in mid-Wales and parts of England and Scotland. In addition, all carrion-feeding birds, including many birds of prey, do a good job of cleaning up the countryside of road-kill.

Most sightings of raptors tend to be distant and often of birds in flight seen from below. Look for the shape and proportions of the wings and tail. Habitat and hunting styles are also clues. Shown below is a merlin with a small bird caught on the wing.

5 Merlin
Falco columbarius

The merlin is our smallest bird of prey, with the male being much smaller (and rarer) than a kestrel. The merlin is a stocky little raptor, with a square-ended tail and shortish wings, broad where they join the body and tapering to pointed tips. The male is warm slate-grey above, with black wing-tips and beige underparts streaked with light brown. Merlins hunt low over the ground and catch small birds on the wing.

HABITAT Most often seen in the breeding season in Scotland, Wales and the north of England. Summer: on heather moors. Winter: much more widespread, including rough grassland and coastal marshes.

SIZE 25–30cm (10–12in)

EGGS 4, cream with lots of tiny, rust-coloured dots

NEST Shallow dip in the heather.

FOOD Small birds, mostly songbirds in spring, meadow pipits in summer and small waders in winter.

SIMILAR TO Other smaller birds of prey but does not hover like the kestrel, or live in woods like the sparrowhawk. Also resembles the hobby, but this bird is only a summer visitor to southern England and its favoured habitat does not coincide.

VARIATIONS Females are a great deal larger than the males and have brown upperparts.

Moorland

Moorlands are found mostly in the north and west of Britain – roughly from Land's End to the Highlands of Scotland and the Shetland Islands – and they are mostly (though not always) at fairly high altitudes. The scenery is typically wild and unspoiled, making places such as the Brecon Beacons, Dartmoor, Exmoor and the North York Moors great favourites for walkers and tourists. Even though the habitat is rather specialized, it has stunning wildlife.

The moorland landscape predominantly features heather, dotted with damp- and acid-loving plants such as bog myrtle, bilberry, crowberry, cotton grass and, in the wetter areas, sphagnum moss – all species that need open conditions to do well. These

The wild and unspoiled moorland landscape of the Cairngorms, in Scotland, is covered in beautiful mauve-pink heather flowers from late summer to autumn.

plants do not thrive in shade, but then there are very few trees here, simply because our native trees do not tend to take to moorland conditions very successfully. You will find some pines and birches in places, especially in the lower moorlands such as Dartmoor and Exmoor, and the Lake District moors also feature a considerable number of trees. What you will see a good deal of today are forestry plantations, because moorland areas were thought to be the most suitable areas for cultivating timber when we needed to produce more in response to wartime shortages. However, in Orkney and Shetland, conditions were too cold and windy for trees to do well, so these islands have always retained a treeless arctic tundra type of landscape.

Sheep have been a great feature of moorland landscapes for centuries, and have helped to maintain the habitat by grazing. In some parts of the country, specific breeds evolved by a process of selection, to suit local conditions – Blackface, Herdwick and Cheviot, for instance. The best moorlands were taken over for grouse, which were far more profitable, but in both cases heather is burnt off regularly to encourage young shoots, which give better grazing, and to keep bracken and scrub under control. The combination of grazing and burning provides open habitats that favour wildlife. Curlew and snipe return to northern moorlands to breed each summer. And high northern moorlands are the habitat of pockets of ice-age creatures such as mountain hare and ptarmigan. On moorland you may also see birds of prey, including hen harriers, golden eagles, buzzards, merlins and peregrine falcons, as well as game birds, especially red and black grouse. You can also see golden plovers, skylarks and meadow pipits and many other birds whose numbers have fallen drastically as their natural habitat has vanished.

6 Hobby
Falco subbuteo

This is a small, slim, very elegant, streamlined bird of prey (the size of a kestrel) that is an increasingly seen summer visitor in the southern half of England. It is usually spotted only as a dark, anchor-shaped silhouette – like a swift – high in the sky. Look for a slender outline with narrow wings pointed at the tips, stiffish wing-beats and a short, blunt-ended tail. During hunting, the flight is very fast, agile and twisting; dragonflies and other flying insects are caught with one talon and eaten in flight. If given a good view of a perching bird, you can see a dark blue-grey head, back, wings and tail, with

dark-streaked, pale-buff-and-white underparts and blackish-streaked fawn undersides of the wings; the face has a black 'moustache' and white throat and collar markings, with bright chestnut 'trousers' over the thighs, extending under the base of the tail.

HABITAT May–September: mostly in wetlands, where its prey is mainly found, but often also over heaths and farmland. Winter: Africa.
SIZE 30–36cm (12–14in)
EGGS 2–3, cream with dark markings
NEST Takes over abandoned crows' nests in trees.
FOOD Dragonflies and other flying insects, also young swallows, house martins, pipits and other small birds.
SIMILAR TO Kestrel (but the hobby never hovers when hunting) and merlin.

7 Peregrine falcon
Falco peregrinus

The world's fastest bird, the peregrine falcon is capable of power-dives of at least 180km (112 miles) per hour. When the bird is in flight, look for a chunky body with wide, thickset wings with tapering tips; the silhouette is roughly anchor-shaped. Normal flight consists of several flaps, then a short glide, but when hunting it soars with level wings, then makes a steep, high-speed power-dive on to prey, particularly pigeons, doves or waders, which are knocked out of the sky by the collision and carried off. It will perch on posts, where you can see the blue-grey back, off-white underparts patterned with dark bars and dark markings on the head, like a jagged balaclava helmet, with a big, dark 'moustache' either side of the short, strong, hooked, yellow-and-grey beak. Suspect a peregrine is around if all the usual wading birds suddenly take flight or are absent; they'll have spotted it first.
HABITAT Coastal inlets, estuaries, salt marshes and nearby marshy fields or moorland. Sometimes also seen over farmland, round remote quarries or even in cities, especially now that so many of their natural prey – pigeons – have moved inland and to cities.
SIZE 45cm (17½in), wingspan 80–110cm (31–43in)

EGGS 3–4, light brown, speckled
NEST Eggs are laid directly on ledges on sea cliffs, quarries or tall buildings such as cathedrals (which they see as modern cliffs).
FOOD Mostly pigeons, doves, waders, sometimes ducks or larger songbirds.
SIMILAR TO Other falcons, but the merlin, kestrel and hobby are smaller (dove-sized). The sparrowhawk is also similar but is smaller and less chunky, flies lower, doesn't soar and prefers wooded habitats, including gardens.
VARIATIONS Male and female birds look almost identical apart from size – the female is larger, as is often the case with birds of prey. Young birds are browner and their underparts are streaked, not barred, and are buff rather than off-white.

8 Red grouse
Lagopus lagopus

This is the well-known grouse of the whisky labels: a plump, squat, short-necked bird the size of a small chicken, with all-over dark rust-brown coloration and raised red 'eyebrows'. Its call is a slow, cackling 'go-back, go-back'. In flight, the red grouse glides with low, arching wings, looking hump-shaped in outline.
HABITAT Managed heather moors in Scotland and the north of England. Red grouse have quite small territories and do not roam far.
SIZE 40cm (16in)
EGGS 6–9, cream with brownish blotches
NEST On the ground, in heather.
FOOD Young heather shoots.
SIMILAR TO Female red grouse are similar to female black grouse but the female black grouse does not have red 'eyebrows'. Also resembles the ptarmigan in summer, but the ptarmigan has white wings and is not all-over dark rust-brown like the red grouse.
VARIATIONS Females are lighter brown and more speckled than males, and have smaller 'eyebrows'.

Keeping warm
Coming from cold, inhospitable countryside, where conditions are particularly bleak in winter, red and black grouse and ptarmigan are unusual in having densely feathered legs and feet, unlike other birds. Their relative the capercaillie, which lives in ancient native Scots pine forest, has slightly feathery legs, but less so than the others.

9 Ptarmigan
Lagopus mutus

The ptarmigan, which is the only British bird to turn white in winter, is a scarce relic from our ice-age past and survives here in only a few remaining high-mountain outposts. In summer it is a grouse-like bird, in dull brindled-brown with white underparts and white wings, which are most noticeable

in flight. It has red 'eyebrows' and creeps low to the ground.
HABITAT High up on bleak, rocky Scottish mountain tops; sometimes seen on slightly lower moorland.
SIZE 35cm (14in)
EGGS 6–10, off-white with brown spots
NEST On the ground.
FOOD Young shoots of heather and other vegetation.
SIMILAR TO Summer plumage is similar to that of female grouse.
VARIATIONS Females lack red 'eyebrows'. In winter, both sexes turn white, contrasting with the black tail and eyes; males retain the red 'eyebrows'.

10 Black grouse
Tetrao tetrix

This rich blue-black bird has striking red 'eyebrows', a long neck and legs, and a black, lyre-shaped tail above a white 'powderpuff'. In flight, its white wing-bars are visible; these are seen only faintly on a bird standing on the ground. Birds roost in woodland, but males (known as 'blackcocks') display dramatically at regularly used areas called 'leks' on nearby moorland – they stretch out their inflated necks horizontally, arch their wings and puff themselves up with the tail fanned out and held upright, while making a strange loud, cooing and bubbling sound. In spring they do this to impress nearby females, but males continue to display for the rest of the year (except in early autumn).
HABITAT Conifer plantations and woods close to moorland, mostly in Scotland but also in some parts of Wales and Ireland.
SIZE 40–50cm (16–20in)
EGGS 6–10, beige with brownish spots
NEST On the ground, in grass.
FOOD Buds and young shoots of birch and pine.
SIMILAR TO Female is similar to the female red grouse (except the female black grouse has a forked tail and the red grouse a square tail), and ptarmigan in summer plumage (which has all-white

wings instead of the all-brown colour of the female black grouse).
VARIATIONS Female lacks the red 'eyebrows' and, unlike the black male, is grey-brown all over with a pale bar on the wings; juveniles look similar to females.

11 Dotterel
Charadrius morinellus

The dotterel is a very scarce, blackbird-sized plover with distinctive markings. It has a chestnut belly, a large white patch under the tail, a white band above the breast, a grey-brown throat, a streaky grey-brown back and boldly striped and speckled grey-brown wings. The head is white with a short black beak, and the legs and feet are yellow. The female is brighter than the male. This bird runs in short dashes and is unusually tame – I've lain on my stomach with my nose barely a foot away from a nesting dotterel! It is a summer visitor that may be seen at the same few resting places each year along its migration route up the east of Britain.
HABITAT April–end of August: virtually barren plateaux on northern mountain tops. Winter: North Africa.
SIZE 22cm (8¾in)
EGGS 3, grey with dark brown blotches
NEST Bare scrape on the ground.
FOOD Insects.

12 Golden plover
Pluvialis apricaria

This is an attractive, elusive, pigeon-sized wader with a black breast, throat and face outlined in white with a gold-speckled, dark brown back and wings. In winter, it groups in loose, open flocks in fields to feed, with birds some distance apart but moving in the same direction; gold, sparkly specks can be seen easily when the birds are in sunlight. In summer, large flocks wheel in the air in much the same way as lapwings, flashing white or gold-brown as they change direction. The call is very evocative of summer moorlands – a plaintive, rising whistle, 'too-eee', through the mist.
HABITAT Summer: northern moorlands. Winter: more widespread, mostly on farmland.
SIZE 28cm (11in)
EGGS 3–4, beige, speckled dark brown
NEST Barely lined hollow in peaty ground on moorland.
FOOD Insects, worms, some seeds.
VARIATIONS In winter, birds lack the black breast and face; they are uniformly grey-brown with gold speckling, fading to beige speckling on the breast with white underparts.

13 Short-eared owl
Asio flammeus

Found throughout England and Scotland, this owl is about the size of the far more common tawny owl, but is longer and less portly, with a tapering rear end owing to its very long wings and short tail. The upperparts are boldly streaked and barred brown and golden-buff. The breast is also heavily streaked but the rest of the underparts are pale, with 2 or 3 black bands at the wing-tips. It flies in daylight but is easier to identify when perched: it does not sit upright like other owls, but with its body horizontal or at an angle. Look for a round face with a Y-shaped white 'face mask', large, glaring yellow eyes boldly outlined in black, and a short, blackish beak. The ear-tufts are very short and not usually visible.

HABITAT Summer: breeds on moorland and young conifer plantations, mainly in uplands. Winter: coastal marshes, rough grassland and other open places.
SIZE 38cm (15in)
EGGS 4–8, white
NEST Shallow scrape on the ground.
FOOD Short-tailed voles and other small mammals and birds.
SIMILAR TO May be mistaken for other owls sometimes seen by day,

such as the little owl, but the latter is much smaller (blackbird-sized). In flight, the long-eared owl looks very like the short-eared owl, but it has darker and more streaked underparts. Unlike the short-eared owl, the long-eared owl is usually a strictly nocturnal hunter. In Ireland, expect to see the more common long-eared owl; the short-eared owl is a scarce winter visitor only.

14 Nightjar
Caprimulgus europaeus

The nightjar is a scarce, secretive, nocturnal bird, usually heard rather than seen. It makes a prolonged, far-carrying, rising and falling, low-vibrating, 'churring' sound that blankets whole areas of heathland on hot, sunny summer evenings. During the day, birds crouch low to the ground or stretch out along logs or branches, where they are camouflaged. Nightjars are best seen at dusk, where they fly swift-like after moths – you'll see only silhouettes floating, twisting and turning, and, with luck, flashes of white on the wing-tips and tail patches on males. The in-flight call is a sharp, quizzical 'quoo-ick?' at intervals. Males display by pausing in mid-air to clap their wings loudly

together overhead. If bird-watchers throw a white handkerchief up into the air, nightjars may approach, mistaking the handkerchief for the white markings on the male.

HABITAT Heathland with gorse and sparse trees, though also found on moors and newly planted or cleared forestry.
SIZE 27cm (11in)
EGGS 2, dappled grey and brownish
NEST Shallow scrape on the ground, superbly camouflaged.
FOOD Beetles, moths and other night-flying insects.

15 Woodlark
Lullula arborea

A scarce but increasing summer visitor to parts of the south and east of England, this bird is well known for its exceptionally lovely song delivered night and day. It has streaky brown upperparts and brown-speckled white underparts, and a dark, stripy head with bright chestnut cheeks and pale cream 'eyebrows' that meet at the back of the head. The orange-red legs have exceptionally long claws. In flight, it looks like a stumpy, very short-tailed skylark, but rather than soaring, males flutter round in wide circles to display, or drift high across their territory.

HABITAT Summer: heathland and downs, scrub, young conifer plantations and woodland clearings. Winter: in fields.
SIZE 15cm (6in)
EGGS 3–4, light buff with darker, brown freckles
NEST Cup of grass lined with hair in a hollow in the ground.
FOOD Mainly insects, small seeds.
SIMILAR TO Skylark, which is more common and is distinctly larger with a longer crest and has a soaring song in flight.

16 Tree pipit
Anthus trivialis

Arriving in Britain around April, this is a solitary, sparrow-sized bird. It has a fine beak and streaky brown upperparts, white underparts speckled brown and orange-buff legs. Unlike other pipits, it spends most of the time in trees or bushes, and flies confidently between trees with no fluttering; in late spring, males fly up from trees in vertical display flight, then parachute down with open wings to land back on a perch.

HABITAT April–early October: throughout Britain (not Ireland) in woodland edges and clearings and lowland heaths and downs. Winter: Africa.

SIZE 15cm (6in)

EGGS 4–6, bluish, greenish or pinkish with darker markings

NEST Cup of grass on the ground or on a bank, lined with moss and hair.

FOOD Mainly insects, some seeds.

SIMILAR TO Meadow pipit, although the meadow pipit prefers open, treeless countryside.

17 Whinchat
Saxicola rubetra

Particularly evident in north and west Britain, the male of this almost robin-sized summer visitor has a brindled-brown back, wings and crown, a blackish face underlined with white, white 'eyebrows', a bright orange-buff breast and an off-white belly. In flight, a white flash is visible down each side of the tail and a white bar at the base and middle of each wing. The male spends time perched on top of bushes, which he uses as a lookout.

HABITAT Summer: upland heaths, hillsides, young conifer plantations and open ground bordering on moorland with scattered bushes. Winter: Africa.

SIZE 13cm (5in)

EGGS 5–6, bluish with brown specks

NEST Cup of grass on the ground.

FOOD Insects, fruit in autumn.

SIMILAR TO Stonechat, which has a bigger head but lacks the white tail-flashes and white 'eyebrows'.

VARIATIONS Females are duller and have brindled-brown 'cheeks'. Juveniles have a streaked breast.

18 Stonechat
Saxicola torquata

Present across the British Isles all year, this lively little bird is smaller than a robin, with a similar upright stance, but with a shorter tail and bigger head. The breeding male has a black hood, beak and legs, a white neck patch, a very dark brown-black back and tail, a small white rump patch, a bright chestnut-orange-red breast fading to tan round the edges and off-white underparts. Males like to perch on top of a gorse bush or a post, or the top of a scrubby tree, where they stay still for long periods. If they fly off (looking like outsized bumblebees) they often return quickly, so it's easy to get a good view. Stonechats are usually seen together in pairs or in family parties.

HABITAT Young conifer plantations, lowland heaths and heath-like coastlines where there is gorse.

SIZE 12cm (4¾in)

EGGS 5–6, greenish, speckled with reddish brown

NEST Cup of grass on the ground.

FOOD Mainly insects, some seeds and berries in autumn and winter.

SIMILAR TO Whinchat and the male bullfinch, which is finch-shaped rather than robin-shaped and has a rosy red breast and a larger, more prominent white rump. Although the bullfinch is an orchard/woodland bird, its habitat can overlap with the stonechat's in hedgerows and at woodland edges.

VARIATIONS Female lacks the black hood; instead, she has a brindled-brown back and head and a paler apricot-tinged breast, with little or no white neck patch. Juveniles are similar to baby robins – speckly brown and dumpy.

19 Wheatear
Oenanthe oenanthe

Usually seen on the ground or perched on top of a post – bobbing and flicking its tail – this summer visitor is larger than a robin but has an upright, robin-like stance. The plumage changes according to the season; in spring, males have light blue-grey upperparts with blackish wings, tail and a broad black 'mask' on the face, and an apricot-buff breast and underparts. The beak, eyes and legs are black. In flight, the bird looks dark grey with a conspicuous white rump and a black 'T' pattern on the short, square-ended tail. By autumn, the back is tan and the underparts are tinted a warm orange-buff.

HABITAT Summer: open countryside, mainly on mountains, moors and heathland in western and northern Britain and throughout Ireland; often seen close to the coast in spring and autumn. Winter: Africa.

SIZE 15cm (6in)

EGGS 5–6, light blue

NEST Old rabbit hole, hole among rocks or in a drystone wall.

FOOD Insects.

SIMILAR TO In the air, easily mistaken for the skylark or the meadow pipit, whose habitats overlap with that of the wheatear; all 3 have hovering song flights. Use binoculars to look for a broad, dark tip to the fanned tail of a hovering wheatear. Birds on the ground are much easier to identify.

VARIATIONS Females are similar to males in plumage pattern, but duller and browner grey and lacking the black 'face mask'. As in males, the legs, eyes, beak and tip of the tail are black; juveniles are similar to females but browner and have a white rump.

20 Dartford warbler
Sylvia undata

This is a scarce but increasing, blue-tit-sized bird with a rather short, chunky body and a very long, semi-cocked, slim, greyish brown tail. Look for the triangular, dark grey head with red eyes, ringed with orange-red, dark brownish grey upperparts, and rich wine-red underparts with a large white patch on the belly. The Dartford warbler flies jerkily between gorse bushes with whirring wings, then creeps about furtively inside the bushes, except in spring and early summer when males sing from the tops of gorse bushes.
HABITAT Restricted to lowland heaths with gorse and heather, especially in Hampshire and Dorset, though it has recently increased and spread across much of southern England near the coast

21

20

and along the coasts of Essex and Suffolk. Dartford warblers are particularly dependent on their specialized habitat for survival.
SIZE 13cm (5in)
EGGS 4, greenish white mottled pale brown
NEST Cup-shaped nest in gorse or heather above ground-level.
FOOD Insects, spiders and other small invertebrates.

21 Ring ouzel
Turdus torquatus

A relatively scarce and declining localized summer visitor, the ring ouzel is a shy, secretive, mountain and moorland version of the blackbird, with a white 'bib'. If you get a close look, you'll see the yellow beak but no yellow ring round the eye (as the blackbird has) and pale silvery grey edges round the feathers, particularly the long wing feathers, giving it a slightly lacy-patterned look. It flies with very deep wing-beats, so the wing-tips nearly touch underneath the bird.
HABITAT Wild, remote places, in uplands in the north and west.
SIZE 24cm (9½in)
EGGS 5, blue-green with reddish brown blotches
NEST Cup of grass on the ground, in rocks, heather or other vegetation.
FOOD Insects and other invertebrates, berries in autumn.
SIMILAR TO Blackbird, but this ouzel has a white, crescent-shaped 'bib'.
VARIATIONS Female is brown with a faint 'tracery' of grey outlining the feathers and a duller whitish buff 'bib'. Juveniles are lightly mottled and lack the white 'bib'.

22 Twite
Carduelis flavirostris

This scarce, declining finch lives in the British Isles all year round but is most numerous in winter. Since it looks much like many other little, streaky brown birds, it is often overlooked. It has dark-streaked, tawny brown upperparts, a beige face and head covered in narrow brown stripes, a buff throat, a peachy beige breast, brown-flecked flanks and a white belly. Look for the short, thick beak (yellow with a dark tip in autumn and winter, brownish grey from early spring to the breeding season), dark legs, wing-tips and tail, which has a strongly notched tip. The twite is seen mostly on the ground in small groups.

22

HABITAT Breeds mainly on uplands, moors and mountainsides of northern Scotland and northern England (especially the Pennines), but also elsewhere in Scotland and in western Ireland. Most migrate south to the lowlands, especially along Britain's east coast.
SIZE 14cm (5½in)
EGGS 4–6, very pale blue speckled and streaked dark grey
NEST Near the ground, in heather.
FOOD Mainly seeds.
SIMILAR TO Sparrows, skylarks, pipits and female linnets, but all lack the dark-tipped yellow beak of the twite in autumn and winter. Also very similar to the lesser redpoll, but the latter is smaller with a neat black 'bib' on the chin and a red forehead.

23 Snow bunting
Plectrophenax nivalis

Resembling a strange, whitish sparrow, but slightly larger, this mainly Arctic bird regularly visits the British Isles in winter. At this time of year, it has a sparrow-patterned back and wings, but is paler, with a whitish face, throat and underparts, and a bright-buff crown and 'cheek' patch and patches on the side of the breast. It occurs in sociable, sparrow-like flocks of fluttering beige and white that look like snowflakes. If given a good view, you will see the dark-tipped yellow beak. The breeding plumage of male birds is very distinctive – clean-cut white with black wings – but you'd be lucky to see this in Britain, as most breed in the Arctic Circle, although a rare few do nest on the highest Scottish mountains.

HABITAT Winter: along the north and east coasts of Britain, sometimes in the hills of north-east England, north Wales, Scotland and parts of Ireland.

SIZE 16.5cm (6½in)

EGGS 4–6, white

NEST Cup of grass, moss and lichen, lined with hair, wool and feathers.

FOOD Insects, seeds.

24 Hooded crow
Corvus cornix

Almost magpie-like in its plumage pattern, but in grey instead of white, this crow has a black head, wings and tail that contrast with a pale grey back and underparts, as if wearing a waistcoat. A close relative of the carrion crow, the 'hoodie' is resident in north-west Scotland, but also throughout Ireland and on the Isle of Man; small numbers of continental birds visit eastern Britain in winter.

HABITAT Wide range of habitats including open country, farmland, woods, moors, coasts and towns.

SIZE 46cm (18in)

EGGS 3–6, pale greenish grey mottled with darker grey

NEST Stick nest in large trees, but not communally like rooks.

FOOD Extremely wide and varied diet – both meat and veg – including scraps and carrion.

SIMILAR TO Magpie, which is slightly smaller with a longer tail and more crisply black and white.

25 Raven
Corvus corax

The world's largest member of the crow family and the biggest of all songbirds, the raven is nearly twice the size of rooks and other crows. It is entirely black, including the beak and legs, with a 'beard' of shaggy feathers under the chin. Slower and more stately in flight than rooks or other crows, the raven also soars like a bird of prey.

HABITAT Sea cliffs, mountains, moorland, crags and quarries. Most abundant in north Scotland and Wales, but also frequent in south-west England and Ireland, slowly spreading eastwards.

SIZE 65cm (26in), wingspan 1.2m (4ft)

EGGS 4–6, pale grey or buff-grey speckled with darker grey and black

NEST Large and untidy, made from twigs and sometimes seaweed, on rock ledges or in woodland trees.

FOOD Mainly dead sheep but also mice, rabbits and other small mammals, birds and eggs, insects.

SIMILAR TO Carrion crow, which is much smaller and more lightweight in build; the rook has a bald face and is also much smaller.

VARIATIONS Juveniles are duller with paler eyes.

1 Emperor moth
Saturnia pavonia

Britain's only member of the silk-moth family, this is a large, glamorous moth with a wingspan of 8cm (3¼in). Males fly by day; their forewings are cream and brown and their hind wings are orange, vividly patterned with brown, wiggly lines and shaded areas, with a large, false eye on each wing. Females have the same pattern but do not have the orange hind wings. Both have a deep pink flush at the tip of each forewing. The females fly at night; by day they sit and wait for the males.
HABITAT In heathlands in the south and upland moors in northern Britain, usually seen April to June.

CATERPILLAR Green, dotted with yellow warts from which grow tufts of short, dark bristles; feeds mainly on heather but also sometimes brambles, blackthorn, elder or purple loosestrife.

2 Oak eggar
Lasiocampa quercus

This is a plainish, light brown-coloured moth (6cm/2½in wingspan), with a wavy line and white spot on each forewing.
HABITAT Hedgerows and scrub, usually seen flying only in sunny weather in July and August.
CATERPILLAR Up to 9cm (3½in) long, buff-coloured with a row of off-white spots down each side, covered in bristly, warm-yellow-brown-to-gingery hairs; patterned to look as if divided into short, jointed segments; feeds on oak or hawthorn, sometimes blackthorn.

3 Northern eggar
Lasiocampa quercus
subsp. *callunae*

Mostly seen in sunny weather, this is the larger, darker-coloured, northern form of the oak eggar. It is a plainish brown moth (6–9cm/2½–3½in wingspan), with a single light-coloured spot on each forewing and a cream stripe running straight across, further back. The male sports a large pair of feathery brown antennae growing moustache-like from the head.
HABITAT The moors of Scotland and northern England, in May and June.
CATERPILLAR Up to 9cm (3½in) long, lightly clad in short, bristly hairs; feeds mainly on heather, sometimes birch or brambles.

4 Large heath
Coenonympha tullia

This is a real northern mountain butterfly, normally seen in June and July, sitting with its wings folded shut. It has one large, false eye on each forewing, which is dull orange with an off-white panel, and a row of small, false eyes along the edge of the hind wings. The hind wings are beige with a light brown fan shape near the body.

HABITAT Scattered locations in Wales, Ireland and upland Britain, especially in the Cheviot Hills, Snowdonia and the Cairngorms.
CATERPILLAR Plain green and perfectly camouflaged when on a grassy blade of hare's-tail cotton grass, its main food plant.

5 Scotch argus
Erebia aethiops

Mostly found in Scotland, this butterfly is believed to have been in Britain since the ice age. It is medium-sized (4.5cm/1¾in wingspan) with dark brown wings patterned with an almost continuous row of small, black-and-white false eyes set in an orange strip along the edges of the wings. Females look the same but are a shade or two lighter.
HABITAT Seen July and August, mainly in the north-west of Scotland and northern England, especially the Cheviot Hills, in sheltered, sunny places on moors and on hillsides where purple moor grass grows.
CATERPILLAR Dull beige, slightly 'ribbed' caterpillars that feed at night (on purple or blue moor grass); by day they hide down at the base of the grass.

6 Grayling
Hipparchia semele

The grayling is a rare, large brown butterfly, 5cm (2in) across. When it is flying, you can see the brown upper surface of the wings, but at rest the wings are kept closed, showing lightly marbled, ash-grey undersides. The forewings are warm buff – each with 2 black eyespots – but these are often tucked under the hind wings, making the butterfly more inconspicuous, dull and moth-like. Rarely still, it constantly takes short flights to new flowerheads or settles on the ground, where it is instantly camouflaged.
HABITAT Scattered locations, mainly in dry heathlands of southern England, including the New Forest, and grassy cliff-tops round the south and west coast of Britain and in Ireland. The grayling is seen from May to August.
CATERPILLAR Horizontally striped buff, pale green and light brown, feeding on grasses. It is seen through the winter.

7 Green hairstreak
Callophrys rubi

The vivid coloration of this small, striking species (2.5cm/1in wingspan), our only green butterfly, is so remarkable that it looks almost artificial. It always sits with folded wings, showing the brilliant green colour, which is only on the undersides of the wings; the uppersides are brown. When it is resting, you can see a curved row of faint white spots across the underside of the hind wings. The long antennae and legs are patterned with black-and-white bands, as if the butterfly were wearing stripy leg-warmers. Adult green hairstreak butterflies are rarely seen feeding on flowers; they tend to group together in sheltered glades, perching on prominent twigs of trees or flitting about in small clouds.
HABITAT Mostly on heaths and downs in southern England, but also in scattered pockets throughout the rest of the British Isles. Seen from March to July.
CATERPILLAR Green with a row of yellow chevrons; feeds on gorse, broom, brambles and dogwood.

8 Silver-studded blue
Plebejus argus

This butterfly gets its name from the pale blue background colour of the undersides of the hind wings, which are unevenly 'studded' with dark speckling and a touch of metallic silver. The uppersides of the wings of the male are blue with a conspicuous black outline edged in white; the females' wings are brown on the uppersides, edged with a row of small orange scallop shapes. The wingspan is 3cm (1¼in).

HABITAT Found locally on sandy heaths and open grassland in southern and western England, mostly in the New Forest and Ashdown Forest, and on heathland in Surrey. It can be seen in flight between May and September.
CATERPILLAR Green with black-and-white stripes; feeds on broom, gorse and heather. The caterpillars of the silver-studded blue butterfly are 'farmed' by ants, which move them from plant to plant to 'graze' and then 'milk' them by drinking their nutritious secretions.

9 Bilberry bumblebee
Bombus monticola

One of our less common moorland bumblebees, about 2cm (¾in) long, this is slightly smaller than the buff-tailed bumblebee and is less plump and furry. The head, thorax and legs are black with a narrow yellow collar between the head and thorax; the abdomen is orange-red with a small black 'waist'. It is seen in spring and summer; as is the case with all bumblebees, only queens survive winter.

HABITAT Moors and uplands in Scotland, Wales, northern England and the far south-west.

10 Potter wasp
Eumenes coarctatus

This is a solitary, black-and-yellow wasp that is superficially similar to the common wasp seen in gardens and at picnics, except the potter wasp has a curved abdomen and a less pronounced stripy pattern, the yellow being found as circles and bands close to the tip of the abdomen. Look on heather stems for the small 'pottery vases' constructed by the female wasps from clay and saliva: these act as 'larders' for the small caterpillars collected to feed the single wasp grub that lives in each 'pot.'

HABITAT Heathland with heather, mostly in Surrey, Hampshire and Dorset, from June to September.

11 Sand digger wasp
Ammophila sabulosa

A rather unusual, long, thin, ungainly insect that hardly looks capable of flying, and nothing at all like a conventional wasp. It is a long (2cm/¾in), lean insect with a black head, thorax and legs, and a slightly more bulbous abdomen, which is a rich chestnut colour with a black tip. It flies rather slowly and ponderously. The adult collects caterpillars, which it paralyzes and subsequently buries in a burrow in dry sand along with a single egg; it then seals up the entry hole so that the caterpillars act as a supply of fresh, live food for the emerging grub.

HABITAT Heathland of south and central England, from May to September.

12 Biting midges
Culicoides obsoletus

These are the large clouds of tiny, silent, leggy flies that make walking in the open almost unbearable in some parts of Scotland in summer. It is the females that bite, leaving the skin itching and smarting; they lack the warning buzz made by common gnats and mosquitoes.

HABITAT Mainly western Scotland, though they also occur in moorland and wet areas elsewhere, particularly in northern uplands of Britain in summer; they breed in boggy ground.

Bumblebee colonies

Unlike the better-known honeybees, bumblebees live in small colonies of up to 150, nesting in holes in the ground, often taking over old mouse nests. They make just enough honey to feed their young, with no winter stores, so only young queens survive the winter – in hibernation – and have to start a new colony from scratch each spring. Bumblebees start foraging earlier in the year than honeybees, and also work longer hours. They aren't as fussy about the weather, so you'll often see bumblebees in the wind and wet when there are no honeybees.

13 Cleg-fly
Haematopota pluvialis

The cleg-fly is one of the commonest members of the horse-fly family. It resembles a large, mottled grey house-fly, 1cm (⅜in) long, with a long, straight body (not rounded like a bluebottle's). Particularly prevalent in thundery

weather, it approaches silently, and does not buzz like a mosquito – the bite is very painful. The cleg-fly is not to be confused with the familiar yellow-and-brown-banded horse-fly, which is half as big again and occurs mainly in southern Britain.

HABITAT Throughout the British Isles, especially in or near damp, well-wooded countryside where livestock is present.

14 Minotaur beetle
Typhaeus typhoeus

The bulldozer-like minotaur beetle is one of the countryside's sewage workers, found 'tidying up' after sheep and rabbits. It is a chunky, almost round, shiny black creature, 1.5cm (⅝in) long. It has a grooved, scarab-like back, which is extremely hard, with shiny shoulders and head from which 3 horns protrude on the male – one pair points forwards and a shorter, single horn points upwards. The female lacks the horns, as only male minotaurs need them to fight each other for females. Males and females then work together, pushing round balls of rabbit or sheep droppings into a deep burrow, in which the eggs are laid. Anything unused is 'recycled' naturally back into the ground and helps to feed plant life.

HABITAT Anywhere south of the Scottish border, particularly on sandy soil where sheep and rabbits graze, in spring and early summer.

15 Green tiger beetle
Cicindela campestris

This is the commonest, fastest and most spectacular of the tiger beetles, looking like an animated enamel brooch. It has a long, slim, straight body, up to 1.5cm (⅝in) long, in bright leaf-green, with a pair of conspicuous cream spots on the wing-cases and a row of smaller matching spots evenly spaced round the edges. The large eyes and ferocious, strong, almost mantis-like jaws show up well with a magnifying glass. It chases insects across the ground, and eats caterpillars too, but may also fly in short dashes between vegetation.

HABITAT Sandy heaths and chalk downs inland, and large dune systems round the coast; seen on sunny days in early summer.

16 Leafhopper
Ulopa reticulata

This is a small, fat, squat, buff-brown, rather bug-eyed bug, 4mm (⁵⁄₃₂in) long, with a short, blunt head and large eyes either side of its face. It has a steeply angled, mottled-brown-and-off-white back, and moves by making large jumps for its size.

HABITAT Commonly found on heather, all year round.

17 Heather crab spider
Thomisus onustus

The crab spider doesn't make webs or chase its prey, but instead sits in flowers waiting for suitable insects to come along, since its intended victims are honeybees. This species is a fat-bodied spider that can be white, yellow or pinkish violet – this is because it has the ability to change colour to match its background. The first 2 pairs of legs are longer and stronger than the rest. It often hides deep inside flowers – so the legs look like stamens – for effective camouflage.

HABITAT Mainly on heather flowers on heaths and moorland in southern England.

Reptiles

1 Adder
Vipera berus

Our only venomous snake, the adder is vividly patterned with a nearly black zig-zag running the whole length of the body with dots alongside, over a beige or grey background. Most are about 30cm (12in) long but they can reach 60cm (24in) and females can be slightly longer. Look for them sunbathing in patches of sunshine in spring. On nature reserves they are often found sheltering under pieces of corrugated-iron sheeting, strategically placed in warm, sunny spots. Though technically venomous – the venom is enough to subdue the snake's prey of small rodents and amphibians – the adder is unlikely to cause healthy humans much of a problem. Adders are normally shy and slither away out of sight if disturbed. Spring is the only time they stay out in the open, so 'look but don't touch'. If you are bitten, play safe and call in at the hospital casualty department.
HABITAT Open countryside, mostly on heathland but also dry parts of moors and open areas on lightly wooded hillsides, especially with dry, sandy ground. In winter, adders hibernate in holes underground, emerging in March.
FOOD Mice, voles, frogs.

2 Smooth snake
Coronella austriaca

This is one of the rarest animals in the British Isles, and certainly our rarest native reptile. A slim snake, up to 60cm (24in) long, it is light grey to buff with a double row of small, light brown, diamond-shaped spots running down the centre of the body, with a larger spot on the back of the head. It could at first glance be mistaken for an adder, but the zigzag pattern of the adder is all connected, while the dots on the smooth snake are separate. The smooth snake spends most of its time underground – it is very shy and elusive – so sightings are extremely uncommon, but it is most likely to be seen in April or May sunbathing among heather.
HABITAT A few locations in heathlands of Dorset, Hampshire and Surrey. Hibernates in holes underground over winter and emerges in spring.
FOOD Mostly lizards, but also small rodents and insects.

3 Sand lizard
Lacerta agilis

This scarce beige lizard is heavily speckled with brown blotches, each with a white speck in the centre and a white stripe down each side of the back, which may have a broken brown stripe or a line of brown, blocky blotches down the centre. During the breeding season, in spring, males have a green flash down each flank, incorporating the chin and front legs. Adults shed their skin in spring, so cast-off skins are often a clue that lizards are in the area.
HABITAT Mostly found in dry, sandy heathlands in Surrey, Dorset and Hampshire, from March to October. Hibernates in a burrow in the sand in winter.
FOOD Grasshoppers, beetles.

Lowland heaths

Lowland heaths occur mostly in the south and east of England, in places where the soil is slightly acidic, usually with a thin layer of peat over pale grey or white sandy soil. Their landscape is characterized by birch, heather and gorse. It's the typical scenery of the Brecklands of East Anglia and parts of Surrey, Dorset and the New Forest.

Heathland is the result of early man's agriculture. In these particular areas the soil was naturally shallow and infertile, which meant that farmers had to move on to new ground every few years – they didn't have artificial fertilizers to keep yields high – and the ground was not recolonized by woodland (which happened naturally elsewhere), so they remained largely grassland, used for rough grazing. Sheep and rabbits were the main crop. Large rabbit warrens were once quite commonplace in Breckland, so much so that they have given rise to place names such as Lakenheath Warren. (Look at a road map and you'll find quite a number of 'warrens' in some parts of the country.) Areas of scrubby bracken and heather were also cut occasionally to provide fuel for fires and thatching material.

Sheep and rabbits did a great deal to keep the heathland growth short, which encouraged a particular range of wildflowers and their associated butterflies, but heaths were also managed by regular burning, in much the same way as moors, to improve the quality of the grazing and to control the spread of bracken and scrub. Heaths continued to be managed in this way until the demand for home-grown food in wartime brought some heathland back into agricultural production, and modern farming methods have made them 'more worthwhile' as cropping areas ever since.

Today, heathland is one of our most at-risk habitats. It needs regular maintenance to remove birch seedlings, rejuvenate heather and control bracken. Most of this work is done by nature conservancy organizations, often with the help of volunteers. But it pays off. Heaths are home to all sorts of rare wildlife, including the Dartford warbler, woodlark, tree pipit and nightjar, all six native British reptiles including the rare sand lizard and smooth snake, and in boggy areas within heathland you can find pockets of the bog plant sundew, with its sticky hairs that trap insects.

Headley Heath, in Surrey, is typical of heathland landscape, with its open expanses of grassland and beautiful yellow gorse on thin chalk soil.

Mammals

1 Reindeer
Rangifer tarandus

Although reindeer were British natives about 10,000 years ago, today they are seen only in the Cairngorms, where a domesticated herd was introduced from Lapland in 1952. They are large deer (bulls stand as tall as 1.2m/4ft at the shoulder) in a donkey-like shade of grey-brown, with white 'ankle socks', chest-tufts, rump and underparts. The feet are wide, with cloven hoofs that look rather like large mussel shells; these spread the weight so the animals don't sink in when walking in snow. Females and calves form herds in summer, and bulls live in isolation except in the mating season, which is in autumn. Unusually for deer, both male and female reindeer (known as bulls and cows respectively) have antlers but those of the bulls are larger. Even calves have small, pointed stubs. Antlers can reach impressive proportions on mature bulls, with one large set curving backwards over the neck. Bulls shed their antlers in autumn after the rut, but cows keep theirs until spring, using them to clear snow to find food for the calves.
HABITAT Arctic tundra.
FOOD Lichen, sedge, grass, young tree shoots.

2 Red deer
Cervus elaphus

Our largest native land animal, thought to have been here since before the ice age, the red deer stag stands up to 1.2m (4ft) at the shoulder. In summer, the coat is red-brown but in winter it turns a duller brown, always with slightly paler underparts. Look for the short tail, which is held down and outlined by the buff-coloured rump patch. The red deer was originally a forest species, but after early man cut down all the trees it adapted to life on open moorland, lower slopes of mountains and wild, rugged heathland. Red deer herds are sometimes kept in parks and they are often farmed for venison, particularly in Scotland. Males (stags) and females (hinds) live in separate herds except during the breeding season, when mature males have shaggy 'beards' on the front of their neck and chest and grow large, branching sets of antlers, which are cast in April – the dominant male is usually the biggest, strongest one with the largest antlers and 'beard'. Juvenile males have short spikes instead of antlers, which are sometimes retained until late summer.
HABITAT Mostly on moors, mountains and heathland in Scotland but there are some in other large, wild places in Britain including Exmoor, the New Forest, the Lake District and East Anglia.
FOOD Heather, grass, young shoots, deciduous tree leaves.

OVERLEAF Dartmoor ponies are small and rugged with thick, furry coats. They are capable of fending for themselves in even the hardest of winters on the moors.

3 Native ponies
Equus caballus

These are small, hardy, wild ponies that evolved into the characteristic breeds we now know as a result of geographic isolation and natural or human selection. Today they are becoming scarce in the wild but are increasingly used for conservation grazing in nature reserves. By eating young saplings they maintain the habitat of heathland, preventing trees from taking over and altering the balance of nature. They all stand roughly 1.2m (4ft) at the shoulder. The Exmoor pony is small and dark brown, with lighter shading on the legs and belly, a long, very dark mane and tail, black nostrils and a pale muzzle that makes the pony look as if it's just taken its nose out of a bucket of meal. The Dartmoor pony is a tough, stocky pony in black, bay (very dark brown) or mid-brown, with a shaggy mane and tail; the coat is far shaggier in winter, when weather on the moors can be atrocious. The New Forest pony (shown above) is pretty and graceful, in light colours, mostly with a sandy-to-light-chestnut-brown coat and a dark mane and tail, often with paler legs or white blazes on the forehead. It is very agile and good at crossing the occasional boggy patches found in the New Forest. The Welsh mountain pony is very pretty, with a slightly 'dished' face, in various colours but mostly grey or light or dark brown. Our native ponies are descendants of bred and domestic animals and they are all owned by somebody. The ponies are rounded up once a year so that new foals can be branded with the owner's mark, and some of them are sold. The annual round-up is best known in the New Forest. The rest of the year, the ponies run free and form their own herds, made up of females and 1- or 2-year-old foals with a resident stallion, which keeps a watchful eye on them and fathers the next crop of foals. Older youngsters and stray males are driven off to start new herds of their own. Domesticated native ponies, sometimes bred in studs, are popular as children's riding ponies. The ones you see running wild on moors and heathland are not tame, so don't attempt to feed or handle them.

HABITAT Moors in Exmoor, Dartmoor, New Forest, Wales and on nature reserves country-wide.

FOOD Grass, sedges and young shoots of wild shrubs and trees, including young saplings.

4 Mountain hare
Lepus timidus

Also known as the blue hare, this scarce animal, 50cm (20in) long, is slightly smaller than the brown hare, with short ears. In the breeding season, in spring and early summer, the brown coat is slightly blue-grey but it grows progressively lighter over the summer and in winter it turns white, apart from the tips of the ears which stay black all year round. Irish mountain hares usually remain brown throughout the year.

HABITAT Mostly found on high heather moors in Scotland and on many Scottish islands, where hares are food for golden eagles. In Ireland they are frequently found on farmland, where they are more common than the brown hare.

FOOD Chiefly heather, with shoots of other moorland plants including bilberry and sedges.

5 Field vole
Microtus agrestis

The field vole is generally reckoned to be the most important of all our small mammals, since so many other creatures rely on it for their food. It makes up 90 per cent of the diet of barn owls, and short-eared owls feed on this species almost exclusively – so much so that the short-eared owl population fluctuates to match the supply of voles. Also known as the short-tailed vole, it is a common and widespread, small rodent with a yellowish brown body, 12cm (4¾in) long, and a short tail (4cm/1½in). It is easily confused with the bank vole (*Clethrionomys glareolus*), which lives in more heavily wooded situations, has reddish brown fur and is slightly smaller (9cm/3½in) but with a longer tail (6cm/2½in). All voles are more hamster-like than mouse-like in appearance, with shortish tails, small ears and dumpy bodies.

HABITAT In fairly open vegetation on moors and in fields, woods and hedges throughout the British Isles.

6 Pygmy shrew
Sorex minutus

This is Britain's smallest mammal, with the typical shrew colour and shape – a small, stout, brown body with an elongated nose, round head and shortish, furry tail. The pygmy shrew's body is about 4–6cm (1½–2½in) long and the tail

another 4cm (1½in). Although generally not as common as the common shrew, the pygmy shrew completely replaces the common shrew in mountain and moorland habitats. Being so tiny creates a big problem for the pygmy shrew: it has to eat almost constantly to get enough energy to maintain its body temperature and keep itself alive. Every day it needs to catch and eat its own bodyweight in food – that's the equivalent of a human being putting away about 60kg (10 stone) or more of pie and chips every 24 hours – or, for healthy eaters, a van-load of fruit, veg and salads.

HABITAT Throughout the British Isles, in areas where low vegetation cover is available.

FOOD Small insects, spiders.

1 Silver birch
Betula pendula

A native species and one of our early post-ice-age colonizers, the silver birch is unmistakable for its shining white bark with black markings. The bark peels off as the tree expands in girth to reveal fresh, new layers underneath. It has small, almost-triangular leaves that create a light, airy canopy that casts little shade and permits a wide range of wildflowers and associated insect life to live underneath. In spring it has small, yellowish green catkins.
HABITAT Widespread throughout the British Isles, particularly on heaths, but it is also often found as isolated trees in mixed woodland.

2 Scots pine
Pinus sylvestris

The Scots pine is a tall, upright tree with a reddish trunk of heavily cracked bark with reddish tinged fissures. Young trees are roughly conical but with age they shed

Haven for wildlife

Venerable specimens of Scots pine, one of the original 3 post-ice-age native trees that once covered Great Britain, are still found in our ancient Caledonian forest. Here it is particularly associated with wildlife such as the capercaillie, red squirrel and osprey, which likes to nest on top of a large, flat-topped pine tree.

their lower branches to leave long, bare trunks and develop a rounded top that becomes flat in time, making a great nesting platform and lookout point for large birds. It flowers in May; the male flowers are lumpy clusters of golden anthers set back a short distance from the tips of the shoots. Female flowers are small, reddish globes at the tips of new shoots; when they

are fertilized, small green cones slowly develop, taking 2 years to mature and turning brown before opening to shed their seeds. The pine needles grow in pairs, connected at the base by a small, brownish sheath.
HABITAT Native in the Highlands but widely planted in commercial plantations elsewhere; has become naturalized on lowland heaths.

3 Dwarf willows
Salix species

Several species of willow are leftovers from the days when Britain was covered in tundra. It's enough for most people to recognize a dwarf willow, but for anyone interested there are several distinct species. All are deciduous. The reticulate or netted willow (*Salix reticulata*, shown below) grows low over the ground; it has small, rounded, deep green leaves, about 3cm (1¼in) long, with smooth edges; their upper surface is faintly leathery, and on the

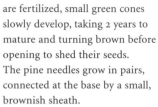

underside a conspicuous network of veins stands out (hence the name). It bears small, oval, reddish catkins on red-tinged stalks from June to August. The least willow (*Salix herbacea*) is very similar, but the leaves have a shiny underside and are faintly toothed around the edges. The woolly willow (*Salix lanata*) is an upright, bushy, branching plant, 1–2m (3–6½ft) high, resembling a natural bonsai, with rounded, grey-green, felty leaves and felty young twigs. In May and June it bears short, wide, furry, silvery catkins smothered in yellow, pollen-tipped anthers. The eared sallow (*Salix aurita*) is a bushy shrub, to 2.5m (8ft) high, with shiny, red-brown young twigs and elongated-oval leaves arranged alternately along the stems, which are dull green above, grey-green and downy below. It bears pussy-willow-like catkins on bare stems in early spring.
HABITAT Mountainous areas and rugged hillsides.

4 Mountain ash
Sorbus aucuparia

Also known as rowan, this attractive deciduous tree is capable of growing at the highest altitude of virtually any native tree. Individual mountain ash trees can grow up to 20m (65ft) but normally reach only half that. It has compound leaves, up to 20cm (8in) long, made up of many pairs of long, narrow leaflets. In May it bears flat-topped clusters of cream flowers, followed by tight bunches of bright red berries ripening in late summer or early autumn – these are attractive to birds. In autumn the foliage takes on bright orange-red tints.
HABITAT High up in mountains and moorland as well as at lower levels; thrives in poor or rocky soils.

5 Gorse
Ulex europaeus

Also known as furze, this is a very common, dense, prickly, impenetrable evergreen shrub. It can grow to 2m (6½ft) and is composed entirely of stiff stems clad in clusters of green spines, which double as leaves. The yellow flowers are very similar to those of broom, and peak in May and June

('When gorse is in bloom, kissin's in season,' runs the old saying). The related western gorse (*Ulex gallii*) flowers in autumn in many western areas of the British Isles. The flowers of *U. europaeus* are sweetly scented (like coconut), and a large area of gorse can be detected from a distance by its smell when it is in full bloom.

Both gorse and broom belong to the pea family. The keeled flowers are the same shape as those of garden peas, but are often slightly bigger, showier and in larger groups. The flowers are followed by pea-like seedpods, up to 3cm (1¼in) long, which dry to a light brown, then burst open with a sharp crack in hot, sunny weather in summer, sending the hard, round seeds flying. If you wonder what is making loud 'pops' or shooting tiny pellets at you when you have a picnic on heathland, don't worry – it'll be the nearby gorse. Gorse dries out in a hot summer, becoming highly flammable – camping stoves, barbecues and cigarette ends thrown out of cars often cause large fires over heathland.

Gorse is a favourite nesting and perching plant for certain birds – notably the stonechat, whinchat and Dartford warbler – and the soft young stems are grazed by animals such as wild ponies.
HABITAT Mostly heathland; also other areas with infertile, light, well-drained soil.

6 Bog myrtle
Myrica gale

Also known as sweet myrtle and sweet gale, this is a very tough plant that can grow where little else survives. It is a rather upright, deciduous shrub, to 1.5m (5ft), that sends out suckers and spreads into good-sized thickets. In late spring it bears small, khaki-coloured catkins, 1.5cm (⅝in) long, followed by tiny, khaki-coloured fruit. Look for red-brown young stems and lance-shaped leaves, 5–6cm (2–2½in) long, that are slightly toothed at the ends and smell of resin when bruised. (A good tip for making a natural midge repellent is to crush a couple of bog myrtle leaves and rub them on exposed arms and legs.) No great beauty, bog myrtle is a bit of a curiosity. Living in poor, wet soil where there are low nutrient levels, the plant has nitrogen-fixing nodules on its roots. These nodules are inhabited by 'friendly' fungal organisms that extract nitrogen from the air and convert it into storable form, allowing the plant literally to make its own nitrogen fertilizer. It's very similar to the way domestic peas and beans 'fix' atmospheric nitrogen.
HABITAT Bleak fens and windswept moors, in acidic, peaty ground that's boggy or even permanently waterlogged (often grows with sphagnum moss). Mostly seen in Scotland and the north of England, but can be spotted in similar habitats throughout Britain, especially the New Forest.

7 Heather
Calluna vulgaris

From late summer to early autumn, the deep mauve-pink flowers of this heather – the most common in Britain – create a purple, hazy effect on the moors when viewed from a distance. Also known as ling, it is a short, shrubby evergreen, to 60cm (24in) high, with thin, wiry, branching stems clad in stemless leaves that overlap each other, creating rather a green, scaly effect. The flowers are arranged in short spikes at the tips of the stems. Some plants have all-white flowers; these are sometimes sold as 'lucky heather'.
HABITAT Moorland and heathland throughout the British Isles, but especially prevalent on managed grouse moors in Scotland and the north of England.

8 Bell heather
Erica cinerea

The distinctly bell-shaped, light mauve-pink flowers, borne from June to September, give this small, branching, spreading, evergreen heather its name. It reaches 60cm (24in) high, and its wiry stems hold needle-like leaves arranged in whorls of 3.
HABITAT On dry moorland and on raised knolls among boggy areas.

9 Cross-leaved heath
Erica tetralix

Much smaller than the more common heathers, the cross-leaved heath is a short, grey, downy-looking evergreen, up to 30cm (12in) high. The leaves are arranged round the stems in whorls of 4 – seen sideways on, they look like rows of evenly spaced Xs. From July to September, the cross-leaved heath bears light mauve-pink, bell-shaped flowers, roughly 5mm (³⁄₁₆in) long, in short, rather rounded clusters at the tips of the wiry, relatively unbranched stems.
HABITAT Moorland, boggy patches on heaths, but on ground that dries out in summer.

10 Crowberry
Empetrum nigrum

A low, mat-forming, evergreen, moorland fruit bush, the crowberry could easily be mistaken for heather, but is less common. The plants are low and spreading or completely prostrate, with creeping, heather-like stems clad in dark green, in-rolled leaves. The leafy stems are punctuated by tiny pink, solitary flowers in early summer, followed by berries that start out green in midsummer, then turn pink, purple and finally black in early autumn, when they are fully ripe. They are not worth picking for eating but are enjoyed by many moorland birds.
HABITAT Boggy, acidic moors.

11 Bilberry
Vaccinium myrtillus

Also known as the whortleberry, this is a short, deciduous, upright, fruiting shrub that thrives in wild, remote, inhospitable places. It grows to 35cm (14in) tall, with 3-angled stems bearing thick, leathery, slightly toothed, ovate leaves (up to 3cm/1¼in long) that take on warm orange tints in autumn. The pink, bell-shaped flowers (up to 5mm/³⁄₁₆in long) are followed by sweet, edible, blue-black berries, which look very much like small blueberries. Some northern moorlands are so thickly carpeted with bilberries that the plants have taken over from heather, the normal dominant plant. Local people once used to come out from nearby towns each summer especially to pick the fruit from what were known as 'bilberry moors'.
HABITAT Mountains and high moorland are its favoured habitats but it is also found in some woodlands with poor acid soil. Mostly seen in northern and western Britain, though on some southern heathlands too.

12 Cowberry
Vaccinium vitis-idaea

This is a low, spreading or prostrate evergreen (sometimes known as lingonberry) with smallish, oval, shiny, leathery, evergreen leaves. From May to July it bears clusters of tiny, pale pink, pixie-hat-shaped flowers, followed in late summer by edible, orange-red fruits (similar to cranberries), which are very popular in Scandinavia.
HABITAT Mountains, moorland and light woodland, where the ground is boggy and acidic.

13 Cloudberry
Rubus chamaemorus

An unusual member of the bramble family, the cloudberry is slightly downy-looking, with low, creeping stems and large-lobed, mallow-like leaves. It flowers sparsely from June to August, bearing white, bramble-like blooms, followed by upward-standing berries that ripen to orange towards the end of summer or early autumn, and which are made up of a few large, rather coarse segments. They aren't worth eating, nor will they do you harm.
HABITAT Moors and boggy ground in northern Britain.

14 Purple moor grass
Molinia caerulea

These dense tussocks of coarse, wiry grass are seen throughout the British Isles in acidic marshes and moors. The leaves, to 45cm (17½in) long, are purplish at the base, and from May to September the clumps produce stiff, straight flower stems, up to 1.5m (5ft) tall, topped with long, slender sprays of purple-tinged flowers. The foliage dies off in winter, making a flat, straw-like circle round the foot of the few broken bases of flower stems. Caterpillars of the Scotch argus butterfly feed on the leaves.
HABITAT Widespread in fens, marshes and moors; also present in wet areas of heathland.

The importance of undergrowth

Undergrowth is all around us in the countryside, and is so common that most people don't notice it – but undergrowth plays a huge part in the natural environment. Different types of undergrowth provide cover for all sorts of creatures (heather and grouse are inseparable), grazing for animals such as deer and food for caterpillars with specialized eating habits. A great number of birds and animals rely on the moorland fruits and berries to fatten them up for winter, to provide fuel for their long journey south, so think twice before you dismiss undergrowth as boring!

15 Common cotton grass
Eriophorum angustifolium

Despite its name, this is in fact not a grass but a sedge. It is a rather stiff, upright, brownish plant, 20–60cm (8–24in) tall, that grows in large groups, with individual plants well spaced out. Look for wiry, 3-sided stems bearing narrow leaves, which wrap round the stems at their base; the leaves themselves are 'folded' lengthways to form a long channel with a 3-sided point at the tip. Each plant is topped by a nodding flower spike that is made up of several short-stalked flowerheads; these are followed by seedheads consisting of long white hairs, looking like loose balls of cotton wool. Cotton grass forms large, sparse carpets over quite wide areas, and is easily seen from a distance. Watch out, as its presence indicates soft, boggy ground that you'll sink into.

HABITAT Widespread on soggy, acid moorland, permanently wet areas of heathland and peat bogs. Cotton grass often grows with sundews and bog asphodel.

16 Hare's tail cotton grass
Eriophorum vaginatum

A close cousin of common cotton grass, this is a tussock-forming plant, 20–60cm (8–24in) high, with upright clusters of flowers at the tops of the stems followed by a white, fluffy 'hare's tail'. The seedheads stand upright from the tops of the plants instead of nodding over and forming loose tufts as in common cotton grass.

HABITAT Moorland, peat bogs and wet areas of heathland, but mostly in northern Britain; rarely seen in the south.

17 Common sedge
Carex nigra

This sedge is a coarse, grassy-looking plant with long, narrow, wiry leaves, often with in-rolled edges, and upright, 3-sided stems topped with a loose spike of flowers. Male and female flowers are nearly always on separate spikes (but not separate plants); you need a magnifying glass to see them properly – male flowers are brown scales from which stamens curve out; female flowers are green and scale-shaped, with an oval brown bract along one side and short, curving anthers at the tip. It's these dark scales on the young female flower spikes that give this species its Latin name *Carex nigra* (meaning black sedge).

HABITAT Acid conditions near water, boggy ground, moorland and permanently waterlogged patches of heathland.

How to tell grasses from sedges

Grasses and sedges can be extremely similar. To tell the difference, look at the stems in close-up – sedges usually have 3-sided stems, and those of grasses are flat or tubular. A few wildflowers also have 3-sided stems, in particular the 3-cornered leek (*Allium triquetum*) – a close relative of wild garlic – but though the leaves are vaguely grass-like, the distinctive garlic smell and the white, typically allium-shaped flower should tell you straight away that this isn't a grass or a sedge.

18 Bracken
Pteridium aquilinum

Our commonest and most widespread fern, bracken spreads rapidly by strong, underground rhizomes and can become a serious pest. A tall, upright plant, to 1–2m (3–6½ft) tall, it appears above ground in May as scaly 'shepherd's crooks', which uncoil

and open out to fresh green, ladder-like fronds. These die down in autumn, leaving rusty brown dead leaves that decompose slowly and build up quite a deep layer of leaf litter. The whole plant is poisonous, although hill sheep and some other animals appear to be able to eat small amounts without apparent harm – most grazing animals simply avoid it when there's other food around.
HABITAT Hillsides, moors, heaths and light woodland, wherever the soil is light and acidic.

19 Alpine lady's mantle
Alchemilla alpina

This is the wild, mountain cousin of the lady's mantle that we grow in our gardens. A short plant, 5–20cm (2–8in) high, it grows from brown, scaly rhizomes that creep along the surface of the ground, with leaves made up of 5 leaflets joining directly to the top of the leaf stalk (unlike the better-known garden lady's mantle, which has pleated, fan-shaped leaves that are only lightly lobed). Tiny, yellowish green flowers are clustered tightly at the tips of flower stems from June to September.
HABITAT Grassy areas on mountains and hillsides above an altitude of 600m (1970ft), mostly in Scotland and the north of England.

20 Harebell
Campanula rotundifolia

Known as the bluebell in Scotland, this is a fragile-looking perennial, 15–20cm (6–8in) high, with slender stems and narrow, grass-like foliage, except for the basal leaves which are round. From July to September it has nodding, bluebell-shaped flowers, up to 2cm (¾in) long, carried on short, arching side stalks that branch out towards the tips of the flower stems. Harebell stems appear to vanish between flowering grasses, so the flowers look as if they are hovering in space.
HABITAT Short turf on hillsides, downs and heathland, in areas where the soil is thin, dry and impoverished.

21 Bog asphodel
Narthecium ossifragum

A real bog plant, this resembles a chunky, coarse grass, with long, narrow, often curving, linear leaves arising from a central crown at ground-level. In July and August the bright yellow, star-shaped flowers grow in tall, upright spikes, quite well spaced out along the stem. In autumn they are followed by small, fruiting capsules, which are surrounded by the deep orange-brown remains of the dead flowers. The capsules themselves are quite colourful and could almost be mistaken for flowers from a distance.
HABITAT Only moors, bogs and soggy, acidic mountainsides and heathland, particularly in northern Britain; sometimes found in wet heathland further south.

22 Common butterwort
Pinguicula vulgaris

This is an unusual insectivorous plant; look for a small rosette (10–20cm/4–8in wide) made up of roughly 5 or 6 pale green, oval-shaped, slightly sticky leaves with

in-rolled edges. Several flower spikes, 5–10cm (2–4in) high, grow from the centre in May and June. In close-up, the flowers look rather like violets – light purple, with a slender spur standing out behind them, and a wider, lip-like lower petal that is cleft in the centre. The plants catch insects to replace the nitrogen that is lacking in the boggy soil where they live; the edges of the leaves curl up over insects trapped on the sticky surface and slowly digest them, extracting the nutrients; once the insect has been sucked dry, the leaf unrolls again, revealing a dry, browny beige husk.
HABITAT Bogs, fens, moors, boggy areas in heathland, also found in permanently wet, rocky places; less common in most of southern Britain.

23 Sundew
Drosera rotundifolia

Another insectivorous plant, sundew produces a small, green-to-reddish-tinged rosette (4–7.5cm/1½–3in across) of short-stemmed, thick, fleshy, almost succulent-looking, circular leaves, which are fringed in short, reddish hairs, each tipped with a blob of transparent 'glue' that traps any insects that land on them before they are digested. From June to August slender flowering spikes, 20cm (8in) long, tipped with tiny white flowers, grow from the centre of each rosette.

HABITAT Common in boggy heaths in the north and west of the British Isles but is rare in southern and eastern areas.

24 Spring gentian
Gentiana verna

A scarce little alpine charmer, the spring gentian makes a short tuft or small rosette with bright green, elliptical leaves. It is most easily spotted when in bloom from April to June. The upward-facing, bright indigo-blue flowers grow singly on short stems, with several pairs of small leaves well spaced out along them. Each blue flower is shaped like a star on the end of a short tube (2cm/¾in long), with a green calyx at the base.

HABITAT Spring gentian grows only at high altitudes and favours short turf on stony mountainsides and steep hillsides, usually on chalky ground.

25 Heath spotted orchid
Dactylorhiza maculata

Flowering in June and July, this is our commonest orchid. It is a striking perennial with a rather upright rosette of lance-shaped leaves with a 'keel' down the middle, heavily patterned with regularly spaced, dark, round spots of different sizes. The flower spike grows up through the centre of the rosette and has 2 or 3 leaves clasping it, sheath-like, part of the way up; at the tip is a broad-based, conical cluster of flowers, which can be anything from pale pink to deep mauve-pink. It frequently grows alongside the cross-leaved heath, a small heather. The whole plant dies down shortly after flowering.

HABITAT Moorland and heathland, on ground that is damp and acidic, but not boggy.

26 Tormentil
Potentilla erecta

A slightly straggly, floppy yet upright perennial, 25–80cm (10–31in) high, with strawberry-like leaves in groups of 3 towards the base of the plant and narrower, more pointed leaves higher up. From May to October it bears yellow, buttercup-like flowers (always with 4 petals), sparsely dotted over the plant, growing one per stalk.

HABITAT Chiefly heathland but sometimes grassland, grassy hillsides and drier parts of fens, in areas with light, acid soil.

27 Purple saxifrage
Saxifraga oppositifolia

One of our few native alpines, this is a tiny but delightful rarity, worth watching out for in mountainous areas. It is a short, branching perennial plant, with creeping stems – rather like green, furry caterpillars – that form small, irregularly shaped mats lying flat to the ground, studded with

solitary, pink-to-mauve-pink flowers that are stemless, or nearly so. It flowers mostly in April and May, but has scattered flowers until August. It will be instantly recognizable as a saxifrage to anyone who grows cultivated species in a rock feature or an alpine sink in the garden.
HABITAT Dampish patches in screes and rocky places in mountainous areas.

28 Dodder
Cuscuta epithymum

An extraordinary annual parasitic plant, seen only in summer, dodder is unusual in completely lacking chlorophyll. Look for masses of reddish, thread-like stems – resembling airy candy-floss – engulfing parts of host plants, from which it 'steals' its food. From July to September dodder bears tight clusters of very tiny, pink or white, bell-shaped flowers. Each cluster is only 1cm (⅜in) across. The seeds germinate in the ground; if the emerging threads find a suitable host, they climb up and sink suckers into it and quickly spread into a dense network of threads that can be 30cm (12in) or more across.
HABITAT Mostly heathland, using heather and gorse as its hosts, although sometimes found on other plants in other habitats.

29 Sphagnum moss
Sphagnum recurvum

This is a rather coarse, thick, fluffy, spongy-textured moss, with a slightly spiky-feathery look even though it is actually very soft. It spreads over the ground, fallen tree trunks or damp rocks to make thick carpets, and is hugely absorbent – a handful of moss, wrung out, yields a surprising amount of water.
HABITAT In stagnant water in acidic bogs, only in areas of high rainfall – mostly northern and western areas of Britain and Ireland.

30 Lichen

Widespread on heaths and moors, lichens are very ancient organisms, the first life that colonized the bare landscape left behind after the glaciers retreated at the end of the ice age. Today they are generally considered to be a sign of unpolluted air. Lichens are remarkable – not true plants, they are a working partnership between an alga (plural: algae) and a fungus (plural: fungi) that combine to create silvery green, moss-like strands hanging in tree branches, or circular grey or yellowish encrustations on bark or stone. They are incredibly slow-growing, most manage to grow only up to 2mm (¹⁄₁₆in) every year, so it's easy to work out how old a large colony

might be – several hundred years isn't unusual. There are hundreds of different species and very few have common names. The pixie-cup lichen (*Cladonia coccifera*, shown above) is one of the easiest to identify. The base is made up of scaly encrustations from which grow tiny silver 'bowls' on stalks.
HABITAT On rocks, fallen trees and open ground in peaty moors, and on tree bark and branches, stones, walls, gravestones and old buildings in open countryside.

Peat bogs

Sphagnum moss grows only on acidic ground where there is stagnant water. Here, normal decomposition cannot take place because of a lack of oxygen, so large expanses of sphagnum moss slowly turn into peat, which builds up over thousands of years into thick layers. Blanket bog – where the ground is densely covered in sphagnum moss – is often found on top of peat moors. The ground in blanket bogs can be extremely soft, so keep to designated tracks, especially where boardwalks have been put in.

Also found on moors, heaths or mountains

Carrion crow (see p.304)
Common gull (see p.28)
Common snipe (see p.236)
Cuckoo (see p.164)
Curlew (see p.43)
Dunlin (see p.40)
Foxglove (see p.118)
Greenshank (see p.42)
Kestrel (see p.298)
Linnet (see p.165)
Meadow pipit (see p.165)
Rabbit (see p.278)
Scottish wildcat (see p.103)
Wood sage (see p.116)

Limestone and
chalk hills and downs

The earliest limestone landscapes of Britain were formed under the sea around 360 million years ago, resulting in spectacular and often dramatic scenery. Chalk landscapes, which were also formed underwater, were laid down some 70 million years ago. These chalk hills and downs were the first areas in Britain to be settled by early man and hold many attractions for wildlife today.

Natural features

What's the difference between limestone and chalk? Not a lot, you might think; they are both forms of rock containing the same main element – calcium. The difference boils down to age, hardness and the percentage of calcium carbonate in the rock. Limestones – and there are several different types – are older, harder rocks and contain over 50 per cent calcium carbonate, while chalk is younger, softer and a good deal purer, consisting of up to 98 per cent calcium carbonate; good enough to write on a blackboard with. Both chalk and limestone were formed underwater, normally beneath the sea.

It's a fact that's hard to believe when you look at towering natural features such as the White Cliffs of Dover, Cheddar Gorge or the peaks of Ingleborough in Yorkshire – until you think back to Britain's very up-and-down geological history. A whole series of alternate dunkings and dryings-out have added layer after layer of limestone to the 'bones' of our islands. You might think one set of limestone landscapes would be very much like another: scenic, owing to the comparative ease and speed at which these relatively soft rocks 'weather', and with similar flora and fauna, since in each case the ground is alkaline. However, the character of limestone landscapes varies quite dramatically.

Limestone landscapes

Our story begins around 360 million years ago, at the start of the Carboniferous era, when the sea level rose, pretty well inundating us. Under the sea, sediments piled up, gradually squashing the lower layers down, so that over millions of years a combination of pressure and time turned them to stone – carboniferous limestone.

This geological activity formed what is now our very oldest limestone, which gives us the spectacular scenery in places like the Yorkshire and Derbyshire Dales, the Burren in Ireland, Malham Tarn, Ingleborough and Cheddar Gorge. But limestone is a notoriously soft type of stone, as stone goes, and it's particularly prone to erosion and weathering. It reacts with anything even slightly acid, which 'eats it away' all the faster. The biggest dissolver of limestone is rain. As rain falls through the atmosphere it picks up carbon dioxide, which makes it mildly acid, so the softest limestone is dissolved, leaving the harder parts, eventually creating dramatic scenery with waterfalls, gorges and ravines, before rivers disappear down sink holes, 'swallows' and potholes into underground cave systems. Limestone caves often contain stalactites and stalagmites, formed from dissolved calcium salts, which are deposited by dripping water into pointy

shapes. (The *mites* go up and the *tites* come down – it's quite a handy mnemonic.) They are both a great feature of Carboniferous limestone landscapes.

Towards the end of the Carboniferous era, approximately 290 million years ago, the seas were shallower. Giant horsetails – which created the coal forests – covered much of the land, which was still distinctly swampy. The underwater sediments that were being laid down at that time formed the limestone scenery of much of Northumberland, South Wales and southern Scotland.

But deep below the earth the tectonic plates were still shifting. As the two supercontinents of the time joined together to make one giant land mass called Pangea, Britain was pushed back into desert conditions again, for some 80 million years. The land dried out and subsequently limestone formation was halted.

By the start of the Jurassic era, 208 million years ago, conditions changed again and we were once more inundated by seawater. Jurassic limestone was being laid down, later to emerge as what is now much of Dorset, North Yorkshire and the Cotswolds. Portland stone, one of the purest forms of limestone and very popular as a building material, dates back to this time.

The cycle continued, and 150 million years ago (when dinosaurs ruled) we rose above the waves again. The Jurassic Coast of Dorset was formed, along with the south coast of what is now the Isle of Wight. Until as recently as 8000 years ago, after the end of the last ice age, the Isle of Wight was a part of mainland Britain. Today both these coasts are rich in the bones of dinosaurs, such as ichthyosaurs and plesiosaurs, as well as in fossilized ammonites. Important finds are still made as rock falls expose new seams of stone and its long-since buried treasures, but you can find all sorts of fascinating things on the beach. Regular fossil-hunters soon recognize which pebbles to tap with a hammer to split in two and reveal buried fossil treasures.

PREVIOUS PAGES The dramatic chalk stacks of the Needles, off the Isle of Wight (main picture), and the clustered bellflower (small picture).
BELOW LEFT Limestone pavement at Malham, Yorkshire.
BELOW CENTRE Flamborough Head, which juts into the North Sea on the east Yorkshire coast, is one of Britain's most spectacular areas of chalk cliffs, standing 400 feet high. It is home to a wide variety of plants and wildlife, including nesting sea birds, and attracts many bird migrants in autumn.
BELOW RIGHT Lulworth Cove, Dorset, showing the natural horseshoe-shaped harbour. The shoreline is formed of Portland limestone.

Chalk landscapes

In the late Cretaceous era, some 60–100 million years ago, the sea level was on the way up again. The dinosaurs were dying out, and in the sea microscopic planktonic organisms died in droves. Their tiny bodies sank to the seabed like dandruff and it was these skeletal remains that then compressed over time to make chalk, the youngest type of limestone. Chalk settled in most of Britain, although further north it was chiefly eroded away by glaciers in the ice age two and half million years ago. The scarp of the Chilterns and the East Anglian Heights mark the northern and western margins of the remaining chalk, and a few isolated pockets also formed in the area round Flamborough Head in Yorkshire and the North and South Downs of Kent and Sussex – today these are our very youngest limestone landscapes.

The big differences between the chalk landscapes found in northern and southern Britain are the result of glaciation. Chalklands in the north often received a layer of silty or clay sediments left by the melting ice. This is the reason why much of East Anglia – though basically chalkland – has soil that isn't particularly alkaline. By contrast, chalklands of the south, which were never covered by glaciers, remained much chalkier and the soils can often be very alkaline indeed. The southern chalk landscape consists of typical downlands – gently undulating hills with thin, stony soil on top.

Chalklands house a wide and varied crop of wildlife today, but their unique features made them ideal for one particular form of wildlife – early man. When people first took to farming in Britain, some 6000 years ago, they seem to have settled on chalklands first of all. One of the reasons for this was that the light, free-draining chalk soils were easy to work with simple farming tools – very basic 'digging sticks' made of bone or antlers. Chalky soil also warms up early, so they'd have been able to harvest their crops before bad weather set in. Another big attraction of some chalkland areas for early people was the flint, which they used for building materials and for chipping to make tools.

Where there were open areas without trees, particularly once the wildwoods were cleared for farming, rain quickly washed the thin, fragile soil away down the slopes of the downs; native plants and wild grasses colonized the chalky, impoverished ground and people grazed sheep on the land. The reconstructed Iron Age roundhouse at Butser Hill in Hampshire shows what a typical farm and its crops and livestock looked like at the time. Areas like the East Anglian Brecklands and the South Downs have traditionally been used for grazing ever since, as trees didn't easily regrow on the poorer soil. Sheep have historically been responsible for maintaining the short, springy turf and wealth of downland flowers and their associated butterflies – a situation that continues even now, although rabbits are also crucial in keeping the grass down in many areas.

Limestone and chalkland flora

Generally, limestone rocks weather to produce alkaline soil, which is what gives limestone countryside its unique flora. You can often tell that you are walking on a limestone landscape – even if you can't actually see lumps of chalk or limestone sticking out of the ground – just by the type of wildflowers that grow there. A lot of them don't grow anywhere else – they are the true calcicoles or lime-lovers. Some calcicoles grow commonly on any type of limestone landscape, including Carboniferous limestone and chalk, for example bird's foot trefoil, clustered bellflower and horseshoe vetch. Others are much fussier about having precisely the right set of growing conditions; indeed, some of the very rarest grow only at particular locations.

As a general rule, chalk landscapes warm up quickly in spring, so their characteristic wildflowers come out early – in May and June – and then die down to spend hot, dry summers safely dormant underground, as is the case with wild orchids. Other chalkland flowers are either fairly drought-tolerant, or they have deep or far-ranging roots that can make use of very limited water. Typical downland flowers include species such as wild marjoram and thyme and small scabious, which is a great favourite with butterflies.

Just as some wildflowers grow exclusively on limestone or chalk landscapes, there are some that never do. These are the calcifuges (lime-haters), so if you see wild rhododendrons, whortleberry and sheep's sorrel, you'll know you're on acid soil. Both the true calcicoles and true calcifuges are 'indicator plants', meaning they indicate the nature of the terrain.

OPPOSITE This hillside chalk carving of a white horse galloping above the Channel Tunnel at Folkestone, Kent, was created to celebrate the Millennium.

1 Quail
Coturnix coturnix

A summer visitor to the British Isles, this very small, scarce, extremely hard-to-see game bird has a plump, rounded appearance, with a short neck, tail and legs. If seen at all, it is usually glimpsed scurrying, hunched and head-down, along rows of crops, or standing more upright, craning its neck to look round. It has brown upperparts, streaked pale yellowish buff, and a warm brown breast fading out to warm buff under-parts that are nearly white under the tail. The head has a streaked dark-brown-and-fawn pattern, with 2 dark bands curving down to surround the off-white throat, and a short, dark, blunt beak. It flies

rarely, and only a short distance, on fast-whirring wings. The loud, far-carrying, 'wet-my-lips' song is heard mostly in early mornings and evenings, and often at night.
HABITAT Late April–September: usually hidden among growing crops in arable fields in chalk or limestone countryside, including downs of southern and south-central England. Winter: Africa.
SIZE 18cm (7in)
EGGS 10–15, buff blotched with dark brown
NEST Bare scrape in grass on the ground among growing crops.
FOOD Seeds, insects, soft shoots.
VARIATIONS Females have a dark spotted breast and a duller head pattern than males.

2 Stone curlew
Burhinus oedicnemus

This plover-shaped bird, which is the length of a woodpigeon but with a less bulky, more tapering body, is perfectly camouflaged against bare soil by its dark-flecked, sandy brown plumage. Look for a large, round head with huge yellow, staring eyes, a yellow, black-tipped beak and long yellow legs and feet. You may also see whitish 'eyebrows' and brown and white lines under the eyes, as well as the white throat, wing-flash, belly and undertail. It is a very scarce and localized summer visitor, but numbers are slowly increasing, thanks to conservation efforts by farmers and wildlife groups.
HABITAT April–late July: mainly in arable crops and sandy heaths of the Brecklands of East Anglia, where there is short grass dotted with patches of bare soil; some on chalk downs in southern England.
SIZE 42cm (16½in)
EGGS 2, greyish white with reddish brown streaks and spots
NEST Bare scrape on the ground.
FOOD Worms, insects, spiders.

3 Cuckoo
Cuculus canorus

This is a summer visitor that is more often heard than seen, making its far-carrying 'cuckoo' calls. Other male calls include a harsh 'gwork gwork gwork'; the female has a distinctive, bubbling call. A good view of a perching bird shows a very streamlined, collared-dove-sized body with a blue-grey head, back and breast; the rest of the underparts are white with dark grey barring. It has long, pointed wings, with darker wing-tips, and a darker, white-spotted tail. The beak is short, slender and slightly down-curved.

HABITAT Very wide range including downland, farmland, heaths, reed-beds, moorland and woodland.
SIZE 33cm (13in)
EGGS Up to 25 eggs in a season but each one is laid in a different host bird's nest; the colour usually mimics that of the host's eggs.

Parasitic birds

The cuckoo famously lays its eggs in the nests of other, smaller birds and leaves them to rear its young. The female cuckoo keeps an eye out for suitable host birds in the area, then lays her eggs – one in each nest – when the hosts are not at home; she takes no further interest in her young. Cuckoos' eggs hatch earlier than the host bird's eggs, leaving the coast clear for the baby cuckoo to heave the other eggs or nestlings out over the side of the nest to enjoy the undivided attention of its 'parents', who keep the gaping mouth of their single 'offspring' (which quickly grows far bigger than them) filled. Shown above is a cuckoo chick (right) being fed by its tiny reed-warbler 'parent'.

NEST Uses nests mainly of meadow pipits, dunnocks and reed warblers (but over 100 host species have been recorded).

FOOD Insects, caterpillars.

4 Great grey shrike
Lanius excubitor

This is an uncommon winter visitor, which is the size of a blackbird, with smart, grey-black-and-white plumage. Look for a grey head, back and rump, and a black beak, 'burglar's mask', wings, legs and a longish black tail. The

underparts, including the undertail, are white. Seen from below, when perched in a tree, the bird looks almost entirely white; in flight, it looks magpie-like, with a bold white wing-flash on black wings. Shrikes are great hunters and store their catch of lizards, large insects and small mammals and birds in a 'larder', by impaling several corpses close together on thorns. When you don't see the bird – and they are not easy to spot – the presence of the 'larder' tells you for sure that a shrike is active in the area.

HABITAT October–late March: downland, coastal dunes, heathland and young conifer plantations, all over Britain (rare in Ireland), especially along the eastern edge, from north-east Scotland down to the Isle of Wight. Summer: northern Europe.

SIZE 24cm (9½in)

FOOD Small birds, mammals, reptiles, large insects.

5 Linnet
Carduelis cannabina

Locally common throughout the British Isles, except in the far north of Scotland, these little, mainly brown-buff finches look like small sparrows from a distance. However, males in spring and summer have a bright crimson patch on the forehead and one on either side of the breast. The linnet's head is grey, its back is unstreaked rich reddish brown, the underparts are white at the centre and the flanks are buff. The blackish wing-tips and tail (which is notched) have prominent white lines along the edges. Towards dusk, linnets tend to flock to the same few trees, making a musical twittering when at roost.

HABITAT Open countryside, including downland, gorse heaths and foreshores close to the sea.

SIZE 13cm (5in)

EGGS 4–5, blue-grey with darker spots

NEST Cup of grass, rootlets and twigs, low down in hedgerows and dense scrub.

FOOD Mainly seeds; some insects.

VARIATIONS Female is far more streaky and sparrow-like than the male and lacks the red patches. The juvenile is paler and more heavily streaked all over.

6 Meadow pipit
Anthus pratensis

Although it's not one of our better-known birds, the meadow pipit is surprisingly common and widespread in the British Isles. It makes up a large part of the diet of several birds of prey, especially the merlin, and is also one of the 3 major host birds used by cuckoos. The meadow pipit is easily overlooked because of its rather furtive habits and dull appearance (streaky brown and sparrow-sized). Mostly seen on the ground, it bobs its tail frequently; the call is a squeaky, high 'tseeep', repeated regularly. If disturbed, it flies off in an irregular pattern, changing direction and height all the time. For its song flight, it rises almost straight up from the ground, singing, then parachutes down to the ground on half-open wings in a 'V' shape, often descending very quickly. The meadow pipit is present throughout the year, but in winter most tend to forsake the highest ground for the lowlands.

HABITAT Summer: wide, open, tree-less countryside, especially downs, but also meadows, moors and coastal wasteland. Winter: more widespread in lowlands and round the coast.

SIZE 14cm (5½in)

EGGS 4–5, entirely streaked brown and grey

NEST On the ground, in short grass

FOOD Mainly insects and other invertebrates; some seeds.

SIMILAR TO Most similar to the tree pipit, which lives in woodland clearings and scrubby lowland heaths in summer and winters in Africa. Also resembles the skylark, which is distinctly larger and has a crest (in flight, it hovers high up, giving its warbling song). Also looks like the female house sparrow, which is more strongly patterned and has a much stouter, conical beak; the sparrow is more assertive and does not bob.

1 Chalkhill blue
Lysandra coridon

An unusual butterfly of chalk hills, the male is the only blue butterfly with silvery blue wings (wingspan just over 3cm/1¼in). These are outlined in black, with narrow, black-and-white, almost-chequer-patterned margins; the hind wings have a row of black spots. The female has similar markings but in brown, with light orange dots along the hind wing. The undersides of the wings are light

buff with a sprinkling of darker spots, greenish bases to the wings, and a row of light orange spots along the edges of the hind wings. Adults live only 2–3 weeks; they feed on nectar from various wildflowers growing on chalk and take moisture from fresh dung.
HABITAT Grassy, chalky hillsides covered in wildflowers, in central and southern England, particularly the South Downs and Chiltern Hills, in July and August.
CATERPILLAR Green with faint yellow stripes running the full length of the body; found exclusively on horseshoe vetch from April to June.

2 Adonis blue
Lysandra bellargus

This is Britain's brightest blue butterfly. Males have sky-blue wings (wingspan about 3cm/1¼in) with faint, black-and-white-chequered borders. Females are brown with a row of orange spots round the edges of the hind wings. The undersides are buff with dark spots and greenish bases to the wings, with a row of plain dots round the edges of the forewings and faint orange spots round the edges of the hind wings. Adult males may be found drinking fluid from fresh dung, and both sexes drink nectar from downland flowers, especially vetches and trefoils, but also wild marjoram.
HABITAT Sunny, grass-covered chalk or limestone slopes rich in chalk-loving wildflowers, only in the south of England, in the Downs and the Chilterns, in May and June or August and September.
CATERPILLAR Green with several faint yellow stripes; found on horseshoe vetch in June and July or during the winter.

3 Small blue
Cupido minimus

Our smallest butterfly (2cm/¾in wingspan), this fragile-looking species is a member of the blue family; however, despite its name it is a dull, brownish species with narrow white wing margins. The

undersides are light buff, sprinkled with darker spots, and the wings are outlined in black with narrow white margins; the bases of the wings are bluish. Look for its fast, flitting flight between plants.
HABITAT Chalk hills, especially the Chilterns and South Downs, but also in scattered localities round the coasts of Scotland, Ireland and Wales, in May and June.
CATERPILLAR Nondescript, buff-coloured grub found on kidney vetch at any time of year.

4 Common blue
Polyommatus icarus

As its name suggests, this is our commonest and most widespread blue butterfly. The male is violet-blue, with a faint blackish band and a white margin round the outer edges of all the wings; the underside is light buff with a bluish base to the wings and a row of faint orange spots along the outer edges. The female is usually brown but may be vaguely blue, with orange spots on both sides of the wings, but most heavily on the hind wings. Adults are often found sipping nectar from fleabane, wild marjoram and wild thyme, or resting on grasses or flowers. It is small-to-medium-sized, with a wingspan of just over 3cm (1¼in).
HABITAT Widespread throughout the British Isles. Found in the north from May to July, but further south it has 2 or even 3 hatchings per year so may be seen from April to October. Very common on the South Downs, along with rarer blue butterflies.
CATERPILLAR Green, found on a wide range of plants, especially bird's foot trefoil and black medick, from June to August or through the winter.

OPPOSITE The northern brown argus, a member of the blue family, is a close relative of the brown argus but is found only in northern Britain.

Blue butterflies

There are quite a few blue butterflies, all of which look very similar (the females of most blue butterflies are brown and spotted). When trying to identify them, take note of the location, habitat, time of year, and which flowers the adults are taking nectar from. Try also to get a good look at the undersides of the wings as well as the top and, if you can, do a quick sketch in a notebook. As much as anything it's a process of elimination – anticipate the commonest species being the likeliest find. If handling butterflies, treat them very carefully and release them as soon as you've had a look.

Some blue butterflies have a curious relationship with ants. Ants protect the caterpillars of the Adonis blue and chalkhill blue from predators, in return for which the caterpillars secrete a sticky, honeydew-like

substance, which is released when the ants gently stroke them. The relationship is taken much further by the large blue butterfly, which lays its eggs on the flower buds of wild thyme; when the eggs hatch, the young caterpillars initially feed on thyme but are then carried off by a particular species of red ant, which takes them back to its underground nests, where the growing caterpillars are 'milked' and feed on ant larvae. The defenceless pupae remain in the ants' nest until they are ready to hatch, before being returned above ground to allow the butterfly to complete its life cycle.

5 Large blue
Maculinea arion

Britain's rarest butterfly and our largest blue (4cm/1½in wingspan), this species became extinct in Britain but has been reintroduced; it is now found in very few places, including the Glastonbury area. The forewings are edged with a broad black outline and the hind wings are edged with a row of black spots; there are black dots on both the forewings and the hind wings. (It is the only blue butterfly to have black spots on the forewings – a useful identification feature.) The undersides of the wings are light buff-coloured, with light blue bases and a sprinkling of darker spots in a scallop pattern round the edges. Adults feed on the nectar of wild thyme and other flowers. Unusually for blues, both the male and female are blue.
HABITAT Open, closely grazed grassland and where there are both anthills and wild thyme plants.
CATERPILLAR Tiny, buff-coloured grubs briefly seen on thyme flowers until collected by ants (see box, p.166).

6 Brown argus
Aricia agestis

This rather uncommon, small butterfly (3cm/1¼in wingspan) is a member of the blue family, despite the fact that it is brown. The wings are warm mid-brown, with all but the leading edges neatly outlined with a row of orange half-moon shapes. The undersides are light brown with darker dots and an edging of orange half-moons backed by brown dots, with a light blue patch where the wings join the body. It is usually seen in groups, basking on flowers with its wings open in sunny weather or feeding on nectar of downland flowers, sometimes bramble.
HABITAT Chalk downs and limestone hills of southern and central England and Wales, from May to August.
CATERPILLAR Green with a thin red stripe down each side, feeding on the underside of common rock rose and common storksbill leaves from August to April.

7 Small heath
Coenonympha pamphilus

This is an unspectacular, small butterfly (3cm/1¼in wingspan), which always keeps its wings closed together when at rest (rather than basking with open wings, as many species do). In this position, the forewings are light tan with orange at the base, and there is a conspicuous, dark 'eye' in the top corner that is seen only on the underside of the wing. The hind wings are buff-coloured with a brown splotch at the base and a very faint row of buff spots near the edge. In flight, the butterfly is a tawny brown, with faintly darker wing margins edged in white. Adults are seen all summer, often with blue butterflies, and feed on the nectar of a wide range of wildflowers including fleabane. Although once common and widespread, it is becoming more localized in many areas.
HABITAT Grassy places.
CATERPILLAR Slender, grass-green, found feeding on stems of long grass from June to April.

8 Marbled white
Melanargia galathea

Our only black-and-white-chequered butterfly, this species has black wings (about 5cm/2in wingspan) patterned with white, block-shaped spots and a row of small, white, often half-circular spots around the edges of the wings. The undersides of the wings have the same pattern but are paler, in 2 shades of grey. Adults, which are usually found singly, are conspicuously slow-flying, and rest with their wings held wide open. They feed on nectar of wildflowers, especially scabious and knapweeds.
HABITAT Fairly widespread in southern and western Britain in July and August, especially on wildflower-rich chalky grassland, downs and in glades in forestry plantations, though occasionally further north or in large gardens surrounded by grassy countryside.
CATERPILLAR Grass-green, found on long grasses, especially fescues, virtually all year round.

9 Grizzled skipper
Pyrgus malvae

Faint grey hairs give this butterfly its grizzled appearance. It is a small, bitter-chocolate-brown-and-white species, with a wingspan of slightly under 3cm (1¼in). The dark brown wings are speckled with white, and a row of square white spots outlines the entire shape. Unusually for skippers, this species basks in the sun with its wings opened out flat rather than 'tented'; when the sun isn't out, the wings remain completely shut.
HABITAT Flowery downland meadows in the southern half of England and Wales, in May and June; also sometimes a second batch in August and September.
CATERPILLAR Dull khaki-green, seen feeding on wild potentilla, cinquefoil, wild strawberry, silverweed and sometimes bramble, between May and early August.

10 Dingy skipper
Erynnis tages

This is a rather unusual and very small, ash-grey-mottled butterfly (2.5cm/1in wingspan), with slightly browner mottling on the forewings; the browner hind wings are outlined with a faintly furry grey fringe. The antennae are ringed in black and white. Adults are never found far from bird's foot trefoil.
HABITAT In May and June, seen in downlands of southern and central England, also limestone areas of Wales, Scotland, northern England and Ireland (it is the only species of skipper to be found in Ireland).
CATERPILLAR Small and green, found from July to April, feeding exclusively on bird's foot trefoil. Generally, skipper caterpillars hide from potential predators, especially while they are small, by trussing the leaves of their food plant together with silken threads to make a loose 'tent' inside which they feed. The dingy skipper caterpillar hibernates over winter in such a 'tent'.

11 Wart biter
Decticus verrucivorus

This is an intriguingly named but rare cricket that, years ago, really was used in Scandinavia for biting off warts. It is a stocky bush-cricket, 2–3cm (¾–1¼in) long, in green or brown marked with a heavily mottled pattern, and with

antennae slightly longer than the body. It is capable of giving a sharp nip if handled.
HABITAT Open, hilly, grassy pastures in a few locations on the South Downs, mainly just east of Brighton; active only on warm, sunny days in midsummer.

12 Dark bush-cricket
Pholidoptera griseoaptera

Once known as the long-horned grasshopper, this is our commonest bush-cricket. It is fairly large, up to 2cm (¾in) long, but with antennae up to twice that length in mature adults. The colour varies from light to dark brown. The female has a single, curving 'claw' (which is her egg-laying apparatus) protruding from the base of her abdomen. This cricket feeds on plants and other insects.
HABITAT Widespread in central and southern England, on hills and downs, in hedgerows, woodland edges, roadside verges, grassland and also gardens.

Differences between grasshoppers and crickets

It's often thought that grasshoppers are green and crickets are brown; it's not true. Both can be either colour, depending on the species – and some are very variable. Grasshoppers have short antennae, and they chirp by rubbing the stiff bristles present along the last section of the hind legs against the forewings; they readily leap out of the grass, sometimes using their wings briefly to glide if they want to travel greater distances. Crickets have longer antennae and chirp by rubbing their forewings together (their songs are usually more high-pitched than those of grasshoppers); they are also less likely to jump, preferring to crawl around in grass. Female bush-crickets have a fearsome, curved 'claw' (which is actually the sheath of the ovipositor) protruding from the end of their abdomen, which is absent in grasshoppers. Real experts can distinguish different species of grasshoppers just by their chirps!

The best time to see grasshoppers, crickets and bush-crickets is in summer, on fine, sunny days, since this is when they are most active. They live for only a single season, and lay eggs that survive the winter in the ground or on grasses, hatching the following year.

13 Common field grasshopper
Chorthippus brunneus

One of our commonest grasshoppers, this species is very variable in colour, from green or buff to warm brown, with short antennae and plump, chicken-drumstick-shaped thighs; the females are up to 2cm (¾in) long, males are a little smaller. They feed exclusively on grass and only the males chirp.

HABITAT Undisturbed, grassy meadows and downs, but particularly south-facing slopes, where it's warmest.

14 Glow-worm
Lampyris noctiluca

The glow-worm is a secretive insect, related to the firefly, found in small colonies. It is most easily seen at night, when the wingless female 'lights up' to attract a mate; look for widely spaced groups of greenish yellow pinpoints in the grass and undergrowth. The male is a small, long, narrow, mid-brown flying beetle, 1.5cm (⅝in) long; the female, which is the same size as the male, looks like a strange brown-and-pink-segmented larva; she climbs up into low vegetation at night and directs her abdomen upwards to show off its greenish yellow light. The light is produced in the last 3 segments of the female's abdomen, using a special enzyme. She can turn her light on and off, to advertise her intentions. Males have very good eyesight and soon

'drop in' to visit. The larvae of glow-worms resemble the females.
HABITAT Generally in meadows in chalk or limestone countryside, mainly in southern England and East Anglia.

15 Bloody-nosed beetle
Timarcha tenebricosa

This is a round, shiny, jet-black beetle with a hard, domed back, 2cm (¾in) long, like an animated pill, with short legs and antennae about half its body length, found walking around on bare ground or

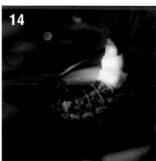

in short grass. When alarmed, it exudes a drop of red liquid from its mouth as a defence mechanism, hence its common name.
HABITAT Meadows in the chalk countryside of southern England, where bedstraw or goosegrass grows, in spring and summer.
LARVA Short, black and slightly concertina-like, seen April to September, feeding on bedstraw or goosegrass.

16 Purse-web spider
Atypus affinis

The purse-web spider is a rare, rather sinister-sounding creature that lives in a burrow and emerges when a passing insect steps on the tubular web that protrudes slightly from the mouth of it; the prey is immobilized with venom and then pulled back into the burrow. It is a plump, short-legged spider (1cm/⅜in long), with brown legs and thorax and a spherical, slightly furry, chestnut-brown-and-black face.
HABITAT Rough grassland, most frequently seen in September and October.

17 Roman snail
Helix pomatia

Britain's largest snail, and sometimes known as the edible snail, this is the species that gourmets buy in tins for stuffing back into a bag of shells along with garlic butter. It has a large, rounded shell (up to 5cm/2in across) in pale cream marked with a few buff bands, and is rather rare. It feeds on vegetation. Snails can live only on ground that contains chalk or lime, since they need to take in calcium constantly in their diet in order to make their shells. They depend on these to avoid dehydration as well as for protection from predators, so it is very unusual to find snail populations in areas without at least some chalk in the soil.
HABITAT In scrub in calcium-rich environments including chalk, limestone and border clay, in southern England.

1 Common lizard
Lacerta vivipara

Ireland's only reptile, this brownish fawn or greyish lizard, 10–15cm (4–6in) long including its tail, is usually seen sunbathing on rocks or logs by day. It has darker spots and 1 or 2 stripes down the entire length of its back. The underside of the male is orange and that of the female is light fawny yellow. A lot of creatures are partial to lizard on the menu, but lizards have a cunning plan – their long tail is the easiest thing for a potential predator to grab, so lizards can shed the tail in order to escape. The stump seals up instantly, so you sometimes find short, stubby individuals wandering about, before their new tail has started to grow back again.

HABITAT Open countryside with light, fast-draining soil, especially chalk downlands and rocky or sandy banks, heaths and coastal areas throughout Britain and Ireland. Seen from March to late October as it hibernates in winter.
FOOD Spiders and other small invertebrates.

Chalk downland

Downland is the typical rolling landscape of countryside overlying chalk, and is mostly found in the south and east of Britain. What we refer to as 'the downs' are the North and South Downs of Kent and Sussex, but you'll also find the same sort of scenery in the Berkshire and Hampshire Downs. All these areas were created by the soft chalk being eroded by rain into low, gently rolling mounds, and have also been landscaped by centuries of sheep-grazing.

Formerly a quarry, these chalk downs in Dorset are covered in pink common spotted orchids and yellow bird's foot trefoil in summer.

Although the scenery is not nearly as spectacular as limestone country with its crags, ravines and peaks, downland is a wonderful habitat with its own set of wildlife, of which plants are the highlight. They have adapted to growing in poor, thin, alkaline soil containing very few nutrients, since these have long since been washed away by rain. When you go out walking on downland, you can't help noticing the short, rather wiry turf and the enormous range of small flowering plants it contains. Most of the common downland flowers are superb plants for butterflies – an accolade that belongs to the likes of bird's foot trefoil, kidney vetch, scabious and several wild herbs such as wild thymes and wild marjoram. Many species of wild orchid thrive on downs too, since they flower fairly early and have short growing seasons that enable them to survive hot, dry summer conditions safely dormant, underground. But many of the later-flowering downland plants, such as perfoliate St John's wort, have penetrating roots that enable them to tap into deep underground reserves. Downland also houses its own range of rare wildflowers. The pasqueflower can occur in fair-sized groups but you'll find it at only a few locations, and the real rarity, the round-headed rampion, grows on the downs and nowhere else.

On the higher and driest areas of the downs, woody plants are rather limited. The wayfaring tree, dogwood and juniper can be seen, and traveller's joy scrambles wildly through the hedgerows. Trees such as beech grow where the ground is lower and richer, at the foot of the downs or in 'hanging woods' or 'beech hangers', such as you'll find at Selborne in Hampshire, home of the eighteenth-century English naturalist and author Gilbert White (his house and gardens are open to the public), where the trees clothe the side of steep downs. You'll also discover ancient yews, especially at Kingley Vale Nature Reserve in Sussex, and box at Box Hill, in Surrey, made famous as the scene of the picnic in Jane Austen's novel *Emma*.

But it's not just the upper slopes of the downs that have their own character. In the countryside at the foot of downland you'll find small, meandering, chalk streams that support watercress farms, trout and crustaceans such as crayfish, which need lime to make their shells.

Mammals

1 Sheep
Ovis species

The short, grassy turf and typical wildflowers and butterflies of the downs are all with us today, thanks to 6000–7000 years of continuous grazing by sheep, which maintain the turf and keep down scrub and invasive species. Several meat-producing breeds, which were developed in the 18th century as a result of selective breeding — for example the Southdown – specialize in grassy downland habitats. Although most of the sheep you see on open downs today are modern, high-yielding breeds, older breeds, such as the the Hampshire Down and the Dorset Horn (one of Britain's oldest breeds), are still sometimes used for conservation grazing. Today, rabbits replace sheep as main grazers in many areas of short grassland.

Other old, rare breeds of sheep were selected for hardiness in mountains, fells or moorland locations, and in the Midlands many long-fleeced breeds were developed for supplying the wool trade. On offshore islands, primitive sheep, such as the Soay, developed in isolation, without selective breeding, relying on survival of the fittest.
HABITAT Pasture, downs, moors and hilly country.
FOOD Grass, supplemented by hay and sometimes concentrates.

Plants

1 Common juniper
Juniperus communis

One of the 'big 3' original trees of the ancient Caledonian forests (the others being birch and Scots pine), this is a prickly, blue-grey conifer with dense clusters of short, sharp-pointed leaves, rather like prickly moss, and round, green, pea-sized berries that ripen to black in late summer and autumn. On exposed hills it grows as a squat, ground-hugging bush, but in more sheltered places it makes a small, columnar tree up to 6m (20ft).
HABITAT In Scotland, Ireland and Wales, and on chalk downs and heaths in southern England.

2 Yew
Taxus baccata

This is an upright evergreen tree that in time spreads out and develops a broad, rounded or pointed top, eventually reaching up to 20m (65ft). The bark is reddish and flaking and an old tree has deep fissures in the trunk. It has dense evergreen foliage, consisting of rows of small (1.5cm/⅝in), dark green needles growing along the young stems, and casts very deep shade – nothing grows under an old yew tree, and all you see is a deep layer of dead, brown needles that builds up over the years. Male and female flowers form on separate trees as tiny, insignificant tufts in the leaf axils near the tips of the shoots; female flowers are green, males yellow. The flowers are followed by red berries, borne singly on female trees. All parts of the yew are toxic.
HABITAT Mostly grows on chalk. Old yew woodland is now found only in a few locations including Kingley Vale Nature Reserve on the Hampshire/West Sussex border. However, yew is becoming common as a self-sown tree in woods elsewhere in the British Isles.

3 Bird cherry
Prunus padus

The bird cherry is a fairly compact, upright tree or bushy shrub, to about 6m (20ft) high, with leaves that resemble those of an ornamental garden cherry – they are 10cm (4in) long, oval with pointed tips and slightly serrated edges, with dark red stalks. In May it bears tassels of small white, almond-scented flowers, 7.5cm (3in) long, followed by small, round, bitter-tasting fruit that ripens through maroon to black

Ancient tree
Yew is one of our longest-lived trees. Some specimens are believed to be over 1000 years old, and a well-known example at Fortingall in Scotland is claimed to be 4000 years old. Yew is the traditional churchyard tree (often planted to repel livestock) and is also familiar as a popular garden hedging plant.

in autumn. (The fruits are known as 'hags' in Scotland, and the tree as the 'hagberry'.) The leaves usually take on gold or orange-red autumnal tints.

HABITAT Lightly wooded, hilly countryside in limestone regions, especially in northern Britain, usually close to streams.

4 Whitebeam
Sorbus aria

A familiar and attractive relative of the mountain ash, the whitebeam makes a tidy, compact, shapely, rather upright tree to roughly 15m (50ft), with large, wide, toothed, oval leaves that have silky-textured white backs. When the buds first break in spring, all the new foliage looks shining silvery white – almost like that of a small-flowered magnolia – especially when seen from a distance. It flowers in May, producing tight, dome-shaped clusters of small white flowers, which are followed by loose bunches of scarlet-red berries that are great favourites with birds. The whitebeam takes on attractive, gold leaf tints in autumn.

HABITAT Chalk hills and limestone countryside.

5 Buckthorn
Rhamnus cathartica

Also known as purging buckthorn, this is a close relative of the old-fashioned laxative, cascara. It is a common though unexceptional-looking, spiny shrub or small tree, up to 3–4m (10–13ft) tall and wide. The slightly toothed, oval leaves are arranged in pairs opposite each other and are concentrated more towards the ends of young shoots, leaving a fair bit of bare stem showing – each shoot has a strong spine at the tip. In May it bears clusters of yellowish green flowers near the tips of the shoots, followed by berries that ripen to shiny black in autumn. Buckthorn leaves are one of the chief food plants of caterpillars of the brimstone butterfly (the male butterfly is bright yellow, females are paler). It is inadvisable for humans to eat the berries because of their powerful medicinal properties.

HABITAT Downs, wasteland, hedgerows and edges of woodland on chalk or limestone, mostly in southern and central England.

6 Box
Buxus sempervirens

More familiar to gardeners as an evergreen hedging plant, box is a British native that still grows wild at a few locations, the best known of which – Box Hill – is in Surrey. Usually seen as an untidy bush a few metres high and the same across, box can also form a small, rounded tree up to 6m (20ft) high. The leaves are easily recognized by anyone familiar with the garden plants: small, dark green and roughly oval, with pointed tips and a deep fold along the central vein. Flowers appear in the leaf axils in April; they are tiny, fluffy clusters of yellow anthers round a green female style, followed by bluish green, pea-like fruit capsules with 3 small points at the tip, ripening to black at the end of summer.

HABITAT Chalky hillsides.

7 Wild privet
Ligustrum vulgare

The narrow-leaved wild privet is our native species, not to be confused with the better-known, oval-leaved privet from Japan (*Ligustrum ovalifolium*), which is used for garden hedging. It is a semi-evergreen shrub with narrow, pointed leaves, 3–5cm (1½–2in) long, and from May to June bears loose, conical clusters of small, strongly scented white flowers followed by small, black, pea-like (poisonous) berries.

Wild privet (*L. vulgare*) was used as a hedging plant in Elizabethan gardens, but it fell from favour once the more lush-looking, round-leaved privet (*L. ovalifolium*) was introduced during Victorian times. Our native plant did not retain its fresh green appearance in winter, and even shed its leaves if the weather was particularly severe. Japanese privet was the choice of the middle classes for planting round suburban villas. However, since wild privet was easily raised from readily available seed, it continued to be used by thrifty country gardeners and is still sometimes seen as a garden hedge.

HABITAT Lightly wooded hillsides in chalky or limestone regions of the British Isles.

8 Old man's beard
Clematis vitalba

Also known as traveller's joy, this well-known wild clematis makes a large, untidy climber, to 20m (65ft) high, with leaves very similar to those of a garden clematis, but smaller and sparser. It has clusters of insignificant, petal-less flowers consisting of short, cream stamens surrounded by small, arching green bracts in July and August. The flowers are shortly followed by the familiar, fluffy seedheads in late summer and autumn.

HABITAT Grows through hedgerows and trees in chalky or limestone areas, particularly in Wales and the south of England.

9 Burnet rose
Rosa pimpinellifolia

This is a rather uncommon wild rose. It has small-to-medium-sized, single, white, 5-petalled flowers carried at the start of summer, from May to July, followed by blueberry-sized hips that ripen to black in late summer to early autumn, with 5 long sepals sticking out of the end. The bushes are low and spreading, 60–90cm

(24–36in) high; they are also very prickly, with dark stems bearing 2 types of prickles – longer, back-curved 'climbing' spines, and stiff, straight bristles that are mixed among them. The compound leaves are made up of 7–9 small, oval, slightly toothed leaflets, arranged in pairs along the stem with a single leaf at the end.

HABITAT Sandy or chalky soils, especially near the coast, also in sand dunes and at fairly high altitudes on limestone hills.

10 Clustered bellflower
Campanula glomerata

The clustered bellflower is a perennial plant with loose clusters of upright stems, to 30cm (12in) tall, bearing elongated, oval leaves arranged alternately. It flowers from May to September, when each stem is topped with a tight cluster of upward-facing, purple-blue, bell-shaped flowers.

HABITAT Locally common on downs and chalky grasslands throughout the British Isles except the far north.

11 Horseshoe vetch

Hippocrepis comosa

Horseshoe vetch is a perennial plant in the pea family. It forms a ground-hugging mat 20–30cm (8–12in) wide, or a loose, untidy mound up to 20cm (8in) high and the same wide, growing from a central rootstock. The weak stems have ladder-like, compound leaves arranged alternately along them. The plant flowers from May to August, bearing loose rings of pale yellow flowers near the tip of each stem. After flowering, the distinctive seedpods make for easy identification – they are slender, approximately 2cm (¾in) long, and are strongly spiralled.

HABITAT Grasslands, downs and grassy hillsides, particularly in chalky and limestone landscapes.

12 Salad burnet

Sanguisorba minor

This is a small, clump-forming perennial, 15–30cm (6–12in) high and wide, with pairs of toothed leaves arranged opposite each other to make ladder-like, compound leaves set along faintly reddish tinged stems. The flowers, seen from May to September, are like a cluster of small green blobs with reddish bristles at the tips of the stems; the flowers later dry to a brownish shade. Salad burnet is sometimes grown as a garden herb for its cucumber-flavoured leaves used in salads.

HABITAT Downs and dry, grassy, limestone countryside.

13 Perforate St John's wort

Hypericum perforatum

This common perennial forms rather stiffly upright clumps, usually 30–60cm (12–24in) high, with short sideshoots growing at regular intervals from the main stem and bearing pairs of small, oval leaves arranged opposite each other. Pale yellow flowers are produced from June to September on sideshoots near the tips of the main stems; they are 2.5cm (1in) in diameter with 5 petals. Under a hand lens you may see a row of faint black dots round the edge of each petal, and tiny, translucent dots on the leaves.

HABITAT Wasteland, scrub, grassland, bottoms of hedges and around the edges of fields and woodland, especially in chalk or limestone landscapes.

14 Large wild thyme

Thymus pulegioides

From May to August, the tips of the stems of this unusual, rather upright perennial, usually 12–15cm (4¾–6in) high, are clustered with small pink flowers much loved by bees. It has small, pointed-oval leaves, clustered at intervals along the rather wiry stems, which are roughly rectangular in cross-section. The plant is strongly aromatic when crushed.

HABITAT Dry, sunny chalk hills and downs, mainly in southern England and East Anglia.

Chalk and limestone countryside

Limestone landscapes and chalk downs may be a tad short of 'larger' wildlife, such as birds and mammals, predominantly because of the lack of cover, but they more than make up for it when it comes to interesting wildflowers. A lot of rare and unusual flowers can be found in these habitats and very often they are species that grow nowhere else, so a day's botanizing can prove very rewarding.

15 Rock rose
Helianthemum nummularium
This is a fairly common subshrub
that forms a very loose, open mat,
15–30cm (6–12in) in height and
spread. The leaves are small and
oval, arranged in pairs and sparsely
dotted along the stems. The yellow,
buttercup-like flowers are borne
from May to September, each one
growing on a short stalk near the
tips of the main stems.
HABITAT Dry, sunny, well-drained
places from grassy downs to rocky
hillsides, often on chalk and
limestone (though not restricted to
them) throughout the British Isles,
except northern Scotland.

16 Bloody cranesbill
Geranium sanguineum
The parent of many garden
cultivars, this unusual perennial
cranesbill has instantly
recognizable, typical hardy-
geranium foliage. It is a low-
growing, loose, spreading plant,
with a height and spread of
10–20cm (4–8in) and very deeply
cut leaves. The large, 5-petalled
magenta flowers, up to 3cm (1¼in)
in diameter, are produced from
June to August.
HABITAT Meadows and grassy
hillsides in limestone landscapes
of northern and western Britain,
but not on chalk hills or downs.

17 Kidney vetch
Anthyllis vulneraria
This fairly common, chalk-loving
perennial, up to 30cm (12in) high,
is frequently found growing
among grasses, which provide
support for its floppy stems. Its
silky textured, compound leaves
consist of several pairs of small,
lance-shaped leaflets arranged
opposite each other, with a single,
much larger terminal leaflet at the
tip. From June to September it
bears roughly spherical heads of
pea-like flowers, usually yellow but
they may be creamish, pinkish,
orange or red-tinged, with a ring
of green bracts round their base.
Old flowers dry out to a brownish
shade and are retained on the
plants for some time. Kidney vetch
is the food plant of the small blue
butterfly caterpillar.
HABITAT Dry, chalky grassland
and hillsides, particularly on
downs and round the coast
including cliff-tops.

18 Hoary plantain
Plantago media
Although it might, at first glance,
be mistaken for the greater
plantain that grows as a common
weed in lawns, the hoary plantain
is an altogether more upmarket
plant. A perennial to 30cm (12in)
high, including flowers, and
10–15cm (4–6in) across, it makes a
rosette of large, rounded leaves
with a light frosting of fine white
hairs (hence the name, as the hairs
resemble hoar frost). From May to
August it has tall, straight stems
topped by long green heads that
carry a haze of soft, spiky flowers
with lavender-pink anthers, which
stand out quite well from a
distance. (The anthers of the
greater plantain are deeper purple,
fading to brown, and it lacks the
hoary hairs on the leaves.)
HABITAT Grassland on chalk and
limestone landscapes throughout
most of the British Isles, but less
common in Scotland and
northern England.

Limestone pavements

Certain areas within our oldest limestone landscapes are noted for their limestone pavements. These are spectacular geological features that look very much the way a patch of muddy clay soil does when it dries out fast in summer – flat, and covered in a series of squarish slabs with cracks in between. Limestone pavements happen on a huge scale, with many acres of vast stone blocks fissured with steep, narrow ravines.

They were created during the ice ages, when the weight of the massive glacier on top was so great that it caused stress fractures in the underlying rock. The result was the extraordinary, shattered, rocky sheets you see

tough trees and shrubs can survive, and even they appear rather stunted. But if you look down into the deep fissures or 'grykes', where conditions are humid and sheltered, you'll find a fair range of plants, including bloody cranesbill, bird's foot trefoil, herb Robert, holly fern, fragrant orchid and hart's tongue fern, growing in pockets of soil. Limestone pavements also house rare flowers found almost nowhere else in the British Isles, including orchids such as the dark red helleborine and autumn lady's tresses. It's plants like these that the enthusiasts are excited about and are prepared to make a special trip to see.

ABOVE LEFT The ancient, windswept limestone pavements of Ingleborough, in the Yorkshire Dales.
ABOVE RIGHT Bird's foot trefoil flourishing in the 'grykes' in the limestone pavement of the Burren, County Clare, Ireland.

today in the Yorkshire Dales at Malham and Ingleborough, in Lancashire at Gait's Barrow in Silverdale, and in the Burren in County Clare, western Ireland. There are also a few areas of limestone pavement in the Lake District and North Wales.

Although the surface seems quite hard, bare and lifeless, limestone pavements are, in fact, a very specialist habitat for plant life. On the surface, the wind whistles over the top of the blocky stone 'clints', so only a few very

Today, limestone pavements cover less of the countryside than they did 150 years ago, because of the Victorian craze for rockeries. This passion for a garden feature that emulated nature resulted in a lot of limestone slabs being ripped up and transported to the gardens of the gentry countrywide. Mercifully, that trend has now been halted and, justifiably, there is now legislation in place to ensure that limestone pavements are protected.

19 Bird's foot trefoil
Lotus corniculatus

This is a common and widespread wildflower in the pea family, with low, spreading, straggly, often prostrate stems, 5cm (2in) high and 10–30cm (4–12in) long, sparsely furnished with clover-like leaves. From May to September it bears bright yellow, pea-like flowers, sometimes streaked with orange or red, arranged in a ring round the tips of the main stems, like a wagon wheel. These are followed by long, narrow seedpods that again splay out from the tip of the stem in the shape of a bird's foot (hence the common name).
HABITAT Dry, sunny banks, grassland, downs, hillsides and roadside verges, usually growing among grass.

22 Eyebright
Euphrasia officinalis

This is a small, common, upright or slightly trailing, branching annual, up to 30cm (12in), which is semi-parasitic on grasses and several common grassland plants such as plantain. It has slender stems with short, wide leaves that have deeply jagged edges, and from July to September it bears flowers in the leaf axils around the tips of the stems. The flowers are under 1cm (⅜in) long, each comprising a small white upper petal marked with a large, light purple spot and a larger, white lower petal with 3 lobes, each with a cleft up the centre and patterned with fine, purplish lines. There is a yellow spot near the centre of the flower.
HABITAT Grassy downs, hills, fields and heaths, particularly on chalky or limestone soils. Occurs throughout the British Isles but is less common in Scotland.

Derivation of names

Some wildflowers include the word 'lady's' in their name, for example lady's bedstraw, lady's mantle and lady's tresses. People often assume the word should be spelt 'ladies' but 'lady's' is correct, since the plants have been named because of ancient legends associating the plant with the Virgin Mary, Our Lady. Lady's bedstraw is believed to be the plant that Mary laid on as her bed in the stable in Bethlehem, where Jesus was born.

20 Lady's bedstraw
Galium verum

A common if unspectacular wildflower, this is a small, sprawling perennial, 15–30cm (6–12in) high, with floppy stems that are square in cross-section, like goosegrass stems, and sparse foliage. The stems carry widely spaced whorls of about 10 small, linear-shaped leaves that circle the stem like a jester's collar and branch towards the tip, where the tiny yellow, 4-petalled flowers are clustered in large, loose heads in July and August.
HABITAT Fairly dry pastures, grassland and downs.

21 Rough hawkbit
Leontodon hispidus

Also known as greater hawkbit, this upright, rosette-shaped perennial superficially resembles a dandelion but is more delicate-looking. Its leaves are like those of a dandelion but they are less strongly toothed; the surface texture is rough like sandpaper, and unlike those of dandelions the leaves do not leak white sap when broken. The flowers, carried from July to September, are yellow, to 4cm (1½in) across, with a ring of ray-florets round the outer edge and the centre filled with shorter petals, with a small, greyish calyx at the base. They are followed by dandelion-type seedheads.
HABITAT Common in chalk and limestone landscapes but sometimes also seen elsewhere in grassy places.

construction is visible when seen through a magnifying glass – what appear to be petals are in fact long, coloured sepals, with the real petals folded inside.

The common milkwort's rarer relation, the chalk milkwort (*Polygala calcarea*), has prostrate stems, to 15cm (6in), with dark blue flowers from May to July. Unlike the common milkwort, it is found only on chalk.
HABITAT Grassland, mainly on downs of southern England but also occasionally on heaths and behind dunes near the coast.

25 Small scabious
Scabiosa columbaria
A favourite of butterflies and bees, this is an attractive, small-to-medium-sized wildflower, 25–70cm (10–28in) high, with a loose rosette of leaves at the base, from which grow wiry green stems bearing a few sparse, feathery leaves near the ground. Each branching stem is topped with a single, small, pin-cushion-like, pale lavender-blue flower, 1cm (⅜in) across.
HABITAT Close-cropped turf in downs throughout the British Isles, except northern Scotland.

23 English stonecrop
Sedum anglicum
Also known as wall pepper, this is an unmistakable, sun-loving, drought-tolerant, succulent plant made up of short, fat leaves strung on slender, creeping stems. It forms a greyish, evergreen mat, tinged with scarlet, that grows to 3–10cm (1¼–4in) high and spreads up to 30cm (12in) or more. The flowers, borne from June to September, are small, white, upward-facing 'stars', with 5 petals grouped loosely at the tips of the short stems.
HABITAT On drystone walls, rocky hillsides and arid slopes, mainly in western Britain.

24 Common milkwort
Polygala vulgaris
This is a fairly common but easily overlooked, clump-forming perennial, to 20cm (8in) high, with upright stems that are woody at the very base, and lance-shaped leaves, 1cm (⅜in) long, arranged alternately up the stem. It flowers from May to September, bearing short spikes of small, slightly fringed flowers ranging in colour from light blue to pink, mauve or white; like the leaves, these are arranged alternately along the stem. Their curious internal

26 Sainfoin
Onobrychis viciifolia
Sainfoin is a most attractive member of the pea family, with showy, almost lupin-like flowers from May to September. It is an airy, upright yet floppy perennial, to 50cm (20in) high, often semi-supported by the longish grass it grows in. The leaves are delicate-looking and ladder-like, made up of many pairs of small, faintly downy, oval leaflets, tapering off slightly in size towards the tip. The flowers are bright pink, clustered in short, conical groups at the tips of the stems; each individual flower looks like a conical snapdragon in close-up. The seedpods are round and slightly spiny, about 5mm (⅛in) across.
HABITAT Locally fairly common on grasslands and roadside verges in chalk and limestone landscapes throughout Wales and the southern half of England.

27 Stemless thistle
Cirsium acaule

This is a low thistle, with prickly leaves arranged in a rough, ground-hugging rosette to 15cm (6in) wide. Throughout late summer, from July to September, the centre of this plant sends out a series of large, stemless, magenta thistle flowers, to 4cm (1½in) wide, each with a big green, scaly, pineapple-shaped knob at the base.
HABITAT Short turf in chalk and limestone regions.

28 Carline thistle
Carlina vulgaris

This is a slightly unusual biennial thistle that starts as a rosette of thistly leaves with rather weak or even soft spikes and produces its flowering spike in the second year. The upright stem, 10–30cm (4–12in) high, grows through the centre of the plant, branching towards the top, with each stem-tip carrying (usually) only one large, tough, yellow thistle flower just over 3cm (1¼in) wide. The seedheads, which dry to a rosette of buff-coloured spikes round a yellowish brown centre, are held well into winter on the dead stems.
HABITAT Very well-drained, sandy, chalky or limestone areas, also along the coast behind dunes or along cliff-top paths, throughout lowland areas in the British Isles.

29 Common spotted orchid
Dactylorhiza fuchsii

With its strongly spotted foliage, and flowers borne between June and August, this is the alkaline-soil-loving equivalent of the heath spotted orchid (which is found only on acid soils). It is an upright, single-stemmed perennial plant, 15–45cm (6–17½in) tall, with 2 or 3 rather broad, arching leaves that clasp round the stem at their base, each with a regular pattern of large, roundish, purple-black spots; the leaves further up the stem are narrow and almost grass-like but still spotted. At the top of the stem is a long, cylindrical flower spike made up of many small pink flowers heavily spotted with mauve. Individual flowers consist of a small, arching hood flanked by a pair of small, upward-curving petals; the large lip has a single tooth in the centre. Common orchids tend to grow in colonies.
HABITAT Locally common growing in rough grass in chalk and limestone landscapes, in places with fairly poor, undisturbed and unimproved ground.

30 Pyramidal orchid
Anacamptis pyramidalis

The characteristic pyramidal shape of the young flowerhead makes this showy wild orchid relatively easy to identify. It grows in colonies, with individuals spaced fairly well apart. Plants are slender and upright, having a single, strong green stem with usually 4 or 5 slightly ribbed leaves, strongly folded upwards either side of the midrib to make a boat shape, clasped round the stem at the base. From June to August it bears spikes of small, mauve-purple, strangely musky, scented flowers, which are tightly grouped in a short, conical shape when young; the spike gradually loosens, becoming more rounded as the flowers open out fully. Individual flowers have a very small hood with a small, down-curved petal on each side and a 3-toothed lip – a complete flower looks rather like a tiny, mauve, 3-legged man.
HABITAT Chalk and limestone landscapes, growing in grass in quite large colonies in some areas.

OPPOSITE The exotic-looking bee orchid is easily identified by the bumblebee-like lip on the flower.

31

31 Fragrant orchid
Gymnadenia conopsea

This is a rather rare orchid, which is locally common in some years, flowering from June to August. The plant is upright and single-stemmed, 5–30cm (2–12in) tall, with 5 or 6 long, narrow, keel-shaped leaves, rather like coarse grasses seen edgeways-on, which clasp right round the stem at their base. The flowers are bright rosy-pink, arranged in a tall, upright spike, with a clove scent that is most noticeable in the evening. Individual flowers of the fragrant orchid have a long, conspicuous, curving spur at the back, a very loose, open hood flanked by 2 short, floppy, horizontal petals, and a broad lip, which is roughly 3-toothed and curved slightly inwards round the edges.
HABITAT Old chalk grassland.

32 Bee orchid
Ophrys apifera

The bee orchid grows in particular sites in colonies, which fluctuate considerably in size from year to year. Upright in habit, it produces a single stem, 15–40cm (6–16in) high, with 4 or 5 broad, oval, ribbed leaves clasped around the base. The large flowers, borne from June to July, resemble bumblebees so much that male bees are sometimes fooled into mating with them. Each flower consists of 3 pale-pink-to-off-white, triangular petals and a brown, furry central lip, which resembles the bumblebee's body, with a pale green 'head' and pair of 'forelegs'.
HABITAT Short, poor grass, mostly in chalk and limestone landscapes.

33

33 Dark red helleborine
Epipactis atrorubens

Flowering in June and July, this is a very rare wild orchid. It is an upright, single-stemmed plant, up to 30–45cm (12–17½in) tall, with a downy, maroon-tinged stem and leaves, which are keeled and oval, clasped round the stem of the plant at their base. The scented, nodding flowers may be greenish to maroon, and are arranged in a long, loose spike. Individual flowers are made up of 5 small, rounded, inward-curving petals, with a yellow blob in the centre of the flower and a tiny, darker lip at the base, with a maroonish calyx.
HABITAT Found locally in grassland or rocky limestone landscapes and in the walls of 'grykes' in limestone pavements, only in northern and western Britain and Ireland.

Identifying orchids

Wild orchid plants are present only in the flowering season – they die down soon after the flowers are over, so timing can help to eliminate some species, as can presence or lack of spots on the foliage. The flowers of most orchids are superficially very similar: don't rely on colour alone when identifying them, because coloration of some species can be variable. Take a hand lens with you and examine the shape of the individual flowers closely. Notice in particular the pattern of spots, if any, on the flowers, and the shape of the hood and lip and any spurs or long, trailing 'tongues'. Make a careful sketch so you can check the details against close-ups in a reference book. Never pick orchid flowers to study back home – you are removing the plant's seed-making capabilities.

32

35 Hart's tongue fern
Phyllitis scolopendrium

This is a well-known and easily identified evergreen fern. Each plant makes a tall, splaying urn or shuttlecock shape, 30–45cm (12–17½in) high and the same across, of large, fairly tough, deep green, tongue-shaped leaves growing out from a central crown, in which the paler green, young fronds can be seen unfurling in spring and summer. Plants eventually form large clumps.
HABITAT Found in a wide range of habitats, sometimes in drier conditions than many ferns tolerate, often inhabiting walls and damp, shady places down the 'grykes' of limestone pavements. It is not restricted to limestone or chalk landscapes, though it is often common there.

36 Common morel
Morchella esculenta

This is an easily identified but bizarre-looking toadstool, 5–10cm (2–4in) high, with a white stalk and a spherical or slightly conical, honey-coloured, honeycombed top instead of the traditional mushroom-like cap. It is a much sought-after edible species found only in spring.
HABITAT In chalk or limestone districts, usually in quite open

34 Autumn lady's tresses
Spiranthes spiralis

Easily overlooked, this is an uncommon, small and inconspicuous wild orchid that flowers in August and September. Each plant is a rosette of wide, oval, ribbed, rather plantain-like leaves, from which grows a short flower spike, 10–15cm (4–6in) long, bearing tiny, wispy white flowers that grow out from green 'scales' that spiral round the spike. At first glance, the spike can give the impression of being an unusual grass seedhead.
HABITAT Downland, dry grassy meadows and sandy places, in chalky regions.

ground that has been fairly recently disturbed by cultivation or earthworks, or where there has been a fire.

37 St George's mushroom
Calocybe gambosa

Emerging at the end of April – around St George's Day (23rd April) – this medium-sized, edible mushroom is short-lived, dying down for the year by mid-June. It has a thick, cream cap, 5–15cm (2–6in) wide, with a pronounced, mealy scent, white to off-white gills and spores, and a white stem with no ring and no thickened fleshy base. Rarely solitary, it usually

grows in rows, rings or segments of rings. It is a good edible species that resembles a cultivated mushroom; however, it is easily confused with a very similar poisonous toadstool that grows in the same habitats. Picking is best left to experts.
HABITAT Well-drained grassland on chalky ground, particularly evident on downland.

Also found on limestone or chalk hills and downs

Adder (see p.144)
Brown hare (see p.199)
Buzzard (see p.130)
Cowslip (see p.204)
Green tiger beetle (see p.143)
Green woodpecker (see p.83)
Kestrel (see p.298)
Rabbit (see p.278)
Red-legged partridge (see p.270)
Rook (see p.191)
Silver-studded blue (see p.141)
Six-spot burnet moth (see p.194)
Skylark (see p.191)
Starling (see p.304)
Tree pipit (see p.137)
Weasel (see p.278)
Wild carrot (see p.75)
Wild strawberry (see p.120)
Yellowhammer (see p.272)

Fields and meadows

Today's patchwork of arable
fields and grassy meadows is
a fairly recent development
that came about when
agriculture became more
profitable. Farmland has
always had a fairly chequered
history as a habitat for wildlife,
but at last there are signs that
we are starting to farm the
land in harmony with nature.

Primitive farming

Some 6000 years ago, Stone-Age people started cutting down the trees that made up Britain's ancient woods to form clearings, which they used for cultivating crops and keeping livestock. These were the very first fields. Once the land had been cleared, it was either sown with field crops, or it was roughly enclosed and allowed to grow its own covering of wild grasses and wildflowers to use for grazing. The presence of such an unusual concentration of seeds, grasses and flowers in these primitive clearings attracted large numbers of insects, rodents and their predators, as well as wild herbivores looking for food, so the first fields were more like nature reserves. At this time, there was no way of keeping wildlife out, so like it or not people had to share their crops.

Prehistoric fields would have looked a bit strange to us – they were not the nice, neat, rectangular shapes with straight edges that we expect today. People who had only basic stone tools and manpower to clear the ground tended to take the easy route round obstacles like huge rocks, and avoided unusable areas such as bogs when they needed to be enclosed to hold livestock. This meant that fields were small with fairly irregular outlines, and they remained pretty much this shape and size well into Anglo-Saxon times.

Medieval strip farming

By the time of the Domesday Book in 1086, big landowners – the church, the crown, and noblemen – had organized all the best farmland into the open-field strip-farming system that persisted throughout the medieval period. The strip-farming system came about as a means of ensuring fair shares for all. Landowners naturally didn't farm the land themselves – most of it was rented out to tenants who did the work and paid their rents in kind by handing over a percentage of the crops as 'tithes' – hence the tithe barns, which you can still see dotted across the countryside. Strip farming first developed around settlements, hamlets and villages so that workers didn't have too far to walk to work. But since the ground near a village would vary in quality, each tenant was allocated several small plots of land scattered round the locality, so everyone had a mixture of good and mediocre ground.

To make this system work efficiently, the farmland was divided up into strips, all growing the same crop; each strip was then divided up into smaller fields, which were rented by different tenants. This arrangement worked very well, mainly because it was organized cooperatively – everyone helping each other out at busy times. Some strips were put down to long-term grazing, while others were used for arable crops on

a strict rotation system. Since the same crop wasn't grown in the same ground again for at least four years, they'd avoid a build-up of pests or diseases by natural means, long before the advent of pesticides.

To restore soil fertility in the absence of fertilizers, entire strips would be left fallow every few years. They would be given over to foraging livestock, which allowed them to be manured and recover their fertility at the same time as weeds and pests were eradicated – again, using natural means. Pigs and poultry do a brilliant job at removing roots and seeds, as well as soil pests, slugs, snails, grubs and larvae. Without their knowing it, medieval peasants were the first organic farmers, although the strip-farming system meant that the countryside looked very different from the way it does now, as you can see from medieval woodcuts.

After the Black Death killed one-third of the population, many medieval hamlets were abandoned. Today all that's left of these 'lost villages' are the outlines of buildings, seen quite clearly from the air in dry summers. Landowners found it hard to get labour or find tenants, so much arable farmland was allowed to revert to grassland and was used for grazing sheep. The market for wool grew, and as sheep became more valuable, strip farming was dropped in good sheep-rearing areas, particularly the Midlands. Where this happened, the land was divided up into more efficient fields surrounded by secure boundaries such as walls or hedges. As the population slowly recovered, the demand for farmland rose, and by the 1700s a lot of the more marginal land, such as heaths and wetlands, was brought into cultivation.

The Industrial Revolution

The eighteenth century saw the end of the strip-farming system and the start of the patchwork of fields that make up today's landscape. Farming was paying handsomely – at least it was for the large landowners, whose income came from rents paid by tenants who did all the manual work. This was

PREVIOUS PAGES A flower-filled summer meadow (main picture), and a meadow brown feeding on a marsh thistle (small picture).
BELOW LEFT The romantic, landscaped gardens at Blenheim Palace, in Oxfordshire. They were designed by Lancelot 'Capability' Brown, who created naturalized woodland, a serpentine lake and grassy clearings.
BELOW CENTRE Prairie farming (here, in Norfolk) creates its own problems with erosion, caused by strong winds.
BELOW RIGHT A patchwork of fields at Abney, in Derbyshire – so typical of traditional English countryside.

the time when the gentry were rebuilding their old family homes or moving away from manor houses on the edges of medieval villages and building themselves grand country houses in beauty spots. And to go with their newly improved country houses they wanted stunning views.

The land round the large house was treated to a massive make-over. Landscape designers such as William Kent and Lancelot 'Capability' Brown were called upon to restyle the grounds into romantic visions of lakes, follies and classical-style ruins amid rolling grass meadows and knolls topped with clumps of trees. Round the edge of the grounds there was sometimes a ha-ha – a deep ditch with one steep, vertical side reinforced with a wall – this was designed to keep livestock at bay but be invisible from the Big House, making it look as if your garden ran off into the surrounding farmland, which was itself restyled. Eyesores, such as dilapidated villages, decaying hovels or unsightly farm buildings, were simply cleared away, and open fields were enclosed and divided up with hedges. The countryside became a series of picturesque fields populated by prize-winning cattle and horses that were as much about one-upmanship as genuine agriculture. And since landowners had nothing much to do other than collect rents and socialize, they took to country sports. Fox-hunting became all the rage, and the new layout of fields, criss-crossed by hedges and dotted with small copses, provided the perfect habitat for foxes.

But although the gentry had never had it so good, farm workers weren't faring quite so well. As the Industrial Revolution took off, many of them moved to the towns in search of better wages. The huge advances in house-building, roads and railways during the reign of Queen Victoria left the countryside way behind. Farming suffered a further decline; Helen Allingham's charming watercolours of quaint cottages with roses round the door depicted a romance that didn't exist – in real life, farm workers scraped by; it was a pitiful existence. If you want to understand what the day-to-day life of a farm worker's family of the time was really like, read Flora Thompson's *Lark Rise to Candleford*, set in Oxfordshire – rough doesn't begin to describe it. With no money for reinvestment, farming stood still. It stayed unprofitable into the start of the twentieth century.

The big wartime self-sufficiency drive

It wasn't until the First World War that the government became concerned about farming. With so much of our food by now being imported from abroad, and merchant shipping at risk from enemy action, we could easily have been starved into submission. A system of subsidies was introduced to persuade farmers to step up production. By the Second World War, farmers were required by the War Agriculture Committee to plough up ancient pastures, and a lot of heathlands were brought into cultivation.

Farms at this time were still the traditional kind that produced a bit of everything – they kept some livestock and grew some arable crops. Sheep were turned out to feed on the stubble fields after the harvest, straw was used for bedding down livestock, and this plus manure from the cattle stalls was spread in autumn and ploughed into the land, so farms were fairly self-sufficient and had relatively little impact on the environment.

But after the Second World War, agriculture had to change. Labour was in short supply, so farms became more mechanized and horses were replaced by tractors. As tractors and combine harvesters became larger and more powerful, hedges were taken out to create bigger fields that allowed the new machinery to work efficiently. Now, instead of growing a bit of everything, farms began specializing in a single crop to justify the high price of the machinery needed to handle it. This in turn meant using large quantities of pesticides and fertilizers to keep yields high.

Farmers with large, flat areas of land went in for grain or sugar beet, which suited large-scale cultivation methods, thus creating the prairie-land scenery of much of East Anglia. The land that was unsuitable for field crops was used for intensive livestock production – animals were kept close together under cover, which created a massive disposal problem. Today, somewhat ironically, manure is classed as industrial waste. Mono-cropping, plus the loss of hedges and heavy use of agricultural pesticides and weedkillers, brought about a huge drop in the numbers of wildflowers, insects and birds in the countryside, since they are all dependent on each other. By the mid-twentieth century, the countryside was in crisis as far as wildlife was concerned – a fact that is illustrated in Rachel Carson's excellent book, *Silent Spring*.

Wildlife-friendly farming

Over the last 30 years, enlightenment has set in. The green movement, plus the rising demand for organic food, have pricked the nation's conscience and made it much more aware of its responsibilities to the land and to the future of British wildlife. Despite frequent complaints that such a system cannot work, the opposite has proved to be the case.

Large estates, for instance the Duchy of Cornwall, under the leadership of HRH The Prince of Wales, have led the way. The Countryside Stewardship Scheme has been introduced, whereby farmers are, in effect, paid to manage the countryside rather than being expected to earn their living entirely from selling crops; and various groups such as the Farming and Wildlife Advisory Group provide advice on 'going green' to farmers. Although farming incomes have fallen dramatically, especially since the epidemics of foot-and-mouth and mad-cow disease, it now seems there is a greater willingness to consider wildlife. All over the country, headlands are being sown with wildflower mixtures, and wider margins are being left at the edges of fields as conservation areas. Farmers have long been aware of their responsibilities as custodians of the land, and it seems that now there is a chance that the Government, too, can play its part in encouraging such stewardship.

Meanwhile, many farmers have diversified into tourism. This may mean anything from taking in B&B guests to turning small fields into touring caravan sites or converting unwanted barns and outhouses into tourist cabins and inviting holidaying families to watch the lambing. One of the biggest success stories comes from Wales, where farmers discovered that 'townies' would travel miles to watch the wild red kites being fed on scraps of offal. The kite population has soared, and the farmers have found themselves an unusual new cash crop.

Conservation headlands, such as this poppy-filled one in Norfolk, are now sanctuaries for wildflowers and wildlife.

1 Lapwing
Vanellus vanellus

The classic farmland birds, lapwings are often seen in flocks. They have a glossy, dark green back with iridescent purple patches (particularly noticeable in bright sunlight), white underparts and a wide black band across the top of the breast. The face is white with a black beak, with 'false eyelashes' under and sometimes also above each eye, and a conspicuous, curved, upswept plume of black feathers (longer in the male) extending back from the back of the head. The wings are broad and blunt-ended, unlike those of other waders. In flight, lapwings flicker alternate black and white as the wings flap, so flocks appear to ripple. In spring, males display by making steep, twisting dives. Lapwings are also known as 'peewits' because of their fluctuating 'peeeee-wit' call.
HABITAT Pastures and farmland; also on inland and coastal salt marshes and muddy estuaries, especially in winter.

SIZE 30cm (12in)
EGGS 4, buff or greenish grey with dark brown spots
NEST Lays eggs in a scrape on the ground.
FOOD Insect larvae, worms and other small invertebrates, on or near the soil surface.

2 Corncrake
Crex crex

Once known as the land rail, this rare summer visitor has dark-streaked, rich brown camouflaged upperparts, a blue-grey breast and head with a sandy patch behind each eye, a dark-streaked brown crown and a short, pointed, sandy beak. In flight, the red-brown wings and long, trailing, dull olive-brown legs are visible. The call is a monotonously repeated 'crex, crex', like the rasping sound of a comb drawn across a piece of wood. After 150 or so years of decline numbers are slowly increasing, thanks to conservation measures.
HABITAT May–August: old-fashioned hayfields, restricted to a few areas on the western Scottish mainland and especially the Hebrides and parts of western Ireland. Winter: Africa.
SIZE 28cm (11in)
EGGS 8–12, beige with reddish brown mottling
NEST Shallow cup lined with leaves on the ground, in long grass.
FOOD Worms, insects.

3 Woodpigeon
Columba palumbus

Our largest pigeon, this is a familiar and very widespread bird. From a distance, it looks a uniform grey, but seen close up it has a blue-grey head and greyer back with pale pinkish breast, black-tipped, grey wings and a blue-grey tail with a broad black band at the tip. There is a prominent white patch on either side of the neck, just below an iridescent, blue-green patch on the nape. The eyes are yellow and the beak is yellow with a red-and-white base. The lovely song is a 5-note, husky 'coo-COO-coo, coo-coo'. One of the reasons that woodpigeons are so successful is that they have a long breeding season; given a mild winter, a good location or a town microclimate, they have been recorded breeding in every month of the year (up to 3 broods a year) and can continue raising families as late as September, though most breed between June and September.
HABITAT Mainly in arable farmland with trees and hedges, also in woodland and increasingly in towns and gardens.
SIZE 40cm (16in)
EGGS 2, white
NEST An inadequate-looking jumble of sticks arranged in a tree to make a loose, flattish platform.
FOOD Seeds, grain, soft young foliage, especially of brassica crops.
SIMILAR TO Feral pigeon, except this is found mostly in towns rather than the countryside, is smaller, usually overall pale blue-grey with a darker head and tail (the woodpigeon looks all grey) and has an iridescent, purple-and-green neck, no white collar, and 2 broad black wing-bars, also often a white rump.

4 Barn owl
Tyto alba

Hunting largely at night, this scarce but well-known, much-loved owl is most often seen as a ghostly white shape in car headlights. It hunts by flying low over the ground (so is often struck by tall vehicles) and pounces on rodents, then carries them off. Look for a pale golden-fawn bird with white underparts and a large, round head with a circular white face, large, round black eyes and a small, pale, curved beak. The muscular legs are clad in fine white feathers and end in strong, curved claws. It flies on totally silent wings and does not hoot or make 'too-whit, too-whoo' owl-calls, but it does make very loud, piercing shrieks, especially during courtship.
HABITAT Throughout the British Isles, in open farmland, grassland, parkland and coastal marshes.
SIZE 33cm (13in)
EGGS 4–6, white
NEST On ledges inside barns, in holes in trees, or in large nestboxes.
FOOD Mainly rodents, also shrews, bats and occasionally birds.

5 Little owl
Athene noctua

This scarce, dumpy owl – the smallest in Britain – is sometimes seen roosting on a post or on a wall in broad daylight. It has a white-dappled, grey-brown back and head, fawn underparts streaked brown, and a goggle-like face, with large yellow eyes under white 'bushy eyebrows'. At roost, the bird looks almost circular, but it can stretch upright – becoming long and thin if alarmed – and

may stretch its neck and weave from side to side or turn its head upside-down to view potential threats. It typically hunts from dusk to midnight and then again before dawn.
HABITAT Scattered throughout England, Wales and southernmost Scotland, on farmland or in open countryside with a few trees.
SIZE 22cm (8¾in)
EGGS 2–5, white
NEST In a hollow tree or a hole in rocks or cliffs, in a rabbit burrow, in an outbuilding or sometimes in a nestbox.
FOOD Insects, worms and other invertebrates, small rodents, birds.

6 Rook
Corvus frugilegus

Large flocks of these scruffy black, crow-sized birds, which make loud 'cawing' sounds, live in rowdy and quarrelsome colonies high up in tall trees. The birds are jet-black, with an iridescent, purplish sheen when seen in sunlight. Look for the bald area on the front of the face and mostly dark grey beak. The shaggy feathers round the legs make the rook look as if it is wearing baggy trousers.
HABITAT Farmland, parkland and around villages and towns but not city centres.
SIZE 45cm (17½in)
EGGS 3–5, pale bluish to grey-green, speckled darker grey and brown
NEST Large, untidy cup of sticks and twigs in large groups in tall tree tops; old nests are refurnished in spring and reused.

FOOD Mostly insects and larvae, also worms, cereal grains, roots, potatoes and berries.
SIMILAR TO Crows, which do not fly in really large flocks like rooks and are less angular. Look also for the bald face and grey beak of the rook (the base of the crow's beak is fully feathered and black, not pale).

7 Skylark
Alauda arvensis

The streaky-brown skylark is about halfway in size between a sparrow and a song thrush. Given a good view of a standing bird, you may see the short crest on top of the head, especially if it is raised. Although present year round, the bird is seen mostly in summer, silhouetted against the sky when on the wing, hovering in mid-air or soaring above an open field, pouring out its long, continuous, silvery, bubbling song. It never perches in trees. When disturbed on the ground, it often makes a short, fluttering flight and quickly lands again. Skylarks are far less common than they once were.

HABITAT Summer: open fields, grassland and downs but also heaths, moors and coastal marshes. Winter: congregates in flocks on the ground in fields.
SIZE 18cm (7in)
EGGS 3–5, white with brown speckles
NEST On the ground, in short grass.
FOOD Seeds, insects and other invertebrates.
SIMILAR TO Meadow pipit, which unlike the skylark has a high-pitched, squeaky call, wags its tail when walking and has a parabolic, parachuting song flight.

Owl left-overs

The parts of their prey that owls cannot digest – larger bones, claws, skulls and suchlike – are regurgitated in the form of small, greyish or blackish 'pellets', 1.5–7cm (⅝–2¾in) long. They can often be found at the foot of fence posts or other perches where the owls have rested in order to get rid of these indigestible remains.

8 Yellow wagtail
Motacilla flava

This is a yellow-and-greenish bird that resembles the much more frequently seen pied wagtail in shape and behaviour but has a shorter tail and is a summer visitor only. Look for the yellow face, throat, breast and underparts, dark-brown-and-white wings and olive-green back and top of head. The tail is blackish brown with white outer feathers.

HABITAT April–September: dampish farmland, fields, water meadows and moors. Winter: Africa.

SIZE 17cm (6¾in)

EGGS 4–6, beige, densely spotted with pale brown

NEST Neat cup of grass on the ground, hidden among vegetation.

FOOD Insects, especially flies and beetles, and other invertebrates.

SIMILAR TO Grey wagtail, which is found beside water, not in fields, and has a blue-grey head and back (rather than green). In summer, male grey wagtails have a black throat, unlike the yellow wagtail.

VARIATIONS Female is a duller, browner-tinged version of the male, juveniles have a brown head and back with a dark, speckled 'necklace' at the top of the breast.

9 Fieldfare
Turdus pilaris

These large, colourful thrushes are winter visitors that appear from autumn in flocks, often with redwings, then feed and move on.

They are sturdy, big-bellied birds, bigger and longer-tailed than the song thrush, with a grey head and white 'eyebrows', a grey rump, a chestnut-brown back and black wing-edges, wing-tips and tail. The breast is orange-buff and the underparts are heavily marked with black spots and chevrons; the beak is yellow with a black tip.

HABITAT October–May: farmland and parkland, especially where there are hedgerows with berries or ploughed fields with worms; in colder weather, may visit large gardens for berries or windfall apples. Summer: breed in northern and central Europe (a very few

pairs stay to breed in Britain).

SIZE 25cm (10in)

FOOD Insects and larvae, worms, berries and other fruit.

10 Redwing
Turdus iliacus

Redwings are small thrushes, seen in groups or small flocks from autumn to spring. They have a dark brown back, wings and head with conspicuous, creamy buff 'eyebrows'. The creamy buff breast and belly sides are heavily speckled dark brown; the lower belly, rear flanks and undertail are unmarked white. Look for the bright chestnut-red 'armpits': the colour

is so noticeable that people sometimes think they are song thrushes that have been injured and are bleeding.

HABITAT October–April: farmland, parkland and, in cold weather, large gardens. Summer: Iceland and Scandinavia (a very few pairs breed in northern Scotland).

SIZE 21cm (8¼in)

FOOD Insects, including grubs and worms, also eats berries and windfall apples.

OPPOSITE A skylark adult with its young demanding food in a nest under scarlet pimpernel, in Norfolk.

11 Tree sparrow
Passer montanus

Once a common countryside bird, the tree sparrow is now rare, owing mainly to loss of winter stubble fields. Both sexes have a black-streaked, chestnut-brown back and pale grey-buff underparts, an all-chestnut-brown hood over the upper half of the head, a white collar round the back of the neck and a black smudge in the centre of each 'cheek'. It is usually seen hopping jerkily on the ground, feeding in small groups; in winter, the tree sparrow mixes with finches and house sparrows.

HABITAT Throughout most of England, the southern half of Scotland and eastern Ireland, on farmland with open fields, in buildings and woodland, especially where farmers practise conservation measures.

SIZE 14cm (5½in)

EGGS 4–6, whitish with heavy brown speckles

NEST Pile of straw and grass in tree holes, crevices and nestboxes.

FOOD Insects, seeds.

SIMILAR TO Male house sparrow, which lacks the black 'cheek' patches and white collar and has a small grey cap rather than a brown hood on top of the head; also, it is a little bigger.

12 Corn bunting
Miliaria calandra

Seen in flocks in winter, this increasingly scarce, sparrow-like bird has a streaky-brown head, back and wings, a darker tail and a lighter beige breast and underparts, with dark speckling and streaks on the breast and flanks. When it is making short flights, the legs are often trailing. The birds are sometimes seen perching on wire fences or posts; look for a very upright stance, short tail and stout, finch-like beak.

HABITAT Mostly seen in southern and eastern England, in large, wide-open, prairie-like cornfields; in winter, larger flocks feed on stubble fields or rough grassland.

SIZE 18cm (7in)

EGGS 3–5, off-white with grey and dark brown blotches and squiggles

NEST Deep, loose cup of grass and roots, on the ground.

FOOD Mainly seeds; also insects.

SIMILAR TO Female or juvenile house sparrow, which is much smaller, less thickset and does not have the speckled breast. Skylark is the same size, but has a crest. Meadow pipit is slightly smaller, has a long, slim beak and rarely perches. However, both the skylark and meadow pipit have different display flights.

1 Cinnabar moth
Tyria jacobaeae

This is a small-to-medium-sized moth (4.5cm/1¾in wingspan) that flies by day and night with weak, fluttering movements. The forewings are black, conspicuously marked with a scarlet stripe along the leading edges and 2 large scarlet spots along the adjacent edge; the hind wings are orange-red with a black border.

HABITAT Common in unmanaged meadows and wild, grassy places where ragwort (the food plant of the caterpillar) grows, mainly in Wales and southern England but scattered elsewhere in Britain, from May to July.

CATERPILLAR Far better known than the parent – boldly striped with black and-orange-yellow rings, like a football jersey, found in large colonies, mainly on ragwort, but also sometimes groundsel, from June to August.

2 Six-spot burnet moth
Zygaena filipendulae

This is a small and common, day-flying moth, which has rather narrow wings (wingspan 3–4cm/1¼–1½in). The forewings are deep glossy green to black, patterned with 6 red spots on each wing (there is also a five-spot burnet moth, *Zygaena lonicerae*). The hind wings are matching red with a faint black border round the edges. Adults feed predominantly on nectar of knapweed and scabious, but also other flowers.

HABITAT Throughout the British Isles, in downland and grassy meadows on chalky soils, and sometimes in gardens, from May or June to August.

CATERPILLAR Light yellow, with several long, straight rows of black dots, found on bird's foot trefoil from August to May.

3 Green-veined white
Picris napi

The green-veined white is a medium-sized (4–5cm/1½–2in wingspan) white butterfly with faint green veins outlined in grey patterning the undersides of the wings. The uppersides of the wing-tips are smudged faintly with black; the male has a single black spot and the female has 2.
HABITAT Widespread throughout the British Isles, in ditches, damp meadows, hedgerows and woodland edges, in May or June with a second generation in July or August.
CATERPILLAR Green with a row of yellow dots down each side, found June to September, feeding mainly on charlock or garlic mustard (unlike 'cabbage whites', which are pests to gardeners, the green-veined white isn't found on cultivated brassicas).

4 Orange tip
Anthocharis cardamines

Seen in April and May, the male of this common white butterfly (4.5cm/1¾in wingspan) can be identified by the warm orange tips edged in brown on each forewing. The female looks very much like a 'cabbage white', as she lacks the orange tips and has dark grey wing-tips instead. The undersides of the wings on both sexes are very

pale green – this tells the females apart from 'cabbage whites'. Adults feed on the nectar of a wide range of flowers.
HABITAT Throughout the British Isles, in damp meadows, woodland rides, verges and riverbanks, from April to June. Males appear a week or so before the females.
CATERPILLAR Deep green, found June or July, chiefly on garlic mustard and lady's smock, but also other wild members of the crucifer family, though not cultivated brassicas.

5 Brimstone
Gonepteryx rhamni

Often the first butterfly seen on the wing in spring, this is a common and easily identified, medium-to-large species (5.5cm/2¼in wingspan), with pointed, sulphur-yellow wings (paler in the female) with a single, faint orange spot in the centre of each. Adults fly between flowers with confident wing-beats (no fluttering) and feed on nectar of a wide variety of wildflowers, with wings held shut.
HABITAT Southern England and parts of Wales and Ireland, in woodland edges, gardens, hedgerows and scrub, especially on downland or chalkland habitats where buckthorn is present, from February to November.
CATERPILLAR Plain green, feeding on buckthorn or alder buckthorn, in June and July.

6 Clouded yellow
Colias croceusa

Rarely resident, this is an uncommon, large butterfly (5–6cm/2–2½in wingspan) that usually migrates to the British Isles early each summer from southern Europe. It is a rich, egg-yolk yellow with broad, mid-brown edges to the wings and a single dark spot on each forewing; the undersides are a slightly greener yellow with a light brown spot on each forewing and a pair of overlapping white spots on the hind wings. The female is similar but lighter in colour all over, and with light brown hind wings and light yellow blotches along the

edges of both wings. Adults are fast-flying and feed on the nectar of clovers, thistles, knapweed and wild marjoram.
HABITAT Mainly round the eastern and southern coasts of the British Isles, in grassy fields with clovers or downland wildflowers, in May or June and then again in September or October.
CATERPILLAR Green with a light yellow stripe along the full length of the body, on either side, on lucerne and clovers, in June or July and September or October.

9 Ringlet
Aphantopus hyperantus

The ringlet is a fairly common, medium-sized butterfly (4–5cm/1½–2in wingspan) in a uniform mid-to-dark brown. It has a series of darker spots, often (but not always) with a white speck in the very centre, and each outlined with a lighter ring, giving the impression of tiny eyes. The forewings have 2 or 3 spots per wing, the hind wings have 5, and these markings show up on both the uppersides and undersides. Adults fly even on dull, wet days.

HABITAT Almost any place where there is long grass, including meadows, parkland and roadside verges throughout southern Scotland, England, Wales and Ireland, from June to late August.
CATERPILLAR Dull beige grub with a slightly darker centre stripe, found on grass stems any time except July.

7 Meadow brown
Maniola jurtina

Our commonest butterfly of all, this medium-to-large species (5cm/2in wingspan) is predominantly brown. The female has a false eye on each forewing, surrounded by an orange patch. The male is uniform dull brown with a dark false eye. The undersides of both sexes have orange-and-brown forewings, on which the reverse of the false eye is visible, and dark brown hind wings with a broad, jagged beige strip round the edge. Adults are active at all times of day, in all weathers, which is very unusual for butterflies, most of which are on the wing only on still, dry, sunny days, outside the heat of the day. If, in midsummer, you walk through a field of long, undisturbed grass, for instance a haymeadow or roadside verge that hasn't been mowed, the clouds of brownish butterflies that rise up all round you are most likely to be meadow browns.

HABITAT Widespread throughout the British Isles, in areas of long grass, except at high altitudes, from June to late August.
CATERPILLAR Solitary, striped in light and mid-green; feeds on grass, mainly cocksfoot, but nearly invisible against the stems. A slow developer, it can be found at any time except June.

8 Wall brown
Lasiommata megera

Also known as the wall, this is a medium-to-large, bright-orange-and-brown butterfly (5cm/2in wingspan) with marbled patterning, a large eyespot on each forewing and a row of smaller ones in a curved row close to the edge of the hind wings. The eyespots show clearly against the rather silvery underside when the butterfly is at rest with folded wings. Males have darker markings than females. Wall browns often bask on walls or wayside flowers alongside paths with wings spread open, and rise up when disturbed by people walking past, often accompanying them for a short distance before settling again.
HABITAT Sunny, grassy places throughout England and Wales,

with scattered populations in Ireland and southern Scotland (not found further north), in May or June and then the next generation in July or August.
CATERPILLAR Plain green, found on long grasses in June or July, and through winter from September to April.

10

10 Small skipper
Thymelicus sylvestris

There are several different kinds of skipper, but as a group they are easily identified by their habit of holding their wings in the same characteristic way when sunbathing – with the forewings half-raised, like a tent, and the hind wings out flat. This makes them look even more moth-like, though they are officially butterflies. The small skipper is a little, tawny orange-brown, moth-like butterfly with narrow black edges to the wings (3cm/1¼in wingspan). The undersides are plain amber tinged ash-grey. Adults dart rapidly about, feeding on a wide variety of wildflowers including dandelions, scabious, thistles and fleabane.

HABITAT Grassy places, including gardens, in Wales and England, in July and August.

CATERPILLAR Slim, plain green, feeding on long grass – rolls the leaf round into a tube and lives inside. Found all year round except July.

11 Essex skipper
Thymelicus lineola

The Essex skipper is almost identical to the small skipper, but under a magnifying glass the undersides of the tips of the antennae are black. Also, instead of overwintering as caterpillars, like the small skipper, it overwinters as eggs on grasses.

11

HABITAT Once rare, it was originally found only at a single location in Essex, but it is now widespread in grassy places throughout the south-east of England and in East Anglia, in July and August.

CATERPILLAR Pale green, feeding on grasses, which are pulled together with silk to make a rough, leafy shelter. Seen from April to June.

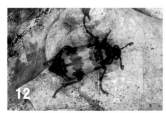

12

12 Sexton beetles
Nicrophorus species

Also known as burying beetles, these are useful but unglamorous beetles that bury the bodies of dead birds, rodents and small mammals, by excavating soil out from below the corpse, into which they then lay their eggs – the grubs use the carcass as their food source, which also helps the tidying-up process. *Nicrophorus humator* is cigar-shaped, 2.5cm (1in) long, black and shiny, with orange blobs on the tips of its antennae; *N. vespilloides* is almost 2cm (¾in) long, chunky and black, with 2 irregular orange bands around the body.

HABITAT Fields, meadows and woods.

13 Dor beetle
Geotrupes stercorarius

The dor beetle is our best-known dung beetle. It is black and scarab-shaped, 2cm (¾in) long and 1cm (⅜in) wide, with shiny 'shoulders' and ribbed wing-cases; the underside is green or dark blue. Adults excavate a deep tunnel system under a cowpat, bury balls of cow dung and lay a single egg on each dung ball. The larvae then feed on the dung.

HABITAT In pastures from April to October.

13

Dung beetles

Dung beetle is the common name for a number of species of small, blackish and brownish beetles of various shapes and sizes that live on dung. They may eat, tunnel in or lay their eggs in the dung where they find it, or they may roll the dung up into balls and bury them, sometimes moving them to another spot for burial. They are responsible for doing a lot of cleaning-up of the countryside and also help increase soil fertility by digging in manure or causing it to break down so that plant food is washed in by the rain.

14 Great green bush-cricket
Tettigonia viridissima

Our biggest bush-cricket, this has a large body, 5cm (2in) long, with antennae the same length, and is grassy green all over, sometimes with a faint brown stripe down the back. It is active on late afternoons and evenings during the summer and has a loud, strident chirp that sometimes continues at night, when it is often mistaken for a cicada (which doesn't live here, only in southern Europe). It may bite if handled carelessly.
HABITAT Mostly found along the south coast and South Downs, often hiding in brambles and gorse; also visits gardens.

15 Meadow grasshopper
Chorthippus parallelus

This is the only flightless grasshopper in the British Isles, although wings are present. It is a fairly common species, 2–2.5cm (¾–1cm) long, with a green head and thorax and brown legs, abdomen, back and wing-cases, which may be streaked with green or purplish brown.

HABITAT Not-too-dry meadows throughout the British Isles (but not Ireland), from June to October.

16 Yellow dung fly
Scathophaga stercoraria

Common in the countryside, this is a fairly large, furry, golden-yellow fly, 1cm (⅜in) long. The males are seen flying round fresh cowpats; females are greyish and less furry and lay eggs on the manure, on which the emerging grubs feed. Adults eat other flies attracted to the dung. The yellow dung fly does not spread disease.
HABITAT Throughout the British Isles, in fields where there is fresh cow manure or, as second best, horse manure.

17 St Mark's fly
Bibio marci

This is a rather thickset black fly, so called as it emerges around St Mark's day (25th April). Fairly commonly seen in swarms near vegetation or sitting on foliage, it is a biggish fly, 1.2cm (½in) long, with transparent wings and rather long legs, which are left dangling in flight.
HABITAT Fields and meadows.

18 Yellow meadow ant
Lasius flavus

The yellow meadow ant is the same size (3mm/⅛in) and shape as the common black garden ant, with similar behaviour, but it has a pale yellow body. The yellow ant makes colonies in mounds of soil in grassland and feeds on the honeydew exuded by aphids.
HABITAT Widespread in grassland, pastures and meadows of southern England, but it is occasionally found elsewhere.

19 Wolf spiders

This is a group name for several common species of greyish brown spider. Instead of making webs, they hunt their prey by sitting in wait and then running it down – hence the name of wolf spider. They are most easily seen on sunny summer days, when they come out to sunbathe on leaves or on bare soil patches, with 2 pairs of front legs stretched out in front of them. *Pisaura mirabilis* is 2.5cm (1in) long, including its legs, with beige, white and black, wavy stripes. It is often found on clumps of nettles. *Pardosa amentata* (shown right), 2cm (¾in) long including legs, has a grey body with black spots and brown-and-buff-ringed legs. It is quite common in gardens as well as in the countryside.
HABITAT Vegetation, shortish grass or bare soil throughout the British Isles.

20 Crab spider
Xysticus cristatus

The crab spider is a non-web-making species that runs about in low vegetation or on the soil, hunting its prey. It has a fat body with a light brown abdomen and thorax patterned with buff lines – the 2 pairs of front legs are elongated and reddish from the 'elbows' to the tip.
HABITAT Vegetation throughout the British Isles from April to September.

1 Slow worm
Anguis fragilis

Often thought to be a snake, the slow worm is in fact a legless lizard. It is reasonably common in Britain but is rarely seen, as it is very reclusive. It has a slender, snake-like shape, up to 45cm (17½in) long but more commonly 30cm (12in), varying in colour from copper to light brown, sometimes with faint stripes or spots. It will sometimes shed its tail when caught by a predator.
HABITAT On sunny banks and hillsides throughout England, Scotland and Wales from March to October (hibernates in winter). Frequently found in garden compost heaps.

1 Brown hare
Lepus europaeus

Widespread throughout Britain but rarely seen because it is so timid, this is an increasingly scarce, long-legged, rabbit-like animal, 55cm (22in) long. It has a shaggy, reddish grey-brown coat, white underparts and tail underside, and long ears (10cm/4in), tipped with black. In spring (the best time for sightings) hares chase each other round fields in long, leaping bounds, or stand up on their hind legs face to face and appear to box.
HABITAT Throughout the British Isles (very rare in Ireland), in wide, open, agricultural land and grassy hills, in untouched countryside away from houses and roads.
FOOD Grass, farmland crops.

2 Irish hare
Lepus timidus subspecies

In Ireland (where brown hares are rare) mountain hares developed in isolation and the Irish hare eventually emerged as a separate subspecies. Exactly like a British mountain hare in shape, size and appearance, the Irish hare is 55cm (22in) long with short, black-tipped ears, but unlike the mountain hare, the Irish hare stays brown all year round, even in winter.
HABITAT Only in Ireland; unlike British mountain hares, the Irish version is found predominantly in farmland.
FOOD Grass, farm crops and other vegetation.

OVERLEAF Hares often 'box' in spring. These bouts may involve a pair of rival males or a female fending off unwanted attention.

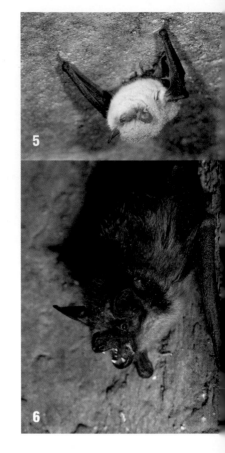

summer, but it needs a spacious cave to hibernate in as, unlike most other bats, it does not crawl into position – it must fly straight to its resting place.

FOOD Dung flies, chafers and other large beetles.

5 Natterer's bat
Myotis nattereri

This is a medium-sized bat (body 4.5cm/1¾in long, wingspan 25–30cm/10–12in), with light brown upperparts and a very light buff or white underside. It flies rather slowly, with its tail pointing down instead of trailing behind it.

HABITAT Throughout the British Isles, seen hunting in fields, open parkland and lightly wooded river valleys. Roosts in trees and roofs in summer; hibernates in caves in winter.

FOOD Moths and other small flying insects caught in flight or sometimes grabbed from foliage.

6 Serotine bat
Eptesicus serotinus

The serotine bat is a large, relatively slow-flying brown bat (body 6–8cm/2½–3¼in long, wingspan 35cm/14in) with rather shaggy-looking fur and a slightly darker head.

HABITAT Mostly restricted to south and east England, seen hunting over parkland and pastures, from April to August. Roosts in colonies in house roofs. Hibernates in buildings, occasionally caves.

FOOD Moths, beetles.

3 Mole
Talpa europaea

Rarely seen but well known and widespread, the mole is a small black, subterranean creature, 14cm (5½in) long, with very soft, velvet-like fur, tiny eyes and a very short, stumpy tail. It has a pointed, pink-tipped snout and large pink, spade-like feet, which are used for digging. It makes its presence known by pushing up fresh soil into molehills and heaving the ground into loose ridges above its shallow feeding tunnels.

HABITAT Arable land, grassland, pastures and woods; also invades garden lawns. Absent from Ireland and from most islands, with the curious exceptions of Jersey, the Isle of Wight, Anglesey, Alderney, Mull and the Isle of Skye.

FOOD Worms.

4 Greater horseshoe bat
Rhinolophus ferrumequinum

This is a fairly rare, large bat (body 6–7cm/2½–2¾in long, wingspan 33–40cm/13–16in) with broad, blunt-tipped wings moving with fairly slow, steady wing-beats – both are good identification features. The face has a horseshoe-shaped flap of skin that gives this bat its common name.

HABITAT Limited to south-west England and the south-western tip of Wales. It is usually seen hunting low over old pastureland and occasionally roosts in attics in

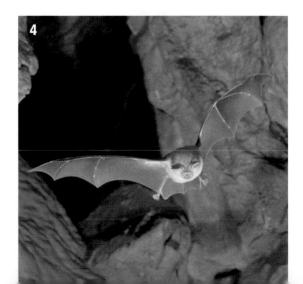

Bat behaviour

Female bats of most species produce a single baby in June or July. Females and young live in communal nursery roosts, while the males return to separate roosts in smaller groups. In winter, bats move to new roosts to hibernate, either singly or in small groups.

7 Polecat
Mustela putorius

The polecat is a rare, long, lean, ferret-like animal, about 38–40cm (15–16in) long excluding the tail. It has blonde fur on the body, sprinkled thickly with long, darker guard hairs that give it a flecked appearance. The shoulders, legs and tail are darker, and the face has a black 'bandit's mask'; the ears are small, rounded and blackish, outlined in white. Polecats live in old rabbit burrows, coming out to feed mostly at night but they are sometimes seen by day. Once almost extinct in England, the polecat has made a good comeback, but it is often confused with domestic ferrets that have escaped and gone wild. It is famed for its extremely unpleasant, pungent smell.
HABITAT Throughout Wales and rapidly recolonizing England and parts of southern Scotland, particularly in farmland.
FOOD Rabbits, small rodents.

8 Feral cat
Felis species

Domestic cats that have turned feral breed indiscriminately and have a huge impact on local wildlife, by competing with predators, such as barn owls and stoats, for the same food supplies.
HABITAT Mostly around farms and factories.
FOOD Small rodents, birds, rabbits.

1 Horse chestnut
Aesculus hippocastanum

This is a tall, stately, spreading tree, to 30m (100ft) high, easily recognized by the palmate (hand-shaped) leaves, which are made up of 5–7 ovate leaves – each with a conspicuous, fishbone pattern of ribs – arranged like a fan at the end of a stiff leaf stalk. The showy, candle-shaped spikes of white, pink-centred flowers in May are followed in autumn by spiky, round seed cases, 3cm (1¼in) across, which contain 'conkers'. The bark is scaly and grey-brown with occasional reddish brown tints.
HABITAT Once widely planted as a street tree, or forming an avenue along the drive up to stately homes, and in parkland.

2 Sycamore
Acer pseudoplatanus

The sycamore is a tall maple, rather upright at first but later becoming dome-shaped, to 35m (115ft) tall. The foliage is typical of maples, having 3 or 5 lobes, but – unusually for the acer family – the sycamore has little or no autumn colour. The leaves are often affected in summer by tar spot – a fungal disease that causes irregular black spots on the leaves (this is a handy identification feature). Dangling clusters of inconspicuous, greenish yellow flowers in May are followed by the familiar strings of green 'keys', which turn light brown when ripe and spiral down on the breeze, often travelling considerable distances. Sycamore seedlings grow extremely fast and the deep-rooted saplings can be a notorious weed in gardens where there is a large, mature tree growing in the vicinity.
HABITAT Throughout the British Isles, growing almost anywhere including along the coast and at high altitude.

3 Snake's head fritillary
Fritillaria meleagris

A rare, wild, spring bulb belonging to the lily family, the snake's head fritillary flowers in April and May, with grassy foliage 20–30cm (8–12in) high. The spectacular flowers are solitary, nodding and bell-shaped, 2–3cm (¾–1¼in) across, in mauve-pink, chequered with tiny mauve squares; you occasionally find a white flower with a pearly grey, chequerboard pattern. The whole plant dies down quickly after flowering.
HABITAT In old meadows that have never been ploughed, in damp areas, mostly in the southern half of Britain.

4 Cowslip
Primula veris

This is a distinctly polyanthus-like spring flower, with foliage similar to that of a primrose, except the leaves of the cowslip taper off more to make a pronounced stalk at the base. Clusters of small, nodding, cup-shaped, primrose-yellow flowers, each with a cluster of large green sepals at the base, are borne on top of flower stems 15–20cm (6–8in) tall. Although the plant flowers only from April to May, its leaves persist for some months after flowering.
HABITAT Open grassland, especially on chalky soils, particularly in the south of England.

5 Ragwort
Senecio jacobaea

Often viewed by farmers and gardeners as a weed, this very common perennial flowers from July to September. It starts as a neat rosette of finely cut, jagged leaves; the tall flower spike grows from the centre, with leaves of decreasing size arranged alternately right to the top, where the flattish, domed cluster of yellow, daisy-like flowers opens. Ragwort is poisonous to livestock, especially horses, but it is the food plant of the cinnabar moth caterpillar and is an important source of nectar for many other insects.
HABITAT Wasteland, roadside verges and unmanaged livestock pastures.

6 Dandelion
Taraxacum officinale

This is a very common perennial wildflower, well known for its 'dandelion clock' seedheads. It has a deep taproot, from which grows a rosette of long, narrow, deeply toothed leaves and, from March to October, a series of individual, bright yellow, double, daisy-like flowers, each supported on its own hollow stem, 15–20cm (6–8in) tall. These are followed by fluffy, spherical seedheads that blow away in the wind, carrying a single seed on each silken 'parachute'. There are over 300 different dandelions in the British Isles.
HABITAT Meadows, rough grass, wasteland, roadside verges and gardens.

Vigorous dandelions

One of the reasons dandelions are so remarkably successful at taking over a wide range of habitats is that they have an extremely efficient seed-distribution system and the plants can adapt themselves to growing in long or short grass. In a lawn, dandelions form neat, flat rosettes that the mower passes safely over, but in long grass the leaves grow tall and upright, which allows them to compete with their neighbours without being swamped.

7 Dock
Rumex obtusifolius

Also known as broad-leaved dock, this is a very common wayside plant with large, broad leaves that are traditionally rubbed on nettle stings to neutralize the irritation. Dock is a tenacious perennial with a deep, branching taproot, from which grows a spreading clump, 60–90cm (2–3ft) high and wide, of large, elongated, heart-shaped leaves (each up to 30cm/12in long and 15cm/6in wide). In summer, several tall, upright, flowering stems push up through the centre of the clump bearing clusters of small, rather insignificant green flowers, followed by dense, spire-like heads of greenish bracts (maturing to rusty red), which house the seeds.
HABITAT Fields, hedgerows, wasteland, roadside verges, cultivated ground and gardens.

8 Ox-eye daisy
Leucanthemum vulgare

Also known as marguerite, this is a common but showy perennial wildflower, often seen in large colonies, flowering from June to August. The plant is upright (to 1m/3ft high) with serrated leaves and long, wiry, upright stems, each topped by a single, large daisy with white petals surrounding a flat, round, yellow centre.
HABITAT Long grass in meadows, wasteland and on roadside verges throughout the British Isles.

9 Meadow cranesbill
Geranium pratense

The meadow cranesbill is a reasonably common perennial plant that looks almost too pretty to be a wildflower, flowering from June to September. It forms a low, loose clump, 30–60cm (12–24in) high and the same across, of deeply divided, slightly hairy, palmate leaves on short stems. The flowering stems have lacy-looking foliage, spaced out at intervals along them with many large, bluish-to-mauve, 5-petalled flowers, very similar in appearance to hardy garden cranesbills.
HABITAT Meadows and roadside verges.

10 Common knapweed
Centaurea nigra

This is a reasonably common, upright-growing perennial wildflower, 30–60cm (12–24in) tall, with long, linear leaves with a few toothed protuberances and wiry,

upright stems branching near the top of the plant. The tip of each stem bears a single, rather thistle-like flower, 2cm (¾in) across, made up of short magenta tufts, which grow in a 'crew-cut' on top of a very hard, round, brown structure (with a texture like that of flock wallpaper) that resembles a door knob, hence the plant's

alternative name of hardheads. Forms also occur with a row of ray-florets, which give the flower the appearance of a cornflower.
HABITAT Grassland, hedgerows and unkempt roadside verges.

11 Selfheal
Prunella vulgaris

Selfheal takes its name from medieval times, when the foliage was thought to heal cuts, especially those caused by farming or carpentry tools. A common, low, creeping perennial wildflower, it has small, wrinkled, oval-to-triangular leaves arranged in pairs, forming a loose network through grass or other plants. From June

to September, it produces upright flowering stems, 10–20cm (4–8in) high, topped by tight-packed heads of tiny, 2-lipped, pink-and-purple flowers.
HABITAT Grassland, verges and rough ground.

14 Charlock
Sinapis arvensis

A common and prolific wildflower, flowering from May to July, charlock is usually regarded as a weed by farmers. It is an annual member of the cabbage family, similar to oilseed rape, with bristly leaves and rather upright-growing, coarse, prickly stems, 30–60cm (12–24in) high, topped by spikes of small, yellow, 4-petalled flowers. As new flowers open at the top of the spike, old flowers lower down die and are replaced by small green pods, which ripen to brown before shedding their seeds.

HABITAT Farmland, hedgerows, roadside verges and wasteland.

15 Scentless mayweed
Matricaria inodora

This common annual or biennial wildflower – a welcome sight on wasteland in summer – makes a low, bushy plant, 30–60cm (12–24in), with sparse, curly, thread-like, ferny foliage, flowering from July to September. The stems are each topped by a solitary, daisy-like flower, about 2cm (¾in) wide, made up of a ring of white petals round a yellow centre.

HABITAT Wastleland and any cultivated ground, occasionally including gardens.

12 Field poppy
Papaver rhoeas

The field poppy is a traditional annual cornfield wildflower that has 'escaped' and is now widespread throughout the countryside, flowering from May to October. It is a fragile-looking plant, 20–45cm (8–17½in) high, with feathery foliage and slender, wiry, slightly hairy stems, each topped by a large, solitary red flower, 4–5cm (1½–2in) wide, that lasts only a day; however, replacements are plentifully produced so that plants stay in flower continuously all summer. Selected forms of the field poppy have given us various hardy annual cottage-garden plants with double or semi-double flowers in a wide range of colours, including Shirley poppies.

HABITAT Roadside verges, wasteland, cultivated land and gardens in all but the far north of Britain.

13 Cornflower
Centaurea cyanus

This is a rare annual cornfield wildflower, flowering from June to late August, with fairly upright, branching, greyish stems, to 75cm (30in), sparsely clad in narrow leaves. Each flowerhead is a tight-packed cluster of tiny blue flowers that are arranged to make a flat head growing from a knapweed-like, hard, round 'knob'.

HABITAT Rare in the countryside, cornflowers are now seen mostly as cultivated forms grown as old-fashioned, hardy annual cottage-garden flowers; the wild species is sometimes grown in natural or wild gardens.

Cornfields and haymeadows

When early people first ventured into agriculture, their fields would have been a blaze of colour, thanks to the annual weeds that grew in among their crops. Some of these weeds would have been native species that took advantage of the new habitat, but others arrived with the crop seeds that were

A meadow in Norfolk, containing a typical mixture of cornfield 'weeds' including cornflowers, field poppies and corn marigolds.

introduced from the Near East. Their flowers attracted insects, which in turn brought in birds and small mammals that depended on them for their diet, followed by the larger predators that preyed on them both – all of this adding greatly to ancient biodiversity.

Weed seeds didn't do early man any harm either; they were milled together with grain when it was made into flour, and ended up in the bread or pottage, adding much-needed flavour and extra nutrients. Adulteration with weed seeds continued through medieval times, until processing methods became more sophisticated.

Even so, annual field weeds flourished. It wasn't until the development of modern agricultural methods, and particularly the use of chemical fertilizers and weedkillers, that crops had fields largely to themselves. Crop yields might have improved, but the countryside has been a poorer place for it.

Some cornfield weeds, such as Venus's looking glass, became rare or died out owing to loss of habitat. A lot of the old field weeds found a new role in life as annual flowers – for example, plants such as cornflower, pheasant's eye and corn cockle can be readily found in seed catalogues for growing in old-fashioned, cottage-style flower gardens. Improved forms of some of these flowers also became very popular – think of Shirley poppies, which were bred from selected forms of the field poppy. Some of the more adaptable species managed to take over rural wasteland, so now you'll often see field weeds such as wild oats and charlock growing round the edges of fields. Field bindweed turns up on dryish banks and roadside verges, and some of the most successful outcasts have reinvented themselves as garden weeds – the likes of chickweed, groundsel, mayweed and shepherd's purse, for example.

But in recent years we've come to think nostalgically of old-fashioned haymeadow and cornfield wildflowers. Today wildflower meadows containing a mixture of grasses and the more romantic, pretty varieties of haymeadow or cornfield wildflowers are a much sought-after feature of modern, natural-style gardens. If you have the chance to see one or grow one of your own, check out the insect life – particularly butterflies and moths – and you'll see what we've been missing all these years.

16 Field bindweed
Convolvulus arvensis

Sometimes known as devil's guts, this is a common, invasive perennial, well known as a weed to farmers and gardeners. It scrambles over other plants, using twining stems that turn anti-clockwise, to maximize exposure of the arrow-head-shaped leaves to sunlight, helping it out-compete rivals for space in a crowded environment. From June to September, it produces pretty, pink-and-white-striped, circular flowers, 2cm (¾in) wide, that close up to narrow, pointed buds at night. The plant has a wide-ranging root system, and is easily spread by broken pieces of root

that regrow and make a new plant, so cultivation actually spreads it.
HABITAT Edges of fields, wasteland, allotments and gardens.

17 Chickweed
Stellaria media

This is an extremely common, widespread and fast-growing weed that flowers all year round, except in the coldest spells in winter, and is one of the first plants to colonize newly disturbed ground. It is a low, spreading annual, up to 15cm (6in) high, forming mats about 45–60cm (17½–24in) across, with soft, weak stems and small, succulent, oval leaves with pointed tips arranged in pairs along the stems; the leaves are larger and fleshier near the stem-tips. The tiny white, star-like flowers grow on short stalks clustered loosely at the tips of the stems.
HABITAT Gardens and allotments; less often found in the countryside, as it likes loose, freshly turned ground. However, chickweed is widespread in secondary grassland and plantation woodland.

18 Sow-thistle
Sonchus oleraceus

The sow-thistle is a very common annual, flowering from June to August, which quickly colonizes cultivated soil. A young plant makes a loose rosette of broad, smooth, semi-shiny, grey-green leaves that are notched close to the point where they join the stem of the plant, but by the time it reaches flowering size it is a bushy clump of branching stems with elongated, soft-prickly, triangular-shaped leaves, topped with clusters of double, yellow flowers. Plants carry open flowers and thistledown seedheads of earlier flowers at the same time.
HABITAT Field edges, wasteland, allotments and gardens.

19 Shepherd's purse
Capsella bursa-pastoris

Flowering from March to November, this is a common and easily identified, small annual weed, 10–15cm (4–6in) tall. It makes a fairly flat, circular rosette of deeply toothed leaves, with spikes of tiny, white, 4-petalled flowers growing from the centre. As the flower spike elongates, new buds appear at the top and small, heart-shaped seedpods form lower down, on short stalks.
HABITAT Cultivated ground, wasteland, allotments and gardens.

flowered, cultivated violas, but narrower. The colour is rather variable – pale purple with a faint orange or yellow eye, sometimes all-yellow. The plant can be confused with derivatives of the hybrid garden pansy.

HABITAT Cornfields, wasteland and cultivated ground. Occasionally in gardens, usually in unfed lawns.

23 Scarlet pimpernel
Anagallis arvensis

The flowers of scarlet pimpernel open from approximately 8am to 3pm every day, and only on fine, bright days, so it was traditionally used by country people years ago as a combined watch and weather forecast, and was known as 'poor man's weather-glass'. It is a common, low, creeping annual, with pointed, oval leaves arranged opposite each other, and small, solitary, 5-petalled, bright orange-red flowers, 1cm (⅜in) across,

which grow at the ends of short stems from the leaf axils towards the tips of the stems from June to August. There is also a blue-flowered form of *Anagallis arvensis*.

HABITAT Cultivated ground, sometimes found in gardens.

20 Fumitory
Fumaria officinalis

Once a cornfield weed, this is an attractive plant that is still fairly common on cultivated ground, flowering from May to August. It is an annual with weak, scrambling stems, to 45cm (17½in) long, sparsely clad with small, smooth, blue-green, ferny leaves, and short, straight flower spikes growing out (usually horizontally) from the leaf joints near the top of the plant. The flowers are small, tubular and pale mauve-pink, flaring slightly at the tip, which is a deeper shade of mauve-pink.

HABITAT Roadsides, field edges, wasteland and any disturbed or cultivated ground, including allotments and gardens, in well-drained conditions.

21 Field pansy
Viola arvensis

Also known as heartsease, the field pansy is a fairly common, upright-growing annual, which looks very similar to the wild pansy but with smaller flowers, 5–10mm (³⁄₁₆–⅜in), in white with a cream lower lip, sometimes tinged purple, flowering from April to September.

HABITAT Cornfields, cultivated ground and wasteland.

22 Wild pansy
Viola tricolor

This is an upright-growing annual wildflower, flowering from April to September, with leaves very similar to the cultivated pansy, but smaller and narrower. The flowers are small, 1–2cm (⅜–¾in), with flat faces that resemble those of small-

24 Blue pimpernel
Anagallis foemina

An enchanting, uncommon, blue-flowered relative of the scarlet pimpernel, flowering from May to August. It is a low, sprawling annual with pointed-oval leaves, arranged along the creeping stems in pairs, and starry blue flowers. It can be confused with the blue-flowered form of the scarlet pimpernel (*Anagallis arvensis*), but in close-up you can see the difference: the petals of the blue pimpernel are slightly separated, while they are slightly overlapping in *A. arvensis*.

HABITAT Found locally in the south and west of England, in cultivated ground.

25 Germander speedwell
Veronica chamaedrys

This is a very common perennial wildflower with fairly vigorous, creeping, reddish stems that root as they run along the ground, helping the plant to form large mats, 40cm (16in) or more wide and 5cm (2in) high. The leaves are oval with neatly toothed edges arranged in pairs along the stems, and from March to July short spikes of blue, forget-me-not-like flowers appear on short stalks from the leaf joints, near the tips of the stems.

HABITAT Usually in old grassland but sometimes in established garden lawns or wasteland.

26 Sun spurge
Euphorbia helioscopia

This is a reasonably common, upright-to-bushy annual, with small, oval leaves arranged alternately along the stems, topped by a whorl of (usually) 4 leaves from which a broad, flat, circular cluster of greenish yellow flowers grows, from April to September. Technically, the 'flowers' are greenish bracts cupping a small collection of yellowy stamens, with no petals.

HABITAT Sunny areas in well-drained-to-dryish cultivated land.

27 Pheasant's eye
Adonis aestivalis

Today pheasant's eye is almost extinct in the wild, but it is sometimes grown in gardens as an old-fashioned cottage-garden flower. A short, upright-growing annual, 20–25cm (8–10in) high, it has finely divided, ferny foliage and wide-open, striking, rich red flowers from June to August, each with a very noticeably black centre and black anthers.

HABITAT Originally a cornfield flower, once also found in other cultivated ground in limy areas of the British Isles.

OPPOSITE Field poppies near Faringdon, in Oxfordshire.

28 Venus's looking glass
Legousia hybrida

This is a rare cornfield flower. Its rarity in most places is a result of modern herbicides and the plant's inability to adapt to other habitats. Unlike some other more successful cornfield flowers, it is not sufficiently spectacular to be taken into cultivation. It is a branching annual, 20cm (8in) high, with elongated-oval leaves, about 3cm (1¼in) long, that have pointed tips but no stems. The leaves are arranged in pairs along the stems; at the tips of the stems are loose clusters of (usually) 3 star-shaped, pale blue flowers, each with a long, tubular green calyx, similar to flowering tobacco (*Nicotiana*) but tiny, from May to July or August.
HABITAT Cornfields on chalky soils.

29 Meadow buttercup
Ranunculus acris

The meadow buttercup is a very common wildflower, seen from May to October. It is an upright-growing, clump-forming perennial, 30–60cm (12–24in) high, with slightly hairy, wiry stems, deeply dissected, palmate leaves and shiny yellow flowers with 5 petals, backed by 5 green sepals that clasp the base of the flower. Each flower stem bears several flowers following one after another.
HABITAT Damp, grassy meadows and rough pastures.

30 Lady's smock
Cardamine pratensis

Also known as the cuckoo flower, this is a common and very attractive, short, loosely upright perennial plant, usually 15–30cm (6–12in) tall, with ladder-like, compound leaves arranged alternately along fleshy stems. It flowers in April and May, producing loose spikes of 4-petalled, lilac-pink flowers.
HABITAT Grass, damp meadows, ditches and stream banks.

31 Green-winged orchid
Orchis morio

Flowering in meadows in May and June, this fairly uncommon orchid makes an upright rosette of unspotted, light green leaves that are 10cm (4in) long and elongated-oval in shape with pointed tips. From the centre of this grows a flower spike, 25cm (8in) high, made up of mauve-pink flowers. In close-up, each flower has a domed top, which is greenish or green-veined above a broad, mauve-pink lip, with a small white centre lightly patterned with small purple dots. The whole plant dies down quickly after flowering.
HABITAT Open, grassy meadows, especially in downland in the southern half of Britain.

32 Field mushroom
Agaricus campestris

Looking very much like the cultivated mushroom, to which it is closely related, this common, medium-to-large mushroom is found in autumn, growing in rings or larger colonies. It starts as a white 'button mushroom', which slowly expands to a large, wide, shallow cap, 4–8cm (1½–3¼in) across, with slightly scaly white skin and a stem 4–6cm (1½–2½in) high, with a ragged fringe of skin forming a ring near the top. The gills underneath the cap are pinkish in a young specimen, turning fawn, then brown with age. When cut, the flesh is white and may take on a faintly pinkish tinge; the spores are dark brown. It is a good edible mushroom, but you need to be sure of your identification – many similar species are not edible.
HABITAT Pastureland, grassy fields, roadside verges and sometimes lawns.

33 Horse mushroom
Agaricus arvensis

This is a big, edible mushroom, like a very large field mushroom, growing as isolated specimens or in rather loose fairy-rings, in autumn. The cap is 5–10cm (2–4in) across, eventually opening out almost flat, with a scattering of scales near the centre, and grows on a tall stem, 8–12cm (3¼–4¾in) high, with a ring near the top. The gills are white in young specimens (never pink as with the field mushroom), becoming brown with age, and the flesh turns yellow if bruised (a good aid to identification, although beware of yellow stainer mushrooms, which turn bright yellow in the stem when cut and can be mildly poisonous). The horse mushroom smells faintly of aniseed.
HABITAT Grassland and in grassy orchards.

34 Parasol mushroom
Macrolepiota procera

Parasol mushrooms are occasionally seen in late summer and autumn, growing as widely scattered individuals in grass close to woodland. Look for tall mushrooms, 20cm (8in) high, with a fairly slender, scaly stem with a ring near the top and a wide, umbrella-like, creamy white cap, 10–20cm (4–8in) across, covered in brownish scales that are arranged in rather regular rows, with a pronounced 'boss' in the centre. The gills underneath the cap are white, with white spores. Young mushrooms have a conical beige cap and a beige and white stem. This is a good edible species if you are certain of your identification.
HABITAT Pastures and rough grass just outside woodland.

37 Giant puffball
Calvatia gigantea
This is Britain's largest fungus, seen in summer and autumn. It is a rounded, white-to-off-white puffball that can grow as big as a human head, with soft skin the texture of chamois-leather and white flesh inside. Older specimens have darker beige or light brown skin and yellowish flesh; eventually the top splits open to release the spores. Although edible when young (it needs to be gathered soon after it emerges from the ground), it is fairly tasteless. **HABITAT** Grassland and at the base of hedges.

35 Shaggy inkcap
Coprinus comatus
Also known as the lawyer's wig, this common and easily identified, tall, slim toadstool, 10–20cm (4–8in) high, grows in colonies in summer and autumn, with bell-shaped caps thickly covered in loose, shaggy, slightly upcurling scales, perched on a long, slender stem with a ring just over halfway up. Old specimens start to curl up at the base and produce slimy black 'ink'. Young specimens look like slightly scaly white lollipops before the cap opens out. **HABITAT** Grassy places including meadows, roadside verges and sometimes gardens.

36 Meadow puffball
Vascellum pratense
Edible when young, this is a very common puffball that grows in colonies, or sometimes rings, from early summer to late autumn. Look for small, off-white, pear-shaped puffballs, 2–4cm (¾–1½in) across, with the dome uppermost and the pointed end down in the grass. The upper surface has a slightly scurfy texture. Old specimens turn beige or brown and have a smooth surface that splits open to release the spores, leaving a crater in the centre. **HABITAT** Short grass on dryish grazing land, village greens, sports fields and lawns.

Also found in fields or meadows

Badger (see pp.98–99)
Common blue (see p.166)
Common lizard (see p.170)
Common shrew (see p.279)
Common toad (see p.314)
Crows (see pp.139, 304)
Curlew (see p.43)
Doves (see pp.93, 299)
Fallow and roe deer (see p.99)
Golden plover (see p.135)
Kestrel (see p.298)
Partridges (see p.270)
Pheasant (see p.271)
Pied wagtail (see p.300)
Reeves' muntjac (see p.102)
Starling (see p.304)
Yarrow (see p.322)

Agricultural crops

When early people first started to practise agriculture, their fields were small, and they cultivated a far wider range of crops than we do today. Some of the plants we now think of as weeds were once deliberately cultivated as food crops: fat hen and pale persicaria were grown in medieval times, and the opium poppy was introduced by the Romans and cultivated for its seeds, which were used as a seasoning. They've all since escaped and become part of our native flora. In the early days, much more land was 'wasted' – wide headlands were left round the edges of fields so that ox teams could turn round; informal pathways were left between fields, allowing villagers to reach their 'patch'; and hedgerows marking parish boundaries or longer-distance routes between settlements all grew their fair share of wildflowers, which in turn supported insects and other wildlife, all the way up the food chain.

Today's mono-cropped and chemically treated prairies certainly don't offer a lot to wildlife. However, you'll still see flocks of swallows swooping down low over cornfields catching airborne insects, and just before the crop is ready to harvest thousands of sparrows congregate for a free meal. In winter, the land may temporarily host flocks of lapwings or other countryside birds, and

hedgerows and roadside verges still act as wildlife corridors through the countryside.

Since people driving, cycling, riding or walking through areas of fields often like to know what it is they are looking at, and what it is used for, I've taken a slight diversion from wildlife to look at what grows in the countryside between the genuinely wild bits.

Oilseed rape

This is a widespread crop that produces bright yellow fields of flowers in April and May and has a strong, distinctive, honey-like scent, which may be noticed even when the field isn't in sight. It is grown for its seeds, which yield vegetable oil used in margarine manufacture and for cooking, as well as in biofuel production. Sown in August and September, the plants are upright and mustard-like, up to 90–120cm (3–4ft) high, with glaucous foliage, rather like that of a run-to-seed cabbage. Thick stems are topped by spikes of bright yellow, 4-petalled flowers, which in close-up look a bit like wallflowers. New flowers continue to open as the spike develops, while the older flowers lower down die and are replaced by long, slim, greenish pods that contain the seeds, which gradually ripen to brown. The plants are left until all the pods have matured and ripened before being harvested in July and August.

Flax, linseed

Fields that appear to be covered with a sky-blue haze when viewed from a distance are generally planted with flax. This is grown for its seeds (linseeds), which are used to make paper, linen, vegetable oil for margarine and high-quality cooking oil. Grown throughout the southern half of Britain, it flowers in June. In close-up, the plants are very similar to the ornamental flax (*Linum* species) grown in gardens as annuals – they are short

A field of oilseed rape in full flower – a common sight in the British Isles in spring. The seeds are used in the manufacture of margarine, cooking oil and biodiesel.

A field of barley – a staple crop, used for making animal feed and beer. The tall, tufted plants are harvested in midsummer.

and bushy, 30–45cm (12–17½in) high, with small leaves and rounded, 5-petalled, sky-blue flowers. When the flowers are over, the plants are left to run to seed. The tiny black seedpods are harvested in October.

Wheat

Wheat is the most widely grown agricultural crop throughout Britain, but particularly in the huge, prairie-like fields of East Anglia. It is used for animal feed, biscuits or as an agricultural seed crop (to produce next year's crops). 'Hard' wheat, grown for bread-making, is a different variety, mainly grown in the USA and Canada. British wheat is sown in autumn (sometimes spring) and grows slowly through the winter, looking like rows of shaggy grass in the fields. Plants are tall, upright and grassy, each making a small tuft branching from the base, up to 75cm (30in) high. From June onwards, green seed-heads can be seen containing neat rows of oval seeds packed close together in a chevron pattern, slowly ripening to beige during the summer, until they are harvested in August.

Barley

Widely grown throughout Britain, barley is easily recognized from a distance as fields of waving wisps. It is used for making beer or animal feed, or to produce seed for the

following year's crops. Sown in autumn, barley grows slowly through the winter, looking like rows of rough grass in the fields. It forms tall, upright, grassy plants, up to 75cm (30in) high, each making a small tuft that branches from the base. From June onwards, green seedheads are visible, consisting of rows of oval seeds interspersed with long, straight, stiff, greenish wisps, which protrude 5–10cm (2–4in) and form a head like a paintbrush. These slowly ripen to beige during the summer and are harvested in July.

Agricultural lupins

Lupins are a relatively new and very attractive crop, giving rise to fields that have a blue-grey haze from a distance. Flowers appear in July and August. The crop is grown for its seed, which is used for vegetable oil and making high-protein animal feed. Medium-tall plants, up to 75cm (30in), they are very much like garden lupins, with the same leaves, shaped like the spokes of wagon wheels, and upright spikes of flower but in shorter spikes and all of the same colour – a slatey-blue. After flowering, plants are left to run to seed, so you see large numbers of the familiar, small, pea-like pods. Lupins are sown in spring and harvested in September.

Field beans

This is a traditional crop with a strong, characteristic scent when the plants are in full flower in June. Field beans are grown for the seeds, which are used as a source of protein in animal feed and human food. Plants look exactly like garden broad beans, up to 75cm (30in) high, but are grown closely together in rows in much the same way as a field of corn, so they stand upright without supports. After flowering, plants are left to produce pods, which are allowed to ripen fully and dry out, turning black on the plants. Field beans are sown in spring and harvested in September and October.

Agricultural peas

Another traditional crop, this is grown in much the same way as field beans, to yield dry peas that are used for making animal feed. (These are also known as marrowfat peas, the same sort made into mushy peas that are eaten with fish and chips.) They are sown in April, reach 60cm (24in) high, and look just like garden peas but are spaced more closely together. The pods are allowed to remain on the plant until they dry out; by August (harvest time) the plants are yellowing and the pods are dried and brown. Even when young, the peas inside are large, coarse and tasteless.

Vining peas

In some parts of the country, particularly Lincolnshire and East Anglia, peas are grown for freezing, often for the big frozen-food firms; you may see large acreages devoted to this crop close to the processing factories, but not elsewhere. Plants look just like short varieties of garden peas, reaching 45cm (17½in) high, but they are grown in rows close together so they hold each other up

without supports. When judged to be exactly ready, a harvester clears the lot very quickly so the peas can be frozen within 30 minutes of leaving the field. They are sown in early April and harvested in June and July.

Sugar beet

Sugar beet is a traditional crop still widely grown in certain parts of the British Isles, particularly East Anglia, within a convenient distance of the processing factory (which can be detected in autumn at harvest time by the faint smell of burning toffee in the air). It is used for making granulated sugar, as an alternative to imported sugar from sugar cane. Sugar-beet pulp left over from processing is used in animal feed. The crop is sown in spring; in summer, sugar-beet fields contain close rows of bright green, beetroot-like leaves. The crop is lifted in autumn and winter, when you may see piles of the big, fat, white, parsnip-like roots in trailers being transported to factories.

Hay/silage

Long grass is used for making hay, which is later baled and used to feed horses, sheep or cattle in winter, or to make silage, which is fermented grass used for feeding bullocks in winter. Hayfields are cut in June and July, when the grass is roughly 1m (3ft) high, and sometimes again in August; long grass in hayfields looks a bit pale, with a lot of wildflowers and seedheads. After cutting, it is then left on the fields to dry out. Grassy fields intended for silage-making are heavily fed so the grass grows fast and looks bright green and leafy. Silage is cut 2 or 3 times from May through to summer. You can usually tell fields used for hay or silage – they are not fenced and the grass is left to grow long. Even if it's empty, a field used for grazing will have short grass and will be fenced.

Although they resemble garden and vining peas, these agricultural peas are less palatable and are used mainly in animal feed.

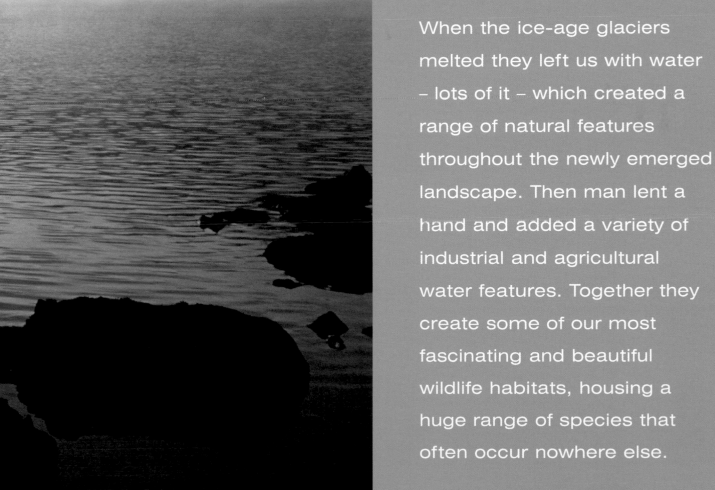

Rivers, lakes and streams

When the ice-age glaciers melted they left us with water – lots of it – which created a range of natural features throughout the newly emerged landscape. Then man lent a hand and added a variety of industrial and agricultural water features. Together they create some of our most fascinating and beautiful wildlife habitats, housing a huge range of species that often occur nowhere else.

The great meltwater run-off

Snowfall might be less frequent than it used to be, but if you think back to the last time we had a couple of inches, can you remember the mess when it melted? Slush, mud and water everywhere for a week or more – the ground simply couldn't soak it up fast enough. Now, imagine Britain as it was at the time of the ice age, covered with solid ice, which in places was a mile and a half thick, and consider what happened when that began to melt. It produced one heck of a lot of water, and it all had to go somewhere.

When climate change made the ice-age glaciers melt, the great thaw gained momentum rapidly. As the area of shiny white ice shrank, less sunlight was reflected back into outer space, so the atmosphere warmed up faster. At the same time, the newly revealed rock and soil, being dark-coloured, absorbed and stored the heat, which helped the ice to melt faster still.

Even so, experts reckon it took a couple of thousand years for the ice-age glaciers to melt completely, and during that time the country must have been awash. Water always takes the shortest route downhill, so it would have been streaming down mountains and hills and rushing through valleys and gorges, washing away anything in its path. As it wore away deeper channels, it formed the first riverbeds.

During the ice age, the ice was thickest in the north of Britain, so that's where its impact on the ground underneath was greatest. Any natural depressions left by the departing glaciers filled with water from the melted ice. Scottish lochs and the lakes that make up the Lake District were all created in this way. The melting glaciers also left us with some strange features known as 'kettle hole lakes', which are deep, round 'ponds', created where a glacier deposited a big lump of ice that sank into the boggy ground and left a crater full of water behind when it melted.

When the raging rivers of ice-age meltwater reached flatter ground, the water slowed down, so instead of wearing away deep channels it spread out to form a lot of smaller tributaries – all heading for the coast – where they branched out into large networks of creeks running into estuaries on their way to the sea. But in flat, low-lying inland regions – places where the water couldn't run away fast enough – the ground soaked up the surplus water like a sponge, and became either bog (a wet area with peaty, acid ground), fenland (a low-lying wetland with peaty soil over limestone rock, causing neutral conditions) or marsh (an area of fine, silty mud that is always wet). Around muddy coastlines and along estuaries, you'll find the seaside version – salt marsh –

which floods with seawater at high tide and drains at low tide to leave saline mud.

The basic landscape probably remained much the same for the next few thousand years, except that it grew a covering of wildwoods (see page 78). The arrival of Stone Age man, as we've already seen, had a big impact, as he started clearing ground for agriculture. River valleys were a popular place for early settlements, since the silty, alluvial soil that had been washed down from higher ground over thousands of years by rain was deep, rich and easy to cultivate. There was also no shortage of water, which was essential for human habitation.

Broads and fenlands

As the population grew, man began colonizing all sorts of 'borderline' areas. Fenlands were notoriously marshy, since they were flat, low-lying regions intersected by many slow-running rivers taking water from higher ground on their way to the sea. But they offered plenty of fish and wildfowl, plus a good supply of reeds for thatching. All of this our ancestors would have appreciated, even if living conditions were a little trying because of the constant damp, with dangerously soft ground that the unwary could sink into easily. We know that there was a resident population living in the Fens, in East

Anglia, during the twelfth century; people inhabited patches of slightly higher ground, where conditions weren't quite so boggy. They dug peat, which they dried to use as fuel for cooking and heating, since trees didn't grow well in very boggy regions. Centuries of peat-digging in the boggy parts of Norfolk and Suffolk eventually created the Broads, which filled with water naturally from all the rivers that ran into them. In the seventeenth century, Dutch engineers were brought over to drain the Fens to turn more of them into good farmland, using techniques they'd perfected when creating their own *polders*. A mixture of artificial waterways and windmills was put in to beef up the existing rivers. They also drained other low-lying land, including Romney Marsh

PREVIOUS PAGES Scottish lochs, such as this one near the Kyle of Lochalsh (main picture) are filled with an abundance of wildlife; Scotland is also a stronghold for otters (small picture). **BELOW LEFT** The North Norfolk coast (here, Burnham Overy Staithe) is characterized by tidal creeks, salt marshes and freshwater meadows.

The grasses, reeds and mud provide ideal conditions for wetland birds. **BELOW CENTRE** The Norfolk and Suffolk Broads are Britain's largest area of protected wetland. **BELOW RIGHT** The Brecon Canal, Wales, is a beautiful rural waterway; swans, kingfishers, herons and buzzards are all common.

in Kent and the Somerset Levels, and an area of Norfolk around the Broads. Over time, the layout of the waterways was altered slightly, as a result of natural silting-up and man-made improvements. People straightened out kinks in the existing rivers and connected stretches of river or drainage dykes together to make it easier to get about by boat. Other than that, little changed for three centuries.

Wars in the twentieth century meant that more land had to be brought into cultivation for crops, so a second round of drainage took place. By then, drainage techniques had improved a great deal. Windmills were replaced by motorized pumps and water levels were controlled by sluice gates, which were much more efficient. As the water table fell and the fenland soil dried out, much more useable farmland was created. The rich, moist, highly organic fenland soil proved particularly good for growing carrots and celery. But as the land dried out, it shrank. The reason is easy to understand: peat consists of plant remains that are only partly decomposed, being held in 'suspended animation' by the lack of oxygen in the acidic water where it forms. Everything changes when such 'earth' is drained. As the water runs out, air moves in. It takes over the spaces in the fibrous structure, so decomposition starts up again and, as the rotting process speeds up, the ground-level drops. Look what happens in your compost bin at home: you fill it to the top with plant remains, then as the stuff rots it shrinks down to less than a quarter of the original bulk. The same thing happened to the Fens – but on a grand scale.

Fields in the Fens are now sometimes 10 feet or more below the level of modern roads. Old tracks and houses sank down along with the ground, and East Anglia is one of the few places where you can travel uphill to reach a river – the banks have to be artificially shored up to keep them from breaking and flooding the surrounding land. The other problem with draining the Fens was that without water keeping the surface layer nice and sticky, the very fine topsoil dried out to a powder-like texture, which was at great risk from wind erosion. Fen 'blows' were common, and even in recent years farmers have lost entire fields of newly sown carrot seed, complete with the top inch of soil, on dry, windy days.

Quite apart from East Anglia's Fens and Broads, other parts of the country have low-lying areas with rivers running through them flanked by water meadows – think of the 'backs' at Cambridge, where the students go punting. They are not just there to look picturesque; they have a serious purpose – to soak up excess winter water that the rivers can't move away quickly enough. Since water meadows are flooded most winters, they provide great inland habitats for waders and other wildfowl, then in summer the water dries out, leaving rich, silty land that provides great summer pasture for livestock while still housing a healthy population of wildlife. When the natural process is stopped and water meadows are used for building on, the surplus water has nowhere else to go in winter, and there's a real risk of flooded houses.

Canals

As the Industrial Revolution took off, we badly needed a means of moving goods around the country. Since there were few good roads, and no railways as yet, boats were seen as the best way of doing the job. An extensive network of artificial waterways was built – the canal system. Long, narrow, horse-drawn barges shifted coal, raw materials and finished goods very efficiently. Alongside each canal was a towpath for the horses to walk on, and when hills got in the way engineers simply created a flight of locks – so the canal went 'upstairs', and then came down again on the other side. If there was a valley to cross, they built a bridge for the canal to flow over, borrowing an idea first invented by the ancient Romans for shifting water supplies into cities set in hilly countryside – the aqueduct.

As the railways appeared and the road network grew, canals became redundant, and the old towpaths, banks and waterways turned into a good habitat for elusive wildlife such as the water vole (Ratty from *The Wind in the Willows*) and a fringe of waterside wildflowers such as figwort, meadowsweet and hairy willowherb. The canals acquired a new use – for leisure – and the old barges were replaced by sleek, well-fitted-out domestic versions: canal boats. The canals were cleared out and cleaned up, which encouraged more wildlife as well as holidaymakers. Today they are a superb place for freshwater fish such as carp, tench, roach, bream, perch and pike, and you may be able to see these elusive creatures in anglers' keep-nets along the banks. These are mostly what are known as 'coarse fish', and they are put back in the water at the end of the day. It's not considered good sportsmanship to take home and eat coarse fish, plus they don't taste very good.

Ponds, lakes and reservoirs

How do you tell a pond from a lake? It's largely a matter of size; lakes are bigger than ponds. Both of them can be natural holes in the ground that have filled with water, but a lot of them are man-made. Ponds were mostly created for serious agricultural purposes, often in medieval times, when they were dug to make drinking places for livestock, or to keep ducks to provide meat and eggs. If the ground didn't hold water naturally, a pond would be lined with clay and 'puddled', by allowing cattle to tread around in it, creating a thick waterproof layer that was well tamped down. Many of today's village ponds were originally agricultural, in the centre of what's left of the old village green. Some ponds were holes or pits left behind after clay or marl had been dug out, which then filled with rainwater. (Certain types of clay were once frequently used for making bricks and roof tiles. Marl is a natural mixture of chalk and clay, which was originally spread on the fields in the same way that lime was used later, to 'sweeten' the ground.)

Some of our more northern lakes, lochs and tarns are glacial features, scooped out by glaciers and filled with meltwater. But a lot of lakes are far from natural: they were often dug as ornamental features for grand country houses in the eighteenth century, when landscape gardens were the Big New Thing. Lancelot 'Capability' Brown and his colleagues spared no expense in rearranging the natural features of the landscape, and that included redirecting the course of rivers and streams, inserting waterfalls or making artificial lakes, often on a very grand scale. In 1763 the entire village of Milton Abbas, in Dorset, was moved several miles to make room for a new lake, to enhance the views for the local landowner, Lord Milton. In more recent times, ponds and lakes have been joined by even more unnatural forms of water – reservoirs and worked-out gravel pits that have filled with water. These house a multitude of water wildlife, in addition to providing leisure facilities and storing the nation's drinking water. They are often conveniently close to big cities, for example the London Wetland Centre at Barnes.

Rivers and streams

Rivers and streams comprise one of Britain's richest habitats, not only in their clear water, but also at their margins. When unpolluted (and we are considerably better off in terms of water cleanliness than we were 50 years ago) the water is home to a wide variety of fish and aquatic creatures, and the riverbank offers sustenance and shelter to an extensive range of mammals, insects and birds. Chalk streams are prized by fishermen for their trout; in Scotland, especially, salmon-fishing is the sport of kings and queens. You could argue that fishing would seem to be at odds with nature conservation, but when you consider the amount of weed-cutting, riverbank reparation, tree-planting and general maintenance that is involved in keeping good 'fishing beats' going, the beneficial effect on wildlife, from insects to birds and mammals, is considerable.

Found throughout wetlands in the British Isles, the mute swan is Britain's biggest bird and the only resident swan. It has to run some distance over water, flapping its wings, before it can get airborne.

1 Marsh harrier
Circus aeruginosus

Usually seen gliding with raised wings in a shallow 'V' shape, or soaring in circles over reed-beds, the marsh harrier is a large, scarce, slow-flying bird of prey – the size of a buzzard but less bulky and more elegant-looking in flight. Males and females differ. A male (seen from below) looks 3-coloured, with a pale head finely streaked brown

and a chestnut-streaked-buff body and leading edges of wings; the rest of the wings and tail are a very pale blue-grey with sharply demarcated black wing-tips.
HABITAT Near reed-beds, mostly in East Anglia in summer. Many spend winter in southern Europe or Africa (those that stay are usually female).
SIZE 52cm (21in); wingspan 1.3m (4¼ft)
EGGS 4–5, pale bluish white
NEST Platform of grass, reeds and sticks in reed-beds or among crops.
FOOD Ducklings, adult birds, frogs, voles and other mammals.
SIMILAR TO Other large birds of prey from a distance, but its location and size help identification.
VARIATIONS Female (shown above) is larger and looks all-brown from below, apart from a cream flash along the wings' leading edges and a cream head. Juveniles are all-brown with a gingery yellow flash.

2 Osprey
Pandion haliaetus

This is one of Britain's most exciting, rare birds of prey. In flight, it looks buzzard-sized, dark brown above and white below, with very long wings and a short, square-ended tail; given a decent view, you may see the wings are tipped a few shades darker and have roundish black patches at the 'kink' roughly halfway along each leading edge, with a dotted band extending from the patches to the body. If you get a good look at a perching bird, you can see a dark brown stripe running from either side of the neck to the eyes. The osprey is a summer visitor, found only close to wide expanses of open water, particularly in Scotland where it nests, although occasional ospreys are spotted at other large bodies of water, for example at Rutland Water, while passing through on migration (introduced birds now breed there too). Its contact call is a sharp, repeated 'chip, chip'.

HABITAT Summer: lakes, large reservoirs and rivers. Winter: West Africa.
SIZE 55cm (22in); wingspan 1.5–1.7m (5–5½ft)
EGGS 2–3, creamy white with reddish brown blotches
NEST Eagle-like eyrie made of sticks on top of a tall tree, usually pine.
FOOD Fish.
SIMILAR TO Could be mistaken for a gull in flight; look for the short, hooked, bird-of-prey beak and hunting technique.

3 Little grebe
Tachybaptus ruficollis

Also known as the dabchick, this is a common and widespread, small, dumpy, rounded diving bird with a short beak and a blunt, apparently tail-less, fluffy rear end. In the breeding season, it has a dark grey-brown face, top of head, back of neck, back and wings, and reddish chestnut 'cheeks' and throat and a light-coloured spot at the base of the beak. Birds dive frequently, stay under for some time and bob up

like a cork some distance away. Shy and furtive, they often disappear into reeds and vegetation.
HABITAT Throughout the British Isles; breeds along canals, slow-flowing rivers, ponds and small lakes and sometimes in inland marinas; in winter, moves to larger lakes and sheltered estuaries.
SIZE 27cm (11in)
EGGS 4–6, white
NEST Heap of floating vegetation tethered to anchored water plants or overhanging branches.
FOOD Aquatic invertebrates, small fish.
VARIATIONS In winter, duller with a dark brownish crown, back and wings and buff underparts.

How and where to spot an osprey

It's often very difficult to get a good view of a fast-moving bird of prey, but the location – over water – and the hunting technique are a great help with a possible osprey sighting. The hunting technique is to circle or hover kestrel-like over the water, then dive down with feet outstretched and grab a fish with its talons; after a successful strike, the fish is carried off – still held in the claws – usually pointing head-first, so as not to create 'drag' and slow the bird down. If you want to see a rare bird such as an osprey, don't rely on luck – visit a known location. The very best for osprey is the RSPB reserve at Loch Garten in the Cairngorms National Park, between April and August.

4 Great crested grebe
Podiceps cristatus

The great crested grebe is a relatively common, easily seen, long, slim diving bird that floats low in the water. Its neck, which is held at right angles to the body when the bird is alert, and its long, dagger-like beak give the bird an angular outline. The upperparts are dark greyish with reddish buff flanks and it has a white face and front of neck; the top of the head is black and has 2 tufts of plumes that are often erect. In spring and summer this grebe has a broad frill of long, chestnut facial feathers tipped with black, which are raised during courtship displays to make a round ruff encircling the face. Usually seen swimming, it stays well out in open water. It dives often, without a splash, staying under for a while and then reappearing some distance away, and prefers to swim rather than fly. Great crested grebes are well known for their spectacular courtship 'dances'. During the breeding season in late spring, pairs of grebes face each other and rise up in the water vertically, like penguins, erect their crests and perform ritual head-shaking, often with beaks full of waterweeds, while paddling like mad with their feet to stay upright.
HABITAT Throughout the British Isles, except northern Scotland and parts of Ireland, on lakes, reservoirs, flooded gravel pits and large rivers; in winter, also on estuaries and sheltered coastlines.
SIZE 50cm (20in)

EGGS 2–6, white
NEST Platform of vegetation tethered to anchored waterweeds.
FOOD Mainly small fish and some aquatic invertebrates.
VARIATIONS At first, the young are black-and-white-striped all over with red spots on the face and head. Later, the stripes become restricted to the head in juveniles. In autumn and winter, adults lose their breeding plumage (including the ruff) and become a plain, dullish grey and brown and the crown lacks the distinctive crest.

5 Bittern
Botaurus stellaris

This is a large, rare and very elusive bird, which resembles a thickset, black-streaked, brown-and-buff-mottled heron. When alarmed, it stands upright among the reeds, where it is superbly camouflaged. It is regularly seen at certain RSPB reserves, such as Leighton Moss in Lancashire, where its presence always creates great excitement at hides. The male's song is a far-carrying, low-pitched boom in spring, repeated 3 or 4 times. Although present in the British Isles throughout the year, it is more likely to be seen in winter, when numbers are higher because of the arrival of migrants from Europe.
HABITAT Very large areas of reed-beds, in relatively few locations.
SIZE 75cm (30in)
EGGS 4–6, buff-brown
NEST Platform of water plants on the ground, deep inside reed-beds.
FOOD Mainly fish, also frogs, insects, small mammals and birds.

6 Grey heron
Ardea cinerea

The grey heron is common, widespread and easily recognized. It is a large, upright, waterside bird with a white breast and neck that has a long, thin black line up the

centre. It can usually be seen standing motionless in shallow water or on the bank, fishing with a sudden stabbing motion of its long, dagger-like beak (normally yellow but orange-pink in spring, at the start of the breeding season). Look for long yellow legs and a white head with a broad black eye-stripe extended into narrow black plumes at the back of the head. When the bird is in flight, its large, lean body and huge, broad wings are visible; the wings show black tips and edges to the uppersides, and the neck is conspicuously doubled back to make a 'bump' at the front of the bird. It is usually silent, but its occasional in-flight call is a loud, sudden, reedy 'frank'.
HABITAT All sorts of freshwater habitats and estuaries; known to raid garden ponds in winter.
SIZE 94cm (37in) high; wingspan to 1.6m (5¼ft)
EGGS 3–4, light blue
NEST Large, untidy, stick nests in noisy colonies in tree tops.
FOOD Mainly eels and other fish, frogs, mice and other small rodents.

7 Mute swan
Cygnus olor

Britain's biggest bird, the mute swan is also very common, widespread and well known. It is huge and white, with a black-tipped, orange-red beak with a black knob at the top; it is often seen swimming, with its long neck held in an elegant 'S' shape. In the breeding season, the male (cob) often raises arched wings, like sails. When it up-ends to feed, the long tail appears markedly pointed. To get airborne, swans have to run some distance over the water, flapping their wings; in the air, the wings make a loud, throbbing noise. Sometimes swans utter various snorting sounds and, when angry, they hiss.

HABITAT Throughout the British Isles (except extreme north), in wetlands, lakes, rivers, reservoirs, flooded gravel pits, estuaries, salt marshes, sheltered coasts.

Swan colony

The biggest concentration of mute swans in the country can be seen at the Swannery at Abbotsbury, near Weymouth, in Dorset. Although swans are normally very territorial and do not put up with rival swans coming close to their nests or young in the breeding season, at Abbotsbury hundreds of them live at very close quarters in a huge colony, with public access to much of the area, yet remain well mannered. The birds are fed here, and injured swans and orphaned cygnets are cared for in pens.

SIZE 1.5m (5ft); wingspan up to 2.2m (7ft)

EGGS 5–7, very large, off-white

NEST Enormous flattened pile of reeds and vegetation, with the eggs in a slight hollow in the centre; on dry land but near water. (Don't get close: swans defend their eggs and young aggressively.)

FOOD Aquatic vegetation, dry-land grasses, salt-marsh plants, invertebrates.

VARIATIONS Cygnets are pale grey and fluffy; juvenile swans are pale brownish grey with dark grey beaks.

SIMILAR TO Whooper and Bewick's swans, but both these have yellow-and-black beaks with no orange-red; also, their wings don't make a loud, throbbing noise in flight.

8 Whooper swan
Cygnus cygnus

A regular winter visitor, this large white bird is similar to a mute swan but it has a long, straight neck that is usually held vertical when swimming. It has a large yellow beak (without the black knob) with a black tip broadening smoothly into a long, narrow head, creating a wedge-shaped outline that is very different from that of the mute swan. Its call is a loud, strangulated, bugling sound.

HABITAT Winter: mainly in northern Britain and Ireland but also the Ouse Washes in East Anglia, on wetlands, lakes, at sea, inshore along sheltered coasts and estuaries and in damp, remote farmland close to lakes or flooded water meadows. Summer: Iceland.

SIZE 1.5m (5ft); wingspan up to 2m (6½ft)

FOOD Aquatic plants, spilt or leftover grain in stubble fields, potatoes, grass, winter cereals.

SIMILAR TO Bewick's swan (which is smaller, with a shorter neck, rounder head and a beak that has more black than yellow) and the mute swan (which has an S-shaped neck when swimming and a bright orange-red beak with a black knob on top).

9 Bewick's swan
Cygnus columbianus

This regular winter visitor from Siberia is a small swan with a proportionately shorter but similarly upright neck to the whooper swan. It also has a bigger, more rounded head and a beak with more black than yellow. It often swims with its tail cocked and can be found in large flocks.

HABITAT Winter: wetlands, particularly the Ouse Washes in East Anglia, and the WWT reserve at Slimbridge in Gloucestershire. Summer: Siberia.

SIZE 1.2m (4ft); wingspan 1.8m (6ft)

FOOD Aquatic plants, grain, potatoes, grass, winter cereals.

SIMILAR TO Mute swan and whooper swan.

OPPOSITE When in flight, the elegant grey heron makes slow, stately flaps with its large, broad wings.

10 Greylag goose
Anser anser

The original ancestor of the domestic goose, the greylag is a large, solid-looking bird with brown wings laced with grey and white, a white undertail, a bright orange beak with a paler tip and dull pink legs. In winter, large flocks of migrants arrive in Scotland from Iceland, although introduced birds can be found in small numbers on water almost anywhere in the British Isles at any time of year.

HABITAT Wetlands and water.
SIZE 82cm (32in)
EGGS 4–6, off-white
NEST Mound of vegetation and sticks on the ground near water.
FOOD Seeds of grasses, sedges and rushes, potatoes and other root crops growing in arable fields, spilt grain.
SIMILAR TO Bean goose (which lives almost entirely in Norfolk and has a black tip to the beak and orange legs) and the pink-footed goose (which has a smaller, darker head and a dark tip to the smaller beak).

11 Bean goose
Anser fabalis

This is a rare goose that visits Britain in winter and is seen only at a few places in Norfolk and with a tiny population in central Scotland. It has very similar plumage to the greylag and pink-footed goose and has a white rear, orange legs and feet and a long, wedge-shaped orange beak with a darker tip.

HABITAT Late September–March: open, grassy pastures. Summer: breeds in northern Russia.
SIZE 75cm (30in)
FOOD Grass, clover, crops.
SIMILAR TO Greylag, but the bean goose is more elegant in shape, has a much darker head and neck, and the neck is more slender and swan-like. Also similar to the pink-footed goose but the legs and feet of the bean goose are orange.

12 Pink-footed goose
Anser brachyrhynchus

By far the most numerous of the 'grey' geese in Britain, the pink-footed goose is dark to pinkish grey, heavily barred on its back and wings. It has a white undertail, a short, thickish neck, a neat, rounded head and a short, dark beak with a pink band near the tip and bright pink legs and feet.

HABITAT Winter: estuaries, salt marshes and coastal farmland, in Scotland, northern England and the Wash, East Anglia. Summer: Iceland, Greenland.

SIZE 70cm (28in)
FOOD Grass, potatoes, grain and other root crops.
SIMILAR TO Greylag and bean goose.

13 White-fronted goose
Anser albifrons

A quite common, noisy winter visitor, in grey-brown with darker wings, back, head and neck, conspicuously patterned with irregular black bars across the breast and belly, and a white undertail. It has orange feet and beak and a small white forehead.

HABITAT October–March: large numbers found in scattered wetland locations in Britain, including the Severn estuary, parts of Norfolk and north Kent, also north-west and extreme south-west of Ireland, parts of Wales and isolated pockets in Scotland.

Summer: Russia, Greenland.
SIZE 70cm (28in)
FOOD Grass crops.
SIMILAR TO Greylag, bean and pink-footed geese, but the white forehead is the key distinguishing feature of the white-fronted goose.

Temporary visitors

'Migrants' is the term used for birds that visit the British Isles from other countries for part of the year. Spring migrants, such as swallows, come here to breed, while autumn migrants, such as geese, come to spend winter in a milder climate than their own, where food supplies may have been cut off by snow. Passage migrants migrate from one place to another and drop in to sites in the British Isles only temporarily, to rest and refuel, before moving on to complete their journey. In some cases, their route takes them over the Continent and they reach us only when they are blown off course by storms or strong winds, which is why many passage migrants are such rare birds. Arctic terns are among our most long-distance passage migrants, spending summer here and winter in the Antarctic, and have been found to travel as far as 35,400km (22,000 miles).

14

winter. Males have a chestnut-coloured head with a large, bold, dark green band around the eyes to the back of the head, outlined in cream. The fawn body has a broad, horizontal white stripe above a narrower black one along the edge of each folded wing, a black-spotted, pale buff breast and a cream-yellow triangle on the rump, under the tail. It feeds in shallow water with a muddy bottom and may up-end but does not dive. The piping 'crick-crick-crick' call is easily recognized with practice.
HABITAT Autumn–spring: most widespread, on lakes, flooded gravel pits, reservoirs, ponds, coastal lagoons and estuaries.

16

14 Mallard
Anas platyrhynchos

This is our most common and widespread duck. The drake has a distinctive, metallic-green head and neck with a bright yellow beak, a white ring round the collar, a brown breast, an off-white back and a black rump with curly black tail feathers. The wings have an iridescent blue flash bordered with white. The mallard dabbles in mud and shallow water and up-ends to feed in deeper water.
HABITAT Any coastal and inland water throughout the British Isles, including parks, where it becomes quite tame.
SIZE 60cm (24in)
EGGS 8–13, pale blue to grey-green or buff
NEST Shallow depression on the ground among vegetation or sometimes in crooks of trees.
FOOD Very varied diet that includes vegetation, seeds, invertebrates, crustaceans and bread.
VARIATIONS Female is overall beige-brown when seen from a distance; in close-up, you can see a distinct tracery/chevron pattern over the body and a white-bordered blue flash on each wing. The beak is mainly dull orange.

15 Gadwall
Anas strepera

The gadwall is a fairly scarce duck, slightly smaller than a mallard. Both sexes look rather dull and brown, so are often assumed to be females of other species. On the water, the male gadwall has a streaky brown back and folded wings, often showing a small white wing-flash, a grey-brown head and a dark grey beak, plus a finely barred grey lower neck and underparts. When it up-ends to feed, you can see the black undertail and rump and orange-yellow legs.
HABITAT Lakes and marshy ground inland. Some breed in the British Isles in summer, mostly in East Anglia, but the rest of the year they are found across central England and parts of Wales and Ireland.

SIZE 50cm (20in)
EGGS 8–12, creamy white
NEST Hollow lined with grass and female's down, near water.
FOOD Waterweeds and other vegetation, seeds.
SIMILAR TO Female mallard, which has more extensive orange and tan colouring.
VARIATIONS Female is light brown, flecked on the body with dark brown chevrons, with a small white wing-flash but no black undertail patch; the beak of the female is edged with orange.

16 Teal
Anas crecca

The teal is a common, very small, short-necked duck – only a little more than half the size of the mallard – seen in flocks, mostly in

Summer: breeds chiefly on wet moorland, marshes and bogs in uplands of northern England and north and west Scotland, with some on lowland/coastal marshes.
SIZE 35cm (14in)
EGGS 8–10, cream to pale olive
NEST Hollow lined with leaves and grass in undergrowth close to water.
FOOD Mainly seeds, invertebrates.
SIMILAR TO Males could be mistaken at a distance for the male wigeon (which is larger and does not have the green eye patch or cream triangle under the tail). Females are difficult to tell from other brown, camouflage-patterned female ducks, particularly the female mallard, but teal are smaller and the female mallard has a blue wing-flash instead of green.

15

17

17 Pintail
Anas acuta

This is a large, striking, elegant and easily identified but uncommon duck, with a long, low shape. The male has a chocolate-brown head and upper neck, a grey beak, a long, thin white neck and lower breast, and a mid-grey body with long, pointed, stripy, black-and-tan feathers drooping over the back and wings. Look for a cream patch at the rear end, followed by a black triangle leading up to the black-and-white tail, with 2 very long, spiky central tail feathers that often whip about. It up-ends to feed and very occasionally dives. Apart from a very small British breeding population (fewer than 50 pairs), it occurs as a winter visitor and is locally common in certain areas.
HABITAT Winter: in fresh water close to the coast and in sheltered estuaries, especially along the Mersey, eastern and south-west England, Wales and Ireland. Summer: Scandinavia, Russia.
SIZE 65cm (26in)
EGGS 7–9, pale cream to pale green
NEST Hollow lined with leaves, grass and female's breast down, on the ground.
FOOD Aquatic vegetation, invertebrates.
VARIATIONS Females are pale brown and lack the long tail feathers of the males.

18 Garganey
Anas querquedula

This uncommon summer visitor – a small, chunky, teal-shaped duck – is mostly seen in central and eastern England. The male has a brown-mottled breast and rear end, with a broad panel of grey stripes running down the centre of each side. The top of the head is charcoal-grey, with huge, bushy white 'eyebrows' on either side. Long, pointed black-and-white feathers droop over the back. The beak, feet and legs are dark grey.
HABITAT Late March–September: flooded fields, marshes, ditches and shallow fresh water.
SIZE 38cm (15in)
EGGS 8–10, creamy buff
NEST Hollow lined with leaves on the ground in tall vegetation.
FOOD Invertebrates, waterweeds.
SIMILAR TO Female teal, but the female teal is darker and less

18

boldly patterned. It has a distinct pale stripe above the eyes, too, and lacks the female garganey's whitish patch behind the beak and on the throat. Also female mallard, but the female garganey is smaller.
VARIATIONS Female is an overall light brown with a darker, almost chevron-like pattern; the uppersides and head are darker with fainter brown patches. The beak is charcoal-grey.

19 Shoveler
Anas clypeata

This is a striking, easily identified duck – mainly a winter visitor – that looks front-end-heavy, owing to an outsized beak ending in a wide spoon shape. It swims along in groups with its beak angled down, touching the surface and filtering the water to obtain food. The drake has a bottle-green head with yellow eyes, a black beak, a

black-and-white-striped back and tail, a white breast and white underparts with a large, chestnut-red patch halfway down the body. When the bird takes off, its wings create a distinctive 'woof, woof' sound, making it easy to identify if you don't get a good view.
HABITAT Winter: shallow lakes, estuaries and coastal lagoons in most of the British Isles (not northern Scotland or Ireland). Summer: some breed in East Anglia.

19

SIZE 50cm (20in)
EGGS 8–12, olive or buff
NEST Hollow lined with vegetation on dry ground near water.
FOOD Invertebrates and seeds, floating near the water's surface.
VARIATIONS Female is overall dappled brown, similar to the female mallard except for the oversized beak.

Male and female ducks

Females of many species of duck look very similar to one another, often being a drab brown, in stark contrast to the brightly coloured males – this is so that females are well camouflaged when nesting. Faced with a large flock of ducks, identify the males first, then spot the females that accompany them. In late summer, all male ducks moult and their plumage becomes dull and more like the female's. It is known as 'eclipse' plumage and lasts for about 4–6 weeks.

Wetlands, fenlands and the Broads

When wetlands are managed carefully they are great habitats for wildlife. Reed-beds are the dominant feature, attracting a wealth of small brown, reed-bed birds such as reed and sedge warblers, and scarce birds of prey like the marsh harrier, which is seen mainly in wetland habitats, mostly in East Anglia in summer. In reed-beds you may also be lucky enough to see – or more likely hear – rarities like the bittern (a large, chunky brown heron with a foghorn-like boom) or bearded tit (a long-tailed, gingery brown bird with a

In summer, the water meadows at Welney, East Anglia, are grazed by cattle, but in winter the meadows flood and thousands of migrating ducks, geese and swans throng here from their Arctic breeding grounds.

distinctive, regular, 'ping, ping' call, found in coastal reed-beds). In winter, large areas of flooded fields are a fabulous venue for watching waterfowl.

The Ouse Washes – which consist mainly of giant water meadows in the middle of East Anglia – are a great place to see migrating swans, geese and ducks that arrive in autumn from the far north to spend winter with us. The Wildfowl and Wetland Trust (WWT) at Welney and the Ouse Washes RSPB reserve are the best places to see them. In other parts of the country, wetlands and reed-beds have

been incorporated into wildlife reserves, such as Slimbridge in Gloucestershire (once the home of the late Sir Peter Scott, the great conservationist, painter and wildlife expert), the WWT's reserves at Martin Mere and the RSPB reserve at Leighton Moss in Lancashire, as well as their relatively new reserve at Pulborough Brooks in West Sussex. In the heart of the Fens, the National Trust's nature reserve at Wicken Fen, Cambridgeshire, hosts all sorts of typical fenland wildlife, including the elusive grasshopper warbler, which is hard to spot but easily heard – its distinctive call sounds remarkably like a fisherman reeling in his line.

The Broads remained a superb wildlife habitat until the waterways opened up to holiday craft, which brought in a whole load of new problems. Motor boats racing along the narrow waterways created wash that wore away the banks and made it impossible for the usual fringe of reeds and other water plants to survive, thus reducing the habitat for waterside birds and wildlife. Pollution – from petrol spills to sewage and litter – didn't help. But conservation came to their aid, rules were tightened up for boats on inland waterways – speed limits and sewage both have to be contained – and today the quieter parts of the Broads and surrounding wetlands still provide a rich wildlife habitat.

Now that the coypu (a non-native rodent resembling a large water rat) has been eradicated, otters are making a welcome comeback, and are thought to be pushing out the mink (which, like coypu, are foreign imports that escaped from fur farms). Since mink are believed to be responsible for the dramatic decline in water-vole numbers, it's hoped that they, too, will recover. Swallowtail butterflies – our largest butterfly species – have now also been successfully reintroduced into the area around the Broads.

20

20 Pochard
Aythya ferina

The pochard is a reasonably common diving duck. The drake is easily identified by its bright chestnut head and grey body with a black breast and tail, giving it a distinctive tricolor effect; if given a good view, you can see the black beak with a large grey chevron midway down, and the long, sloping forehead. Birds are usually seen floating, asleep, by day – they feed mostly at night. It is mainly a winter visitor, often observed with tufted ducks.

HABITAT Winter: present throughout most of the British Isles, on lakes, reservoirs and large ponds with plenty of vegetation in the water. Most winter visitors breed in northern and eastern Europe and central Russia, though about 500 pairs nest in Britain and about 50 pairs in Ireland.
SIZE 45cm (17½in)
EGGS 6–10, greenish grey
NEST Dense mat of vegetation on the ground among reeds.
FOOD Waterweeds, seeds, invertebrates.
SIMILAR TO Drake can be confused with a wigeon drake, which has a chestnut head with a creamy yellow forehead stripe and a small grey, black-tipped beak, a pinkish breast with a grey-and-white body, and black wing-tips and tail.
VARIATIONS Females are almost entirely brown, with a yellowish brown head and breast and grey-streaked brown back and wings; the beak is black with a grey chevron.

21 Tufted duck
Aythya fuligula

This is by far our most common diving duck. In the breeding season, the relatively small drakes are a distinctive black and white, with a short black crest drooping from the back of the head. Swimming birds look mostly black with an oblong white patch on the flanks; in close-up, you can also see the light grey, black-tipped beak, very round head with a high, domed forehead and bright yellow eyes. Usually seen in groups, often with other ducks, they dive frequently for a few seconds and come bobbing up again like corks.

HABITAT Widespread throughout most lowland areas of the British Isles, except northern Scotland, the extreme south-west of England, western Wales and south-west Ireland, on lakes, reservoirs, flooded gravel pits and sometimes rivers.
SIZE 45cm (17½in)
EGGS 8–11, pale blue-green
NEST Hollow lined with vegetation in dense cover near water's edge.
FOOD Molluscs, aquatic insects and plants, other invertebrates.
VARIATIONS Females and juveniles have a dark brown back, tail and head (with a short tuft at the back of the head) and light brown flanks and breast.

21

22 Goosander
Mergus merganser

A long, sleek diving duck of inland waterways, the goosander is locally common at certain regularly used sites but rare elsewhere. It is as big as a mallard drake, with a long, narrow red beak, hooked down at the tip, a large, bottle-green head and upper neck (which appears black from a distance) and a high forehead and mainly black back. The rest of the bird is white with a grey tail and the legs are orange.

HABITAT Lakes, flooded gravel pits, reservoirs, rivers and a few sheltered estuaries. Usually seen in pairs or small groups, mostly in Scotland, the north of England and Wales. In winter it is more widespread throughout the British Isles except in Ireland, where it is a rare visitor.
SIZE 60cm (24in)

22

EGGS 8–12, off-white
NEST In a hole in a tree or tree stump, lined with female's breast down; in special nestboxes; sometimes on the ground.
FOOD Fish, occasionally small mammals and insects.
SIMILAR TO Red-breasted merganser, which is usually seen in winter in sheltered coastal waters, although some may be found on fresh water; mergansers have smaller heads, narrower beaks with only a slightly hooked tip and a more slim-line profile; the male merganser has red eyes, and a far more heavily patterned body than the male goosander, including a white collar round its neck. The female merganser differs from the female goosander in the shape and size of its crest; also, the goosander female has sharper demarcation between the head, neck and chin areas (in the merganser, the colour changes are more gradual).
VARIATIONS Female is the same shape as the drake but has a pearly grey, dappled body and an auburn head with a short, shaggy crest down the back and a white chin.

23 Red-breasted merganser

Mergus serrator

Mergansers are difficult to see well as they frequently dive and swim, usually well out at sea. The outline is often the first clue – look for a long, thin, stiletto-like red beak, a long, narrow, swept-back head tapering into a wispy crest at the back, an S-shaped neck and a long, lean body that floats very low in the water. Given powerful binoculars or a telescope, look for the bright red eyes and beak, which is very slightly up-turned, a broad white ring round the neck, a black-spotted, chestnut breast, a dark bottle-green head with a spiky crest, and a black back with white flashes on the 'shoulders'. The grey underparts and orange-red legs are not normally visible on swimming birds. Males in spring breeding plumage are especially striking, displaying flamboyantly towards the end of winter.

HABITAT Winter: mostly sheltered inlets or estuaries but often some distance offshore. Summer: breeds in Scotland, west Wales, north and west Ireland, on estuaries, large creeks, sea lochs and inland waters.

SIZE 55cm (22in)

EGGS 8–10, light beige

NEST Hollow in the ground among vegetation, close to water.

FOOD Fish.

SIMILAR TO Great crested grebe (which is more common) has a similar outline and often swims

in similar places in winter; however, in winter the grebe is more grey and white, with little or no crest, and its beak is paler and more spear-shaped. Also similar to the goosander.

VARIATIONS Female has a dark chestnut head and smaller crest, duller red or brown eyes, a dark grey back and pale grey underparts.

24 Smew

Mergus albellus

A rare winter visitor to Britain, the smew is a small, striking, teal-sized diving duck. It is often solitary or seen in small numbers in the British Isles. A drake on the water looks black and white – it has a white body, faintly grey-barred flanks, 2 narrow black rings around the base of the neck and across the sides of the breast, a black centre to its back and charcoal-grey wing-tips. Its head is adorned with a small white crest and a black flash on either side, and it has a charcoal-grey beak and

a black patch around each eye.

HABITAT November–late March: mostly in the south-east of England, on reservoirs, lakes and flooded gravel pits, including those round London. Summer: Scandinavia, Russia.

SIZE 40cm (16in)

FOOD Fish.

VARIATIONS Females (known as 'redheads') are much greyer-bodied than the males, and their heads have a chestnut cap, running from the beak to the back of the head, with a black patch around each eye, contrasting with the pure white 'cheeks' and throat. Juveniles look like females but with darker upperparts and browner caps.

25 Mandarin duck

Aix galericulata

This is an unmistakable Southeast Asian duck, which escaped from ornamental wildfowl collections and has now become established in the wild. The drake is very colourful, with a red beak, a shaggy

orange 'beard' and huge, bushy white 'eyebrows'. It has a dark-green-and-purple crest along the top of the head and neck, a glossy dark green back and tail, tan sides and a purple breast edged with 2 pairs of broad, black-and-white stripes. Big, bright orange 'sails' stand up on either side of the back, just before the tail. The mandarin often perches on trees at the waterside, giving a view of its white belly and yellow legs.

HABITAT Lakes surrounded by trees in southern and central England with a few further north.

SIZE 45cm (17½in)

EGGS 12, white

NEST In holes in trees.

FOOD Seeds, nuts, insects, snails.

VARIATIONS Female is duller in colour but patterned. It has a grey head with a white eye-stripe and chin, an ochre, white-tipped beak, a brown back and tail, royal blue wing-tips, a brown breast and sides with white speckles and a white belly.

Saw-billed fish-eaters

Smew, goosander and red-breasted merganser are known as sawbills, since instead of having wide beaks with smooth edges, like most other ducks, their beaks are long and slim with toothed inner edges – these enable them to get a grip on slippery fish, which are their main food. Also, these diving ducks have strong beaks for dealing with molluscs and crabs. Other ducks feed on waterweeds, seeds and invertebrates, which are 'dabbled' for, so spatula-shaped beaks allow them to shovel down food.

26

26 Ruddy duck
Oxyura jamaicensis

This is an unusual and immediately recognizable diving duck that was introduced from the United States into ornamental wildfowl collections and then escaped into the wild. Small and stocky, it has a pert, cheeky look, rather like an animated toy duck for the bath. The drake has a conspicuous, intensely bright blue beak in the breeding season, a black head and neck, white 'cheeks' and a bright chestnut body. Another identifying feature is its long, stiff, dark brown tail, which is carried along the water or held jauntily cocked at an angle or vertically, displaying the white patch underneath. The bird often dives and bobs up again in seconds. Conservationists have mixed feelings about the arrival of the ruddy duck – on the one hand, it is a very endearing charmer, much loved by the general public; however, its arrival presents a threat to the rare European white-headed duck, a close cousin, found in southern Spain.
HABITAT Shallow lakes, reservoirs and ponds with fringing vegetation, mainly in central and southern England but with scattered populations in southern Scotland, Anglesey and northern Ireland.
SIZE 40cm (16in)
EGGS 8–10, off-white
NEST Platform of rushes, reeds and leaves among vegetation in water.
FOOD Aquatic invertebrates, seeds of water plants.
VARIATIONS Female is drab brown, with a darker crown and back and a lighter brown-barred face and paler underparts.

27 Water rail
Rallus aquaticus

An uncommon and furtive bird, the water rail is rarely seen but more often heard, making sudden, bloodcurdling, pig-like squeals or grunts. It is most likely to be seen walking cautiously, flicking its tail nervously, in the mud alongside a reed-bed, or walking down a drainage channel in wetlands. Look for a large, moorhen-shaped bird with a very slim body and longish red beak, a strongly streaked chestnut-and-blackish crown and upperparts, a blue-grey head and neck and flanks barred black, white and buff. It has a short, semi-cocked tail with a white patch underneath, and long legs and toes.
HABITAT Throughout most of the British Isles, except northern Scotland. Breeds in reed-beds and marshes with dense vegetation and in areas of bare mud; also along rivers and edges of lakes and ponds. More widespread in winter.
SIZE 25cm (10in)
EGGS 7–10, buff with sparse red-brown blotches
NEST Cup of stems and leaves deep in reed-beds or drainage channels overgrown with dense vegetation.
FOOD Invertebrates, seeds, berries, frogs, newts, small fish.

28 Moorhen
Gallinula chloropus

The moorhen is a common, widespread and well-known water bird that looks wedge-shaped in the water, with a dark brown back and a black head with a bare red forehead, a red, yellow-tipped beak and a slate-grey neck and underparts. It swims with jerky movements, like a clockwork toy, with the tail held upright, showing a white triangle underneath. It can dive, but doesn't do so very often and quickly resurfaces. On land, you can see its long, yellow-green legs and large, unwebbed feet with very long toes. The moorhen rarely flies, preferring to scuttle away through the undergrowth. On the water, it keeps fairly close to the edge. Its alarm call is a loud, sharp 'karrack'.
HABITAT Throughout lowland areas of the British Isles, in all types of fresh water, including water-filled roadside ditches and village ponds, also reed-beds and undergrowth in damp meadows close to water.
SIZE 34cm (14in)
EGGS 6–10, light buff with reddish brown blotches
NEST Deep cup of twigs and stems lined with grasses among reeds or other dense aquatic vegetation, in

28

waterside bushes or trees, or on a large, messy pile of floating waterweeds that are tethered to sunken branches.
FOOD Water plants, seeds, invertebrates, worms, tadpoles, carrion, human food scraps.
SIMILAR TO Coot, which is slightly larger and dumpier and also differs in having a white forehead and beak, bluish grey legs and flanged feet. The coot is usually less shy than the moorhen.
VARIATIONS Downy chicks are pure black, lacking the red heads of baby coots; juveniles are brown with green beaks.

27

29 Coot
Fulica atra

This is a common, self-confident and easily seen black water bird that is dumpy and rounded, with a bare white forehead and beak and reddish eyes. On the water, it looks very buoyant, swimming well out in the open, and it dives often and deeply for food, staying under for some time. On land, you can see the light, mainly blue-grey-and-olive legs and matching feet, which look too big for the bird – they are not webbed, but lobed with flanges of skin running down the edges of

the toes. When in a hurry, it 'runs' on the surface of the water, flapping its wings, but it is not keen to take off except in emergencies. Its main call is an irate squawk. It also has a less urgent 'coot' sound and a distinctive 'ptik'. The coot can be very quarrelsome and aggressive in the breeding season.

HABITAT Widespread throughout most of the British Isles, except for some parts of the south-west and north-west Scotland, on and near open water, including canals, slow-flowing rivers, large ponds, lakes, flooded gravel pits and reservoirs.

SIZE 38cm (15in)

EGGS 6–9, light buff with dark brown speckles

NEST Untidy, floating pile of waterweeds on a firm foundation.

FOOD Mainly algae, roots, shoots, water-plant seeds, invertebrates.

SIMILAR TO Moorhen.

VARIATIONS Downy chicks are black and fluffy, with red faces and beak bases with blue behind the eyes and a ruff of long orange down; juveniles are grey with a white lower face and breast and a pale grey beak.

30 Little stint
Calidris minuta

This is a very small, sparrow-sized wader, mostly seen in autumn in the British Isles, when it is passing through on migration from Scandinavia or Siberia to its winter grounds. Many birds are juveniles with quite pronounced markings. Look for squat, short-necked birds with a dark-tipped tail and short black legs and beak. The crown and upperparts are boldly chequered with chestnut, black, buff and white, bearing a narrow but distinct, white, double 'V' in the centre, pointing towards the tail (a good identification feature). It has a white throat and underparts and the head is often speckled light brown, with a faint chestnut eye-stripe. The little stint feeds in wet mud, pecking repeatedly at the ground with a fast 'sewing-machine' action; it is often seen with dunlin.

HABITAT August–November: round the south and east coasts of the British Isles, in sheltered, muddy ground near still, shallow water inland, but sometimes also on mud flats at estuaries. Winter: Africa, India.

SIZE 13cm (5in)

FOOD Small marine invertebrates.

SIMILAR TO Dunlin, which is bigger with a longer, down-curved beak. By autumn, when the little stint arrives, the dunlin is often in winter plumage, so looks greyer.

31 Ruff
Philomachus pugnax

An uncommon, rather redshank-like wader, the ruff has long legs but a slightly plumpish body that is topped by a rather elegant, slim neck and a small head. During the breeding season, males sport a spectacular neck ruff, although this is rarely seen in the British Isles. Most birds are seen in autumn, while passing through on migration between Scandinavia or Russia and Africa. At this time, it has dark greyish brown upperparts, paler on the back of the neck and top of the head, and warm buff underparts that grade into a white belly and undertail. Look for the dark, slightly drooping beak and reddish, orange, greenish or buff-brown legs. This wader feeds in mud or shallowish water, probing for food with its beak.

HABITAT Autumn: in various freshwater habitats and in fields beside water. Some spend winter here, mainly near the coast.

SIZE 26cm (10½in)

FOOD Invertebrates, some small fish, frogs and seeds.

SIMILAR TO Redshank, though the redshank has a bright red beak and legs while the ruff has a dark-brown-to-black beak and variable leg colour (may be reddish, greenish or buff-brown).

VARIATIONS Female (reeve) is smaller than the male. In winter plumage (they are often moulting into it in autumn) both sexes have a mottled grey back, a light grey or white head and neck and white underparts.

Breeding plumage

You'd expect that the ruff would be very easy to identify 'in the field', since the male is often depicted in illustrations or seen on TV in its breeding plumage, sporting a huge, shaggy, white, chestnut-brown or brindled ruff round the neck and a big, shaggy crest standing up above a pinkish face. The birds are usually shown displaying communally at special sites known as 'leks' to impress females. But unless you are very lucky indeed and spot them at their breeding grounds (of which there are very few in the British Isles, chiefly on the Ouse Washes of East Anglia) you won't see a male with his ruff. You are much more likely to spot a non-breeding adult, in autumn, which looks very similar to other waders, particularly redshanks.

32 Jack snipe
Lymnocryptes minumus

This is a brown wader that is a scarce winter visitor, with a dumpy shape, short tail and shortish legs. It has brown upperparts, with very striking, horizontal, creamy buff lines running from shoulder to tail, a buff-speckled throat and breast, white underparts and dull grey-green legs. The head is brown on top, with a buff-coloured face striped with brown, and a medium-length beak. Jack snipes lurk in dense vegetation, often bobbing up and down when feeding, but they 'freeze' close to the ground if frightened and fly up only when something threatens to step on them. When this occurs, the birds erupt silently into the air and drop down into cover quickly.

HABITAT September–April: well-vegetated, marshy places scattered around England, Wales and southern Ireland.
SIZE 18cm (7in)
FOOD Insects, molluscs, worms and other invertebrates.
SIMILAR TO Common snipe, which is larger and has a much longer beak. Also, the head patterns differ: the jack snipe has a narrow, dark, horizontal line that runs through each pale buff 'eyebrow', a dark stripe down the very top of the crown (rather than pale buff) and a bold, dark crescent below each eye. The common snipe is not as scarce and is present year round.

33 Common snipe
Gallinago gallinago

The common snipe is a medium-sized, streaky brown wader with darker upperparts and paler underparts. It is so well camouflaged that you could be looking straight at it but see it only when it moves. Look for a brown-and-buff-striped head and a very long, straight beak that is over twice the length of the head and neck. The very long beak is used to probe deeply into mud and soft ground for worms and insects, and is very obvious when the bird is in flight.
HABITAT Throughout Britain and Ireland, in wetlands, marshes, bogs and wet farmland; numbers are considerably higher in winter, when migrants arrive from northern Europe.
SIZE 26cm (10½in)
EGGS 4, pale green with brown blotches

NEST Grass-lined hollow on wet ground.
FOOD Worms, insects and other invertebrates.
SIMILAR TO Woodcock (which lives mainly in woodland and is much larger and stouter, with a more mottled, less 'stripy' appearance and a shorter beak) and Jack snipe.

34 Common sandpiper
Actitis hypoleucos

Not as common as the name suggests, this thrush-sized wader has a medium-length, brownish beak with a darker tip, a mid-brown back, wings, head and neck and short, dull-greenish-to-yellow legs. The bright white of the underparts extends up in a distinctive white wedge between the brown of the breast and the 'shoulders'. It is usually seen alone or in groups of up to 5 or 6, rather than congregating in large flocks, as is the case with many seashore waders. The common sandpiper feeds from the surface of mud while walking, and the tail and rear end bob up and down frequently.
HABITAT Summer: along the edges of streams and rivers, lakes and fast-flowing reservoirs, mainly in northern and western uplands. Migrants are more widespread on wetlands and in sheltered estuaries. Winter: a few stay in the British Isles but most migrate to Africa.
SIZE 20cm (8in)
EGGS 4, beige with darker spots
NEST Hidden in grass, near water.
FOOD Insects and other invertebrates.
SIMILAR TO Green sandpiper.

Identifying snipes by sound
You can often tell you are in snipe territory, even without seeing the bird, if you hear a soft but far-carrying, rhythmic bleating sound in summer, usually early in the morning or in the evening on fine days. This is made by the males, which display by diving down towards the ground with their stiff outer tail feathers spread out at right angles, so creating the familiar sound known as 'drumming'.

35

35 Green sandpiper
Tringa ochropus

This is a widespread, blackbird-sized wader in darkish olive-brown with white underparts, a medium-length beak and dark olive-green legs. The head and neck are a shade lighter grey, with black eyes linked to the black beak by a short, broad, smudged black line with a white area immediately above it, continuing as a white eye-ring (a good identification point). The back is speckled with white. When seen in flight, the undersides of the wings are black against the white body, which identifies it from any other British wader. The green sandpiper is mainly an autumn passage migrant (present in the British Isles from July to October) and is a scarce winter visitor (from November to March). Just a few pairs are known to breed in the Highlands, though this occurs in some years only.
HABITAT Edges of inland water, including lakes, reservoirs and sometimes creeks around tidal estuaries.
SIZE 23cm (9in)
FOOD Invertebrates.
SIMILAR TO Common sandpiper, which lacks the white speckles on the back and has a paler, shorter beak and legs and a white wedge between the breast and 'shoulders'. Also resembles the wood sandpiper, which has longer green legs, pale underwings when seen in flight, and is more dappled than the green sandpiper.

36 Wood sandpiper
Tringa glareola

This is a scarce wader that drops in briefly during its annual migration and may be seen in August and September in the British Isles. It looks like a scaled-down version of the green sandpiper: a size smaller, a little leaner, a shade or two paler-coloured and more dappled, but with much longer, yellower legs than the green and common sandpipers. The white 'eyebrows', reaching from the beak to well behind the eyes, are distinctive, but it still has the green sandpiper's smudgy black line linking the beak to the eyes. In flight, the wood sandpiper has pale underwings and its toes project behind its tail.
HABITAT Inland wetland areas of southern and eastern British Isles.
SIZE 20cm (8in)
FOOD Invertebrates.
SIMILAR TO Green sandpiper and common sandpiper, which is not speckled and has pale buff rather than yellow legs.

36

37 Black tern
Chlidonias niger

The black tern may 'drop in' almost anywhere in England or parts of Wales while on migration in May, but it is seen mostly from July to September. Spring birds in breeding plumage look very different from seaside terns. Viewed in flight from below, black terns have a black head and body with a short, slightly forked white tail; instead of diving into the water for fish they dip down, more like a swallow, to catch insects. A standing bird has an ash-grey lower back and wings contrasting with a black head and body, also short, stumpy, dull red-brown legs, a sharp, slim black beak and long wing-tips and tail – the folded wings stand out slightly from the side of the body. Birds seen in autumn will be taking on or already in winter plumage; the body loses its black coloration and the undersides of a flying bird look white with dark smudges. At this time of year, the upperparts are grey and the white head has a black cap.
HABITAT Inland lakes, pools, marshland, reservoirs and sometimes sheltered coastal inlets.
SIZE 23cm (9in)
FOOD Insects, fish, frogs, tadpoles.

37

38

38 Sand martin
Riparia riparia

This is a small, squat, summer-visiting member of the swallow family, with shortish wings and a short, shallow-forked tail. It is brown and white, with a pronounced brown collar over the white breast. The sand martin has a very fast, jerky, fluttering flight, and is found near fresh water across the British Isles.
HABITAT March–October: lakes, flooded gravel pits or quarries and other places where there are cliffs in which to nest. Winter: just south of the Sahara.
SIZE 12cm (4¾in)
EGGS 4–5, white
NEST At the end of a burrow in vertical cliffs where the rock is soft enough to tunnel.
FOOD Small flying insects, especially midges, flies, aphids.
SIMILAR TO House martin, which is often found hunting over water, like the sand martin. However, the house martin is black and white with a white rump patch (lacking in the sand martin). In flight, the house martin makes more sweeping movements and the underwings are much paler than those of the sand martin.

39

39 Kingfisher
Alcedo atthis

The kingfisher is a striking, colourful but rather shy and elusive resident that is more common than you might think. Barely bigger than a sparrow, it is usually seen as a streak of brilliant orange and turquoise flashing low over the water, often with a brief, loud, shrill, 'peeping' whistle. Given a good view of a perched bird (which sits very upright), you can see the orange 'cheeks', chest and belly, the iridescent greenish-blue-to-turquoise head and wings, the brilliant electric-blue back and tail and the red feet. The beak is long and dagger-like – the lower mandible of the female's beak is orange; the male's beak is all black.

HABITAT Clear, clean, slow-moving rivers throughout the British Isles (absent from much of northern Scotland). May be seen in estuaries in very cold winters.

SIZE 16.5cm (6½in), including a 4cm (1½in) beak

EGGS 6–7, white

NEST At the end of a long tunnel in the riverbank, excavated by the breeding pair, accessed via a hole in a reasonably bare, vertical earth face.

FOOD Fish up to half the bird's own body length; some aquatic insects.

PREVIOUS PAGES The Ouse Washes, in East Anglia, are visited in winter by tens of thousands of swans, many of which have journeyed from northern Europe in search of food.

40 Grey wagtail
Motacilla cinerea

This is the same shape and size as the better-known pied wagtail, with the same bobbing behaviour. It has a blue-grey head with a white stripe above and below the eyes, a blue-grey back, a black tail with white outer feathers and black wings, a light greenish yellow rump patch and, in summer only, a black throat. The underparts are a clear lemon-yellow and the legs are pink.

HABITAT Summer: fast-flowing rivers and streams, mainly in west and north Britain. Winter: on wet farmland, reservoirs, canals, lowland rivers and coasts.

SIZE 18cm (7in)

EGGS 4–6, buff-grey with slightly darker speckles

NEST Cup of grass, rootlets and twigs in holes in steep banks or in walls or bridges near water.

FOOD Aquatic invertebrates.

SIMILAR TO Yellow wagtail, which is present only in summer.

VARIATIONS Female has an off-white or speckled-grey throat in summer; the male in winter looks like the female with very little yellow on the breast and belly.

41 Dipper
Cinclus cinclus

Although they are land birds, dippers are extremely adept in the water – they will dive off stones or walk into water, and when buffeted by 'white water' they will bob up again quite happily. They are the only songbirds to walk underwater on the bed of fast-flowing streams to seek food. They also use their wings to swim underwater, which is remarkable for a land bird. They are squat and very plump-bodied, with a white throat and breast and chestnut belly band separating the white from the brown-and-black rest of the body and wings, and a very short, sawn-off-looking tail. Dippers are usually seen bobbing up and down on rocks, or making brief, rapid flights on short, whirring wings.

HABITAT Mostly in northern and western Britain, along mountain streams and fast-flowing, shallow, rocky rivers; sometimes around weirs or rapids in watercourses at lower levels and, in winter, around lakes and other wetlands.

SIZE 18cm (7in)

EGGS 4–5, white

40

41

NEST Bulky, dome-shaped nest of moss and grass under an overhang, in a hole in the riverbank or behind a waterfall.

FOOD Small fish, aquatic insects and other invertebrates.

VARIATIONS In juveniles, the upperparts are slate-grey with pale markings. The chin and breast are dirty white with grey crescents, the rest of the underparts are grey, barred darker.

Watching kingfishers

Kingfishers are birds with very regular habits. If you see a kingfisher whizzing down the river, keep quite still and wait for a better look, as it often repeats its flight pattern. Eventually, you may see it returning along the same route, or stopping at a favourite perch to watch for fish. When it spots one, it will dive into the water and emerge almost immediately with a small fish, which is bashed on a twig, then swallowed head-first. The birds return regularly to good vantage points – a bare, horizontal branch, standing out on its own about 2–3m (6½–10ft) above the water, or a post in the bank are often used. (They will sometimes stop and hover in mid-air, when they look rather like hummingbirds, with incredibly fast-moving wings.) If you see a bird fly out of a hole in the bank, it will usually be back within 5 or 10 minutes with a fish. Kingfishers are most often seen fishing in summer, when they have young to feed.

42

44 Cetti's warbler
Cettia cetti
Pronounced 'chetty's', this is a furtive and hard-to-see, small bird that has spread here from the Mediterranean region since our winters turned milder. Look for a stocky, short-winged, robin-sized bird in warm chestnut, with a pale grey eye-stripe, and pale grey underparts with a rusty wash on the flanks. The tail is broad and rounded at the tip, brown above and below, and is often held semi-cocked and slightly fanned. The

44

42 Bearded tit
Panurus biarmicus
The distinctive, 'ping, ping, ping' call is often the first indication that bearded tits are around. They are hard to see, occurring in small, loose flocks, clambering about athletically in reed-beds, where they feed, or flying quickly between clumps with whirring wings. Although unusual, these sparrow-sized birds, with a very long, rust-orange, black-edged tail, are easily identified. A perching male has a pale lavender-blue hood, a buff-orange beak and bold, black 'handlebar-moustache' markings from the beak to the top of the breast. The body is rust-coloured, with slightly paler undersides and bold chestnut-black-and-white stripes diagonally across the folded wings. The legs are black. Though present all year round, they are most likely to be seen in spring and autumn, when they move between their summer and winter locations.
HABITAT Found exclusively in dense reed-beds, especially in East Anglia, Lincolnshire and a small strip along the south coast, roughly from Weymouth to Eastbourne.
SIZE 16.5cm (6½in)
EGGS 5–7, white with dark brown speckles
NEST Deep cup of leaves and reeds, near the ground in reed-beds.
FOOD Insects, seeds.
VARIATIONS Female looks like the male but with a rust-orange head and whitish throat and lacks the hood and 'moustache'.

43 Reed bunting
Emberiza schoeniclus
Commonly found mainly in wettish areas in Britain, the reed bunting resembles a sparrow with a conspicuous black cowl over its head and a black 'bib' and white collar. Look for a sparrow-sized bird with a house-sparrow-like pattern on the back, but brighter, in chestnut, blackish and buff, and with a longer black-and-buff tail that has a V-shaped notch at the tip. Look also for a grey neck and breast with slightly streaked flanks. The tail has white outer feathers.
HABITAT Damp places, including riverbanks, reed-beds, marshes, fens; increasingly in drier habitats such as farmland with overgrown hedgerows, ditches, young conifer plantations and even large gardens.
SIZE 15cm (6in)
EGGS 4–6, buff-grey, streaked with blackish brown
NEST Cup of grass and moss in low bushes or young conifer plantations.
FOOD Mainly seeds, also insects and spiders.
SIMILAR TO House sparrow, but the reed bunting has brighter coloration and the male has a black cowl in spring and summer.
VARIATIONS Female lacks the black cowl; the crown and upperparts are dark-streaked and the head is mid-brown with 2 white stripes above and below the dark 'cheeks'.

43

bird makes sudden, short dashes between bushes and lurks low down in deep cover; it is usually located only by its occasional, sudden, loud bursts of song.
HABITAT Low scrub close to inland water, in a broad strip along the south and east coast from the Wash to Falmouth and around the Bristol Channel.
SIZE 14cm (5½in)
EGGS 4, bright brick-red
NEST Deep cup of grass and leaves, low down in dense bushes.
FOOD Small insects and other invertebrates; some seeds.
SIMILAR TO Many other small brown birds if only a fleeting glimpse is obtained. The broad fan-tail is a good give-away.

45 Grasshopper warbler
Locustella naevia

The grasshopper warbler is a fairly scarce, little brown summer visitor that is more often heard than seen. It is smaller than a house sparrow, with mid-olive-brown upperparts marked with broken streaks, tan underparts with some streaks on the chest and flanks and light pink legs. The head is streaky brown on top with matching 'cheeks', a faint tan eye-stripe and a light tan throat with a slim, pointed beak. Hard to see, it creeps mouse-like through the reeds, although it sometimes sits out in the open to sing. Its song is an unmusical, high-pitched mechanical sound, rather like a fisherman's reel being wound in.

HABITAT April–September: in and near marshes, fens or dry habitats such as farmland, young conifer plantations (where some grasshopper warblers breed) and heaths throughout Britain and Ireland (except for the north), but seen and heard with most certainty at fenland nature reserves such as Wicken Fen, in East Anglia.

SIZE 13cm (5in)

EGGS 5–6, white speckled with brown markings

NEST Cup of grass, moss and leaves, low down in dense cover.

FOOD Insects, spiders.

SIMILAR TO Sedge warbler, which has a much more pronounced, creamy white eye-stripe, contrasting with its darker crown.

46 Sedge warbler
Acrocephalus schoenobaenus

A summer visitor to Britain, the sedge warbler is an active, small brown bird with a fairly short, blunt-ended tail, streaky brown upperparts with a gingerish rump, pale buff underparts and reddish brown legs. It has a pale throat and a pronounced, creamy white eye-stripe running from the beak to the back of the head, which has a darker, streaky cap.

HABITAT April–September: throughout the British Isles, mainly along riversides, reed-beds, marshes and other wet places, or in shrubs or other dense vegetation. Winter: Africa.

SIZE 13cm (5in)

EGGS 5–6, light buff with darker grey speckles

NEST Deep cup of grass, woven around low-down stems among brambles or other dense bushes near water.

FOOD Mainly insects and other invertebrates; berries in autumn.

SIMILAR TO Grasshopper warbler and reed warbler, which lacks the conspicuous eye-stripe and darker cap and has an unpatterned head, back, wings and tail and brown legs.

47 Reed warbler
Acrocephalus scirpaceus

A small, shy but active bird, the reed warbler is a plain-plumaged, almost featureless 'little brown job' of reed-beds, where it clings to vertical reeds, hops from stem to stem, and makes short, low flights

through the bed. It has a plain, unpatterned, mid-brown head, back, wings and tail (which is short and blunt-tipped); underneath, it is buff or creamy buff. The legs are brown, the head is slender with a longish, slim, pointed beak and there is a very small, faint, light stripe from the base of the beak to just behind each eye. Reed warblers are the favourite 'surrogate parents' for cuckoos, so if you see a reed warbler's nest you may see a cuckoo's egg inside – the young cuckoo hatches first, and heaves the other occupants out over the side.

HABITAT Reed-beds in England and Wales, with a few in southern Scotland and eastern Ireland.

SIZE 13cm (5in)

EGGS 4, greenish white, blotched olive-brown

NEST Deep cup of grass, leaves and reed flowerheads, built round reed stems, usually above water.

FOOD Insects and other invertebrates; berries in autumn.

SIMILAR TO Sedge warbler. Experts can tell the two apart from their songs. Both are loud and repetitive but the reed warbler's is lower-pitched, less varied and does not end in a crescendo.

Fish

1 Salmon
Salmo salar

Although it's usually thought of as a river fish, the salmon spends much of its life at sea, in the north Atlantic, returning only to the river of its birth to spawn in November and December. It is a large, silvery fish, up to 1.2m (4ft) long, and is dark grey dappled with darker spots along the top, and paler grey fading to white underneath. The tail is slightly forked at the end. The well-known red flesh and hooked jaw of a male salmon in spawning condition don't develop until the fish is on its journey up river.

HABITAT Often seen around the mouths of popular salmon rivers in autumn, particularly in Ireland and Scotland, on its way back from the sea.

2 Brown trout
Salmo trutta

The brown trout is a long, slim, streamlined, speckly brown fish, usually about 30cm (12in) long, with sparse orange spots. It is usually seen 'hovering' almost motionless in small shoals facing into the current; when seen in deeper water on sunny days, it often appears to be black. It feeds on freshwater shrimps, insect larvae and flies. The sea trout is the same species but grows much bigger (up to 1.3m/4ft) and looks more silvery, lacking the orange spots of the river form. It migrates from rivers to sheltered estuaries and sea lochs, particularly in Scotland and Ireland, but is never found far out to sea. To tell a sea trout from a small salmon, look for a row of tiny teeth round each jaw, and a tail that is not forked.

The rainbow trout (*Salmo gairdneri*) is an introduced species, originally from the Rocky Mountains of the United States, and is used to stock fish farms and some sport-fishing facilities. It is occasionally found in trout streams but is not welcomed, as it out-competes the native brown trout.

HABITAT Brown trout is found in rivers and lakes with gravelly bottoms throughout the British Isles, particularly in southern England, where the water is often managed for fly fishing, with excess weed being regularly cleared and competing fish species culled.

3 Grayling
Thymallus thymallus

This is an attractive, long, slender, silvery fish, up to 50cm (20in) long and weighing 2.5kg (5½lb), tinged with slightly metallic mauve or green and with a light sprinkling of black spots. The large, almost half-moon-shaped dorsal fin is a distinctly mauvish pink colour. The Latin name comes from the fact that the flesh is said to smell of thyme.

HABITAT Clean, cool, fast-flowing streams, brooks and rivers throughout the British Isles (especially trout streams such as the Test in Hampshire), though distribution is patchy.

4 Three-spined stickleback
Gasterosteus aculeatus

One of our most widespread fish, often seen in shoals, this is well known to children fishing with bent pins and bits of bread. It is a small, silvery green or blue-green fish, 3–10cm (1¼–4in) long, with silvery white undersides and 3 strong spines on the back. The male has a red throat and belly in the breeding season in spring. (There is also a nine-spined stickleback, which is far less commonly found.) Sticklebacks feed on fish eggs and small baby fish, and they themselves form a major part of the diet of other fish and carnivorous waterside wildlife.

HABITAT Ponds, lakes and rivers throughout the British Isles; even thrives in polluted or brackish water and flooded ditches.

5 Perch
Perca fluviatilis

The perch is a favourite coarse fish with anglers. It can be up to 30cm (12in) long and is rather variable in colour, ranging from light buff through green to nearly black, patterned with regularly spaced, darker, vertical bars. The perch has 2 dorsal fins, the first of which – the larger and more sail-like – has a dark spot at the tail end. The lower fins are tinged red. Both dorsal and anal fins have spines, and the hard, triangular-shaped gill cover has a spine at the tip furthest from the head. Young fish move in shoals, but larger ones are more solitary, often waiting for prey among water plants or reed stems.

HABITAT Slow-flowing rivers, also lakes and ponds throughout lowland areas of the British Isles.

Coarse fish

Coarse fish is the term usually given to freshwater fish other than salmon or trout; they are not generally considered good for eating. Anglers put them in keep-nets close to the bank and release them back into the water at the end of the day. The big exception is the pike, which is often removed from waterways to safeguard stocks of other fish. Pike is considered a delicacy in some countries, including France.

6 Bullhead
Cottus gobio

Also known as miller's thumb, this is a small, common fish, up to 15cm (6in) long, with a very large, bumpy-looking head and a blotchy, olive-brown body that tapers off to a wedge shape with a thin tail and a small tail fin. A nocturnal species, it hides among stones in the riverbed by day and feeds at night.
HABITAT Throughout England and Wales, in shallow rivers and lakes with a stony or gravelly bottom, but not often seen in Scotland and never in Ireland.

7 Common carp
Cyprinus carpio

The common carp is one of the longest-lived freshwater fish, at around 40 years. Often found in small shoals, it has a greenish brown body with paler undersides, large, regular scales and fairly small fins; it is often 25cm (10in) long but can be up to 1m (3ft). Look for 2 pairs of short barbels on the upper lip – one pair drooping down either side of the top lip, and another, slightly longer pair in the corners of the mouth. The carp is a bottom-feeder, taking plants as well as invertebrates and small molluscs.

Although reasonably common today, carp are not native to the British Isles. They originally came from Asia and were probably introduced to Britain by the Romans. Medieval monks, who were not allowed to eat meat on Fridays and during certain religious festivals, kept carp for food in ancient 'stewponds', which can still be seen today at places like Mickleham Priory in Surrey.
HABITAT Throughout the British Isles, mainly in south-east England, in shallow lakes and slow-moving rivers.

8 Tench
Tinca tinca

Tench are chunky, deep-bodied fish, up to 70cm (28in) long, in deep bronze-green or olive-brown, with red eyes and a pair of small barbels in the corners of the mouth. Tench

are a favourite with anglers, since they reach a good size.
HABITAT Mainly found in the south-east of England, in flooded gravel pits, slow flowing rivers and shallow lakes with a soft base and plenty of waterweeds.

9 Minnow
Phoxinus phoxinus

This is a common, small, slim, tubular-shaped fish, up to 10cm (4in) long, found in tight shoals darting around in the shallows. It has a greeny grey back, often faintly patterned with stripes, and a distinct median line halfway up each side of the body. The males have a red belly in spring. Minnows feed on midges, fish eggs (including those of trout), aquatic insects, larvae, small crustaceans and plant algae. Young minnows themselves form a major part of the diet of larger fish and also birds such as herons.
HABITAT Fast-flowing, unpolluted rivers and trout streams throughout the British Isles, except Scotland.

10 Gudgeon
Gobio gobio

This is a rather slender, streamlined fish, up to 20cm (8in), usually seen in dense shoals, with silvery greenish grey or brown upperparts and a distinctly lighter shade below the lateral line (which runs along the body halfway up). There are darker blotches on both the body and the fins. Look for a pair of long, whiskery barbels hanging down, one from either side of the mouth. A bottom-feeder, gudgeon takes small invertebrates and fish eggs, also some water plants, from the riverbed.
HABITAT Flooded gravel pits and other inland watercourses, including canals. Commonest in the south of England but found throughout England and Ireland and (rarely) in Wales and Scotland.

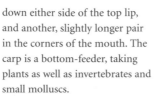

Feeling for food

If you see a fish with barbels, you know straight away that it feeds on the bottom, since these sensitive, fleshy filaments are used to feel around between stones for food, such as the freshwater shrimps, fish eggs and plants that are found there. Some species, such as tench, use barbels for finding larvae among waterweeds. Fish such as trout, which lack barbels, feed on the surface, where they have a different diet – they come up to take flies.

11 Rudd
Scardinius erythrophthalmus
Well known to anglers, the rudd is a green-bronze, herring-like fish with orange-red eyes, red fins and tail and a sharply down-curved mouth. The average size is roughly 12cm (4¾in), though it can grow to 20cm (8in) or more, with a weight of about 1kg (2lb). It feeds on aquatic plants, insects and other invertebrates. The rudd is easily confused with the roach, but the anal fin of the rudd starts well behind the back of the dorsal fin, while in the roach the front of the anal fin is immediately below the base of the dorsal fin.
HABITAT Slow-moving rivers, lakes and canals where there is plenty of aquatic vegetation, in lowland areas of England and Ireland (rare in Wales and Scotland).

12 Roach
Rutilus rutilus
This is our commonest coarse fish, well known to anglers. It is a silvery, herring-like fish with orange-red eyes, amber fins and tail and large scales. Although it is usually up to 20cm (8in) long, specimens of over 35cm (14in) and up to 1.5kg (3lb) in weight have been caught. Males sometimes develop tiny, off-white tubercles on top of the head around spawning time in spring. Roach feed on aquatic insects and larvae.
HABITAT Slow-moving rivers, canals, lakes, reservoirs and flooded gravel pits in most of England and southern Scotland but sporadic in Wales.

13 Dace
Leuciscus leuciscus
The dace is a slim, pale-coloured, rather tubular-shaped fish, up to 30cm (12in) long, with a small, neat head, an olive-green back, silvery sides with just a hint of a greenish tinge, and paler underneath, with slightly darker yellowish fins. It is usually found in large shoals.
HABITAT Clean, fairly fast-flowing rivers throughout England, most of Wales and Ireland.

14 Pike
Esox lucius
Large and carnivorous, the pike hides motionlessly, often under water-lily leaves or in the shade of a bridge, then strikes out at prey, which includes smaller fish (even baby pike), small waterfowl (including ducklings), water voles, frogs and newts. It has an enormous mouth and head, which looks too long for the body, and is greenish tinged, patterned with paler spots or wavy bands and with brown-speckled-buff fins and tail. The pike can live 25 years or more, growing up to 1m (3ft) long and weighing up to 14kg (31lb), especially where it has eliminated all competitors by eating them, but most are much smaller.
HABITAT Found in just about any fresh water in the British Isles, including castle moats, where there is plenty of vegetation to hide in.

15 Stone loach
Noemacheilus barbatulus
The stone loach is a small, common fish that is smooth-skinned, with no scales, reaching 14cm (5½in) long. The face is rather lizard-like, with 6 long barbels protruding downwards from the tip of the upper jaw. The upperside is buff, tinged green and heavily mottled with olive-brown, and the underside is buff, with a fairly obvious, buff lateral line. Nocturnal, it sits on the bottom of the river by day and feeds at night.
HABITAT Found throughout the British Isles (except the north of Scotland) only in clean, unpolluted rivers with stony or occasionally sandy or muddy bottoms.

16 Eel
Anguilla anguilla
The eel is a common, slimy-coated, snake-like fish in brown (males) or olive-green (females). The underside is paler and the fins and tail have fused together to form a continuous 'fringe' along the upper and lower sides of the rear two-thirds of the body. The lower jaw protrudes beyond the upper jaw, giving it a bulldog-like face. Eels can reach up to 1.5m (5ft) long and over 5kg (11lb) in weight, although most are usually much smaller. They spend most of their life (5–10 years) in fresh water, then

return to the Sargasso Sea off Bermuda to spawn. The tiny, translucent, thread-like young (known as elvers) return to fresh water from late winter to late spring, and often form huge shoals heading upstream. Eels are rarely seen, except by fishermen, because they live in the bottom of waterways and are most active at night. They are often mistaken for snakes, since eels will sometimes wriggle over land to reach another stretch of water.
HABITAT Rivers, ditches and streams throughout lowland areas of the British Isles.

1 Swallowtail butterfly
Papilio machaon

Britain's biggest butterfly (9.5cm/3¾in wingspan), this species is easy to identify, as it has a distinctive shape. However, it is very rare. It has yellow-and-black, 'art deco'-patterned wings, with a red spot at the rear of each hind wing, and long, pointed black tail extensions.

HABITAT Only in the Norfolk Broads, East Anglia, in June and early July.

CATERPILLAR Very striking, with a pair of bright orange 'horns' at the

front and a green body, marked with black bands bearing rows of red dots. Feeds only on milk parsley (a rare relative of cow parsley, found mostly in East Anglian wetlands, especially the Fens and round the Norfolk Broads).

2 Mayfly
Ephemera danica

Mayflies are large insects (up to 4cm/1½in wingspan) that form spectacular, mist-like clouds over the water on a few evenings each year in early summer. If you look closely, each mayfly has a pair of large, translucent, silvery-to-light-green, 'stained glass window'-patterned wings; in flight, it has long antennae sticking out ahead and a long, trailing tail behind. Mayfly hatchings attract swarms of swallows, martins and fish to feed. Mayfly larvae resemble tiny, brownish crayfish; they live on the bottom of rivers, streams and lakes

for 2 years and are an important food source for fish and other water wildlife. The larvae emerge from the water on fine, still days in early summer, climb up waterside plants to split their skins and allow their unfurling wings to dry before taking off to mate and drop their eggs back into the water. Adults are short-lived, alive perhaps for just one evening – the water is covered with dead bodies the next day. Not for nothing is the Latin name of the mayfly *Ephemera*. *E. danica* is one of many similar species of mayfly found in Britain.

HABITAT Lakes, streams and rivers.

3 Brown hawker dragonfly
Aeshna grandis

This species is a common, very large dragonfly with a long, lean brown body, 7.5cm (3in) long, and amber wings (10cm/4in wingspan), patterned with a network of very fine brown veins, which are a good identification feature.

HABITAT Lakes, ponds, rivers and other inland waterways in central and south-east England, from June to September.

4 Emperor dragonfly
Anax imperator

Our biggest dragonfly (one of the hawker group), and one of the most colourful, this is a big, fast-flying insect (wingspan up to 10cm/4in and similar body length), with an emerald-green head and thorax and a brightly coloured abdomen – brilliant turquoise-blue in the male and emerald-green in the female, both with a continuous black line down the back.

HABITAT Mainly in south-east England but also in other parts of England and Wales, darting low over lakes, ponds and other large areas of water fringed with upright water plants. Seen from May to October on sunny summer days.

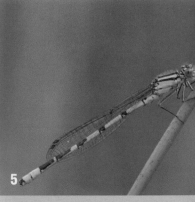

Dragonflies and damselflies

There are dozens of different dragonfly and damselfly species, all of which have 2 pairs of wings. In dragonflies, the hind wings are slightly wider than the forewings; this is seen when the insects are at rest on foliage, as they bask with wings stretched out. Damselflies have narrow wings that are of almost identical size, and they rest on vegetation with their wings folded back. In flight, damselflies look more delicate and fly more slowly than the chunkier dragonflies, which often make a papery, 'whirring' noise. Both feed on smaller insects; dragonflies catch their food in mid-air, while damselflies snatch theirs off vegetation.

There are several groups of dragonflies, including hawkers and darters. The hawkers are always on the wing, patrolling up and down their patch, fending off rivals or looking for food or mates. They have long, slender bodies and a large wingspan. The darters are usually more thickset, with shorter wings; they sit on foliage or cling to vertical reed stems and then dart out to catch nearby insects.

Dragonfly and damselfly larvae live in the bottom of lakes and ponds and are ferocious predators of tadpoles, fish fry and insect larvae. They look like tiny dragons with large face-masks.

7 Pond skater
Gerris lacustris

This is a common but easily overlooked bug, seen skimming across the water's surface. It is small (1.5cm/⅝in long) and narrow, light brown and lozenge-shaped, with 4 long legs held out in the shape of a cross. It feeds on small or dead insects on the water's surface.

HABITAT On fresh water, seen mostly on sunny days, close to the water's edge or near a bridge or jetty in spring to late summer.

8 Water boatman
Notonecta glauca

Also known as the backswimmer, this is one of our commonest and most easily recognized water bugs, with a chunky, rounded-oval shape, 1.5cm (⅝in) long, seen 'rowing' itself under the water in short, sharp jerks with a pair of long, thin, oar-like legs. If you get a close-up view, you'll see it actually swims upside-down and has bright red eyes. The water boatman dives to catch tadpoles, small fish fry and insect larvae.

HABITAT In summer, seen in still, fresh water including ditches, ponds and lakes; usually stays fairly close to the edge, where there's vegetation for cover.

9 Whirligig beetle
Gyrinus substriatus

This is a fairly common, black, oval beetle, 5mm (³⁄₁₆in) long, with no markings except for a faint line down the middle and across the neck and 6 short legs arranged evenly around the edges of the body. These beetles are most commonly seen in groups on the surface of the water, whirling round each other; they dive when frightened. They feed mainly on mosquito larvae.

HABITAT Still or very slow-moving fresh water, in summer.

5 Common blue damselfly
Enallagma cyathigerum

The commonest-seen damselfly, this resembles a very slim dragonfly with an electric-blue abdomen. It has a wingspan of 4cm (1½in) and body length of 3cm (1¼in). When mating, the male damselfly uses pincers at the rear end of his abdomen to clasp the female by the neck. She bends her body around to meet his reproductive organs in a formation known as the 'mating wheel'. The two, so connected, will fly over water and the female will lay her eggs at the foot of iris leaves or reeds just below the surface.

HABITAT Over still inland waters or resting on vegetation, especially water-lily leaves, on sunny days from April to August.

6 Large red damselfly
Pyrrhosoma nymphula

This is a common and easily identified damselfly, with a large, slim, dragonfly-like body, 3cm (1¼in) long with a 5cm (2in) wingspan. It has a bright orange-red body with brown stripes on the thorax and brown rings around the abdomen (the 'tail'), which also has a brown tip.

HABITAT Throughout the British Isles, over still or slow-moving water, from April to August.

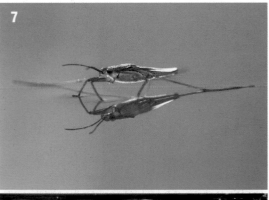

10 Great water beetle
Dytiscus marginalis

Also known as the great diving beetle, this is one of Britain's commonest large water beetles, with an oval body, 3cm (1¼in) long, black with a faint greenish sheen, outlined in beige. The 2 pairs of back legs have hairy edges and are used for propulsion when swimming and diving. The larvae are long, lean, brown-segmented creatures with 3 pairs of hairy legs immediately behind the head, which has powerful, curved jaws. Adults and larvae feed on tadpoles, baby fish and pond invertebrates.
HABITAT Lakes and ponds with plenty of waterweeds and other vegetation, all year round, though less active in winter.

11 Raft spider
Dolomedes fimbriatus

Britain's biggest spider, the raft spider has a body up to 2.5cm (1in) long. This rare, dark brown species is usually seen resting on floating vegetation. As it floats, the front pair of legs is stretched out, touching the water to detect vibrations from potential prey (aquatic insects and larvae) disturbing the surface tension, in much the same way as other spiders keep legs on their webs. Seen in close-up, the raft spider has a narrow, yellow or orange-yellow line along either side of the body; however, size and location are the big identification features.
HABITAT Only in swampy areas, wetlands and on vegetation round the edges of lakes and ponds; best known on southern heathlands; seen mostly on fine summer days.

12 Water spider
Argyroneta aquatica

Unlike the raft spider, which walks on the water's surface, the brown water spider (1.2cm/½in long) lives right under the surface, inside silk 'diving bells' lodged among waterweeds. Each 'bell' contains a bubble of air where the spider lives by day, coming out at night to feed on baby fish and invertebrates. The spider uses hairs on its legs and abdomen to trap air from the surface, which is then released in the underwater web. This is also topped up by oxygen in the water, which diffuses through the silk. Eggs are laid inside nursery 'diving bells'; these hatch into larvae that feed on small water insects.
HABITAT Fairly common in shallow, weedy ponds, including stagnant water in southern England, all year round.

13 Freshwater shrimp
Gammarus pulex

The freshwater shrimp scuttles about on stones or debris in the bottom of a pond or stream. It is essential to the eco-systems of inland waters, and is a good natural monitor, since it thrives only in totally clean, unpolluted water containing plenty of oxygen. Feeding on decaying organic debris, it does a valuable job of keeping the water clean. The freshwater shrimp is itself prey for a wide variety of water wildlife, including birds, water beetles, small mammals and dragonfly larvae.
HABITAT Clean freshwater ponds, lakes, rivers and streams, also healthy garden ponds.

14 Great pond snail
Lymnaea stagnalis

Also known as the freshwater whelk, this is our most conspicuous water snail, with a pointed-conical, light brown shell – up to 5cm (2in) long and with a pronounced spiral from the opening to the tip – containing a dull brown snail. It is often found upside-down just under the surface of the water, using surface tension to keep it in place, or on the undersides of water-lily leaves, where its long, narrow, tubular, translucent masses

of eggs (up to 2cm/¾in long) are deposited. This snail feeds on algae and decaying plant or animal matter, including fish eggs.
HABITAT Present mainly in the southern half of England in ponds, lakes and other still or slow-moving fresh water; also in stagnant water and garden ponds. Found at any time of year but particularly active from spring to early autumn.

15 Ramshorn snail
Planorbis planorbis

A striking water snail, this is far less common than the great pond snail, with a flat, spiral-shaped shell rather like a small ammonite, up to 2cm (¾in) in diameter, in light brown, with a dark brown (or more rarely red) snail inside. It is usually seen creeping about in waterweeds and grazes algae from submerged rocks and water plants.
HABITAT Throughout lowland areas of the British Isles, in ponds, lakes and slow-moving water; often introduced into garden ponds as an alternative to the great pond snail, since it does not damage water plants.

16 Water scorpion
Nepa cinerea

The water scorpion is a strange-looking bug, with a flat, slightly elongated, shield-shaped body, 3cm (1¼in) long, in light brown. It has no visible antennae, but does have a pair of large, strong 'arms'

(with what look like large biceps) on either side of the head, held at right angles, which are used for grabbing prey. It is often seen suspended just below the water's surface, among waterweeds, with its 'tail' acting as a breathing tube up to the surface. The larvae look very similar but with faint, segmented markings ringing the body instead of the folded wing-cases of the adult (it has wings but rarely flies). Adults and larvae feed on tadpoles, baby fish and invertebrates.
HABITAT Shallow, weedy ponds, including stagnant water in southern England, all year round.

17 White-clawed crayfish
Austropotanobius pallipes

Now rare, this is Britain's only native species (also known as the freshwater crayfish). It is a grey-brown, lobster-like creature, up to 10cm (4in) long, which hides among stones in the stream bed or riverbed and comes out only at night to feed on tadpoles and small aquatic invertebrates. The American signal crayfish, which has escaped from captivity, is larger, more brightly coloured and very much commoner. Being an aggressive species, it is taking over territory once held by the native species.
HABITAT Found only in certain fast-flowing chalk streams of central and southern England, well hidden among the pebbles or in holes in the bank by day.

1 Red-eared terrapin
Trachemys scripta elegans

A small, turtle-like creature, up to 30cm (12in) long, the red-eared terrapin has a grey-brown shell and body and a bright red flash on either side of the head. It is not a native species, but it was once popular as a child's pet and was illegally released into waterways, where it has become a problem in the last 10–20 years, as it can live for a long time. (Its lifespan is around 40 years.) It is not thought to breed in the British Isles, but scientists believe that only a small rise in global warming would trigger breeding; nests and eggs (but no young) have been seen in the Southampton area.
HABITAT Occasionally seen basking on sunny banks of ponds, lakes or slow moving waterways, especially round London.
FOOD Aquatic plants, invertebrates, small snails, worms, baby fish and other reptiles and amphibians.

2 Grass snake
Natrix natrix

Britain's biggest snake, this is long and slender (commonly 90cm/36in but may reach 1.5m/5ft) with very variable coloration – it may be dark olive, grey-green, light

sea-green or buff, with a row of dark spots along both sides of the body, or darker scales forming complete rings round the body (these do not show on dark olive snakes, which look uniform in colour). It often has a yellowish or greenish collar just behind the head. Widespread but not very common today, it is usually seen basking in the sun on short-grass banks or open soil, but it may also be seen in water as it swims well, with sinuous movements. The grass snake is non-venomous

to humans and is not to be confused with the venomous adder, which has a broad, dark zig-zag down its back.
HABITAT In lowland areas of England and Wales, in grassy places, especially near water, from April to September; hibernates in winter.
FOOD Frogs, tadpoles, small fish, newts.

3 Common frog
Rana temporaria

The common frog is a widespread and well-known, small amphibian, up to 10cm (4in) long, with smooth skin that is rather variable in colour, usually ochre-yellow or olive-green, strongly marked with black spots and blotches, with a dark ochre, triangular patch behind each eye. The strong hind legs are usually folded into a 'Z' shape, held close to the body to enable it to make large leaps; the webbed feet are used for vigorous, breast-stroke-like kicks when swimming. Its voice is a loud 'ribbett, ribbett' croaking by males from ponds during the breeding season. Frogspawn is produced in huge masses in mild spells from February onwards. It feeds mostly at night but will come out during the day in wet weather or in damp places.

HABITAT Late February–early April: often seen in large numbers in ponds and water-filled ditches during the spawning season in early spring (exact timing depends on the temperature). Summer: fields and ditches in countryside near spawning sites, also gardens, especially with ponds. Winter: hibernates in pond mud or in damp soil.

FOOD Insects, worms, slugs.

4 Marsh frog
Rana ridibunda

There are various uncommon frogs that have been introduced and reintroduced over hundreds of years to Britain, either for food or as ornamental pets for garden ponds; the marsh frog is one of these introduced species. It is very large, the biggest frog in Europe, and measures 12cm (4¾in) long (not counting the extended rear legs), in brown to greenish khaki with white underparts and olive spots on the rear half of the body and hind legs. It croaks very loudly, repeating 'yak-yak-yak-yak', inflating its cheeks as it does so. The closely related edible frog (*Rana esculenta*) is similar to the marsh frog but smaller (roughly the same size as a large common frog) and the background colour is bright green.

HABITAT Isolated locations around London, the south-east of England and parts of East Anglia, especially in ponds or drainage channels between fields. It hibernates in mud at the bottom of ponds for the winter.

FOOD Insects and other aquatic invertebrates, worms.

5 Common newt
Triturus vulgaris

Also known as the smooth newt, this is a lizard-like amphibian, less common than frogs, but fairly widespread. It has smooth skin, which is variable in coloration – from buff to olive with darker spots – and a tail that is flattened laterally and wiggles from side to side when swimming. In spring males take on breeding coloration – orange underparts and large, dark spots on the upperparts – and also sport a crest along the back and tail, often causing them to be mistaken for the much rarer great crested newt. After the breeding season, all that remains of this crest is a small ridge running along the back of the creature. Newts spend much longer living in water than frogs, which pass through water only to breed.

HABITAT Spring and summer: throughout lowland Britain and parts of Ireland, in ponds and slow-moving or still watercourses in the countryside; also often seen in gardens, especially those with ponds. Late summer and autumn: on land around these areas. Hibernates in winter.

FOOD Tadpoles, daphnia (water fleas) and other small aquatic invertebrates.

6 Palmate newt
Triturus helveticus

Britain's smallest newt, up to 7cm (2¾in) long, this has warm olive-brown coloration with a central stripe down the back, sides speckled with faint streaks and spots, a brown eye-stripe and off-white underparts. In spring males have a very small, smooth crest along the back and develop webbed back feet. They leave their ponds in midsummer and return to land.

HABITAT Widely distributed throughout most of the British

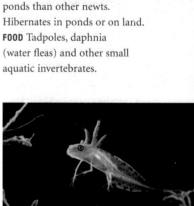

Isles (but not Ireland), mostly in heathland and moorland areas, and more often found in small ponds than other newts. Hibernates in ponds or on land.

FOOD Tadpoles, daphnia (water fleas) and other small aquatic invertebrates.

Life cycle of newts

Like frogs, newts enter water to breed each spring, then from midsummer onwards adults return to life on land. Newt spawn is inconspicuous and laid round waterweeds; it develops into tadpoles, which have feathery external gills just behind the head and a large body with a broad, spotted, semi-translucent tail shaped like a knife-blade. The front legs and hind legs develop at more or less the same time, unlike those of frog tadpoles, so you may see strange, half-developed creatures in the water. Young newts remain in water until the end of their first season, when they leave to hibernate.

7 Great crested newt
Triturus cristatus

This is our biggest and least abundant newt (up to 16cm/6¼in long), in dark olive-brown with indistinct, darker spots on the sides. In the breeding season (spring), males have an orange belly, a large, jagged crest along the back and a wide, knife-blade-shaped tail. Females are the same size as the males but lack the crest, and the orange belly is much less pronounced. The great crested newt is normally seen in ponds, as it spends a much greater proportion of the year in water than any of Britain's other newts.
HABITAT Widespread, but mostly in larger ponds in southern England. Hibernates in winter in or near ponds.
FOOD Tadpoles, daphnia (water fleas) and various other small aquatic invertebrates.

Mammals

1 Cattle
Bos species

A common sight in conventional farm fields, cattle have long been turned out to graze in marshes during the summer to fatten. Some – particularly hardy breeds such as the shaggy, long-horned Highland cattle – are also used for conservation purposes, to prevent undergrowth taking over, and to keep the grass short for ground-nesting birds and other wildlife, duplicating the role of the ancient aurochs (our original wild ox, which stood nearly 2m/6½ft high and had enormous horns). The aurochs became extinct in the British Isles and the last-known records are from Roman times.
HABITAT Pastures, water meadows.
FOOD Grass supplemented by hay, plus concentrates in winter for milking herds.

2 Chinese water deer
Hydropotes inermis

This is a rather small, dog-like deer, 50cm (20in) at the shoulder. In summer it is a rich tan colour, but in winter it is grey-brown, with contrasting black eyes and nose. It has a rounded back and no antlers (it is the only male deer in Britain without antlers), although the males have tusks protruding down from the upper jaw, like long canine teeth, used for defence. Listen for unusual barking and squealing sounds, and watch for cavorting and kicking-up of heels, which easily distinguishes this species from other deer. Originally from swampy parts of northern China and Korea, Chinese water deer were introduced to parkland at stately homes such as Woburn Abbey, Bedfordshire, where visitors can still see them today. Our wild population is descended from escapees; they are elusive and therefore difficult to see.
HABITAT Reed-beds in the Broads and Fens of East Anglia.
FOOD Mostly grass, some scrub or bark in winter.

3 Otter
Lutra lutra

An enchanting but rare creature, the otter has a long, lean, stream-lined body (up to 1.2m/4ft nose to tail; the female is smaller), a broad, flat head with long whiskers, a long, tapering tail and webbed feet. The short fur is brown, with a white 'bib' covering the chin and chest. An adept swimmer, it paddles with its back feet and uses its front feet for manoeuvring or holding freshly caught food while it eats. Numbers declined greatly around the 1970s, but they have been increasing since fewer pesticides have been used on fields and in the absence of hunting. Now otters are thought to be driving out mink along riverbanks, thus opening up habitats for water voles and ground-nesting aquatic birds once more.
HABITAT Usually associated with inland rivers, but most frequently seen on the north-west coast of Scotland or Shetland, where it can often be seen hunting and playing in the sea.
FOOD Mostly eels but also frogs, fish, small birds, mammals.

How to tell water voles from rats

Brown rats are often mistaken for the very much rarer water voles; people will often throw bread and other food to brown rats nesting in holes in banks or swimming in streams and drainage ditches in the mistaken belief they are helping the endearing water vole. Brown rats are bigger – up to 28cm (11in) in body length with a 25cm (10in) tail – a quick glance is enough to see that the tail of a rat is nearly as long as its body, but that of the water vole is only about half the body length. The brown rat looks a more dingy, greyer brown than the rich chocolate-brown water vole. The head of a brown rat looks more streamlined – it has a slim face with a pointed nose and conspicuous, naked ears; the water vole has a distinctly short, chubby face and a short, blunt nose with barely visible ears. Given a good view of the water vole on dry land, you can see the tail is lightly hairy, unlike that of the brown rat, which is naked and scaly. If you see lots of the animals together, on banks or in the water, they are almost certainly brown rats, which live communally. Water voles do live in colonies but only a few are usually seen together at any one time.

4 Water vole
Arvicola terrestris

Also known as the water rat, the water vole ('Ratty', from *The Wind in the Willows*) is now a rare species. Active by day, and usually seen swimming in still water, it has a rat-like, dark reddish, chocolate-brown or occasionally black body, 18cm (7in) long, with a slightly hairy tail, 10cm (4in) long, and a chubby head with a blunt nose and ears that are almost lost in the fur. It makes a distinct 'plop' as it dives into the water from the bank. The water vole is at risk from loss of habitat, but also from predators such as mink.
HABITAT Clear, unpolluted streams, riverbanks and canals, sometimes ponds or lakes, in remote, undisturbed countryside, well away from human habitation, throughout most of lowland Britain. Not found in Ireland.
FOOD Grasses such as reeds and soft, short shoots of waterside plants.

5 Mink
Mustela vison

The mink is a rather small, slender, dark brown, ferret-like creature with a long body (males are 40cm /16in, females 35cm/14in) and a short, furry tail of 18cm (7in). It has a short head with a pointed nose and very sharp teeth. The fur looks shaggy and falls into a series of short, uprightish points when the animal first leaves the water. It is largely nocturnal. Originally from North America, our resident population is descended from fur-farm escapees, and with no natural predators mink have taken over a variety of waterside habitats, often to the detriment of our native wildlife. Control is being exercised in some areas to help water voles increase.
HABITAT Close to water in most of lowland Britain and parts of Ireland.
FOOD Small mammals such as water voles, fish, eggs and the young of waterside birds, especially ground-nesting species, also eels and crustaceans.

6 Water shrew
Neomys fodiens

A widespread shrew, this is slightly larger than the common shrew (body 8cm/3¼in, tail 5.5cm/2¼in), with black or brown-black fur and a silvery white underside and chin. It dives to catch fish and other underwater prey. Its saliva is mildly venomous and helps to subdue animals, even frogs, which it then pulls on to the shore to eat.
HABITAT Patchily distributed throughout the British Isles (though not present in Ireland), living in burrows in banks of streams but also often found on land some distance away from water, for example in wettish fields, ditches beneath hedgerows and in other damp habitats.
FOOD Tadpoles, frogs, small fish, earthworms, other invertebrates.

7 Daubenton's bat
Myotis daubentoni

Flying with very fast, shallow, quivering wing-beats, often regularly up and down the same stretch of water, this is a widespread, medium-sized brown bat (body 4.5cm/1¾in, wingspan 25cm/10in) with short ears and large feet with widely splayed toes. It skims the water's surface to feed.
HABITAT Throughout the British Isles; always inhabits damp habitats with trees, and is seen hunting very low over rivers, lakes and ponds at night. In summer, it roosts by day in hollow trees and crevices between rocks, buildings or bridges over water; in winter, solitary bats hibernate in caves, mines or other underground sites.
FOOD Mayflies and aquatic insects.

OPPOSITE Chinese water deer are the only British deer that give birth to more than one young at a time.

1 Common alder
Alnus glutinosa

The common alder is an ancient native inhabitant of the British Isles and is still common and widespread. It is an attractively shaped deciduous tree, to 22m (72ft) high, though normally much less, with branches very regularly spaced along the trunk, often making an almost geometrical pattern in winter, when the tree is leafless. In February and March it bears long, dangling, hazel-like male catkins and small green, cone-like female catkins on bare branches; the rounded, hazel-like but hairless foliage appears later. Small clusters of dry brown 'cones', dotted all over the bare branches, are conspicuous in winter.
HABITAT Wetlands, riverbanks, boggy places.

2 Black poplar
Populus nigra subsp. *betulifolia*

This is the classic riverside tree, potentially 30m (100ft) high, but usually much shorter in exposed situations. It is now rather rare. It has an upright trunk with grey-brown, fissured bark, often decorated with large knobbles, and a rounded shape with wide-spreading branches. The leaves look rather like birch leaves – they are triangular, 5–7cm (2–2¾in) long, and very slightly toothed round the edges.
HABITAT Throughout the British Isles, especially the Fens, the Broads and wetlands of East Anglia.

3 Grey willow
Salix cinerea

Also known as the grey sallow, this is a common tree but is more often seen as a large shrub, 4–6m (13–20ft) high. It has silvery, 'pussy-willow' catkins in early spring on bare twigs, usually a few weeks ahead of hazel catkins. (It is not the only willow that has 'pussy willow' catkins – the more widespread goat willow, *Salix caprea*, is best known for them.) In summer, the oval leaves are dull green above, greyish white and slightly downy underneath, and the young twigs are shiny.
HABITAT Wet, low-lying wild areas, in hedgerows, scrub, wetlands and fenland.

4 Crack willow
Salix fragilis

A large and familiar willow, this often makes splendid specimens to 20m (65ft), or it is sometimes pollarded to reduce the size, resulting in a trunk with a mass of strong, upright stems growing from the top. The leaves are long, narrow and shiny green, often slightly twisted, and have very slightly serrated edges. The twigs are brittle (hence the name crack willow), and snap off easily, then float downstream, where they take root, starting a new tree. The crack willow flowers in May, with male and female flowers on separate trees; the male flowers are fluffy, dangling, yellow, pollen-bearing catkins, and the female flowers are green, spiky, dangling catkins without pollen. The bark of the mature tree is grey and deeply fissured.
HABITAT A great feature of many riverbanks in the British Isles.

5 Osier
Salix viminalis

A shrubby willow, 3–4m (10–13ft) high, the osier is often coppiced to produce long, slim wands for basket-making. When left to grow naturally, it makes a loose, open-branching shrub with rather stiff stems and exceptionally long, thin leaves that have perfectly smooth edges and a long, pointed tip. Flowers appear in early spring, before the leaves, with both male and female flowers being produced on the same shrub but on different stems. The male flowers are short, rounded-oval, pussy-willow-like catkins (but less fluffy or silvery than the 'real thing'); the female flowers are the same shape and size but green and spiky.

HABITAT Damp or marshy ground; especially common in Somerset, where there is still a thriving basket-making industry.

6 Guelder rose
Viburnum opulus

The guelder rose is a common, dense, rounded deciduous shrub, 3m (10ft) high and the same across, with leaves roughly the same shape and size as sycamore leaves, with 3–5 lobes, turning dull red in autumn. In early summer it bears large, flat, circular clusters of white flowers that resemble those of elder from a distance; in close-up, they are more like lace-cap hydrangeas, having a ring of showy flowers with petals round the edge and masses of smaller flowers (which look like buds that haven't opened) in the centre. These are followed in late summer and autumn by clusters of red berries, which are much loved by birds.

HABITAT Wet or boggy countryside throughout lowland areas of the British Isles, especially the Fens in East Anglia.

7 Reed
Phragmites australis

This is Britain's tallest native grass, 1.5–3m (5–10ft) high, with leaves 60cm (24in) long by 3cm (1¼in) wide, growing from tough, upright stems; these persist as bare brown 'canes' in winter, and were traditionally used as a thatching material (they still are in some areas). From August onwards, buff-coloured, plume-like sprays of flowers are produced at the top of the plants, which droop after a while and persist well into winter. Plants spread rapidly from strong roots and quickly colonize new ground, forming dense reed-beds that support a wealth of birds and other waterside wildlife. The roots of phragmites reeds are also beneficial as they 'filter' impurities from water and absorb nitrates from fertilizers leaching from fields, which cleans up the ecosystem. Reeds are currently used in 'green' sewage treatment systems, such as the one installed at Highgrove, in Gloucestershire.

HABITAT Wetlands, riverbanks and permanently damp ditches.

8 Great reedmace
Typha latifolia

Often called bulrush, this is a common water's-edge plant in the British Isles. (Its American name is cat-tail.) With its tall, upright habit, 1.5–2.5m (5–8ft) high, it resembles a reed but it is less densely packed and leafy than true reeds, with coarse, grassy, straight-edged leaves arranged alternately all the way up the main stem, which terminates in a flowerhead. The female flower is the familiar brown, tubular bulrush that appears in July; the yellow, fluffy, upright 'tail' that stands out from the top of the bulrush in early summer is the cluster of pollen-bearing male flowers. Fluffy, greyish clouds containing the tiny seeds hang on to the seedheads in late summer or early autumn, until they are dispersed by the wind; the bulrush heads persist into late autumn.

HABITAT Boggy ground, lakesides, marshland and damp ditches, especially in southern England.

9 Clubrush
Schoenoplectus lacustris
Clubrush is a relative of the sedges. It is fairly common but far less distinctive than the bulrush – the great reedmace. It is a reedy plant, 1–2m (3–6½ft) high, with long, slender, linear leaves, and in June and July the taller, leafless stems are topped with loose, airy clusters of small brown, sedge-like flowers. The flower stems are always circular in cross-section.
HABITAT Silty edges of lakes, ponds and inland waterways.

10 Duckweed
Lemna minor
This is a tiny plant, growing in huge colonies to make the familiar green blanket over fresh water in summer. Each plant consists of a 1- or 2-lobed green leaf the size of a pair of frozen peas floating on the surface of the water, with a very short, single, thread-like root dangling down beneath. It rapidly spreads by 'buds' and dies back to resting buds in winter, to reappear, as if by magic, next year. Though it is said to be capable of producing flowers, they are rarely if ever seen. Duckweed is something of a mixed blessing. On the one hand, large colonies can become so dense that they block out light and prevent submerged water plants, including oxygenating species, from growing

underneath – this can make it impossible for aquatic wildlife to survive. On the plus side, duckweed acts like a 'living filter', removing nitrates from the water and turning them into high-protein vegetation that is eaten by ducks and swans and other water wildlife. In a swan- or duck-rich environment, it is often the birds' droppings that are the biggest cause of water fouling, so it seems only reasonable to process the waste via fast-growing and easily disposable plants, and 'return to sender'.
HABITAT Ponds, canals, lakes and other still or very slow-moving fresh water, including water-filled ditches and garden ponds.

11 Marsh marigold
Caltha palustris
Also known as water blobs, or kingcup, this is a well-known and widespread, perennial waterside plant. It has large, glossy, deep green, kidney-shaped leaves, which persist all summer, and large, single, yellow, giant-buttercup-like flowers from March to May, which attract large numbers of insects.
HABITAT Shallow water and boggy ground along streams and rivers throughout lowland areas of the British Isles.

12 White water lily
Nymphaea alba
Water lilies are common water plants that grow some distance

from the shore, with the familiar, large, floating leaves and flowers that bloom from June to August or early September. The white water lily has the biggest flower of any native wildflower in Britain, like a large white powder-puff up to 20cm (8in) wide, standing out of the water a few inches. The leaves are glossy, rounded-to-heart-shaped, up to 30cm (12in) across, floating on the surface of the water in a roughly circular group up to 4m (12ft) across; the underside of the leaves is much used as a 'creche' by water snails – the leaves

are often seen bobbing as fish pick off the gelatinous masses of eggs glued on underneath. The plant grows in fairly deep water (up to 2m/6½ft), and dies down to a network of rhizomes in the mud at the bottom of the pond in winter.
HABITAT Lakes, shallow broads, disused canals, backwaters of rivers and other large, sunny expanses of still, fresh water.

13 Yellow water lily
Nuphar lutea

Also known as the brandy bottle, the yellow water lily has large leaves, up to 40cm (16in) across, making them the biggest submerged leaves of any British water plant. It has relatively small yellow flowers, rather like waxy buttercups standing several inches out of the water, from June to August or early September. It can grow in water up to 3m (10ft) deep because it has very long leaf stalks. In winter it dies down to a network of rhizomes. The plant gets its common name of brandy bottle from its green, bottle-shaped seedheads, which form after the flowers are over. These float for some time after being shed by the plant, allowing the seeds to be distributed at a considerable distance from the parent.
HABITAT Lakes, shallow broads, disused canals, backwaters of rivers and other large, sunny expanses of still, fresh water.

14 Water crowfoot
Ranunculus aquatilis

Water crowfoot is a fairly common, perennial water plant. It resembles an aquatic buttercup and is unusual in having 2 different types of leaves: below the water is feathery green, thread-like foliage, and floating on the surface are circular green 'ruffs', which resemble buttercup leaves. White, buttercup-shaped flowers with yellow centres (1.5cm/⅝in wide) are produced in May and June, and stand out a few inches above the water. If you see water crowfoot growing in a faster-flowing stream, as a mat of rather water-weedy-looking foliage studded with yellow-and-white flowers that are lying over in the direction the water flows, it is a different species – possibly the river water crowfoot (*Ranunculus fluitans*), which has only one sort of foliage (thread-like) and lacks the floating foliage of plain water crowfoot.
HABITAT Still or slow-moving, fresh water including ponds, streams and permanently damp ditches throughout lowland areas of the British Isles.

15 Watercress
Rorippa nasturtium-aquaticum

A perennial waterside plant, watercress has a spreading network of creeping stems that root as they run, bearing more upright, branching shoots that carry the foliage. The leaves are slightly more pointed than those of

greengrocer's watercress, and throughout summer the plant produces upright spikes of tiny white flowers, followed by narrow green seedpods. (It is not advisable to pick and eat wild watercress, in case the water and surrounding areas are polluted.)
HABITAT Edges of streams and shallow rivers throughout many lowland areas of the British Isles, particularly chalk streams.

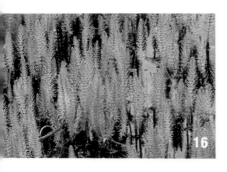

16 Mare's tail
Hippuris vulgaris

This is a fairly uncommon water plant that grows from underwater rhizomes. Colonies of feathery, upright stems, 30–60cm (12–24in) tall, arise out of the water some distance from the shore, looking rather like small Christmas trees; it never grows along the banks. Despite appearances, mare's tail is a flowering plant, bearing tiny, insignificant, greenish flowers without petals in June and July. It is often confused with horsetail (Equisetum arvense), a common weed of damp wasteland, especially where there is clay soil.
HABITAT Medium-depth, still or slow-moving, fresh water in lowland areas of the British Isles.

17 Broad-leaved pondweed
Potamogeton natans

A fairly common, perennial water plant, the broad-leaved pondweed produces 2 kinds of leaves: underwater, the foliage is long, narrow and straw-like and clasps the stems; when the plant reaches the surface, the leaves broaden out and become more oval in shape, 5–10cm (2–4in) long, and they float. A normal view of the plant gives the impression of leaves floating over straw-like waste in the water. Short spikes of insignificant, greenish flowers, 8cm/3¼in high, appear

PREVIOUS PAGES Rivers within the Lake District National Park contain significant populations of fish, together with other wildlife such as native crayfish and otters. The rivers are fed by many fellside streams.

at the tips of the stems from May to September, standing slightly out of the water, and are followed by spikes of small green fruit that are very similar to the seedheads of plantains in a neglected lawn.
HABITAT Still or slow-moving water, in streams, ponds and watercourses throughout lowland areas of the British Isles.

18 Yellow flag iris
Iris pseudacorus

A common and familiar, perennial wildflower found in boggy places, this iris has tall, upright, sword-shaped leaves and stems, 1m (3ft) high, topped by a succession of large yellow, 'flag' flowers from May to July, each lasting only a day or two. Each individual flower consists of 3 large, down-turned petals and 3 small, feathery petals that stand up in the centre. The flowers are followed by a cluster of large, bulbous green seedpods.

HABITAT Fringes of ponds, rivers and streams; also boggy ground and permanently wet ditches.

19 Water forget-me-not
Myosotis scorpioides

Quite a common waterside plant, this is like a garden forget-me-not but scruffier and more spreading, with a longer flowering season, from May to September. The creeping stems root as they run along the ground, forming large, loose, untidy mats of foliage. The flowers are small, pale blue and star-like, but in close-up the petals of this species have blunt ends, each with a slight notch in the centre, unlike the more pointed and unnotched petals of other wild and cultivated forget-me-nots.
HABITAT Shallow water along the edges of streams, ponds and lakes, also ditches and other damp places throughout lowland areas of the British Isles.

Wild water plants in garden ponds

Some native species of water plants are sold in garden centres for growing in ponds at home. The smaller kinds, such as water forget-me-not, flowering rush and bog bean, make quite good plants for a fair-sized pond, but the more fast-growing types, such as yellow flag iris and yellow or white water lilies, are not to be recommended, even in large ponds, as they are so invasive – cultivated varieties are far more suitable. Conversely, many of the water plants sold for growing in garden ponds are tropical species, which are now at risk of running amok in our countryside if they are allowed to 'escape'. Mild winters no longer mean they are reliably killed off each year. Several potential problem species have been withdrawn from sale, but if you grow water hyacinths, water lettuce or curly pondweed, dispose of them on compost heaps at the end of the season and do not allow them to get into waterways. Parrot's feather (Myriophyllum aquaticum) is best steered clear of completely.

22 Purple loosestrife
Lythrum salicaria

A tall and imposing wetland wildflower, purple loosestrife is commonly found in large drifts along riverbanks. It forms upright clumps, 1–1.2m (3–4ft) high, with pointed-tipped leaves arranged in groups of 3 round the stems and producing long, narrow, tapering spikes of mauve-pink flowers, each with 6 petals, in July and August.
HABITAT Riverbanks and water's edges, but also permanently damp ground such as fenland and marshes throughout Wales and the southern half of England.

23 Water figwort
Scrophularia auriculata

The water figwort is a slightly unusual waterside wildflower. It is tall, lean and upright, to 1.2m (4ft) high, with stems that are square in cross-section, accentuated by long flanges running up them, almost to the full height of the plant. The large, spatula-shaped leaves are

faintly notched around the edges and arranged in pairs up the stems. From June to September, bunches of small, strange, brownish, helmet-shaped flowers (no bigger than a child's fingertip) grow out from the leaf axils near the top of the plant. (If you find a figwort growing in damp woods, without winged stems and with deeply toothed, almost fringed leaves, it is likely to be a close relative, the common figwort, *Scrophularia nodosa*.)
HABITAT Damp, sunny places close to water, mostly in the southern half of England.

20 Flowering rush
Butomus umbellatus

The flowering rush is a slightly uncommon, perennial water plant with rush-like foliage, forming clumps 60–90cm (24–36in) high. In July and August it bears clusters of very attractive, pale pink flowers at the top of long, slim, wiry, tubular, upright stems; each flower has a cluster of deeper raspberry-red stamens in the centre.
HABITAT Riverbanks and shallow water round the edges of ponds; found locally in central and southern England.

21 Meadowsweet
Filipendula ulmaria

Meadowsweet is a tall, upright perennial, 60–120cm (24–48in) high, with distinctive, pinnate leaves that have deeply indented veins, growing alternately up the stems. From June to August they are topped with cloud-like sprays of frothy, creamy white flowers. Both flowers and foliage are aromatic.
HABITAT Wet meadows, damp woodland edges, fenland and marshy places.

26 Ragged robin
Lychnis flos-cuculi

The ragged robin is a common but distinctive and easily identified wildflower, 30–75cm (12–30in) high, with delicate, shaggy, bright pink flowers in May and June; in close-up, you can see the petals are deeply divided to create the feathery appearance. The leaves are long, slim and oval, arranged in pairs up the flower stem.
HABITAT Damp meadows and woodland edges.

27 Early marsh orchid
Dactylorhiza incarnata

An uncommon plant, the early marsh orchid is found locally in colonies in wet grassland. Like most native orchids, it is difficult to identify positively as there is a great number of similar species. It has upright flower spikes, 30–60cm (12–24in) high, with long, narrow, non-spotted foliage rather like coarse grass, 20–30cm (8–12in) long. Each leaf base clasps closely round the stem of the plant, and each stem is topped by a short, squat, blunt-topped cluster of flowers, which can be any shade of pink, or light magenta through to an almost brick-red colour. For good identifying features, look at the lip of each flower (the lowest and widest petal), which has its edges turned back, and the flowerhead, which contains a scattering of large bracts that protrude between the flowers.
HABITAT Grassland on damp, chalky soil, also fenland and marshes, mostly in the southern half of England.

24 Bog bean
Menyanthes trifoliata

The bog bean is an unmistakable, attractive and unusual water plant, growing in loose clumps by the waterside with stems that creep out across the water without taking root. The foliage looks very much like that of the broad bean – grey-green and oval, growing in groups of 3 leaves. It flowers from May to July, producing clusters of very pale pink, fringed flowers in short, pyramidal spikes standing 10–15cm (4–6in) out of the water, with reddish buds tightly grouped at the tips of the stems.
HABITAT Locally in bogs, fenland and round the edges of lakes and ponds.

25 Great willowherb
Epilobium hirsutum

A common wetland wildflower, the great willowherb forms tall, bushy clumps, 1–1.5m (3–5ft) high and the same width across, often colonizing large areas. The fairly long, narrow leaves are slightly hairy and lightly toothed round the edges, arranged in pairs up the main stems of the plant. In July and August, it produces pink flowers on short stalks from the leaf axils towards the top of the plant. Each flower has 4 or 5 petals, with a notch at the tip of each. These are followed by short, slender green pods, which eventually burst open to release seeds spread by the wind on silken threads.
HABITAT Riverbanks, edges of ponds and lakes, also fenland and marshy ground.

28 Himalayan balsam
Impatiens glandulifera

The Himalayan balsam is a stout, fast-growing, upright, bushy annual, 1–2m (3–6½ft) tall, with fleshy stems that are sometimes reddish tinged, and large, oval, busy-lizzie-like leaves with slightly notched edges arranged in pairs along them. It flowers from July to October, producing loose clusters of mauve-pink (sometimes also pale pink or white), helmet-shaped flowers towards the top of the plant. The ripe seed capsules

open with a 'pop', shooting seeds some distance away – it self-seeds very freely.

Originally introduced from the Himalayas in the early 1800s as a garden plant, Himalayan balsam has now 'escaped' into the countryside. Although very pretty, it is not welcomed by environmentalists for its highly invasive nature, which has enabled it to take over huge expanses of riverbanks (in places like the 'backs' at Cambridge) and squeeze out native vegetation. It is one of the plants that is actively being removed from sensitive sites, together with the similarly invasive Japanese knotweed (*Fallopia japonica*) and *Rhododendron ponticum*, which, coincidentally, were both introduced as garden plants and have now 'escaped' to make a nuisance of themselves in the wild.

HABITAT Riverbanks and other damp places throughout lowland areas of the British Isles.

29 Comfrey
Symphytum officinale

Comfrey is a well-known and widespread perennial, growing in dense, bushy, mound-shaped clumps, up to 1m (3ft) high and the same across, with thick, bristly stems; the large, coarse, pointed-oval leaves have a rough, sandpaper-like texture. In June and July it bears clusters of nodding, creamy white bells at the end of sideshoots near the top of the plant; these are very popular with bees.

HABITAT Undisturbed, damp ground, usually near water or on wasteland.

30 Wild teasel
Dipsacus fullonum

This is a striking and easily identified perennial plant, with tall, upright, prickly stems, 1–1.5m (3–5ft) high, and long, narrow leaves with toothed edges arranged in pairs all along them. The main stems branch out at the top of the plant, with each short sideshoot producing a large, solitary, pine-cone-like flowerhead, 5cm (2in) long, dotted with rings of tiny lavender florets. Long, narrow, spiny green bracts make a shaggy collar round the base. The lower leaves are fused and often act as a reservoir for water. The 'pine-cone' seedheads persist late into winter, and are often visited by

flocks of goldfinches, who feed on the small seeds they contain.

HABITAT Damp ground, especially in hedgerows and wasteland, also found along paths and roadside hedgerows, throughout the British Isles (except northern Scotland).

Also found in or around rivers, lakes or streams

Arctic tern (see p.32)
Black-headed gull (see p.28)
Black-necked grebe (see p.25)
Black-throated diver (see p.24)
Canada goose (see p.298)
Common tern (see p.32)
Cuckoo (see p.164)
Greenshank (see p.42)
Harvest mouse (see p.279)
Herring gull (see p.29)
Lady's smock (see p.212)
Lesser black-backed gull (see p.29)
Little egret (see p.44)
Oystercatcher (see p.39)
Polecat (see p.203)
Red-throated diver (see p.24)
Ringed plover (see p.39)
Shelduck (see p.37)
Slavonian grebe (see p.25)
Wigeon (see p.38)
Yellow wagtail (see p.192)

Hedgerows

The fortunes of hedgerows have ebbed and flowed down the centuries. Initially erected as defensive barricades, they later became boundary markers, as well as living larders for country folk. In the twentieth century, hedgerows were deemed unprofitable and many were removed to create space for farming; luckily, we've realized their value to wildlife in the nick of time.

Natural defences

When early people first began making small clearings in the wildwoods to use for growing crops and keeping livestock, the local wildlife descended in hordes to take advantage of the sudden increase in food supplies. So they left the band of scrub that grew up naturally in the shady strip round the edge of the clearings, where crops wouldn't grow anyway. This border of shrubs thickened and created a natural barrier that helped to keep deer and other foragers out of their grain crops and protect their livestock from predators.

During the Bronze and Iron Ages, a lot of hedges would have grown up in much the same way – accidentally – but they'd have been more like shaggy shelterbelts than today's neatly shaped and clipped versions. It's also very likely that when our ancestors needed a boundary in a hurry they'd put in an artificial hedge, consisting of a row of posts stuck in the ground – similar to the arrangement they used to surround hill forts to defend them from unfriendly tribes, only smaller, since the ones round fields were mostly to keep livestock in and thieving wildlife or pilfering neighbours out. Once the posts were in place, wild plants grew up from wind-blown seeds between and around them, so the defensive 'fedge' (fence-cum-hedge) would soon be clad in plants, which took over as the original timber rotted away. Hedgerows continued in this informal way for a very long time.

Roman interlude

The Romans, who ruled Britain from AD 43 to 410, brought their hedging expertise with them. They'd been using formal hedges for ages in Italy, and so they created extensive and elaborately maintained hedges around their villas in Britain, as archaeological evidence shows at sites such as Fishbourne Roman Palace, in Sussex. They also practised the art of hedge-laying, which reinforces a hedge by weaving the partially cut and angled stems between a row of upright sticks hammered in along the boundary line, to make something very much like a living fence. When they were recalled home, many of their skills and much of their civilization went with them. Although it would be a long time before formal hedging came into being in grand British gardens, the ancient art of hedge-laying helped to shape the face of the countryside.

Medieval markers

After the Romans left, it was very much back to business as usual for the British countryside. Settlements grew slowly,

new ones appeared and regularly trodden routes emerged round the edges of fields between one hamlet and the next. Since almost everyone worked on the land in one way or another, they'd have known better than to walk on growing crops – so they went round the edge instead.

Rough tracks of trodden earth would have deteriorated into a muddy mess in winter, so they were gradually improved by digging ditches alongside to give the surface water somewhere to run away; the soil that was dug out to make a ditch was thrown up next to it to form a bank. Since neither the tracks, ditches or banks could have been used for growing crops, wild scrub would very likely have been allowed to grow up on the bank, where it gave anyone using the path a bit of shelter.

As these informal paths between villages became more strongly defined, they often ended up becoming parish boundaries. And as medieval farmers began taking livestock to market, many of the regular routes widened out, as a result of the passage of hundreds of hooves, to become 'drove roads'. The existence of boundary hedges and ditches alongside these must have made the job of shifting large herds of animals on foot a lot easier, as they couldn't wander off into the surrounding fields. These early hedges didn't follow straight lines – they followed the edges of fields, which were themselves odd shapes in order to fit the contours of the land or to avoid natural obstructions. Many of the curved shapes were created by regular ox-ploughing, where ploughmen needed a generous sweep to turn the team at the top of each field. So next time you are following a public footpath or bridleway and wonder at the strange twists and turns it takes, it's probably because you are following the outline of an ancient field system.

Hedges gradually became the major boundary marker for most of the productive farmland across Britain. Since the majority of hedges still grew up naturally, most medieval hedgerows contained a large mixture of species, including woodland trees such as hazels and hollies, and scramblers such as wild rose and blackberry. Hedges were a useful source of firewood – particularly in Elizabethan times, when fuel

PREVIOUS PAGES A hedgerow lining a rural road in County Armagh, Northern Ireland (main picture), and a harvest mouse foraging at the edge of a field (small picture).
BELOW LEFT The Romans introduced formal hedging to Britain, creating clipped patterns, as seen at Fishbourne Roman Palace, Sussex.
BELOW CENTRE A hawthorn hedge with cow parsley lining the track.
BELOW RIGHT A series of hedges divide up the land surrounding Stokesay Castle, Shropshire.

was in great demand during the 'mini ice age'. Hedgerows could also be 'cropped' of wild fruit, nuts and berries, and they were good places for trapping rabbits. A lot of hedging was planted during the great sheep-farming boom that followed the Black Death (1360–1600), especially in the Midlands, where sheep farming took off in a big way.

In some parts of the country, where conditions didn't encourage hedges to grow naturally, other boundaries were used to outline fields. In high, windy areas with poor, stony soil, stones were piled up to make drystone walls instead. They are still a major feature of the landscape in places like the Yorkshire Dales and the Lake District today. There's an art to drystone-wall building. These barriers may look flimsy, but they are intricately constructed and have surprising strength. Building them is a rural craft, which is currently undergoing something of a resurgence. In the south-west of England, it was more traditional to pile up high banks of turf round the edges of fields, and these were eventually colonized by wild shrubs and scrub, making the characteristic edgings to many of the narrow country lanes still seen in Devon and Cornwall. In wetland areas, such as the Fens, ditches were the most convenient way to mark field boundaries, since hedgerow shrubs didn't cope with the waterlogged ground, and anyway ditches were more useful because they doubled as drainage channels. But in most of the country, where the soil was of reasonable quality and the land sufficiently sheltered, meandering hedgerows became a familiar part of the scenery.

The heyday of hedgerows

The big hedgerow revolution took place in the eighteenth century. This was the time when wealthy landowners were regrouping their resources, building grand country houses and reorganizing the landscape into today's familiar chessboard pattern of fields and hedgerows. This was aided by the Enclosures Acts, when 21 per cent of England was enclosed by Act of Parliament and much common land was appropriated for private use. It's been estimated that 200,000 miles of hedging were planted during this time. Since hedges were being deliberately planted, rather than just allowed to grow up from whatever happened to grow wild in the right place, landowners generally planted solid rows of one type of plant. Hawthorn (also known as 'quickthorn' or simply 'quick') was the popular choice at most country estates, as it

grew quickly and, being prickly, it was ideal for keeping livestock in. As the Industrial Revolution got a grip on the countryside, farmers started planting elms in their hedges – the timber was in great demand for making lock gates for canals and water wheels for powering cornmills.

By the late eighteenth century, fox-hunting had become a popular country pastime with the gentry, and countryside that was intersected with hedges, ditches and occasional copses provided good cover for the quarry. They also created a variety of obstacles for riders to negotiate, making for a more interesting 'chase' and hence a better day's sport. Around the same time, steeple-chasing started up as landowners took wagers on the fastest horse and rider to travel cross-country between the steeples of the churches of two adjacent villages, jumping any hedges they encountered *en route*. Leicestershire and the Midlands were prime fox-hunting territory, and the characteristic countryside of those areas has largely been formed for the sport.

A good many eighteenth-century hedges still remain today, but they've nearly always been invaded by naturally occurring hedgerow species. A rule-of-thumb for estimating the age of a planted hedge is to count the number of species it contains – as a rough guide, each species represents approximately 100 years.

By the nineteenth century, some budding Victorian bean-counter estimated that a tenth of the good farmland in the country was taken up by unprofitable verges, hedges and ditches. He need not have worried – agriculture was in the doldrums and going downhill fast, since speedier, more efficient transport meant that by the start of the twentieth century it was cheaper to bring in much of our food from abroad rather than grow it ourselves. Nobody felt inclined to do anything about wasted space round farmland. The official view was that if our farmers couldn't make a living, they could always find work in towns. So there wasn't really anything to worry about, was there?

Wartime farming

When the First World War began, the Kaiser thought we would be a push-over; since we now imported so much of our food from overseas, all he had to do was cut off our shipping routes and starve us into submission. This notion had the effect of galvanizing the government into action.

Farming received a terrific shot in the arm – a system of subsidies was introduced to encourage farmers to produce more food by guaranteeing them a good return.

In the Second World War the same thing happened again, only more so. Farmers were encouraged to plough up ancient pastures, heaths and even parkland to grow crops. The King allowed 2000 acres of deer park at Windsor Great Park to be turned over to farmland, playing fields and village greens became instant allotments, and householders brought every spare bit of ground into cultivation as part of the 'Dig For Victory' campaign. Every little helped. Farmers started to make a good living and could afford to invest in new equipment. As they bought bigger tractors and combine-harvesters, many hedges were taken out to make larger fields in which machinery could be used more efficiently. And to safeguard our future food supplies, the government continued giving farmers grants and subsidies long after the war.

As agriculture grew steadily more intensive, more hedgerows and copses were ripped out to make larger fields; parts of East Anglia began to look like the prairies of North America. What with the loss of trees, hedgerows and uncultivated corners, and the increased use of pesticides and herbicides, it's little wonder wildlife was dying out. But things were to get worse. The 1970s brought in a craze for stubble-burning, which managed to set fire to a lot of hedges too, then Dutch elm disease killed off enormous numbers of one of our most prolific hedgerow trees, giving farmers and local authorities the perfect excuse to remove them – along with much of the adjacent hedging, too. The countryside was being denuded before our very eyes.

Fortunately, people started seeing sense, and by the 1990s conservation efforts began to pay off. New hedges and trees were being planted, giving wildlife their old green corridors back, linking feeding and nesting sites. And even if farmers were still using the tractor-mounted flail-cutters for hedge-trimming, at least they now did it in winter and not during the bird-nesting season. Over the past couple of decades the general public have became increasingly aware of 'green' issues, and problems such as mad-cow disease and foot-and-mouth have triggered widespread changes in farming. As the use of the countryside for tourism has grown, a change in attitude is really starting to make a difference.

An old, prickly hawthorn hedge boundary offers shelter for wildlife and acts as a wind barrier, even during the winter months.

1 Grey partridge
Perdix perdix

Our native grey partridge is similar in build to the now far more common red-legged partridge but has a different plumage pattern and is shyer and far less numerous (it has suffered a large decline). Although it looks grey-brown at a distance, a closer view reveals a bird with an orange face, bold chestnut bars on the flanks, a delicate grey crown, hind neck and breast, with a variable dark brown, horseshoe-shaped patch on the underside. The tail has chestnut edges, visible in flight. It avoids flying if possible and creeps about in vegetation. It has a distinctive 'keeer-ik' call, like a creaking gate with unoiled hinges.
HABITAT Mainly in lowland areas, particularly in eastern and central England, in arable farmland, heathland and open grassland.
SIZE 30cm (12in)
EGGS 13–17 (sometimes more), buff
NEST Hollow lined with grass and leaves on the ground, in hedgerows.
FOOD Mainly leaves and seeds of weeds, turnip tops, corn, berries; young are fed on insects.
SIMILAR TO Red-legged partridge, which has a stripy head, white

'cheeks', a black-spotted 'necklace', bolder red-brown bars on the flanks, red legs and is less secretive.
VARIATIONS Females have smaller or no horseshoe-shaped patch on the underside. Juveniles lack the stripy flanks and orange face.

2 Red-legged partridge
Alectoris rufa

Also known as the French partridge, this is a plump, rounded, short-legged game bird, with stumpy wings and a rather hump-backed stance, usually seen feeding or walking in flocks on the ground. It flies only when it has to, travelling a short distance. Like the grey partridge, the red-legged partridge is superbly camouflaged against soil when crouching or standing still – it has a plain, grey-brown back and wings and conspicuous, near-vertical, chestnut stripes on the blue-grey flanks. Look for a bold head pattern with bright, rusty red-brown eye-rings and beak. Its creamy white face breaks up into a speckled-black '' on the chest. The legs are rust-coloured and there are rusty red triangles on either side of the tail, visible in flight. The male has a distinct song: a series of chuffing notes like the sound of a distant steam train. Introduced from France just over 200 years ago, this resident has now outstripped our native grey partridge.
HABITAT Mostly in southern, eastern and central England, on arable farmland or occasionally heaths, dunes or coastal shingle.
SIZE 33cm (13in)
EGGS 10–16, buff, speckled brown
NEST Shallow, sparsely lined scrape on the ground, in hedgerows.
FOOD Seeds, roots, leaves of plants; young are fed on insects.

SIMILAR TO Grey partridge.
VARIATIONS Juveniles are dull brown above and buff below, with few stripes on the flanks.

Birds on the ground

Families of red-legged partridges often walk in single file, with a parent at the front and large numbers of babies following in a line behind. Birds frequently follow tractor ruts through crops, as it is easier than pushing through rows of plants. Flocks of adults are sometimes seen walking along quiet country footpaths, tracks and little-used country lanes, and if hurried along by walkers or cyclists they will often scuttle through a gap in a hedge to get back into a field rather than taking off.

3 Pheasant
Phasianus colchicus

Our best-known, commonest and most numerous game bird, the pheasant is thought to have been introduced from southern Asia around 1000 years ago for sport. It is a large, mainly iridescent, copper-coloured bird, heavily marked with black crescents below, with a long, dark-barred ginger tail, a dark, glossy, green-black head and neck, a bright red face and sometimes a white collar round the neck. In spring, its breeding plumage is even brighter and dominant males grow larger with an enlarged red wattle and bigger, erectile, dark green ear-tufts on top of the head. There are many variations in colour owing to regularly introduced forms from the Continent. Dominant males display in spring by stretching upright to 'crow' and shake their feathers. Otherwise, pheasants prefer to 'melt away' into the undergrowth. If alarmed, they will take flight with loud whirrings of wings and 'kok-ok' alarm calls.

HABITAT Well-wooded farmland and parkland, as well as woods and hedgerows; sometimes country gardens. Throughout the British Isles, except north-west Scotland.

SIZE 53–90cm (21–36in)

EGGS 8–15, pale olive-buff

NEST On the ground among vegetation, often in hedgerows.

FOOD Grain and other seeds, insects, berries.

VARIATIONS Young, low-status, non-breeding males lack the bright breeding colours of the older cock birds; females are smaller and dull, speckled, sandy brown to dark rufous brown; juveniles are beige with a much shorter tail.

4 Turtle dove
Streptopelia turtur

This is an increasingly rare summer visitor that has the physique of a collared dove but is a little smaller, with much more striking markings. The basic body colour is light pinkish grey with paler underparts. Most of the upperparts are bright orange-brown with an almost diamond pattern of darker brown; the flight feathers show as a narrow blue-grey panel just above the flanks, with the outer wings dark brownish. The legs and eye-rings are raspberry-red. The beak is short and black, and has a small, black-and-white-barred patch either side of the nape. It is shy, reclusive and flies off easily, with flicking wing-beats and a side-to-side, tilting action during brief glides.

HABITAT Summer visitor mainly to southern and eastern England, with a few birds in northern England and eastern Wales; rare in Scotland and Ireland. Found on farmland with overgrown hedges, also sunny woodland edges. Winter: Africa.

SIZE 28cm (11in)

EGGS 2, white

NEST Flimsy platform of small twigs in trees or overgrown hedges.

FOOD Mainly seeds of wildflowers, some insects, snails.

5 Common whitethroat
Sylvia communis

These active, fidgety little warblers are constantly on the move. When perched, they often fan out their tail or raise a small crest on top of the head. Look for a grey head, white throat, creamy breast and underparts, and a brown back and tail with gingery or reddish brown wings and light-coloured legs. As summer visitors, they are more plentiful in some years, scarcer in others.

HABITAT April–September: across the British Isles, except northern Scotland, in dense scrub, woodland edges, young plantations, parkland and farmland with copses and overgrown hedges. Winter: Africa, south of the Sahara.

SIZE 14cm (5½in)

EGGS 4–5, greenish white, speckled olive-brown

NEST Cup-shaped nest of grass, low down in bushes or scrub.

FOOD Insects; berries in late summer to autumn.

SIMILAR TO Lesser whitethroat, which is smaller and has a uniform, greyer back, tail and wings (no reddish colouring in the wings) and dark grey legs.

VARIATIONS Females and juveniles have brown rather than grey heads.

6 Lesser whitethroat
Sylvia curruca

This is a declining and secretive summer visitor, rather like the more abundant common whitethroat but a little smaller with a much greyer back and wings. It also has a distinctive, smudgy, dark grey patch on each 'cheek'. It may be seen in small flocks on migration, often with common whitethroats. More usually it is heard. The call is a hard 'tac tac', similar to that of the common whitethroat. The best time to see it is in autumn, when it is feeding on berries.

HABITAT May–September: dense thickets, scrub and overgrown hedgerows in England, Wales and southern Scotland (rare in Ireland). Winter: north-east Africa.

SIZE 13cm (5in)

EGGS 4–6, off-white, speckled olive-brown

NEST In thickets or hedgerows.

FOOD Insects, fruit, berries.

SIMILAR TO Common whitethroat.

8 Yellowhammer
Emberiza citrinella

The yellowhammer is roughly the size of a sparrow but slimmer, with a canary-yellow head and underparts and a streaky, chestnut-brown back and tail with a notch at the tip. The warm rust-brown patch on the rump is often visible on a bird flying away from you. Unlike most farmland birds, it continues to sing in summer, even in the middle of the day. Its song sounds like 'little bit of bread and *no-o* cheese', but sometimes it omits the 'cheese'. Numbers have declined greatly (by over 50 per cent) since the 1970s owing to agricultural intensification.
HABITAT Fields, scrub, hillsides and country gardens with hedges or plenty of bushes. Throughout most of the British Isles, particularly eastern and central England and eastern Scotland.
SIZE 16cm (6¼in)
EGGS 3–5, off-white with dark grey squiggles and spots
NEST Bulky cup of straw, grass and moss on the ground or in a bush.
FOOD Mostly seeds, also insects and other invertebrates.
SIMILAR TO Cirl bunting, which is slightly smaller, less yellow overall, with pronounced black markings on the face rather than smaller, grey smudges. The female yellowhammer and female cirl bunting are very similar, except the female yellowhammer has a chestnut rump and black tail but the rump of the female cirl

bunting is greyish brown, which extends down the sides of the tail, and has bolder head markings.
VARIATIONS Female and immature adults look less yellow, rather like unusually bright sparrows patterned in chestnut and yellow. Their head and breast are heavily streaked with brown.

9 Cirl bunting
Emberiza cirlus

This is a rare, yellowhammer-like farmland bird with a chestnut-and-black-flecked back, yellow markings on the face, yellow underparts, a blackish tail with a notched tip, a short, thick grey beak and warm buff legs. Look for the distinctive black crown and eye-stripes on the male and a black chin with a

greenish-tinged breast band. Its song is a rattling trill, 'tacatacataca', very similar to that of the lesser whitethroat. It is reliant on winter stubble fields for survival, which is one of the main reasons why its population has declined, but numbers are increasing where farmers practise conservation.
HABITAT South-west England (virtually all in south Devon), in traditional farmland with plenty of hedges with taller trees and bushy scrubland.
SIZE 15cm (6in)
EGGS 3–5, greenish white with dark brown blotches and squiggles
NEST Cup of grass, stems and moss, lined with hair and other soft materials, in hedgerows and hedgerow trees.
FOOD Insects and other invertebrates, seeds.
SIMILAR TO Yellowhammer.

7 Magpie
Pica pica

The magpie appears black and white from a distance, but close up, in good light, the black areas have a strong iridescence, with a beautiful, blue-green sheen to the wings, bluish purple on the head, breast and back, and mainly bronze-green, bluish and reddish bands on the tail. A large, cocky, assertive member of the crow family, it is common and easily recognized in flight by its bold plumage pattern with a very long, wedge-shaped tail and wings that flare into 'open fingers' at the tips. Its call is a harsh, chattering 'chak-chak-chak'.
HABITAT Throughout the British Isles, except far north of Scotland, in wooded farmland, parkland and gardens with fair-sized trees.
SIZE 46cm (18in)

EGGS 5–8, grey-green, speckled with darker grey and brown
NEST Untidy dome of sticks in a thorny bush or high in a tree.
FOOD Varied diet including fruit, seeds and other plant food, road-kill, scraps, baby birds and eggs taken from nests.

Invertebrates

1 Red admiral
Vanessa atalanta

This is a very common, medium-to-large (6cm/2½in wingspan), black-white-and-orange summer visitor from the Continent. When

it is basking with its wings held open, orange crescents on the individual wings join up to form a continuous, irregular circle that stands out against the black background; there are also scattered white dots on the wings. Adults feed particularly on the nectar of teasel and, in gardens, on scabious, buddleia, Michaelmas daisies and *Sedum spectabile*, as well as on rotting windfall apples.
HABITAT Arrives in May or June and seen all summer, in hedgerows, woodland rides and gardens.
CATERPILLAR Black and spiky, with rows of small white dots, feeding on nettles in summer.

2 Painted lady
Cynthia cardui

The painted lady is a medium-sized butterfly (5.5cm/2¼in wingspan) in tawny-orange with black spots. It is often confused with the small tortoiseshell: look for the distinctive, black-and-white tips to the forewings in the painted lady. A migrant from North Africa and southern Europe, it is widely seen in the British Isles in some years but is scarce in others. Adults feed on the nectar of a variety of wildflowers and garden plants, particularly thistles and buddleia.

HABITAT Throughout the British Isles, in hedgerows, wasteland and gardens with a wide variety of nectar-rich flowers.
CATERPILLAR Black with a thin yellow stripe up each side and spiky yellow 'bristles', feeding on nettles or thistles from June to September.

3 Small tortoiseshell
Aglais urticae

Very common and familiar, the small tortoiseshell is a medium-sized, orange-brown-and-cream butterfly (5cm/2in wingspan). The forewings have a conspicuous band of alternate black and cream rectangles along the front and the hind wings are edged with a scalloped border of small blue half-moons. The undersides have the same pattern but in buff and cream. Adults feed on a range of hedgerow wildflowers, especially thistles; in gardens they are often found on *Sedum spectabile*,

Michaelmas daisies and buddleia.
HABITAT Throughout the British Isles in hedgerows and gardens, from March to September. The last generation of butterflies to hatch in late summer, they often overwinter in hollow trees or outbuildings.
CATERPILLAR Spiky, black and yellow, congregating under silken nets on nettle leaves near the tops of the stems.

4 Gatekeeper
Pyronia tithonus

Often seen following walkers along country paths, and also known as the hedge brown, this is a pretty orange butterfly (3cm/1¼in wingspan) with a brown body and brown 'trimmings'. The orange forewings have a double false eye in the centre and a brown outer edge; the hind wings are brown with an orange stripe across the middle and a small dot near the inner edge of each. Adults feed on

the nectar of brambles and other hedgerow flowers.
HABITAT Hedgerows and orchards throughout the southern half of the British Isles in July and August.
CATERPILLARS Inconspicuous greyish 'grubs' on grasses, all year except July.

A haven for butterflies

An averagely unkempt countryside hedgerow provides a superb habitat for an enormous range of butterflies. The flowers of wild hops and brambles supply nectar for various adult butterflies – the large white, peacock, painted lady and red admiral are frequent visitors. The small white, green-veined white and orange tip prefer flowers of wild members of the crucifer family, such as Jack-by-the-hedge. Hedgerows are also home to several good 'nursery plants' for caterpillars, such as ivy, thistles, hawthorn and various grasses; the most valuable hedgerow plants of all are nettles, which are used as crèches by the peacock, red admiral, small tortoiseshell, painted lady and comma butterflies.

5 Small copper
Lycaena phlaeas

This is a colourful, small, orange-and-brown butterfly, which basks on the ground with its wings spread out (about 3cm/1¼in wingspan) and chases off other butterflies that enter its 'patch'. The forewings are mainly orange, edged with brown and with scattered, dark spots; the hind wings are brown with a wavy orange band round the edges. The undersides of the hind wings are light buff with darker markings. Adults feed on the nectar of fleabane and other flowers.

HABITAT Fairly common throughout the British Isles, less so in Scotland and central Ireland, on downs, grassy meadows, heathland, wasteland, roadside verges and occasionally gardens, from April to October.

CATERPILLAR Small pink and/or green 'grubs' on dock and sorrel, from May to October.

6 White-letter hairstreak
Strymonidia w-album

The white-letter hairstreak is a small-to-medium-sized butterfly (3cm/1¼in wingspan), in mid-brown with a pair of conspicuous, pointed black 'tails' towards the tips of the hind wings. If it is viewed at rest with closed wings, a fine white line crossing the forewing is likely to be visible, as is a distinct white 'W' on the hind wing, which has an irregular orange streak patterned with black dots near the 'tail'. Adults often feed on the nectar of bramble flowers.

HABITAT Scattered locations throughout England (except the far north) and Wales, in hedgerows and woodland glades, in July and August.

CATERPILLAR Short, fat, green, almost slug-shaped 'grubs', patterned as if divided into segments, feeding on leaf-buds and leaves of elm.

7 Angle shades moth
Phlogophora meticulosa

This is a very common but easily overlooked buff moth, with irregular, dull brown 'camouflage jacket' markings, often with small hints of green, red or pink, with jagged trailing edges to the wings. It is seen mostly during the day, looking like a dead leaf resting on vegetation.

HABITAT Throughout the British Isles in hedgerows and gardens, from May to October.

CATERPILLAR Green, to 4–5cm (1½–2in), feeding at night on leaves, buds and flowers of a wide variety of foliage; also sometimes found in greenhouses.

8 Robin's pincushion
Diplolepis rosae

Also known as the rose bedeguar gall, this common, attractive and unmistakable plant gall is made up of fluffy, rosy-red threads forming a shaggy, candyfloss-like head, 1–3cm (⅜–1¼in) across and long, on young stems of wild rose. The gall has a hard centre; if it is sliced open, you will see many tiny chambers, which contain the larvae of a minute gall wasp. You are unlikely to see the adult, which is tiny (5mm/³⁄₁₆in wingspan) with a black thorax and brown abdomen.

HABITAT Throughout the British Isles, on stems of wild roses growing in hedgerows in summer.

9 Buff-tailed bumblebee
Bombus terrestris

Also known as the humblebee, this is our biggest bumblebee – the familiar, big, fat, furry one with 'football jersey' stripes. The background colour is black, with one narrow yellow stripe around the neck and a second yellow stripe around the middle of the abdomen, which has an off-white tip at the rear end.

HABITAT Any countryside with a wide range of wildflowers blooming in succession from early spring onwards.

OPPOSITE A small copper butterfly resting on a leaf.

Jobs for all

Worker bees live for 3 or 4 weeks only. They are the ones you see out and about in flowers, where they gather pollen, which is carried back to the nest in pollen baskets (small, coloured bulges) on their back legs. They also carry back nectar in the stomach, to store for feeding new bees – the nectar is regurgitated as honey into wax cells. There is one queen per nest and she stays inside most of the time, laying eggs. Male bees (drones) gather when a new queen leaves a colony – their sole job is to mate, then they die. Mated queens are the only bees to survive the winter.

10 Green lacewing
Chrysopa carnea

The green lacewing is a long, pale green 'fly', 3cm (1¼in) long, with 4 enormous, translucent, lace-like wings neatly folded over a tubular green body; the head bears a pair of very long antennae and golden eyes. It is not a strong flier, but when it does fly it looks like a large, fluttering mayfly with 2 pairs of wings. The larvae, pale and shuttle-shaped, are found under foliage and feed on aphids. There are 2 similar, closely related species.
HABITAT Seen in summer or autumn, in foliage in hedgerows or gardens throughout the British Isles, but most common in southern England.

11 Scorpion fly
Panorpa communis

This is a rather secretive insect, with a grey-and-yellow-banded body, 1.5cm (⅝in) long, and mottled grey wings, with a wingspan of 3cm (1¼in). A close-up view of the male shows a yellow 'beak' and a large, red, upturned rear like a scorpion's sting (which is not a sting but the claw used to grasp the female during mating). The female is similar but lacks the rear claw. Adults feed on dead insects, grubs and fruit. The larvae resemble off-white, slightly hairy caterpillars and feed on dead insects in the soil under a hedge.
HABITAT Shady hedgerows, hedge-bottoms, nettles or bramble thickets throughout the British Isles, but mostly in southern England, from May to July.

12 Green shield bug
Palomena prasina

One of those 'I can't believe my eyes' bugs, this looks like a bright green badge. The chunky, rounded-triangular body, 2cm (¾in) long, has broad 'shoulders' and a tiny head, from which grow 2 long antennae. Although reasonably common, it is rarely seen as it mostly stays still or creeps in slow motion among stems, where its colour is an exact match for surrounding foliage. It flies loudly and lands with a thump.

HABITAT Throughout the British Isles on foliage in hedgerows, woodland edges and scrub, sometimes gardens, in summer and autumn.

13 Red-and-black froghopper
Cercopis vulnerata

This froghopper is a striking, small, cylindrical bug, 1cm (⅜in) long. The head and legs are black and it has a black-and-red-blotched body. The nymphs live in hardened 'froth' on roots growing underground.
HABITAT On foliage in hedgerows and wooded areas from April through to August. Widespread throughout the British Isles but most common in southern and central England.

14 Hawthorn shieldbug
Acanthosoma haemorrhoidale

The hawthorn shieldbug is a large, common, shield-shaped bug, up to 2cm (¾in) long, with long antennae. Much of it is dark green, with a dull reddish, triangular marking on the back, outlining the wing-cases and 'shoulders'. As its name suggests, it feeds on the berries and leaves of hawthorn, and also oak leaves.
HABITAT Seen mainly in spring and autumn throughout England and Wales, in hedgerows containing hawthorn and oak.

15 Elm-bark beetle
Scolytus scolytus

The carrier of Dutch elm disease is this small, bullet-shaped beetle, 5mm (3⁄16in) long, with chestnut-brown antennae, legs and wing-cases, a black thorax and a grey head. Adult females tunnel underneath elm bark, then the larvae make a characteristic pattern of tunnels that radiate out from a central 'corridor' where the eggs have been laid. The disease is spread by fungal spores inhabiting the burrows, which are then carried to new elm trees when the next generation of beetles hatches and flies off, leaving small, woodworm-like exit holes in the bark.
HABITAT Widespread in hedgerows in southern and central Britain, scarcer in the north; adult beetles are seen from April to September.

16 Soldier beetle
Rhagonycha fulva

This is a common, elongated orange beetle, about 1cm (⅜in) long, which is active by day, usually seen in small groups conducting its courtship or hunting for small insect prey on large, flat-topped flowers such as cow parsley or hogweed.

HABITAT In sunny, sheltered hedgerows, verges, also sometimes gardens, in July and August. In England and Wales, scarcer in Scotland and Ireland.

17 Devil's coach horse
Ocypus olens

The devil's coach horse – a fairly common, ground-living beetle – is a ferocious-looking, stout black creature, up to 2.5cm (1in) long, with a pair of powerful, curved mandibles at the front of the large head. If threatened, it raises its scorpion-like tail and squirts a smelly substance from its rear end

in defence. The jaws are used to break up the caterpillars, earwigs, spiders and occasionally carrion on which it feeds.

HABITAT Countryside, especially hedgerows with fallen logs or leaf litter for cover; also visits gardens and old houses.

18 Yellow ladybirds

Less often seen than the more familiar red forms, yellow ladybirds are very striking and reasonably common. They are a typical ladybird shape and size, but in yellow and black instead of red; the 14-spot ladybird (*Propylea quattuordecimpunctata*), 5mm (³⁄₁₆in) long, has black squares, some of which are joined together across the middle of the back. The 22-spot ladybird (*Thea vigintiduopunctata*, shown here) is 3mm (⅛in) long and has tiny black dots all over.

HABITAT Hedgerow, trees and hedge-bottom vegetation – 14-spot mostly in the southern half of England, 22-spot in scattered pockets throughout Britain and Ireland, from April to September.

19 Speckled bush-cricket
Leptophyes punctatissima

This is an elegant, long-legged and long-antennaed bush-cricket, about 1.5cm (⅝in) long. It is a bright emerald-green, speckled all over with minute black dots.

HABITAT Hedgerows, nettles or bramble patches, but also sometimes in gardens in the southern half of the British Isles, from July to October.

20 Money spiders
Linyphia species

There are many closely related species of minute spiders of which *Linyphia triangularis* is one of the commonest, but they are hard to tell apart; most are very small with a black body and brown legs. They make roundish, 'hammock webs' in grass or low down in bushes to trap aphids and other small insects on which they feed. On sunny days in autumn they release a thread of silk, which is caught in the air currents, carrying them away like a parachute in reverse and allowing them to move around – literally – to new pastures.

HABITAT Throughout the British Isles in grassland, fields of crops and gardens, mostly in late summer and autumn.

21 Hedge snails
Cepaea species

Also known as banded snails, these are fairly common snails with banded patterns spiralling round the shells. We have 2 species and although they both vary in colour and banding from all-yellow or pink to virtually all-black, there is an easy way to tell them apart. The white-lipped hedge snail (*Cepaea hortensis*, shown here) has a pale lip round the shell opening, while the dark-lipped hedge snail (*C. nemoralis*) has a dark shell opening. Both snails reach a size of 2cm (⅜in) across.

HABITAT Hedgerows and also hedge-bottom vegetation, woods and gardens. *C. hortensis* occurs throughout the British Isles but *C. nemoralis* is absent from islands off the north coast of Scotland.

1 Rabbit
Oryctolagus cuniculus

A very familiar, common and widespread mammal, the wild rabbit is usually smaller than the domestic pet rabbit, up to 40cm (16in) long, with straight ears and a neutral grey-brown coat, although an unusual all-black form is sometimes seen. When fleeing from a predator, it flashes its white tail underside (the 'scut') as a warning signal to other rabbits in the vicinity.

Wild rabbits live in colonies and are active by day, particularly in spring, when they are often seen feeding or frolicking. You can tell when rabbits are active in the area, even if you don't see them, since they graze field crops almost down to bare ground in a strip 3m (10ft) or more out from a hedgerow. Although generally considered a pest by farmers and gardeners, rabbits actually do a lot of good in several ways, for example by digging burrows that are later inhabited by other creatures, especially seabirds such as puffins on cliffs and islands. Also, by grazing and keeping turf short on hills, downs and other beauty spots, they help to create conditions in which rare wildflowers thrive.

HABITAT Throughout Britain and and Ireland, in arable fields, pasture, parkland, downs and hedgerows, also scrub – especially bramble patches – and woodland. They are most abundant in cultivated ground, including country gardens, where they can be a real pest.

FOOD Grass, arable crops, weeds and plants, and in winter also nibbles young tree shoots and strips bark from trees.

2 Weasel
Mustela nivalis

This is a slim, slender carnivore. The male is about 21cm (8¼in) long including the tail (the female is shorter), with a rich reddish brown coat, a completely white underside and a short, all-brown tail (the tail of the stoat has a black tip). It moves fast with sinuous, snake-like movements through undergrowth, often investigating holes.

HABITAT Throughout England, Scotland and Wales (not Ireland), in woodland, overgrown hedgerows in farmland, parkland and large woodland gardens.

FOOD Mice, voles, baby rabbits.

3 Stoat
Mustela erminea

The stoat is a long, low, lean, ferret-like carnivore, up to 40cm (16in) long (including a 10cm/4in tail), with brown fur and a white chin and chest and a black tip to the tail. It has a tubular shape, but holds its neck and head at right angles to the body. Generally, it moves fairly sinuously but bounds through the grass when chasing prey. In winter, stoats in some northern parts of the country turn white except for the tip of the tail, which stays black. The weasel is smaller, thinner and redder, with a short tail that never has a black tip – this is the instant give-away.

HABITAT Throughout most of the British Isles, in woodland and dense, overgrown hedgerows near farmland, wherever there is good cover and a supply of rabbits.

FOOD Rabbits, small rodents, birds.

Stoat and weasel relatives

Unlikely though it sounds, stoats and weasels have a lot of close relatives in the countryside – badgers, mink, otters, pine martens and polecats are all members of the same family, known as the mustelids. The ferret that is sometimes kept by countrymen for rabbiting (and often as a family pet these days) is thought by some to be a descendant of the wild polecat; it has been bred in captivity for many generations. Escaped ferrets are sometimes seen in the countryside, but are common only where few foxes are present.

4

the tail of the one in front. Predators (other than owls) rarely take shrews, as they apparently taste terrible.

HABITAT Fields, woodland and hedgerows throughout the British Isles.

FOOD Earthworms, snails, spiders, insects and other invertebrates.

6 Pipistrelles
Pipistrellus species

Pipistrelles are our smallest and commonest bats. Until recently we thought we had only one common pipistrelle but bat experts now

6

4 Harvest mouse
Micromys minutus

Our smallest rodent, this is an agile mouse with a head and body only 6cm (2½in) long plus a tail of the same length. It has bright gingery fur and white underparts. Look for the small, round ears, a naked pink, prehensile tail used for gripping stalks and naked pink hands and feet. Although active day and night it is reclusive and hard to spot; you are more likely to see the round, tennis-ball-sized nests of woven grass attached to several stems in long grass, usually about 60cm (24in) above the ground. Harvest mice are rarely seen but are more common than were once thought.

HABITAT Long grass, hedgerows,

bramble patches and reed-beds. Found in England from Lincolnshire southwards, with a few in Wales and Scotland.

FOOD Grain, fruit, shoots, insects.

5 Common shrew
Sorex araneus

This is a very common and widespread, small, mouse-like creature, 7cm (2¾in) long plus a short tail, 2.5–4.5cm (1–1¾in) long. It is dark brown above, with a paler underside, and has tiny black

5

eyes, an elongated, bottle-shaped nose and very long back feet relative to its body size. Shrews are not seen very often, as they spend most of their time feeding in dense vegetation; however, they are frequently heard in the undergrowth, where they squeak aggressively to deter other shrews from venturing into their patch. Very occasionally you may see a family of shrews 'caravanning', when an adult leads its young in single file, each holding the tip of

agree that there are 2 (or possibly even 3) very similar species, often living alongside one another: the common pipistrelle (*Pipistrellus pipistrellus*) and what is now known as the soprano pipistrelle (*P. pygmaeus*). They are similar in size, 3.5–4.5cm (1½–1¾in) long with a wingspan of about 20–25cm (8–10in), depending on the sex. The main difference is in their voices – the common pipistrelle makes a lower sound (at 45khz) than its cousin (at 55khz).

HABITAT Both occur widely in buildings and around hedgerows, although the soprano pipistrelle seems to prefer wetlands and lives in bigger colonies.

FOOD Small flying insects such as midges and moths.

1 Hawthorn
Crataegus monogyna

This is our most widespread countryside hedge; when left untrimmed, it grows into a tree up to 10m (33ft). It has gooseberry-bush-like leaves, which grow on stems armed with scattered, single, short, straight, sharp-pointed thorns. In May, it produces clusters of small, white, 5-petalled flowers, followed by bunches of small, dangling fruit that ripens to dark red haws and persists well into winter, providing valuable food for redwings, thrushes and blackbirds. **HABITAT** Around fields as trimmed hedges, also as small-to-medium-sized trees growing up through hedges or along country lanes. Throughout Britain and Ireland.

2 Holly
Ilex aquifolium

The common holly is a popular and easily identified, native evergreen tree or shrub, with tough, glossy, prickly-edged leaves and clusters of bright red berries that ripen in winter and are traditionally associated with Christmas. The insignificant male and female flowers occur on separate plants, so only female hollies have berries, provided there's a male growing close enough for pollination to occur. **HABITAT** Throughout the British Isles, in hedgerows and woodland; sometimes found beneath a canopy of deciduous woodland trees. Not in boggy ground.

3 Hazel
Corylus avellana

Hazel is an easily identified tree, to 6m (20ft), carrying the familiar, long, dangling yellow catkins on bare branches in February; these are the pollen-producing male flowers – the female flowers are tiny red tufts dotted around on young twigs (these are wind-pollinated). The large, rounded-to-heart-shaped leaves appear later – they have a slightly frilled edge and a pointed tip. Clusters of green nuts develop from summer onwards, each with a green frill at the base. Hazel trees that have previously been coppiced grow into multi-stemmed trees.

One of our most ancient trees, hazel was an original post-ice-age colonizer, coppiced to supply building and craft materials since the Middle Ages. Old hazel woods nowadays often house carpets of

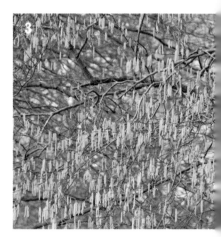

bluebells or wood anemones. The hazel bushes grown in rows in fields in Kent are in fact cultivated strains known as cobnuts or filberts, a different species (*Corylus maxima*) with a much bigger frill enveloping the entire nut; these Kent cobnuts are specially pruned to maximize nut production. **HABITAT** Hedgerows, coppices and woodland throughout the British Isles, except on acid soils.

OPPOSITE Hawthorn trees in blossom in the Olchon Valley, in the border country between England and Wales.

Wind-sculpted trees

In exposed areas, hawthorn trees often grow into particularly gnarled, craggy shapes that appear to lean away from the direction of the prevailing wind. This happens because on the windward side of the tree the developing leaf-buds are scorched by the wind in spring and are therefore prevented from developing as fast as buds growing on the more sheltered, leeward side of the tree. After many years of growing unevenly in this way, the tree becomes lopsided, and usually has a flattish top too, since the buds at the top are also scorched and stunted by the wind.

4 Blackthorn
Prunus spinosa

Also known as sloe, this is a small tree or more commonly a large shrub, growing up to 4m (13ft) high, though it is usually trimmed as a hedge. It has small, oval leaves and long, vicious thorns at the tips of the short sideshoots. The blossom appears on bare bushes in March or early April and, if you look closely, you'll see that it is made up of lots of small, white, 5-petalled flowers growing on short sideshoots. The flowers are followed by small, hard, bitter black fruit, known as sloes, which ripen in late summer and are used for making sloe gin. If left on the bushes, they provide food for berry-eating birds in autumn and early winter. Bushes spread by suckers from the roots, so plants slowly spread along a hedgerow.
HABITAT Hedgerows throughout the British Isles, except in Orkney and Shetland and mountainous areas.

5 Ash
Fraxinus excelsior

The ash is a common and handsome, British countryside tree with widely spaced, spreading branches; it can reach 30m (100ft) high but is usually less than half that size. In winter, ash trees are easily identified by their large black buds, which are arranged in pairs opposite each other and have a large bud at the centre of a small cluster at the shoot tip. In late March to early April, the buds burst and produce clusters of fluffy, greenish or purplish flowers,

which appear on bare branches shortly before the foliage opens. The leaves are made up of several pairs of slightly toothed leaflets, arranged opposite each other. In late summer and autumn, it bears large, conspicuous bunches of dangling, dry fruit (keys), each consisting of one seed and one long green wing (unlike the more familiar, 2-winged sycamore seeds).
HABITAT Throughout the British Isles, especially chalky or limestone areas, in hedgerows, on downland and in woodland; also grows in limestone pavements.

6 Spindle tree
Euonymus europaeus

This is a small, branching tree, to 4m (13ft) high, or a loose, open shrub, 2m (6½ft) high and wide. Spectacular in autumn, the leaves are lance-shaped, approximately 5cm (2in) long and slightly toothed round the edges; they take on brilliant pinkish red autumn tints before falling. The flowers are small and white, with 4 petals around a green centre; they are

followed by curious, 4-lobed seed capsules, 1cm (⅜in) wide, which ripen in autumn to bright pink cases containing orange berries.
HABITAT Hedgerows, woods, thickets and scrub, in chalk and limestone regions (less common in Ireland and Scotland).

7 English elm
Ulmus procera

The English elm is a traditional hedgerow tree originally planted for timber, so it is often grown as a tree rather than trimmed as a hedge. It is rather upright in habit, to 10m (33ft) high, with rounded, hazel-like leaves with a fishbone pattern of veins. The small, inconspicuous, red-tipped, spiky tufts of flowers, borne in spring, are followed by clusters of disc-shaped, winged green fruit that ripens to brown in autumn. Elms are seldom long-lived because of Dutch elm disease (the large elms of the Victorian countryside are a thing of the past in most areas).
HABITAT Hedgerows, particularly in southern and central England.

Dutch elm disease

Although they were once major hedgerow trees, a lot of elms have died out because of Dutch elm disease, which was accidentally brought to this country on imported timber in the 1960s. The disease is spread by elm-bark beetles, which tunnel just under the bark – if you peel back dead bark on infected trees, you'll often see the tell-tale squiggly markings. Many local authorities and landowners fell dead elms, but when dead trees are left alone the trunks usually remain standing and simply shed their branches, which turn brittle when dead. The dead wood makes homes for all sorts of other beetles, besides giving cock birds good places from which to sing their territorial songs or to use as a look-out. (It's much easier to identify birds when they are sitting on bare branches, so knowing a good hedge full of dead elms can be handy.) Elms also regenerate from the roots, provided the stump is not removed, so even after a tree has died it often replaces itself with a thicket of new stems from the base, which makes a bushy clump after a few years.

8 Crab apple
Malus sylvestris

A very ancient, British native tree, this is the ancestor of many attractive, ornamental garden trees. The native, wild crab apple is a very variable, small-to-medium-sized tree, to 9m (30ft), like a very craggy, garden crab apple but with much smaller, semi-stunted leaves and small, white or pink flowers. The fruit is hard and round – green at first, then turning pale yellow – and provides valuable food for various birds and wildlife.
HABITAT Throughout the British Isles in hedgerows, woodland, thickets, scrubland and along roadside verges.

9 Field maple
Acer campestre

Our native maple is usually found in mixed countryside hedges, although it is sometimes seen as a shrubby sapling in scrub; rarely is it a freestanding tree. It has small, rather irregular, 3–5-lobed, typical maple leaves, 3–4cm (1¼–1½in) long, in a delicate pale green, which take on rich, buttery gold autumn tints. The tips of the shoots bear clusters of insignificant greenish flowers in spring, followed by bunches of small, winged, green, sycamore-like, dry fruit (keys) in summer, which ripen to brown in autumn. Two-year-old stems have corky 'wings', which gradually turn into gnarled bark.
HABITAT Mixed country hedges and scrub, found mainly in chalk or limestone ground in England and Wales.

10 Wayfaring tree
Viburnum lantana

Named for the fact that it was once abundant growing along old country lanes and footpaths, the wayfaring tree is a large, loosely rounded, branching shrub, up to 4m (13ft) high and the same across. It has large, almost heart-shaped leaves, which are slightly serrated at the edges and grow in pairs on faintly downy, young stems. Large, domed clusters of small white flowers appear at the tips of the shoots in May and June, followed by red berries, which slowly ripen to black by late summer or early autumn, when the leaves take on rich red autumn tints.
HABITAT Hedgerows, hilly countryside and downs in chalk or limestone country, mainly in the southern half of Britain.

11 Dogwood
Cornus sanguinea

Our native version of the coloured-stemmed garden shrub, wild dogwood makes a noticeable splash of red in the countryside in autumn. It is a tall, suckering shrub, or occasionally it grows as a small tree, up to 3m (10ft). The oval leaves, which have deeply indented ribs, are arranged opposite each other in pairs and take on bright red tints in autumn before falling, revealing the reddish coloured bark of the young shoots.

The flowers are small, unpleasant-smelling and greenish white, and are borne in tight, rounded clusters at the tips of the shoots in June; they are followed by berries, which ripen to black in autumn. The native dogwood is one of the principle food plants of the caterpillar of the green hairstreak butterfly.
HABITAT Hedgerows, thickets, wasteland and woodland, mainly in chalk and limestone country in England and Wales.

12 Honeysuckle
Lonicera periclymenum

Also known as woodbine, this is a common and well-known, highly fragrant climber that scrambles through stronger plants using twining stems. It usually reaches 10–20m (33–65ft) up large trees, but in hedges that are regularly trimmed, honeysuckle spreads and will produce fuller, denser growth. The leaves are oval and grow in pairs, and whorls of scented, tubular flowers appear at the tips of new stems from June to September. The flower colour can be fairly variable and changes as the flowers open and mature – pink and white, orange and yellow or often mauve-tinged. The flowers are followed by small clusters of tight-packed, pea-sized red berries, much loved by birds.
HABITAT Throughout the British Isles in hedgerows, trees in woodland edges or clearings.

13 Ivy
Hedera helix

A very common and well-known evergreen climber, ivy clings on to all sorts of surfaces using aerial roots, which are produced along the stems, making plants hard to detach. Young plants produce 3-to-5-lobed leaves, each lobe with a pointed tip, on climbing stems; as it matures, ivy becomes tree-like, no longer climbing but growing bushy and producing adult leaves, which are more

Ivy as a wildlife habitat

You might think ivy is a rather dull sort of plant, but it's actually extremely good for wildlife. Various birds such as wrens and blackbirds (above) nest in its dense covering of leaves; the flowers produce lots of nectar that attracts out-of-season insects, which in turn attract insect-eating birds such as robins. Later in the year. birds enjoy eating the berries, which ripen in winter and early spring when food is short. Ivy also plays host to the caterpillars of the holly blue butterfly.

triangular-to-heart-shaped and unlobed, with a single, pointed tip. Adult ivies also produce greenish flowers, in tight, round clusters from September to November; these are followed by balls of pea-sized green berries that ripen to black at the end of winter and in early spring.
HABITAT Throughout the British Isles, except Shetland and Orkney, in hedgerows and climbing up walls or trunks of mature trees.

14 Dog rose
Rosa canina

The dog rose is a very common hedgerow scrambler, pushing up through stronger-growing shrubs and using strong, curved prickles as grappling hooks. It bears single pink flowers in June and July, appearing over the outside of hedges. The flowers have 5 large pink petals with white bases and form a loose, open circle with a cluster of golden stamens in the centre. They are followed by large rosehips, which ripen to orange-red in autumn. The leaves are similar to those of garden roses – oval with toothed edges, arranged in groups of 5, with 2 opposite pairs along a short stem and a lone leaf at the end.
HABITAT Throughout most of Britain and Ireland, in hedgerows.

15 Downy rose
Rosa mollis

Similar to the dog rose, the downy rose is a sprawling shrub, 1–3m (3–10ft) tall and the same across, with arching stems and single pink roses with pale yellow stamens in June and July, followed by globular, orange-red hips. The compound leaves are made up of (usually) 7 pale blue-green leaflets, with a very light covering of 'down' on both sides; the thorns are virtually straight (unlike the dog

rose, which has strongly hooked prickles and hairless leaves).
HABITAT Locally common on wasteland and in hedgerows – particularly in the north of England and throughout Wales and Scotland. A related species, *Rosa tomentosa*, occurs in the south.

16 Cow parsley
Anthriscus sylvestris

Also known as Queen Anne's lace, this is a very common and familiar, wayside wildflower. It is a rather upright, bushy perennial, to 75cm (30in) tall, with finely divided, ferny foliage and smooth, slender, branching stems topped by flat heads of tiny, frothy white flowers, arranged in a cartwheel shape, from April to June. After flowering, the narrow seeds, 5mm (³⁄₁₆in) long, stand up from the spent flowerheads, which retain their cartwheel shape. There are several similar, cow-parsley-like plants, sometimes growing in similar sites, but this is the first to flower.
HABITAT Throughout the British Isles in hedgerows, roadside verges and country footpaths; also in cemeteries and on wasteland.

Country lanes

When you're speeding along country lanes in the car, you could be forgiven for thinking that the hedges, ditches and untended verges alongside them are rather featureless. But when you stop and look harder you discover that they form a fascinating network of linear wildlife 'larders' winding through the British countryside. At various times of year they are packed with fruit, seeds, nectar or insects that attract huge numbers of wildlife to feed.

Hedges on the edge of fields are usually composed of prickly hawthorn or blackthorn, but since birds deposit seeds you'll also find bramble, elder, wild hops, dog rose and traveller's joy (a wild clematis). Hedgerow berries are appreciated by all sorts of wildlife – birds, small rodents, even foxes – while the nectar of wild hop and bramble attracts an enormous range of butterflies.

It's very common for occasional trees to be left to grow up through a hedge, so you'll probably find the odd oak, or perhaps an apple tree that has grown up from pips shed by an apple core thrown out of the car window by a

In late spring and early summer, a country hedge bank can be as bright as a herbaceous border in the garden.

passing motorist. These are attractive to nesting birds, such as pigeons or crows, and if there is a good group of tall trees you may spot a noisy rookery. You may also see elm trees, which today are often dead but still house a range of beetles, which in turn provide food for other wild creatures, or hazel bushes, which have grown from nuts buried by squirrels. Hedges outside old country cottages are particularly productive for wildlife, since they were often originally planted with country fruit trees such as damson, bullace and elder, whose produce was used for making wine and preserves, but is nowadays usually left for the birds.

Overgrown hedges are often full of ivy which, if left to grow, eventually reaches its mature phase and, instead of climbing and having the usual three-pointed ivy leaves, becomes bushy and more woody, producing larger, rounder leaves and clusters of greenish flowers in autumn. These attract lots of small insects, which in turn are eaten by wrens, and the flowers are followed by bunches of berries that ripen to black after Christmas and give blackbirds a late feed.

In country areas, where hedge-bottoms are left to grow their traditional range of wildflowers and the narrow roadside verges in front of them remain uncut, conditions are even better for wildlife. Long grasses feed the caterpillars of many butterfly species such as meadow browns, which are now being seen again in significant numbers. They also house a sequence of wildflowers, starting with cuckoo pint, alexanders, cow parsley and hogweed, which play host to soldier beetles, and the year ends with thistles and teasels, whose seeds attract flocks of goldfinches.

Drainage ditches along the edges of lanes act as small-scale wetland habitats for moisture-loving plants, such as primroses and lady's smock, and if the bottom of the ditch stays wet right through the summer there may also be clumps of yellow iris or reedmace. In winter and spring, herons stalk the ditches looking for frogs or small rodents.

17 Hogweed
Heracleum sphondylium

This is a reasonably common, cow-parsley-like wildflower, but taller (to 1.5m/5ft) and chunkier, with roughly hairy, hollow, upright, unbranched stems and larger, more solid, compound leaves (they are almost celery-like, while those of cow parsley are feathery). The flowerheads are larger and later than cow parsley's, often 15cm (6in) wide, and open from June to September. The seeds are fat, 5mm (³⁄₁₆in) long, and dry out on the remains of the old flowerheads – the dead stems persist for several months, like skeletons. Hogweed is not to be confused with the giant hogweed (*Heracleum mantegazzianum*), an introduced rarity over 3m (10ft) high, with flowerheads 30cm (12in) wide, which is notorious for its irritant sap. However, don't take liberties with the sap of native hogweed, as it contains the same ingredient – there's just less of it. **HABITAT** Throughout the British Isles in hedgerows, roadside verges and wasteland.

18 Alexanders
Smyrnium olusatrum

Alexanders is a yellow-flowered, cow-parsley-like plant, less often seen than the 'real thing' but flowering at the same time as its better-known cousin, from April to June, and growing in the same kind of places. It is a rather leggy-looking biennial or short-lived perennial, to 60cm (24in) tall, with upright, non-branching stems and small, parsley-like leaves arranged in groups of 3 to make rather gappy-looking, compound leaves. The stems are topped by heads of yellow, cartwheel-pattern flowers, but unlike those of cow parsley they are not at all frothy.

HABITAT Hedgerows, roadside verges and wasteland, mostly near the coast in England, Wales and Ireland.

19 Greater celandine
Chelidonium majus

This is a reasonably common wildflower which, despite the name, is not related to the lesser celandine and looks nothing like it. It is an untidy, mound-shaped plant with thick, fleshy green stems and compound leaves made up of semi-shiny leaflets that are bright mid-green above and more bluish green below. It flowers from May to August, producing loose clusters of 4-petalled, pale yellow flowers, approximately 1.5cm (⅝in) across, near the top of the plant; these are followed by long, narrow seedpods containing black-and-white seeds. **HABITAT** Usually near habitation, in dryish hedgerows, stony ground and wasteland. Throughout the British Isles, but not the far north of Scotland.

20 Stinging nettle
Urtica dioica

This nettle is an all-too-common plant with a well-known self-defence mechanism: both leaves and stems carry stinging hairs. A fast-spreading perennial, its tall, upright stems, to 1.5m (5ft) high, bear oval leaves with pointed tips, arranged in pairs up the stems. During the summer, strings of tiny green flowers, 5–10cm (2–4in) long, sprout from the leaf joints. Male and female flowers grow on separate plants – the females have long, dangly strings of flowers; those of the male are shorter and stand out horizontally. Nettle is the

food plant of caterpillars of several different species of butterfly, which may use the same plant in succession over the season. **HABITAT** Throughout the British Isles in hedgerows, woodland edges, wasteland and neglected cultivated ground.

A painful sting

The sting that causes the painful nettle rash when plants are handled is the result of the snapping-off of the tips of the hairs, which releases a cocktail of irritant chemicals including formic acid (as produced by ants). The 'antidote' is to rub the affected area immediately with a dock leaf.

21 Rough chervil
Chaerophyllum temulum

Rough chervil is a reasonably common, cow-parsley-like perennial with branching stems to 1m (3ft). It is often mistaken for cow parsley but flowers slightly later – in June and July – and has purple-spotted stems. The leaves are ferny, and the clusters of white flowers are distinctly dome-shaped – look closely, and you'll see that individual flowers in each cluster have different-length stems, unlike those of cow parsley, which are all the same length. Seedheads dry out like cow parsley's, but the seeds are ridged (in cow parsley they are not).
HABITAT Hedgerows, roadside verges and woodland edges in all but the far north of Britain.

22 Upright hedge parsley
Torilis japonica

This is another reasonably common cow-parsley look-alike found in hedgerows, but it flowers much later, in July and August. It is a rather delicate, airy-looking perennial, to 1m (3ft) high, with tall, slender, slightly branched stems and sparse, small, feathery foliage. The stems are topped by domed white flowers, like cow parsley's but more delicate. After flowering, the seeds are oval and spiny (quite unlike those of cow parsley).
HABITAT Throughout the British Isles, except northern Scotland, in hedgerows and verges.

23 Hedge bedstraw
Galium mollugo

This perennial, which scrambles up hedges, is similar to the annual goosegrass (also known as cleavers). The deep green stems of the hedge bedstraw are square in cross-section, with whorls of small, elongated-oval leaves of the same colour, edged with minute prickles and ending with a slightly down-curved point. From June to August, tiny white flowers are clustered tightly in globular, pea-sized heads at the tips of short sideshoots growing from leaf joints near the top of the stems. These are followed by small, round, smooth fruit.
HABITAT Dryish hedgerows throughout the British Isles, but becoming scarcer in the north.

24 Hedge woundwort
Stachys sylvatica

The hedge woundwort is quite a common perennial, to 75cm (30in) high, with upright, hairy, square-sided stems bearing hairy, toothed, heart-shaped leaves arranged in evenly spaced pairs. In July and August, each stem is topped by a long, conical flower spike made up of several whorls of small, dark mauve, helmet-shaped flowers.
HABITAT Hedgerows, woodland edges and shady corners in country gardens. Throughout the British Isles, except Scotland.

25 Jack-by-the-hedge
Alliaria petiolata

Also known as garlic mustard, this is a common perennial wayside wildflower with smooth, unbranched, upright stems, to 90cm (36in), and heart-shaped leaves with toothed edges, around 5cm (2in) long, arranged alternately along the stem. From April to June, each stem is topped by a small, tight cluster of tiny white, 4-petalled flowers. These are followed by clusters of long, slender, slightly ribbed seedpods. The whole plant has a rather pungent, vaguely garlic-like smell if bruised or crushed. Although it looks fairly unexciting to us, this plant (a member of the cabbage family) is a valuable resource for

insects. It is the food plant for caterpillars of the orange tip, small white and green-veined white butterflies, and the nectar is attractive to various butterflies and hoverflies.
HABITAT Shady hedgerows and woodland edges. Throughout most of the British Isles, except mountainous areas.

26 Black bryony
Tamus communis

Black bryony is a fairly common climbing plant seen scrambling over hedgerows in summer. It is a poisonous member of the yam family, with a large, perennial underground tuber producing fast-growing annual stems that climb by twining anti-clockwise round stems of sturdier plants. The leaves are large, smooth and heart-shaped, 7.5–10cm (3–4in) long, and from May to July it has short spikes of tiny white, star-like flowers growing on short stems from the leaf joints. These are followed by dangling strings of red, pea-sized berries in late summer and autumn.
HABITAT Hedgerows, scrub and woodland edges across southern Britain.

27 White bryony
Bryonia cretica

White bryony behaves in a similar way to black bryony – climbing up and over hedgerows in summer – but it looks slightly different. It has tiny, 5-petalled, greenish white flowers in clusters on short stalks growing from the leaf joints, followed by greenish, pea-sized berries that slowly change colour from yellow to orange then red; all stages, including the flowers, can be seen on the same plant at the same time for much of the summer. The leaves are similar in shape to ivy foliage but with a matt surface. The plants cling to surrounding shrubs using tightly coiled tendrils growing from the leaf joints.
HABITAT Hedgerows and scrub, mainly in central and southern England, except Cornwall.

28 Hedge bindweed
Calystegia sepium

Resembling a pure white morning glory, this is a very common perennial climber with thick white underground roots, from which fast-growing annual stems appear; these twine round nearby plants in an anti-clockwise direction – where no other plant is available, bindweed stems twist round each other, making thick 'ropes'. The leaves are large, 5–7.5cm (2–3in) long, smooth, light green and heart-shaped, arranged alternately along the stems. From July to September, solitary flower buds develop on short stems growing from the leaf joints; the buds are long and cylindrical, opening out into large, circular white flowers, 5cm (2in) across.
HABITAT Throughout the British Isles but particularly widespread in the southern half, in hedgerows, on wasteland and in neglected cultivated land including allotments and gardens. It may be replaced by great bindweed (*Calystegia silvatica*) in these sites.

29 Goosegrass
Galium aparine

Also known as cleavers, this very common and well-known, annual scrambling plant is seen throughout summer and autumn. It has weak, square-sided stems, up to 1.5m (5ft) high, growing in sheaves over surrounding plants and using minute, soft hooks all over the backs of the leaves and the stems for support. The leaves are arranged in whorls evenly along the stems. In summer, the stems are dotted with tiny, off-white flowers clustered at the tips of short, thread-like stems growing

from the leaf joints, just beyond a tiny collar of leaves. The flowers are followed by small clusters of fruit, which slowly ripens from green to brown. The whole plant 'sticks' to clothing when you brush past; the ripe fruit is particularly hard to dislodge, being covered in tiny hooks.
HABITAT Throughout the British Isles in hedgerows, woodland edges and wasteland; also found in gardens and on allotments.

30 Lords and ladies
Arum maculatum

Also known as cuckoo pint, this is a fairly common, clump-forming perennial, to 45cm (17½in) high and as wide, growing rapidly in spring, then dying down in summer. The large, arrowhead-shaped leaves, 20cm (8in) long, are a deep glossy green patterned with occasional purplish black spots; the flowers, borne in April and May, are hood-shaped spathes in light green with purplish spots, enclosing a tubular, purplish brown spadix. After flowering, the spathe dies away leaving a tight, cylindrical-shaped cluster of (poisonous) red berries on a short stalk. This persists for a while even after the leaves have died down.
HABITAT Hedgerows and woodland clearings throughout the British Isles, except the far north.

31 Woody nightshade
Solanum dulcamara

Also known as bittersweet, this is a fast-growing climber that scrambles up through hedges for support. It has compound leaves, made up of a pair of small, oval leaves with a larger oval leaf at the tip, growing on short stems arranged alternately along the

semi-woody stems. From June to September, it produces striking, potato-like flowers with 5 purplish blue, backward-curving petals set around a pointed-beak-like, yellow centre. The flowers are followed by clusters of small, round fruit, which ripens from green through yellow to orange and then red. All colours can be seen in the same bunch of berries, and plants often have flowers and berries at the same time for much of the summer. Though not actually deadly poisonous, all parts of this plant can cause sickness and should be treated with caution.
HABITAT Hedgerows throughout the British Isles, except northern Scotland.

32 Greater stitchwort
Stellaria holostea

Greater stitchwort is a common and widespread perennial plant that forms large mats of upright stems, usually 20–30cm (8–12in) high but reaching 45–60cm (17½–24in) when growing through competing plants such as grasses. The stems are smooth and slender, bearing long, thin, almost grass-like foliage arranged in pairs. From April to June, branching, thread-like stems at the top of the plant

each bear a solitary, small, star-like white flower; the petals are so deeply notched in the centre that they are almost divided in two.
HABITAT Hedgerows and woodland edges throughout the British Isles, except a few of the northernmost offshore islands. Grows in light, shady sites.

33 Common vetch
Vicia sativa

A scrambling plant in the pea family, common vetch uses tendrils to hold on to neighbouring plants. It reaches 30–90cm (12–36in), has ladder-like, compound leaves, and flowers throughout summer from June to September, producing small clusters of mauve-pink, pea-like blooms growing from the leaf joints towards the tips of the stems. The seedpods are pea-pod-shaped, but small and slender, about 2.5cm (1in) long, with a curved tip.
HABITAT Scrambling in hedgerows and round the edges of cultivated fields. Fairly common in the south-east of England but far less so elsewhere in the British Isles.

34 Tufted vetch
Vicia cracca

This is an attractive, scrambling wildflower, up to 2m (6½ft) high, with weak, slender, fairly straight stems branching from the base. The ladder-like, compound leaves have branching tendrils at the tips,

which the plant uses to hold on to surrounding stems. In July and August, it produces many small, purple-blue, pea-like flowers growing in long, one-sided spikes, 7.5–15cm (3–6in) long, at the ends of slender, upright stems. These are followed by small green pea pods, about 2cm (¾in) long.
HABITAT Throughout the British Isles in hedgerows and field edges.

35 White clover
Trifolium repens

White clover is a very common grassland wildflower, with creeping rootstocks that send up vertical stems carrying single leaves or flowers. The leaves are the familiar, 3-lobed clover leaves with 'herringbone' ribs and a faint, horseshoe-shaped mark on each leaflet. The flowers are rounded white tufts that turn slightly brown at the base as they mature. Produced throughout summer, they are favourites with both bumblebees and honeybees. **HABITAT** Throughout the British Isles in meadows, roadside verges, rough grass and garden lawns.

36 Spear thistle
Cirsium vulgare

The emblem of Scotland, this is a tall, distinctive, architectural plant, to 1.5m (5ft) high, with stiff, strong, prickly, typically thistle leaves, arranged alternately along robust, thick, spiny stems. The stems branch slightly at the tips and each sideshoot bears a large, chunky, solitary thistle head, up to 5cm (2in) across, which starts as a spiky, round bud from which the bright mauve, spiky flower appears. Flowering occurs from July to October; the thistly seedheads attract goldfinches in autumn and early winter. **HABITAT** Throughout the British Isles in hedgerows, roadside verges or grassland.

37 Silverweed
Potentilla anserina

Silverweed is a locally common wildflower with striking, shaggy, silvery green, jagged-edged, compound leaves, resembling Prince of Wales feathers, growing upright from creeping, horizontal stems. From June to August, it produces solitary, usually 5-petalled yellow flowers, 2–3cm (¾–1¼in) wide, which grow at the ends of long stems that emerge directly from the creeping stems. The plant spreads by overground runners to form loose colonies. **HABITAT** Throughout the British Isles in hedgerows, roadside verges and other undisturbed land.

38 Red dead-nettle
Lamium purpureum

Resembling the closely related, ornamental garden dead-nettle (*Lamium* cultivars), this is a short, squat, bushy annual, to 30cm (12in) high and the same across. Square-sided stems carry small, rounded, plain green leaves with slightly scalloped edges – the leaves do not sting, unlike those of the stinging nettle. From April to October, the red dead-nettle bears small, mauve-pink, hooded flowers that are very similar to those of mint (to which it is related). **HABITAT** Throughout the British Isles in hedgerows, on wasteland and cultivated ground.

39 White dead-nettle
Lamium album

This is an upright, clump-forming perennial, to 60cm (24in) tall, with non-stinging, nettle-like leaves arranged in pairs up the square-sided stems; each pair of leaves bears a whorl of white-hooded flowers in their axils from spring to autumn and sometimes winter. **HABITAT** In England, most of Wales, lowland Scotland and eastern Ireland, in hedge-bottoms, wasteland, field edges, allotments and gardens.

40 Mistletoe
Viscum album

Mistletoe was the mystical plant of the ancient druids and was long associated with the pagan midwinter ceremonies that later became Christmas. It forms a rounded, evergreen dome, up to several metres wide, suspended high in certain deciduous trees. It is most conspicuous in winter, when the trees are bare. In close-up, you can see the familiar Christmas decoration in its wild state, with paired green leaves on a branching network of stems, dotted with small clusters of white berries during November and December. The seeds are spread by birds (mainly mistle thrushes and other thrushes, such as blackbirds and robins) wiping their beaks on a branch after feasting on the berries, which have sticky goo round the seeds. A semi-parasitic plant, mistletoe gains nourishment partly from its host tree and partly from its own chlorophyll, which manufactures food for the plant.
HABITAT Grows wild on several types of tree, particularly lime, apple and poplar, but sometimes willow, oak or hawthorn. Mainly in the southern half of Britain, on mature trees in hedgerows or growing in livestock pasture.

41 Wild hop
Humulus lupulus

Wild hop is a common but easily overlooked climbing plant with woody stems, up to 5–6m (16½–20ft) long, and 3-pointed leaves with toothed edges. The flowers and fruit are produced on separate male and female plants: the male plant has small bunches of tiny, insignificant, greenish yellow flowers in July and August, while female plants carry nodding clusters of papery, lime-green cones, each about the size of your fingertip. (These produce the familiar beery scent only when cut, dried and kept in a warm room.)
HABITAT Southern and central England and Wales, in hedgerows.

42 Hedge mustard
Sisymbrium officinale

A fairly common and easily identified annual wildflower, the hedge mustard produces a rosette of cabbage-like leaves at the base, from the centre of which emerges a tall, skeletal framework of thin, wiry, upright stems – each with sideshoots growing from it at right angles. All the stems are virtually leafless, apart from occasional green scales clinging to them. At the tips of the stems are small clusters of tiny, 4-petalled yellow flowers.
HABITAT Throughout the British Isles in hedgerows, roadsides, wasteland and edges of arable fields, particularly in dry, sunny places.

43 Coral spot
Nectria cinnabarina

Coral spot is a common, brightly coloured and easily identified fungus, mostly seen in spring, summer and early autumn. Look for colonies of small, coral-red spots on dead branches, usually still attached to living trees or shrubs or fairly freshly fallen branches. A new strain has recently appeared that seems to attack living branches that have been damaged, allowing the organism to enter.
HABITAT On dead and, occasionally, damaged living branches, on a wide variety of trees and shrubs (but rarely on conifers) in hedgerows, woodland edges and gardens.

Also found in hedgerows

Bats (see p.202)
Blackbird (see p.302)
Brimstone (see p.195)
Brindled beauty (see p.307)
Comma (see p.306)
Cuckoo (see p.164)
Dunnock (see p.301)
Elephant hawk-moth (see p.308)
Field vole (see p.147)
Fox (see p.314)
Herb Robert (see p.119)
Holly blue (see p.306)
Little owl (see p.191)
Long-tailed tit (see p.88)
Mice (see pp.104, 315)
Mole (see p.202)
Peacock (see p.306)
Pygmy shrew (see p.147)
Robin (see p.301)
Woodpigeon (see p.190)
Wren (see p.301)

Urban jungle

You might think that they are blots on the landscape, and visually that may be true, but one way and another towns and cities have been colonized by and provide shelter and sustenance for a surprising array of wildlife. Urban sprawl is our very latest habitat, and in terms of evolutionary history it is very recent indeed.

Early settlements

Our earliest ancestors lived exclusively by hunting, fishing and gathering fruit or seeds. It was a way of life that needed a great deal of land to support each person – but back then there were only a few thousand people living in Britain. Six thousand years ago, new arrivals to our shores introduced us to farming. Man's dramatic impact on the landscape had begun. Our native forests were cut down to make fields – the woods were harvested for fuel and building materials and livestock was allowed out to forage. Settlements grew and spread. Inevitably, habitats were altered.

When the big Norman census produced the Domesday Book, there were about two million people living in Britain, but numbers increased very slowly. By medieval times, the population was still only four to six million, and most people worked on the land. Hamlets grew into villages and towns were spreading. They were dirty places, crammed with close-packed wood-and-thatch houses, with no running water or proper sanitation, so disease and fire were constant hazards. But still the big towns swelled, and the wildlife that could adapt to this new environment swelled with them.

The Great Plague of London of 1665 – carried by rats – thinned out the population, and the Great Fire, which followed a year later, also took its toll on the capital city. The fire made rebuilding necessary, and the architect Sir Christopher Wren laid out the bones of a new central London. However, urban society as we know it today really started to come about only as a result of the Industrial Revolution, a mere two centuries ago. By 1801 there were ten million people in Britain, and after centuries of being farmers we were becoming a nation of townies.

The Industrial Revolution

The eighteenth and nineteenth centuries saw agriculture declining dramatically at the same time as the first proper industries were spreading over the landscape. Many desperate farm labourers left the land and moved to towns to take jobs in mills and factories. Transport was still basic, so industries developed close to their source of raw materials. The first big industrial towns – Manchester, Huddersfield and Leeds – grew up alongside their supplies of coal; the pottery towns were built near a source of good-quality clay, while the city of Liverpool expanded round its docks with their thriving import/export trade.

The sudden inrush of new workers meant that lots of cheap housing had to be built in a hurry, resulting in all those

rows of Coronation Street-style terraces running up hill and down dale. Welsh quarries were opened up to produce roofing slates, and clay pits were trawled for brick-making materials. The canal system was built to move raw materials and finished goods around and to connect towns and cities across the country.

Habitat destruction was part and parcel of all this development, but in the long term it wasn't entirely bad news for wildlife. Given time, worked-out slate quarries provided plenty of rocky ledges for peregrine falcons, choughs, doves and pigeons, which once were found only on steep sea-cliffs. The empty clay pits filled with water and turned themselves into ponds. Even the canals became extra wildlife habitats later in their life when they were made redundant by the increase in railway and road systems, and they were eventually redeveloped for leisure use.

Although town housing was probably better than accommodation out in the countryside at this stage, water and sanitation were still minimal. Housewives had to fetch water from the pump, and the loos were earth closets down the garden – a situation that would become riskier as larger concentrations of people packed into smaller areas. Diseases such as cholera spread rapidly from small, local outbreaks,

and with so many people now packed into cities like London, disposing of the dead was becoming a real problem. It was the Victorians who laid out the first large cemeteries round the outskirts of the city, landscaped tastefully with trees and shrubs. Today they are the capital's great secret wildlife reserves, where you can spot birds and foxes, deer and rabbits and, at dusk, bats.

Under the encouragement of Queen Victoria's husband, Prince Albert (a great fan of new technology), flush toilets and sewage systems began to be installed; for many years, sewage farms with their ever-present swarms of flies were a great attraction for insectivorous birds, especially in winter when food was short.

The railways were built between 1830 and 1860, connecting London with the major towns. All this construction work created a spate of new jobs for navvies,

PREVIOUS PAGES The grid-like pattern of housing in Milton Keynes, with green areas in the form of gardens and parks built into the plan (main picture), and jackdaws resting on an urban chimney (small picture).

BELOW LEFT Canada geese by the lake in Regent's Park, London.
BELOW CENTRE Derelict industrial sites are surprisingly rich in wildlife.
BELOW RIGHT The adaptable urban fox goes from strength to strength.

grounds of an old royal palace near Richmond were being
redeveloped into Kew Gardens, much along the lines we
know today. The Royal Horticultural Society had gardens at
Chiswick and Kensington, and the Botanical Society started
up its own gardens at Regent's Park.

But all was not rosy. The steam trains and the coal-fired
heating and cooking appliances in the new houses created a
filthy and poisonous atmosphere that left a layer of soot over
everything. Plants didn't survive for long under the
onslaught. That's why London's squares and many of its
residential streets were planted with plane trees, which shed
not only their old leaves but also their outer layer of bark
every year, neatly getting rid of the pollution. Spotted laurel
shrubs and privet hedges were great favourites for planting in
city gardens, since they were among the few plants that
survived the soot. Their legacy remains in many cases today.

The Victorians made other contributions to the
horticultural landscape: they brought us the giant redwood
and named it after a national hero – *Wellingtonia*. Examples
of this tree still stand in parks and country estates and
survived the 1987 hurricane, when many lesser species toppled.
They also introduced the monkey puzzle, for many years a
popular street tree in the suburbs until, in more recent times,
its habit of shedding lower branches unexpectedly on to cars
parked in the street beneath led to its removal.

But by today's standards, the Victorians were not very
environmentally aware. Their great rock-gardening craze was
responsible for stripping limestone pavements and natural
outcrops from beauty spots all round the British Isles.
Rhododendron ponticum, which was widely planted in
woodland in the 1800s, is now being removed by
conservationists as a pernicious weed that's smothering out
natural species. And Japanese knotweed, originally
introduced as a novelty to grace herbaceous borders in the
gardens of Victorian country houses, turned out to be a real
menace, as we know to our cost.

From boom to bust

The two World Wars had their own effect on the urban
landscape. During the First World War, the Kaiser was trying
to starve us into submission and food was being rationed –
so every spare patch of ground was turned over to vegetable-

who built the tracks and embankments and brought a
bonanza of business to the engineering towns of Crewe and
Swindon, which again resulted in more housing and
associated infrastructure. The railways opened up the holiday
trade, and towns like Blackpool, Bournemouth and Bognor
Regis blossomed into prosperous seaside resorts catering for
the newly emerged Victorian middle class. This led, in turn,
to even more building. It had become an obsession. The
Victorians filled cities with new roads, bridges and ornate
municipal buildings, such as libraries and town halls, then
enlarged these densely packed centres by surrounding them
with rings of suburbs, to house all the new middle-class
employees. And their big new craze was for gardens.

The rise of parks and gardens

City people needed to breathe; somewhere to relax and take
the air. A rash of squares and public parks appeared in
London and other major cities during the nineteenth

growing. Local authorities took over vacant land, including city parks and playing fields, to use as allotments. People grew vegetables on odd bits of land alongside railways. The successful 'Dig For Victory' campaign of the Second World War, spearheaded by radio gardener Mr Middleton, saw townspeople digging up their back gardens to grow vegetables and even their own tobacco, which they cured in the shed. When peace finally came, parks were reinstated, requisitioned land was returned to its original owners and allotments outside towns were redeveloped for – you've guessed it – housing.

By then, people had had enough of the practical 'make do and mend' mentality and they wanted to see flowers growing again, so decorative planting schemes were restored to parks and gardens and allotments fell out of favour. These days they are back in demand, now that fruit and vegetable gardening is fashionable, but with inroads made for housing estates, business parks and shopping centres, only 36,000 or so acres of allotments remain round the country today.

Wartime did open up a lot of new opportunities for wildlife, however, not least thanks to bomb damage. Some plants are particularly good at colonizing bare ground – think of Flanders poppies (the first to cover the First World War battlefields), Oxford ragwort and rosebay willowherb, which was so good at taking over bomb sites and railway lines after the surrounding area had been burnt that it was known as fireweed. A lot of today's fast-growing, invasive, common 'weeds' got their big break as a result of bomb sites, and the mass of seeds they shed then infiltrated town and city gardens and paved the way for generations of weed problems ever since.

Post-war rebuilding was just the tip of the iceberg. Urban sprawl has continued. In just two centuries, the population of Great Britain has shot up from 10 to 60 million. And while we are becoming ever conscious of our impact on the landscape and the wildlife that occupies it, some species are doing well in spite of our activities, and others are thriving because of them. It seems that we can't always choose the wildlife that lives among us. Quite the reverse: it usually chooses us, and sites that at first glance seem like eyesores to us can frequently offer rich pickings for the creatures that find food and shelter there.

OPPOSITE Ring-necked parakeets, here roosting in Esher, Surrey, are relatively recent residents in Britain.

BELOW Buckingham Palace gardens offer a tranquil oasis for wildlife in central London.

Birds

1 Kestrel
Falco tinnunculus

Well-known and widespread, this small bird of prey is characterized by its habit of hovering above the ground, facing into the wind with its head down, hunting for mice and voles – most people see it over motorway verges. Like many birds of prey, kestrels also often perch on posts or trees, waiting for meals to turn up. A male kestrel has a blue-grey head, a black-spotted, bright chestnut back, darker plain brown wing-tips, a blue-grey tail with a broad black band almost at the tip (which is white) and black-spotted, buff underparts. Both males and females have a smudgy, dark 'moustache' stripe on the head.

HABITAT Throughout the British Isles in open countryside, roadside verges and towns.

SIZE 33cm (13in)

EGGS 4–5, white heavily spotted and smeared with reddish brown

NEST In holes in trees or walls, also old crows' nests.

FOOD Mostly mice and voles, but also other small mammals, birds and invertebrates.

SIMILAR TO Other falcons and the sparrowhawk, which hunts by chasing small birds through woodland or gardens.

VARIATIONS Female is slightly bigger and duller in colour than the male, but has a barred brown tail instead of blue-grey and black.

2 Canada goose
Branta canadensis

This is a large, common and easily recognized goose, whose numbers have increased greatly since it was introduced from North America in the 17th century. It has a black head and tail, a long black neck with a white patch from the chin almost to the top of the head, a pale buff breast and a brownish grey back with a white undertail.

HABITAT Throughout much of England, Wales, Scotland (except for the north) and north-eastern Ireland, in ponds and on grassland close to water, especially in city parks with lakes, reservoirs and flooded gravel pits.

SIZE 1–1.1m (3–3½ft)

EGGS 5–7, cream

NEST Twigs, reeds, grass, leaves and down, on the ground, close to water.

FOOD Water plants and grass.

SIMILAR TO Brent goose, which is half the size and has a shorter neck with only a small white patch. Also resembles the smaller barnacle goose, which is grey, black and white, with a creamy white face (except for the top of its head).

3 Little ringed plover
Charadrius dubius

A scarce summer visitor, this has a brown cap and back, white under-parts, a black ring round the neck and a black 'burglar's mask' that surrounds the yellow-ringed eyes and extends up as a black bar across the top of the head. Look for white 'eyebrows', linked by a white line across the forehead, a black beak with a white blob above the base and greyish pink legs.

HABITAT Late March–September: throughout most of England (except the far north and the south-west) and in south Wales, in flooded gravel pits, reservoirs and shingly river-edges, including those close to London. Winter: Africa.

SIZE 15cm (6in)

EGGS 4, buff with brown markings

NEST Bare scrape on the ground.

FOOD Small insects and other invertebrates.

SIMILAR TO Ringed plover, which is larger and has a black-tipped, orange beak, orange legs and feet, no prominent yellow eye ring and no white line across the forehead connecting the 'eyebrows'.

4 Ring-necked parakeet
Psittacula krameri

Noisy and colourful, ring-necked parakeets, also known as rose-ringed parakeets, have been breeding wild in Britain at least since the 1960s. It is thought that they escaped from aviaries and/or were deliberately released by sailors and other travellers, who brought them back as novelties from Asia and Africa. They are bright green birds, slim with a very long tail that has a blue streak down the centre and, in the male, a black or pale collar, a dark chin and a blue wash over the nape. They have a red, parrot-like beak – strong, short and curved – and dark grey feet. Their call is a loud, raucous 'keee-ak, keee-ak'; there is often a lot of noisy squabbling from flocks feeding or at nest sites.

HABITAT Parks, sports grounds and in wooded areas and gardens, mainly around London and the south-east of England.

SIZE 40cm (16in), of which the tail is 25cm (10in)

EGGS 3–4, white

NEST In holes in large trees, usually fairly communally.

FOOD Fruit, buds, seeds (including seeds from bird tables).

VARIATIONS Females and juveniles lack the neck ring, dark chin and blue nape of the male.

5 Collared dove
Streptopelia decaocto

This is a rather slim, elegant dove in pale buff-grey with a narrow, white-edged black bar round the back of the neck, very dark red eyes and a black beak. The wing-tips are black and the tail has a broad white band at its end and a black band at its base. Its call is a monotonous, 3-note 'coo-*COO*-coo'. This dove is so well known today it seems hard to believe it's a fairly recent addition to Britain; it reached us only in the 1950s (from south-eastern Europe) and didn't become widespread until the 1970s.
HABITAT Throughout the British Isles, mostly close to human habitation, in parkland, gardens, allotments and farmland with plenty of good-sized trees, and old hedgerows that have been allowed to grow up into taller shelterbelts. (Unlike woodpigeons, it is not seen in large flocks in open fields.)
SIZE 32cm (13in)
EGGS 2, white
NEST Thin platform of twigs in trees, usually where a strong branch joins the trunk.
FOOD Grain, seeds, fruit.

6 Feral pigeon
Columba livia

Descendants of wild rock doves, with domestic racing pigeon and decorative breeds of pigeon in their mix, these variable birds are a common sight in towns and cities, foraging in rubbish and perching in girders under bridges or on street-lamps and rooftops. They are usually blue-grey with a darker head and tail, and hints of bluish or mauve-pink, iridescent tints on the neck.
HABITAT In towns and cities throughout the British Isles, in parks, squares and railway stations.
SIZE 30–34cm (12–14in)
EGGS 2, white
NEST On ledges of buildings and girders – even in window boxes and hanging baskets.
FOOD Seeds and many other foods, including fast-food debris.
VARIATIONS Interbreeding means many have brown, beige, cream or off-white plumage, or a mixture.

7 Swallow
Hirundo rustica

The swallow is a much-loved summer visitor, with a sparrow-sized body but with long, thin wings and an elongated, forked tail extended by very long, thin 'streamers' (shorter in the female and juvenile than in the male). Swallows fly fast, skimming fairly low to the ground, catching insects over fields and water. The glossy blue head, back and wings appear dark seen against the sky but you may catch a glimpse of red on its forehead and chin and its white-to-buff underparts. It's easiest to get a good view when birds return to their nests, so keep an eye out around old outbuildings.
HABITAT April–October: farmland and on house eaves; often seen congregating on telegraph wires in autumn throughout the British Isles. Winter: South Africa.
SIZE 19cm (7½in)
EGGS 4–5, white with reddish brown specks
NEST Deep half-cup shape, made of mud and grass or straw, stuck to a rafter inside old outbuildings with open windows or gaps in the structure to allow access.
FOOD Flying insects.
SIMILAR TO Swifts and house martins (see box, below).

Identifying swallows, swifts and house martins

It is extremely difficult to get a good look at fast-moving birds such as martins, swallows and swifts and they can be very difficult to tell apart, so try comparing the birds' different flying styles and look for features that can be taken in at a glance. Here are some hints:

● Swifts and house martins both tend to fly higher than swallows when feeding.
● Swifts are dark all over, apart from their hard-to-see, pale chin (swallows and house martins have white underparts).
● Swifts are slim with long, curved, scimitar-shaped wings – their flying style is to glide, following this with rapid beating of stiffly held wings.
● House martins are smaller, dumpier birds with a more fluttering action than swallows.
● Swallows have red on the head (lacking in swifts and house martins) and are slim with pointed wing-tips and long, trailing, forked tails; they fly with more leisurely flaps than the swift or house martin.

8

8 Swift
Apus apus

Usually seen in silhouette against the sky, these high-flying visitors have wings that appear to form a continuous, slim, dark crescent shape and a shortish body, ending in a short tail that may be closed to a point or opened to a deep, forked shape. The colour is overall dull brownish black with a paler patch on the throat. Swifts spend most of their time airborne, even sleeping, drinking, bathing, eating and sometimes mating in flight – they never land on the ground (unless injured or forced down in a storm) and never perch on wires – they have tiny legs that are useless for anything except clinging to a vertical surface and getting into their nest.

HABITAT May–August: over fresh water or farmland and round towns and villages throughout the British Isles (less common in Scotland).
SIZE 16cm (6¼in)
EGGS 2–3, white
NEST Shallow cup shape made of feathers, straw and other material in a hole in a roof.
FOOD Flying insects.
SIMILAR TO Swallows and house martins (see box, previous page).

9 House martin
Delichon urbica

This is a small, squat, summer visitor with a glossy, dark blue head and back, white underparts, shortish wings, a short, forked black tail and a white rump.
HABITAT March–October: in towns and villages, almost all nesting on human habitations, throughout the British Isles (except the far north-west of Scotland).
SIZE 12cm (4¾in)

EGGS 4–5, white
NEST Cup-shaped and made of mud with a small entrance hole at the top, under eaves of buildings.
FOOD Flying insects.
SIMILAR TO Swallows and swifts (see box, previous page).

10 Pied wagtail
Motacilla alba

A striking and easily recognized, slender, black-and-white bird, the pied wagtail has a bobbing walk, with the tail flicking up and down constantly. It runs along the ground jumping up or flying up briefly to catch flies.
HABITAT Towns, villages, playing fields, parks and gardens as well as open countryside throughout the British Isles (but less common in northern Scotland).
SIZE 18cm (7in)
EGGS 5–6, off-white, speckled grey-brown
NEST Untidy cup of moss and grass, lined with feathers and hair, in a

11

9

10

hole in a wall, outbuilding, bridge or grassy bank.
FOOD Mainly insects and other invertebrates; some seeds.

11 Waxwing
Bombycilla garrulus

The waxwing is a very scarce but annual winter visitor, present in varying numbers from year to year. It is an exotic-looking bird, pinkish buff below and reddish above, with a striking pink head crest, a small 'eye mask' and a black 'bib'. The wings are patterned halfway down with a white patch ending in a row of sealing-wax-red spots (hence its name). It also has black wing-tips edged in white and yellow, a grey rump and a short, square-ended dark grey tail with a yellow tip. An acrobatic bird, with a long, tinkling call, it is seen mainly in small flocks.
HABITAT Winter: along the east coast of England and Scotland, and in Ireland, in gardens, parks and hedgerows. Summer: northern Europe.
SIZE 18cm (7in)
FOOD Berries, insects.

12 Dunnock
Prunella modularis

Erroneously known as the hedge sparrow and formerly as the hedge accentor, this very common little brown bird – slightly smaller than a house sparrow but slightly bigger than a robin – is often disregarded as dull, but it is the possessor of a delightful song and an outrageous private life. It has a blackish, streaked, rich brown back and wings and a blue-grey head, neck and breast that fades to pale streaky brown on the flanks and undertail, and pinkish brown legs. Its voice is a melodious warbling.

Dunnocks are real avian wife-swappers: both males and females have several other sexual partners. The female invites the male to mate by sticking her tail up and twirling it coquettishly in a clear 'come hither' gesture. The dunnock is one of the birds targeted by cuckoos, so the male dunnock often brings up not only a rival male's young but one of a different species entirely.

HABITAT Hedgerows, woods, parks, farmland and gardens throughout the British Isles, except on high mountains and on Shetland.
SIZE 14cm (5½in)
EGGS 4–5, bright blue
NEST Cup of roots, grass and leaves, low down in hedgerows and bushes.
FOOD Insects, other invertebrates, seeds, grains, berries.
SIMILAR TO Sparrow, but the beak of the dunnock is far more slender, thin and pointed.

13 Wren
Troglodytes troglodytes

Our most widespread and most numerous bird, the wren is tiny, dumpy and brown with a short, often cocked tail. (It is the third-smallest bird in Britain, after the goldcrest and firecrest, and was pictured on the back of the old farthing.) Rarely seen for long in the open, it may be spotted flitting from bush to bush, or scurrying about rather like a clockwork mouse. It has darkish brown upperparts and a paler brown breast and underparts; given a good view of a perching bird, you can see chestnut and mid-brown bars across the folded wings, pale barring on the flanks, dark bars on the tail and a whitish eye-stripe. The call is a mechanical 'tic tic tic' sound, like a bicycle chain being pedalled backwards. The wren has an incredibly loud song – a rapid, explosive torrent of rattling and warbling notes, ending in a trill.
HABITAT Throughout the British Isles (with 4 distinct races found on our offshore islands) in most habitats, from woodland, parkland, hedgerows and gardens to moorland and sea cliffs.
SIZE 9.5cm (3¾in)
EGGS 5–8, white with reddish spots
NEST Feather-lined dome of vegetation and moss, with a side access hole, often in ivy.
FOOD Small insects and other invertebrates including spiders.

14 Robin
Erithacus rubecula

Star of a billion Christmas cards, this is a very common, popular and easily identified bird, with an orange-red breast, face and forehead, separated from the sandy-brown crown and back by a blue-grey band. The flanks are buff-coloured, the rest of the underparts are off-white, and it has a narrow, brownish beak and thin legs the same colour. Robins are among our friendliest wild birds, well known as 'the gardener's friend'; they do not fly away until you approach very closely, and follow anyone weeding or digging, often darting close to grab worms or insect larvae from newly turned soil; they are also regular visitors to bird tables. However, they are often aggressive towards other robins and larger birds.
HABITAT Woods, gardens, scrub and hedgerows throughout the British Isles.

SIZE 14cm (5½in)
EGGS 4–6, white with small red spots
NEST Small and domed, made mainly of leaves and moss, hidden in dense hedges, holes in banks, or inside garden sheds; often in open-fronted nestboxes or any available container, such as an old teapot.
FOOD Insects, other invertebrates, seeds, berries.
VARIATIONS Young birds are spotty with gingery beige speckles and chevrons and lack the adults' red breast, which starts to appear as birds mature, at which point the adults will chase them off.

15 Black redstart
Phoenicurus ochruros

A close relative of the robin, this is a 'townie' bird, whose numbers increased in London and some other urban areas after the war as a result of the good nest sites provided by bomb sites. The male is jet-black, except for a white wing-flash, a bright orange tail with a black stripe down the centre and a peach-coloured undertail.
HABITAT Mainly in south-east England and the Midlands, in buildings including industrial sites and houses.

SIZE 14cm (5½in)
EGGS 4–6, white
NEST Cup of vegetation and moss, lined with hair, in gaps in masonry or on ledges.
FOOD Insects, other invertebrates, fruit, seeds.
VARIATIONS Female is a drab brownish grey with a rusty orange tail with a dark stripe down the centre and a dark beak and legs. Lacks the white wing-flash present on the male.

16 Blackbird
Turdus merula

Often the first bird that children learn to recognize, this is a very common, widespread and well-known thrush. The male is a plumpish, all-black bird with a bright yellow beak, yellow-ringed eyes and brownish legs.
HABITAT Gardens, hedgerows, farmland, parkland and woods throughout the British Isles.
SIZE 25cm (10in)
EGGS 3–5, greenish blue with reddish brown speckles
NEST Cup of grass and small twigs in hedgerows, trees and bushes.
FOOD Insects, worms, seeds, berries, fruit (especially windfall apples).
VARIATIONS Female is dark brown with a slightly darker tail and variable, usually dull, darker spots on the underparts. Juveniles are more reddish brown and are streaked and barred above and below. Males develop their full black plumage in stages, so half-grown males may have black wings and a brown body.

17 Song thrush
Turdus philomelos

The song thrush is a familiar and easily identified bird, smaller than a blackbird and with a more upright stance. It is mid-brown above with a conspicuous, golden buff breast and flanks speckled with black spots. It feeds on the ground, cocking its head to 'listen' for worms and watching for any movement of prey, and flies low from cover to cover. It is usually solitary and has a very distinctive, loud, musical song, consisting of a series of up to 100 or so short phrases, each repeated 3–5 times, with brief pauses in between. The song thrush is one of the few birds able to eat snails, which it does by picking them up and banging them down vigorously against a handy stone, which is usually reused regularly. These 'anvils', littered with broken shells, are a sure sign of a thrush in a garden, even if you don't often see it.
HABITAT Hedgerows, woods and gardens throughout most of the British Isles.
SIZE 23cm (9in)
EGGS 3–5, pale blue speckled with black
NEST Cup of twigs, grass and moss in hedges, bushes and trees.
FOOD Worms, snails, berries.
SIMILAR TO Redwing, which is a winter visitor only and is a darker brown colour overall, with conspicuous red 'armpits' and a bold cream stripe above the eyes.

18 Spotted flycatcher
Muscicapa striata

This is a robin-sized 'little brown job' with a plain, grey-brown head and upperparts and streaky, off-white underparts. It resembles a sparrow, but the spotted flycatcher is easily identified by its feeding behaviour. Alert and fast-moving, it sits with a very upright posture on a favourite bare branch, fence post or other perch and darts out to grab flying insects on the wing, then brings them back to the same perch to swallow. Large insects may be bashed against the branch first, like a fish caught by a kingfisher.
HABITAT May–September: in woodland clearings and edges, large gardens and parks throughout the British Isles. Winter: Africa.
SIZE 14cm (5½in)
EGGS 4–5, white with reddish blobs and blotches
NEST Loose cup of grass, twigs and rootlets, often among dense garden climbers on walls or in ivy on tree trunks. Also in the old nests of other species and nestboxes.

FOOD Mainly flying insects, such as large flies, moths and butterflies.
VARIATIONS Juvenile birds are more mottled, with buff spots above and scaly markings around the edges of the breast.

19 Great tit
Parus major

A common garden bird, this is distinctly larger than a blue tit, with bolder markings. It has a conspicuous black cap that continues down the side of the neck and beneath the white 'cheeks' to join the black 'bib', an olive green back, bright yellow underparts and a long, narrowing black stripe from the 'bib' down the middle of the breast and underparts to the tail. It tends to dominate other tits at the bird table. The great tit has one of the biggest vocabularies of any bird, with over 60 different calls recorded; it has an assertive, repetitive 'teacher-teacher-teacher' song, which has been likened to a squeaky bicycle pump.
HABITAT Throughout the British Isles in gardens, deciduous woods, hedges and forestry plantations.
SIZE 14cm (5½in)
EGGS 5–12, white speckled with red
NEST Cup of moss and plant fibres, lined with wool and hair, in holes in trees and nestboxes.
FOOD Insects, seeds, fruit, nuts.
SIMILAR TO Blue tit, which is smaller and more agile, with more blue in its plumage, including a bright blue cap, and narrower black markings on the head.
VARIATIONS Juveniles have pale yellow 'cheeks' and the greenish areas are more yellowish green.

Unnatural habitats

You might think creeping urbanization would crowd wildlife out as yet more land is concreted over for roads, shops and housing, but some species have adapted remarkably well to their new habitat. As new buildings went up, they provided vast numbers of ledges, which were colonized by birds that originally lived on steep cliffs – initially pigeons, but later followed by their natural predators – peregrine falcons. Urban peregrines now nest regularly in cities like London, Bristol, Exeter and Derby, and a pair also nest regularly on Chichester cathedral.

Wildlife has really taken to city life. Fast food has gone down well with pigeons, which sometimes nest in hanging baskets and window boxes, and dustbins provide easy pickings for urban foxes, which find life easier in town than in the country. Jackdaws nest in chimney pots and grey squirrels take up residence in roof spaces. Meanwhile, the expanding network of urban rubbish dumps

A pair of kittiwakes nesting on the Royal Hotel, Lowestoft, Suffolk. There is also a fair-sized colony of kittiwakes in Newcastle, nesting in the girders of the Tyne Bridge.

is a great hunting ground for seagulls and, together with other opportunists like sparrows and starlings, they have discovered rich pickings at outdoor cafés. In various cities and towns, gulls now prefer to live on the rooftops rather than taking their chance on the coastline. Their nesting areas are often littered with chicken bones scavenged from local eateries, and gull chicks shelter in now rather aptly named gullies.

Even today's well-manicured golf courses provide a certain amount of cover for wildlife in the 'rough' round the edges, and although deer and rabbits are not very welcome lest they damage the greens, the water hazards make good out-of-hours watering holes for birds and other creatures. In addition, wasteland behind warehouses or factories often yields a huge, 'unofficial' crop of weeds that provide nectar, seeds or fruit for urban wildlife. Clumps of nettles can house up to five different species of caterpillar during the course of the summer.

As the road network spreads, motorway verges now represent one of the great undisturbed wildlife reserves. Voles live there, attracting kestrels, and all sorts of wildflowers and roadside trees provide berries and nesting places. On the downside, roughly a million animals are killed on our roads every year. Hedgehogs still haven't learnt that curling up into a ball is a poor defence against a lorry, and deer, foxes and badgers are among the newer casualties now that their numbers are increasing. In country areas, barn owls are often killed or injured as they fly low enough to be hit by vehicles on the road at night.

Although we can't turn the clock back, we can at least ensure we make the most of what we have and preserve it for future generations. It's happening now. Wasteland and old gravel workings around towns and cities are frequently landscaped to make new wildlife sanctuaries, such as the London Wetland Centre at Barnes. And various wildlife conservation groups organize gangs of volunteers to clear tree saplings and restore heathland to make new conservation areas where wildlife thrives.

20 Blue tit
Parus caeruleus

A regular visitor at garden feeders, this is a well-known, widespread and easily identified little bird with a bright blue cap, wings and tail, and a green back and bright yellow breast and underparts. Inquisitive and athletic, it actively works its way over a tree or shrub while feeding, and often hangs upside-down to check underneath foliage.
HABITAT Deciduous woodland, hedgerows and gardens throughout the British Isles.
SIZE 11cm (4¼in)
EGGS 7–12 (occasionally more), tiny and white with brick-red spots
NEST In holes in trees, nestboxes.
FOOD Insects and spiders; berries, nuts and seeds in autumn/winter.
SIMILAR TO Great tit.
VARIATIONS Juveniles are smaller, slightly fluffier, and have a greenish crown instead of bright blue and yellow on the face instead of white.

21 Jackdaw
Corvus monedula

The jackdaw is a cheeky, small crow with a black body and a dark grey nape and back of the head; it has a relatively short beak. Usually seen in groups, it walks with a typical, self-confident crow strut and its call is a harsh 'chack, chack'. Jackdaws are good mimics, often impersonating barking dogs.
HABITAT Widespread throughout the British Isles, in farmland, parks, woods, towns, gardens and old buildings, especially ruins.

SIZE 33cm (13in)
EGGS 4–6, pale blue-green, spotted dark brown and dark grey
NEST Made of sticks, in tree holes, rocks, on buildings, often in disused chimney pots.
FOOD Mainly insects and other invertebrates, but eats almost anything, including road-kill.
SIMILAR TO Carrion crow and rook, which are much larger and lack the grey head markings. The hooded crow is also much bigger with more grey on the body and nape.

22 Carrion crow
Corvus corone

The carrion crow is a familiar and widespread, big black bird with neat plumage, a strong black beak and bare legs (apart from small feathers on the 'thighs'). An intelligent bird, it has a self-confident air and a strutting walk. It is often seen flapping lazily over farmland or scavenging for road-kill and visits gardens for scraps, which it often dunks into a pond or bird bath. The chief call is a harsh, resonant 'karrr'.
HABITAT Open woodland, farmland and parkland, also towns, roadside verges and sometimes gardens, throughout England, Wales and most of Scotland (except north-west and far north); not in Ireland.
SIZE 46cm (18in)
EGGS 4–6, greenish blue, speckled brown and grey
NEST Bulky cup of sticks and other vegetation, usually in a tree.
FOOD Very wide and varied diet, including scraps and road-kill.
SIMILAR TO Rook is the same size but untidier, with a bald face and shaggy 'trousers' round the legs; unlike the carrion crow, it flies in large flocks and nests communally.
VARIATIONS In north-west Scotland and Ireland, a piebald relative of the carrion crow – with a grey body and black wings – is known as the hooded crow.

23 Starling
Sturnus vulgaris

The starling is a familiar, well-known and widespread bird. It is similar in size to a blackbird but with a slimmer build and more upright stance. It is mostly black with lighter speckles all over; in sunlight, the feathers light up with iridescent, greenish, bluish and purplish glints. Look for the sharp, pointed yellow beak, pinkish orange legs and feet and short tail. Starlings have a strutting walk and squabble a lot; they are frequently seen looking for grubs in lawns or in rowdy groups at bird tables. In flight, they are habitually spotted in small flocks, forming larger flocks in early evening when going to roost (usually in hedgerows or trees), and they often wheel around in flowing clouds.
HABITAT Towns, cities, gardens, countryside, also seen feeding on the strand-line of beaches, throughout the British Isles except at high altitudes.
SIZE 21cm (8¼in)
EGGS 4–7, pale blue
NEST Untidy nest of leaves and grass in tree holes or buildings.
FOOD Insects, seeds, scraps.
VARIATIONS Winter plumage is spottier than summer plumage. Juveniles are grey-brown; adult coloration occurs gradually, so halfway stages are seen in summer.

24 House sparrow
Passer domesticus

Small and cheeky, the house sparrow is an extremely familiar bird that is always thought of as very common, although numbers are mysteriously declining in many areas. It has chestnut-and-black-dappled back and wings, a scruffy black 'bib', a blunt, bullet-shaped head with a grey cap, and very light grey 'cheeks', breast and underparts; the beak is short and thick. It hops along the ground, but does not run, and its calls are of a series of monotonous chirps.
HABITAT Throughout the British Isles in cities, towns, villages, parkland and farmland, often in large flocks in fields of cereal crops shortly before harvest.
SIZE 15cm (6in)
EGGS 3–6, off-white with tiny darker speckles
NEST Untidy, rounded pile of grass and straw in a hole or crevice in a tree, shrub, hedge or building. Birds nest communally and may take over house martin's nests, occasionally evicting the owners.
FOOD Seeds of weeds, grasses, ripening cereal crops, food scraps; feeds young on insects.
SIMILAR TO Tree sparrow looks like the male house sparrow but has a black spot on the light grey 'cheeks' and a white collar.
VARIATIONS Females and juveniles are much lighter-coloured and duller, with a plain buff head, breast and underparts and a buff-and-black-striped back and wings.

25 Chaffinch
Fringilla coelebs

The sparrow-sized chaffinch is one of our most abundant birds. The male is particularly colourful in spring, when its pinkish buff face, breast and underparts turn several shades brighter than usual. It also has a blue-grey 'helmet', a chestnut-brown back, blackish wings with 2 parallel white bars, and a blackish tail with white outer feathers. Its call is a sharp, metallic 'pink, pink, pink' or a questioning 'hoo-eet?' Its song is a cheerful, descending series of trills, accelerating to a flourish.
HABITAT Fields, hedgerows, woods, parkland and gardens, throughout the British Isles but less common in north-west Scotland.
SIZE 15cm (6in)
EGGS 4–5, pale greenish or bluish to buff, marked purple-brown
NEST Very neat cup of moss and grass in hedgerows and bushes.
FOOD Seeds, insects.
SIMILAR TO Female chaffinch is fairly similar to the sparrow, except the chaffinch has 2 white flashes on the wing and is unstreaked above.
VARIATIONS Female lacks the bright colours of the male.

26 Greenfinch
Carduelis chloris

Usually seen in flocks, these are common, sparrow-sized birds but stockier. In spring and summer, the males look similar to canaries, with a bright olive-green head and upperparts, greyish 'cheeks', yellow-green underparts and rump and brilliant yellow streaks on the grey-and-black wings and tail. The pinkish beak is short, strong, thick and triangular, adapted for eating hard seeds. The bird appears to be constantly frowning. Large flocks are often seen in fields with sparrows shortly before harvest and often visit garden bird-feeders.
HABITAT Farmland, hedgerows and gardens throughout the British Isles, except for parts of the Highlands and north-west Scotland.
SIZE 15cm (6in)
EGGS 4–6, off white lightly spotted and streaked reddish brown
NEST Sturdy cup of twigs, moss and grass in hedgerows and bushes.
FOOD Mainly grain and seeds.
VARIATIONS Females are not quite as brightly coloured, and both sexes become duller, more green-buff in winter. Juveniles are buff, with fine brown streaks all over.

27 Goldfinch
Carduelis carduelis

Once caught in huge numbers (as they are still in parts of Europe) for cagebirds, this colourful finch is often seen in small flocks and is increasingly found in gardens. It is distinctly smaller and slimmer than a sparrow, but with a bright red face, a white 'bib' and 'cheeks', black 'headphones', a warm beige back with a white-tipped black tail, and white-spotted black wings that have a large, golden-yellow flash running right down the middle.
HABITAT Throughout the British Isles, except in the far north of Scotland, in farmland, orchards, weed-filled wasteland and gardens.
SIZE 12cm (4¾in)
EGGS 4–7, pale blue with darker, speckled markings
NEST Neat cup of moss, rootlets, grass and lichens near branch tips.
FOOD Seeds, insects and (in gardens) hulled sunflower seeds or nyger.
SIMILAR TO Juvenile goldfinch may be mistaken for the juvenile greenfinch, but the goldfinch does not have any yellow in its tail.
VARIATIONS Juvenile lacks the colourful face pattern and the yellow markings are duller.

Collective nouns for birds
A flock of goldfinches is correctly called a 'charm', but other birds have their own equally picturesque yet less well-known collective terms – an 'exultation' of larks, a 'spring' of teals, a 'murder' of crows, a 'doping' of sheldrake, a 'chattering' of choughs, a 'walk' of snipe, a 'parliament' of rooks, a 'sedge' of herons and a 'fall' of woodcock.

1 Large white
Pieris brassicae

Often referred to by gardeners as the cabbage white because of the tendency of the caterpillars to feed on cabbages, this is a common, widespread white butterfly (6cm/2½in wingspan) with bold black wing-tips and 2 large black spots on the forewing of the female; the male has no spots, just black wing-tips. The undersides are very pale cream.

HABITAT Throughout the British Isles in fields and gardens, from March to May, with a second generation June to September.

CATERPILLAR Yellow or greenish yellow, patterned with rows of black dots; feeds in large colonies on brassica crops, wild crucifers and nasturtium leaves, quickly reducing the plants to skeletons, from June to October.

2 Small white
Pieris rapae

Like the large white, this butterfly (the second most common in the British Isles) is often referred to by gardeners as the cabbage white. The forewings (4.5–5cm/1¾–2in wingspan) are white with yellowish tips, and the hind wings are yellowish with light black tips and very small dots on the underside (a single dot indicates a male, 2 dots means it is a female).

HABITAT Throughout the British Isles in farmland and gardens, especially where cabbages or wild members of the crucifer family

grow, from March to September.

CATERPILLAR Small, solitary and plain green, feeding on cultivated cabbages or wild members of the cabbage family including garlic mustard (Jack-by-the-hedge), from June to September.

3 Holly blue
Celastrina argiolus

These are small, fluttering blue butterflies (3cm/1¼in wingspan), often seen on warm, still, sunny days. The forewings have a navy-blue-black edge, the hind wings have a row of dark spots round the edge, and the undersides are very pale blue speckled unevenly with minute, dark dots.

HABITAT Gardens, parkland, allotments and hedgerows, almost anywhere in the southern half of England from April to October.

CATERPILLAR Well camouflaged, small green 'grubs' with tiny, red-and-white markings. Two generations are produced each year: the first feeds on flower buds of holly in spring, the second on flower buds of ivy in October and November.

4 Peacock
Inachis io

This is a very common and easily recognized, rich orange-red butterfly (6cm/2½in wingspan) with 4 very conspicuous, false eyes – one on each wing – visible even when in flight. At rest, when the wings are partly folded, only the

front pair is visible. Adults feed on the nectar of various wildflowers, and in gardens they feed on ice plant (*Sedum spectabile*), buddleia and Michaelmas daisies, as well as rotting windfall apples in autumn; some adults overwinter in hollow trees, outbuildings and shelters.

HABITAT Throughout England and Wales, with a patchy distribution in Ireland and south-west Scotland and virtually absent from the rest

of Scotland. Seen from late May to September, in hedgerows, woodland rides and gardens.

CATERPILLAR Black and hairy, developing orange 'legs' as it grows older; found on nettles in June.

5 Comma
Polygonia c-album

The comma is a common, colourful, medium-sized orange butterfly (wingspan up to 5cm/2in), lightly dappled with brown spots and easily recognized by the very irregular edges to the wings. It is named after the white, comma-like mark on the underside of the hind wings. Adults feed on the nectar of brambles, thistles or hemp agrimony in the wild, and buddleia and Michaelmas daisies in gardens.

HABITAT Gardens and hedgerows throughout most of England and Wales, from March to September.

CATERPILLAR Bristly, black and white, found on nettles or wild hops, from late April to early September.

6 Buff-tip
Phalera bucephala

This large, common, widespread moth (wingspan 6cm/2½in) is mainly dappled brown, with a buff head and rounded buff patches at the ends of the wings — hence the name. It flies at night and spends the days perfectly camouflaged as a bit of broken twig on a tree branch, with its wings folded in a 'V' shape.

HABITAT Throughout the British Isles, but commonest in central and south-east England, in woods, farmland, parkland, towns and gardens, from May to August.

CATERPILLAR Pale yellow, slightly bristly, each segment patterned with black parallel lines. Found in groups from July to September on leaves of deciduous trees, including oak, hazel and whitebeam, which it may defoliate badly.

7 Magpie moth
Abraxas grossulariata

This is a common and conspicuous, medium-sized, day-flying moth (up to 4cm/1½in wingspan) with a ginger body decorated with a row of black spots up the centre, and white or cream, back-swept wings heavily spotted with black, with an orange band across the centre and a small orange patch round the head.

HABITAT Gardens, allotments, wasteland and hedgerows, in July and August, in England, Wales, Ireland and lowland Scotland.

CATERPILLAR White with black spots and orange bands down the sides.

Seen in May and June, often in large numbers in the garden on soft fruit bushes, which are quickly reduced to bare stems; in the countryside, found on blackthorn, hazel, hawthorn and other traditional hedging plants. Known as 'loopers', because they move by curling their body into a loop, then stretching out with the head end before looping up the back end again, rather like a 'slinky' spring.

8 Brindled beauty
Lycia hirtaria

The narrow, wavy brown lines that create a brindled pattern on the warm beige wings give this widespread, small-to-medium-sized moth (up to 4cm/1½in wingspan) its name. The fact that it usually rests on tree trunks by day ensures that it is perfectly camouflaged and hardly ever seen.

HABITAT Throughout the British Isles, but most common in and around London on large street trees and in parks and squares, in April and May.

CATERPILLAR Long and narrow, in chestnut-brown with yellow markings; they feed at night on apple trees, willow, lime, silver birch or elm foliage, from May to July, but resemble twigs so are hard to see.

9 Puss moth
Cerura vinula

Usually seen resting on tree trunks by day, this is an uncommon but widespread, large and relatively ordinary-looking moth (8cm/3¼in wingspan). The cream wings are covered with light brown zigzag markings, and it has a furry, light-brown-and-cream-striped body. It has perhaps the most spectacular caterpillars of any moth.

HABITAT Throughout the British Isles, from May to July, in parks, light woodland, nature reserves and damp places, such as watersides, particularly with willows or poplar.

CATERPILLAR Green with a bold, jagged, black-and-green pattern and a row of tiny white dots down

each side. When threatened, the front end rears up and swells, inflating a red strip that contains 2 large, false eyes and 2 red-tipped, whip-like 'tails', which are held over the rear of the body; as a last resort, the caterpillar spits formic acid at its aggressor. Seen on poplar or willow in July and August.

10 Lime hawk-moth
Mimas tiliae

The lime hawk-moth is a large, night-flying moth (up to 8cm/3¼in wingspan) with a khaki body and camouflage-patterned wings in several shades of chestnut, olive and brown. The shape of this moth at rest, when its back-swept wings with irregular trailing edges are on view, makes it resemble a stealth bomber.

HABITAT Fairly common around lime trees, particularly in south-east England, from May to June.

CATERPILLAR Lime-green with a row of short, thin, slanting, reddish lines and matching dots along each side of the body and a short, pointed 'horn' sticking up at the rear end. Present from July to September, it feeds on lime leaves at night and hides by day.

11 Elephant hawk-moth
Deilephila elpenor

This is a very beautiful but uncommon, pink and olive-beige moth (up to 7cm/2¾in wingspan) with conspicuous white legs. It flies and feeds by night but may be seen resting on plants by day, with back-swept wings. The caterpillars are seen more than the adults.

HABITAT Grassland and on wasteland wherever willowherb grows, also sometimes in gardens feeding on honeysuckle, petunias, bramble, or valerian at dusk. Found mostly in the southern half of England but scattered elsewhere.

CATERPILLAR Long and streaky brown, patterned with rows of black dots and light yellow lines. When the caterpillar is disturbed, its front end rears and swells up, enlarging 1 or 2 pairs of spots into alarming 'eyes' to frighten off potential predators. Sometimes found on willowherb or on fuchsias in gardens in July and August.

12 Hummingbird hawk-moth
Macroglossum stellatarum

Often mistaken for a hummingbird, this is an uncommon, day-flying moth (wingspan 5.5cm/2¼in) that migrates to us from the south of France each summer. It is a rather

dumpy, medium-sized, dull brown moth with gingery 'armpits', usually spotted in flight owing to its faint humming sound and unique habit of darting and hovering in front of flowers, where it feeds like a hummingbird, sticking a long proboscis deep into blooms of honeysuckle, petunias, verbena and a few late summer-flowering shrubs.

HABITAT Mostly in the south-east of England from June to September, though they may be seen all over the British Isles.

CATERPILLAR Long, thin and bright green, bearing a few parallel, yellow and dark blue stripes, with a long, dark bluish 'horn' at the rear end. Rarely found in the British Isles, but sometimes on bedstraw in July or August.

13 Garden tiger moth
Arctia caja

This is a large, common, night-flying moth (wingspan to 7.5cm/3in) that's as pretty as a butterfly. It has a brown head and thorax, a red stripe across the 'shoulders', brown-and-white, camouflage-patterned forewings and bright orange hind wings with bold black spots.

HABITAT Gardens, parkland, allotments, roadside verges, in July and August. Was once common throughout the British Isles, but it

has recently retreated northwards, becoming rare in the south.

CATERPILLAR Well known to children as 'woolly bear', the caterpillar is shaggy, long-haired and black with a dash of ginger near the head. Feeds on foliage of just about any soft garden plants, including annual bedding plants and perennial flowers, from September to June. Handle it with care: it brings some people out in an itchy rash.

14 Brown-tail moth
Euproctis chrysorrhoea

Also known as the brown-tail tussock moth, this is a fairly common but bland moth, best known for its anti-social caterpillars. The adult is slightly furry white with a brown abdomen, usually found resting on twigs or foliage in hedgerows in July.

HABITAT In gardens and hedges in a broad strip along the south-east coast of England.

CATERPILLAR Blackish, marked with indistinct rows of red dots, entirely clad in stiff, irritant hairs. Lives communally under scruffy, silky tents made from matted, spider-web-like material, draped over hedges or in small trees including hawthorn, blackthorn, elm, bramble, fruit trees and general scrub. Found from August to June, large colonies can cover many

yards; major infestations cause serious defoliation. Can cause a nasty rash if touched.

15 Silver 'Y'
Autographa gamma

The silver 'Y' is a common, dull, medium-sized, day-flying moth (4cm/1½in wingspan) that migrates here from Europe each year and is often observed feeding on nectar of buddleia and *Sedum spectabile* in gardens. Seen in flight, the fast-moving wings look like a silvery blur; at rest, the arrowhead shape patterned in brown and silver is perfectly camouflaged against tree bark. It gets its name from the silver shape on each wing that looks like a Greek letter 'Y'.

HABITAT Seen all summer throughout the British Isles, in gardens and other cultivated areas including nurseries and parks.

CATERPILLAR Light green and eats soft garden foliage and flowers, particularly of herbaceous plants, from May to September.

16 Vapourer moth
Orgyia antiqua
This is a curious moth. Only the male has wings – he is small (3cm/1¼in wingspan), slightly hairy, dull and gingery, with a brindle pattern and a conspicuous white spot on each wing (seen at rest); he flies by day. The wingless female looks like a flattened, oval, greenish brown, hairy grub, and is often seen with a silky white cocoon containing the eggs.
HABITAT Throughout Britain (not Shetland) and parts of Ireland in hedgerows and gardens, from July to September.
CATERPILLAR Spectacular black caterpillar with red dots and long tufts of stiff black hairs (which are an irritant to some people), with 4 longer tufts standing out from the head and a single tuft at the rear. Seen from May to August, feeding on hedgerows and a wide variety of deciduous trees and shrubs including roses, fruit trees, ornamental trees in gardens, towns and the countryside.

17 Lackey moth
Malacosoma neustria
This is a small, rarely seen, gingery brown moth with a faint wood-grain pattern in ash-grey, making it very well camouflaged against tree bark, where it normally rests by day. It is on the wing at night (wingspan up to 2cm/¾in) between June and August.
HABITAT Hedgerows, woods, gardens and orchards, from June to August. Throughout most of the British Isles, but not Scotland or far north of England.
CATERPILLAR Up to 3–4cm (1¼–1½in) long, horizontally striped red, black and blue. Seen from April to June, living

communally in silken 'tents' on a variety of hedges including hawthorn and blackthorn, also a variety of deciduous trees in gardens and orchards.

18 Large yellow underwing
Noctua pronuba
This is a common, buff-coloured, night-flying moth (6cm/2½in wingspan) that spends the daylight hours hidden low down in plants with folded wings; it may be seen flying at dusk, when the buff-orange hind wings show up.

Its caterpillar is the cutworm – a serious garden pest, particularly in annual flowerbeds and the vegetable patch.
HABITAT Throughout the British Isles in gardens and allotments, from June to October but most often seen on August evenings.
CATERPILLAR Green or light khaki-brown, hiding in the soil by day and feeding at night low down on plants, often chewing right through stems of lettuce and annual flowers and cutting them off at the base, hence the common name of 'cutworm'.

19 Honey bee
Apis mellifera
The slim brown, 'cultivated' bee of bee-keepers also lives wild in both towns and the countryside where swarms have escaped. It dwells in large colonies of up to 50,000; these are most active in spring and summer – only a small nucleus of workers overwinters with the queen. In the countryside, worker bees are seen gathering pollen from a variety of wildflowers, also fields of oilseed rape; in gardens they visit various flowers.
HABITAT In hives, hollow trees or wall cavities throughout the British Isles.

20 Red-tailed bumblebee
Bombus lapidarius
This is the common, big, fat, black-and-orange bumblebee, with a large, rounded, rather furry-looking black body (2.5cm/1in long) and a conspicuous, orange-red rear end. A worker bee at work will usually have pollen baskets on the back legs.
HABITAT Countryside and flower-beds throughout the British Isles but particularly in the south.

21 Leaf-cutter bee
Megachile centuncularis
Very similar in size and shape to a honeybee, this is a common but rarely seen species. However, you can tell where it's been by the neat, scalloped 'bites' removed round the edges of certain garden plants (particularly roses, lilacs and laburnum) in midsummer. It uses its strong jaws to shear the edge of a leaf, then flies away with the piece, carrying it in its legs, to use for nest construction.
HABITAT Fairly widespread in gardens in southern England in summer.

22 Mason bee
Osmia rufa
Similar to the honeybee in shape and size, but clad in short, reddish fur, this is a common bee, often identified by the characteristic holes it makes in old brickwork. It is usually seen clearing out loose mortar in old brickwork or working on pencil-width holes in firm sandy banks, which are used as egg chambers then sealed with soil.
HABITAT Garden walls and sandy banks in summer, throughout the British Isles.

23 Common wasp
Vespula vulgaris
The common wasp is a very familiar, widespread, black-and-yellow-striped insect, 2cm (¾in) long, capable of delivering a painful sting. The German wasp (*Vespula germanica*) is equally common and almost identical, but has 3 tiny black dots on the face instead of a black anchor smudge down the middle. To most people, wasps are a pest, known for their fondness for boring holes into garden fruit and menacing picnics or outdoor meals in summer. However, earlier in the season they take carrion and are helpful in pest control, carrying aphids and small caterpillars back

to their nest – a large, papery construction made from chewed-up wood, in porch roofs, lofts and hollow trees and under ground. Most of the larvae hatch out into more worker wasps, all of which die off at the end of summer. Only the mated queen wasp survives to hibernate through the winter.
HABITAT Parks and gardens throughout summer; also orchards and allotments in late summer. Throughout the British Isles but commoner in the south.

24 Black garden ant
Lasius niger
These are very common, small, wingless black ants that run around erratically. They are often found on plants where colonies of aphids are present, as they 'milk' aphids for their sticky secretions; they also sometimes enter houses or invade picnics in search of spilt sugary liquids. Their underground nests – made in lawns and rockeries, under paving slabs and in containers of plants – are easily spotted by the numbers of ants coming and going, and the crater-like pile of finely graded grains of soil around the entrance hole. Winged male and female (queen) ants appear only when the colony swarms, usually on warm evenings in midsummer, attracting birds such as swallows to feed.
HABITAT In gardens and allotments, but also found in parkland and grass verges, throughout the British Isles.

25 Daddy long-legs
Tipula paludosa
Also known as the crane fly, this is a long-bodied, light brown insect with angular, spidery legs, 4–5cm (1½–2in) across. It is most commonly seen in large numbers on lawns on August and September evenings, when the adults emerge from underground larvae, mate and lay their eggs. Their khaki larvae, known as leatherjackets, live in lawns and cultivated ground and are well known to gardeners and

allotment-holders for chewing the roots off plants. They attract large numbers of starlings, which probe for the larvae with their beaks.
HABITAT Throughout the British Isles in gardens, allotments and other cultivated ground, from May to October.

26 Hoverflies
Episyrphus species
There are over 250 species of hoverfly in the British Isles. About half are black-and-yellow wasp mimics with aphid-eating larvae. *Episyrphus balteatus* (shown above), about 1.5cm (⅝in) long, is particularly common. Unlike wasps, hoverflies have no sting and often hover or dart swiftly one way, then another in flight. Adults feed on nectar; the larvae are small and slug-like and feed on aphids.
HABITAT Throughout the British Isles in gardens and parks, from April to October but seen predominantly on still, warm, sunny summer days.

27 Housefly
Musca domestica
Our commonest 'indoor' fly, 8mm (⁵⁄₁₆in long), the housefly has large, reddish eyes, a dark grey thorax and legs, a buff abdomen and transparent wings. The larvae are maggots that develop from eggs laid in manure or rotting household refuse.
HABITAT Throughout the British Isles year round, particularly around farms, rubbish dumps, dustbins and often seen inside rooms, buzzing up windows or cruising round kitchens.

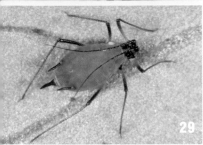

28 Common spittlebug
Philaenus spumarius

One of many species of froghopper, this is a very common and widespread, garden insect whose presence is usually detected by white, frothy 'cuckoo spit' on plants in early summer. The adult is rarely seen. It is a small, elliptical, dark-brown-and-buff-mottled bug, slightly less than 1cm (⅜in) long, that jumps between plants when disturbed. The larva is a small, bright green bug, 5mm (³⁄₁₆in) long – the same shape as the adult but without wings – which excretes the well-known blobs of 'spit' round itself to prevent its body drying out in sunlight.
HABITAT Throughout the British Isles in gardens, allotments and on wasteland, from May to September.

29 Aphids

Aphids are well-known, rounded-to-pear-shaped insects with semi-transparent bodies, roughly 5mm (³⁄₁₆in) long or smaller, with spindly legs, feeding on sap sucked from the soft tips of shoots, flower buds and the undersides of young leaves where the tissue is most tender. There are actually many different types that attack particular plants. The rose aphid (*Macrosiphon rosae*) is a large greenfly in green, beige or pink and is found on roses. The peach-potato aphid

(*Myzus persicae*) is a small green, yellow or pink aphid found on potato plants, also garden flowers and greenhouse and indoor pot plants. The lime leaf aphid (*Eucallipterus tiliae*) is a lime-green greenfly that lives in large numbers in lime trees and sheds sticky honeydew on parked cars underneath. The black bean aphid (*Aphis fabae*) is a black or dark grey, greasy-looking aphid clustered on beans or nasturtiums.
HABITAT Throughout the British Isles in parks, woods, gardens and allotments, from spring to early autumn. The peach-potato aphid can be found all year round in greenhouses or on indoor plants.

30 Seven-spot ladybird
Coccinella 7-punctata

Our best-known and biggest ladybird, this is a small, rounded beetle, 1.3cm/½in long, with bright orange-red wing-cases that are patterned with 7 evenly spaced black spots. Adults feed on aphids, as do the larvae, which look nothing like the adults – more like grey-black grubs dotted with orange.
HABITAT On plants from late spring to early autumn, throughout lowland areas of the British Isles. In winter, adult ladybirds hibernate in large groups in leaf debris, in hedge-bottoms, sheds or under ledges on buildings.

31 Cockchafer
Melolontha melolontha

Also known as the maybug, this is a large, unmistakable, nocturnal beetle, 2.5cm (1in) long and 1cm (⅜in) wide, with chestnut-brown wing-cases and a black thorax. In flight it is clumsy, often bumping into things; the loud, humming noise and whirring, short, stumpy wings are conspicuous. Adults feed on tree leaves. The larvae are large, fat and usually curved (almost banana-shaped), up to 5cm (2in) long, with a white body and brown head. They live underground, feeding on grass roots, often causing bare or brown patches in lawns or other turf. As a result, they are considered a pest by many gardeners.
HABITAT Throughout most of the British Isles in gardens, allotments and meadows, on warm evenings in late May or early June. Often attracted to lighted windows.

32 Ground beetle
Pterostichus madidus

This is a very common and ordinary-looking, medium-sized beetle with a semi-shiny black body, up to 1.5cm (⅝in) long, and roughly one-third as wide. It has 2 pairs of rear-facing legs and a single pair of forward-facing legs, also a pair of leg-length antennae sticking out from the front of the head. The larvae are long, black,

segmented grubs with 3 pairs of short legs near the front and a pair of curved nippers on the front of the head. Both adults and larvae feed on slugs' eggs and small insects, including many species harmful to garden plants, so they are considered beneficial by gardeners.

HABITAT Throughout the British Isles in gardens, allotments, hedgerows, woods and fields; mostly seen in summer, scurrying around hedge bottoms, closely planted beds and vegetable patches or hiding under logs and stones.

Aphid lifestyle

One reason why aphids are so successful is that, without needing a male, females can give birth to live young by a process known as parthenogenesis. These young are all females – they start feeding on plants straight away and soon produce live young of their own.

Aphids have a fascinating symbiotic relationship with ants, which 'milk' greenfly, stroking them in order to stimulate the release of a sticky, honeydew-like secretion on which the ants feed. In exchange, the ants 'farm' the aphids, moving them from plant to plant and protecting them by fiercely attacking potential predators. Although they are pests to gardeners, aphids (especially those on fruit trees and roses) are a valuable resource for many birds, especially blue tits, for feeding chicks in spring.

33 Earwig
Forficula auricularia

Well known and easily identified, the earwig is a tubular, shiny, chestnut-brown-coloured insect, approximately 1.5cm (⅝in) long, with a long pair of antennae on the head, 3 pairs of legs attached at the front of the body (to the thorax), and a long abdomen with a distinctive pair of stout pincers at the rear. It can fly but is rarely seen in flight, since it takes a lot of bother to fold the wings back into their cases. It feeds on flower petals and buds, aphids and other small insects.

HABITAT In gardens, outbuildings and houses, usually hiding in dark, enclosed places, including the rolled petals of flowers such as dahlias and chrysanthemums, but also under logs, stones and similar places. Throughout the British Isles, mostly seen in summer and early autumn.

34 Garden spider
Araneus diadematus

This is a common spider, also known as the diadem spider. Its webs are seen stretched between plants or draped over hedges, sparkling with dew on fine, sunny mornings in late summer and early autumn. The female, which is usually observed lying in wait in the centre of the web, is medium to large, up to 3cm (1¼in) across, including the legs, with a large, globular beige body with a white cross on the back. The male is smaller and narrower.

HABITAT Throughout the British Isles in gardens, allotments and parks as well as in the countryside.

35 Four-spotted orb web spider
Arenus quadratus

Orb web spiders are a small group that includes the familiar garden spider. Most of them don't have

common names. This particular species is one of the largest and commonest; it is almost crab-shaped, with a fat, round, khaki-to-brownish abdomen marked with 4 prominent, pale spots.

HABITAT Throughout the British Isles in gardens and countryside, especially in August and October.

36 Woodlouse spider
Dysdera crocata

The woodlouse spider is a fairly common, nocturnal species (1.2cm/½in long) that specializes in hunting woodlice. It has a brown thorax, a buff abdomen, chestnut-orange legs and unusually large, powerful jaws. This is one of only a handful of British spiders that has jaws that can open wide enough to bite through human skin and will give a painful nip if picked up incautiously. You are most likely to see it while clearing up the garden or spreading compost.

HABITAT Throughout the British Isles, in countryside and gardens, hiding between stones in piles of debris or at the base of hedges, and particularly in compost heaps.

37 House spider
Tegenaria gigantea

Often seen inside the home, this is the well-known, dark, hairy-legged spider found in the bath, behind furniture and in the attic. It constructs flat, roughly triangular webs with a tubular retreat in one corner. If it feels vibrations of an insect crossing the matted silk strands, it rushes out and pounces on its prey. The colour varies from brown to nearly black. Females are up to 4cm (1½in) across, including the legs, and are larger and longer-lived than the males. House spiders are most often seen in autumn, when many come indoors from the garden and males are moving around looking for mates.

Despite the rumours, spiders don't climb up the inside of the waste pipe to get into your bath; they climb up the bathroom wall or bathtub surround and slide down the slippery bath surface and then can't get out. If 'rescued' and put down elsewhere they are often back again the next day, so put them out in the garden if you want to be certain they are expelled.

HABITAT Throughout the British Isles, in houses, sheds, outbuildings or the garden, all year round.

38 Daddy long-legs spider
Pholcus phalangioides

A very long-legged spider, about 4–5cm (1½–2in) across, this looks like a fragile, pale buff daddy long-legs without wings. The body is tiny (5mm/³⁄₁₆in) and dewdrop-shaped with a 'waist'. The legs are very long, each with 2 slightly knobbly 'knees', usually a little darker than the rest of the legs. It is generally seen hanging by its feet from its fragile-looking web and feeds on various small insects. It can go many days or even weeks between meals, conserving energy and moisture by not moving a muscle or twitching a limb.
HABITAT Houses and outbuildings, mainly in southern Britain.

39 Garden snail
Helix aspersa

Our commonest snail, this has a buff-coloured shell, up to 3cm (1¼in) across, banded with darker brown. It is active mostly at night, and climbs up walls and tree trunks as well as feeding at ground level. Several may 'stick together' in clusters to survive long, dry spells in summer or to hibernate for the winter, often choosing crevices in rocks or under rubble, logs and inside empty flowerpots. During the summer, small, white, pearl-like eggs are laid in groups of 30–40 in shallow soil. Snails feed on living and decaying vegetation.
HABITAT Gardens, banks, hedge-bottoms, walls round fields and woods from spring to late autumn.

40 Garden slug
Arion hortensis

One of the commonest garden slugs, this is grey with an orange underside, up to 3cm (1¼in) long. By day it hides under stones, logs or rubbish and by night it comes out to feed on the ground and in low vegetation. It eats most soft plant foliage, particularly seedlings and young annual flowers, vegetables and salads.
HABITAT Throughout the British Isles in gardens, allotments, parks and farmland, also on wasteland, mostly from spring to autumn.

41 Great black slug
Arion ater

Britain's biggest slug, this is quite frequently seen, even though it is mostly nocturnal, because it emerges by day in damp weather. It is black and up to 15cm (6in) long when fully extended, but at rest it contracts to a short, fat, black mound, about 2cm (¾in) long. It eats almost anything – plant material, carrion, insects, even bread put out for birds – so unlike smaller slug species it does very little damage in gardens.
HABITAT Throughout the British Isles, predominantly in gardens, allotments and other cultivated ground, but also hedgerows, from spring to autumn.

42 Field slug
Deroceras reticulatum

Also known as the netted slug, this is another of the commoner garden slugs, up to 5cm (2in) long. It is rather variable in coloration – sometimes yellowish grey, beige or brownish grey. In close-up, you can see a finely patterned network of darker veins. It hides under stones, logs or rubbish by day. At night, it feeds on most soft plant foliage at ground-level; it is also often found inside lettuces or eating seedlings in the greenhouse.
HABITAT Throughout the British Isles in cultivated land such as gardens, parks, allotments and farmland, from spring to autumn.

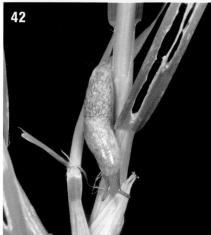

Good news about slugs

You might think 'ooh, nasty' when you find one in your lettuce, or come out one morning to find they've eaten all your newly planted seedlings, but slugs add useful protein to the diet of many garden birds. Hedgehogs love them, and even a fox or badger will eat them if it's hungry enough. Slugs lay clusters of tiny, pearly white eggs in loose soil; you sometimes find them round the garden. These are also eaten by various garden wildlife, including ground beetles, but those that make it through the winter hatch next spring.

Reptiles and amphibians

1 Common toad
Bufo bufo

Superficially frog-like in shape and size, the common toad has rough, warty-textured skin and walks instead of hopping like a frog. The colour is rather variable – brown, khaki or reddish-tinged. Despite its name, this toad is not so common now, and it is more likely to be seen in urban gardens – especially those with ponds – than in the countryside. 'Toad crossings' are not uncommon on roads in spring, on their regularly used routes to spawning ponds. Toad-spawn is produced in long, sticky ribbons draped round water plants in fairly deep water, about 2 weeks later than frogspawn. Soon after spawning, the adult toads leave the water and return to life on land. **HABITAT** Gardens, among damp vegetation or in crevices under stones, plant containers or logs round gardens where people do not use chemicals and there is a good food supply. Hibernates in winter under upturned plant containers, logs, large stones or paving slabs. Mostly in England and Wales, less common in Scotland and absent in Ireland. **FOOD** Slugs, worms.

2 Wall lizard
Podarcis muralis

The wall lizard is a native of southern Europe that has been introduced to a few locations in Britain, where it is rare. It has a buff-brown back with faint black horizontal stripes and much darker sides – almost black, with brown dots – and a buff-brown tail faintly banded with slightly darker rings. The underparts are paler. The tail is long, over twice the length of the body, giving a total size of up to 25cm (10in). The wall lizard also has especially long fingers and toes, good for gripping rough surfaces when running up and down walls. It is often seen basking on sunny walls or banks. **HABITAT** Wild on Jersey, now also in parts of Surrey, Sussex, south London and the Isle of Wight, in dry, sandy or rocky places. **FOOD** Insects.

Mammals

1 Fox
Vulpes vulpes

With its long, bushy tail, or 'brush', the fox is a very familiar and widespread carnivore, about 70cm (28in) long and weighing about 5–6kg (11–13lb). The colour varies from the familiar fox-red to chestnut-brown or nearly black, with variable markings – some have a white tip to the tail, a white 'mask' and chest, or black legs, while others are a more uniform shade. The fox is normally active at night, but it is very likely to be seen by day in spring when there are cubs to feed. **HABITAT** Throughout the British Isles, traditionally in woods, copses, dense hedgerows and bramble thickets amid farmland, also parkland and large woodland gardens. However, there is now a large urban fox population in towns and they are often out by day, sunbathing on flat roofs, or in early evenings visiting gardens or wasteland for food. **FOOD** Earthworms, berries, fruit, snails, beetles, rodents, rabbits, poultry, carrion and scraps of all sorts including discarded fast food.

2 Domestic cats
Felis species

Unusual as it might seem to include a popular domestic pet in a book about natural history, domestic cats are the commonest predators in the British Isles – there can be over 500 of them

per square kilometre in towns and cities and as such they have a considerable impact on urban wildlife, especially rodents, rabbits and birds. In turn, this affects the outlook for other predatory species.

3 Hedgehog
Erinaceus europaeus

The hedgehog is an easily recognized and much-loved, small animal, 25cm (10in) long, covered in beige-tipped, brown spines. The pointed face is clad in long, stiff hairs, with a round black, rubbery nose, black, shiny eyes and small, rounded black ears almost hidden in the hair. When threatened, it rolls into a tight, spiky ball for defence. By day it hides in hedgerows or woods and at night it comes out to feed. Hedgehogs now do better in urban environments than in the wild. There is a race of blonde hedgehogs on the island of Alderney, in the Channel Islands; for some reason, these paler versions do not have the usual population of fleas seen on most hedgehogs.

HABITAT Throughout areas of lowland in the British Isles (except for some Scottish islands) in hedgerows, edges of woods, parkland and gardens.
FOOD Worms, beetles, snails, carrion, eggs of ground-nesting birds.

4 Wood mouse
Apodemus sylvaticus

Also known as the long-tailed field mouse, or often simply called the field mouse, this is one of the most numerous British mammals (after the field vole), even outnumbering the brown rat. It has a rather house-mouse-like shape, with a slender body (up to 9cm/3½in long) and a tail that is slightly shorter. It is easily distinguished from the house mouse by its very large eyes and slightly shaggy, sandy-brown coat with white underparts and lack of smell. (The house mouse is light grey-brown all over.)

HABITAT Throughout the British Isles in woodland, hedgerows, farmland, gardens and houses.
FOOD Seeds, snails, insects, grubs.

5 House mouse
Mus domesticus

This is a familiar, small, long-tailed, light brown-grey mouse with a short, sleek coat, very much like a pet mouse, but largely nocturnal. It has big, round, naked ears, long whiskers and large eyes, with a long, naked, slightly scaly, light brown-grey tail, which is roughly the same length as the body (combined length 17cm/6¾in). House mice are more common in city centres than wood mice, which are found in more rural or suburban areas.

HABITAT Throughout the British Isles, mostly in farm buildings, outbuildings and garages, especially where foodstuffs or suitable nesting materials are stored.
FOOD Domestic foodstuffs, refuse, stored birdseed as well as a more 'normal' rodent diet.

6 Brown rat
Rattus norvegicus

The brown rat is an extremely common animal, far more numerous than is generally realized, as it is secretive and comes out mostly at night. It is a long, lean, grey-brown rodent, up to 28cm (11in) long (females are slightly smaller), with a long, thin head with beady eyes and small, rounded, naked ears, naked hands and feet and a long, scaly, hairless tail. It is often seen swimming in ditches, where it is mistaken for the

much rarer water vole (which has a short, blunt head, short tail and rich brown not grey-brown fur).

HABITAT In almost any habitat throughout the British Isles, particularly hedgerows around farmland, wasteland, riverbanks, shores and ditches where rubbish is dumped or washed up. In urban areas, lives in attics, sewers, rubbish dumps and outbuildings. In autumn, after crops have been harvested, 'country' rats move from the fields to warmer and better-stocked locations closer to human habitation.
FOOD Almost anything edible including rotting rubbish, spilt grain crops, stored fruit, vegetables or tubers in sheds, vegetables growing in gardens and edible waste on compost heaps. Often takes food left out for birds.

Unwelcome visitors

You don't have to see mice to know you are on their visiting list. Droppings, chewed food packaging, gnawed electrical wiring and shredded paper are unmistakable signs of habitation and they can cause considerable damage. You may also notice a distinctive, musty aroma, which is a sign that a house mouse is resident. Mice may live inside the house or outside, in piles of rubble, rockeries and in undisturbed junk in outbuildings. They can enter houses (usually at night) through tiny holes and will reuse the same routes regularly to reach good supplies of food or nesting materials, usually following the edge of a wall or the back of a shelf.

Plants

1 Common lime
Tilia x europaea

Also known as the linden tree, this is the tallest-growing of our broadleaved trees, a hybrid of our native small-leaved lime (*Tilia cordata*) and the large-leaved lime (*T. platyphyllos*). It is a tall, upright, stately tree, to 40m (130ft) high, with large, heart-shaped leaves, 10cm (4in) long. In July, it bears small clusters of scented, creamy yellow flowers hanging from a long, narrow, light green, leafy bract. After pollination, clusters of small, round, green, pea-like fruit form – these fall in early autumn, still attached to their bracts. The trees produce large clusters of suckers from their base. It is the food plant of caterpillars of the lime hawk-moth.

In early summer, huge numbers of aphids are attracted to the soft young leaves of lime, and the insects deposit vast quantities of sticky honeydew on anything beneath, making them unpopular with motorists when they are grown as street trees, as parked cars are soon covered in goo. The leaves on the trees are so heavily covered they glisten; after a while, a blackish sooty mould grows over the sticky surfaces.

HABITAT Parklands and urban streets throughout the British Isles.

2 London plane
Platanus x hispanica

One of the commonest trees in London streets and squares, this is a large deciduous tree, up to 30m (100ft) high, with maple-like leaves. The male flowers are small yellow clusters; the tiny female flowers appear at the very ends of new shoots in spring. Loose

PREVIOUS PAGES Foxes have now become increasingly common in urban environments.

clusters of round, spiky green fruit develop over the summer but aren't easy to see until they ripen red in autumn – they remain on the trees through the winter. The bark has a characteristic patchwork pattern and peels off in dry, jigsaw-puzzle-shaped pieces often seen in piles under the trees. Plane trees were much planted in London by the Victorians, since they could survive the heavy city-centre pollution caused by coal fires and coal-burning steam trains; their habit of shedding bark as well as leaves meant they could cast off the build-up of soot and dust that made life impossible for many other trees.

HABITAT Cities, large towns, parks and stately homes throughout most of England and round cities in Scotland.

3 Elder
Sambucus nigra

This is a very common and widespread, small tree or large shrub, to 6m (20ft) high. (It is not to be confused with ground elder, which is a short, spreading perennial weed.) The trunks of old trees and elderly hedgerow specimens have craggy, ridged bark and young stems are smooth. The compound leaves are arranged in pairs, each being made up of several pairs of toothed, oval leaves

with a lone leaf at the tip; the foliage smells pungent when crushed or bruised. In June, the familiar, flattish heads of creamy white, perfumed flowers appear, followed by large clusters of berries that ripen through wine-red to black in late summer.

HABITAT Hedgerows, scrub and waste ground throughout the British Isles except the far north.

4 Buddleia
Buddleja davidii

Also known as the butterfly bush, this large, bushy deciduous shrub, up to 2.5 (8ft) high and spreading to 3m (10ft), produces long, conical clusters of tiny, 4-petalled, lilac, lavender, mauve or purple flowers in July and August – as the alternative name suggests, these attract several species of butterfly.

The leaves, which are arranged in pairs along the stems, are long, narrow and pointed, with a leathery texture; they are dark green above and felty grey-green below. Mullein moth caterpillars may sometimes be found feeding on the foliage.

HABITAT Originally a garden plant that 'escaped' into the wild and now grows in cracks in brickwork, along railway tracks, on wasteland and along roadsides in towns and cities, throughout most lowland areas in the British Isles.

5 Wallflower
Erysimum cheiri

Wallflowers are short-lived, bushy perennials with semi-woody, upright stems, usually around 30cm (12in) high, with long, narrow, linear leaves, looking like a rather weedy, stunted version of the well-known bedding plant. From April to June they carry 4-petalled yellow flowers, sometimes slightly orange-tinged, to 2.5cm (1in) across, followed by long, narrow, tubular green seedpods, roughly 5cm (2in) long, that ripen to brown. It is generally thought that the first wallflowers to reach us were introduced on stone brought over for building castles following the Norman Conquest. They were popular medieval plants for castle gardens at a time when there were few flowers in cultivation, and later they became common plants of farmhouse and cottage gardens.
HABITAT Self-seeds into chinks in old walls, gaps in paving and similar hot, dry, sunny spots in and round towns and old buildings throughout lowland areas in the British Isles.

6 Valerian
Centranthus ruber

This is a common, tall, rather upright, clump-forming biennial or short-lived perennial, to 1.5m (5ft) high, with smooth green stems bearing pairs of shiny, rather plastic-looking, pointed-oval leaves, 5–8cm (2–3¼in) long. The tiny, pinkish red flowers (occasionally white) are grouped in 'tufts' on short, branching stalks around the tip of the main stems, forming a loose, tiered, roughly pyramidal head. The flowers are attractive to hoverflies, butterflies and bees.
HABITAT Hot, dry, sunny places, including stone walls along lanes, on wasteland and in gardens; also sometimes on cliffs and rocky outcrops or round quarries. Throughout England, Wales and Ireland (localized in Scotland).

7 Ivy-leaved toadflax
Cymbalaria muralis

An enchanting, little, trailing and scrambling plant, this was first introduced as a garden plant in the 17th century and has since 'escaped'. It has prostrate stems that root as they run along the ground, eventually making a mat about 45cm (17½in) high and the same across, covered with small, glossy, ivy-shaped leaves. From May/June to October it has tiny, hooded, rather snapdragon-like flowers in yellow and lilac, each with a short spur on the back.
HABITAT Throughout the British Isles in hot, dry, sunny places, especially near human habitation; also in gaps in paving and old brickwork, gravel, rocks and sandy banks.

8 Fleabane
Pulicaria dysenterica

Fleabane is an upright-branching perennial that grows in groups, often forming fair-sized colonies, with rather wrinkly-textured, long, narrow, faintly pointed, greyish green leaves. In August and September, the tops of the plants are covered in single, yellow, daisy-like flowers. After flowering, the seedheads are an untidy mass of dandelion-like fluff that blows away in the wind.
HABITAT Hedgerows, verges, damp wasteland and ditches in most of the British Isles (not far north).

9 Rosebay willowherb
Chamerion angustifolium

Once known as fireweed for its habit of colonizing burnt-out areas, such as wartime bomb sites and railway embankments that had been set alight by sparks from steam trains, rosebay willowherb is still a very common yet attractive sight today. It is a tall, clump-forming perennial, to 1.2m (4ft) high, with upright, reddish stems bearing long, narrow, pointed leaves arranged in pairs with a heavy, reddish midrib running down the centre. From June to September, each stem is topped by a very pretty, loose, conical spike of 4-petalled, rosy-mauve flowers, with new buds forming at the tip of the spike. After flowering, the fluffy seeds of the willowherb persist into autumn.
HABITAT Throughout the British Isles on wasteland, riverbanks, railway embankments and derelict sites in towns and the countryside.

10 Creeping thistle
Cirsium arvense

An extremely common and persistent thistle, this perennial plant spreads by creeping underground roots and often forms large colonies. The tall, upright, prickly stems grow to 1m (3ft) high and are fiercely armed with jagged, spiny leaves. From July to September, it is topped with clusters of typical thistle flowers consisting of hard, round, bristly knobbles from which grow spiky mauve florets; these attract several species of butterfly. The flowers are followed by masses of untidy, thistledown seedheads, on which goldfinches love to feed.
HABITAT Throughout the British Isles on wasteland, at field-edges, in hedgerows, verges and gardens.

11 Coltsfoot
Tussilago farfara

This is a distinctive, spreading perennial, 20–25cm (8–10in) tall, often forming large, dense colonies and producing clusters of single, yellow, daisy-like flowers on scaly brown stems from late February to May, before the leaves appear. The leaves push up in late spring and early summer; they are large and shield-shaped, up to 20cm (8in), with pointed tips and pinkish- or reddish-tinged leaf stalks and main veins. They have faintly felty backs. After the flowers have finished,

OPPOSITE Every garden can be enriched by a wildlife pond.

coltsfoot plants produce thistledown-like seedheads.
HABITAT Throughout the British Isles, on dry wasteland and other disturbed ground in cities, towns and in the country, especially on clay soil.

12 Oxford ragwort
Senecio squalidus

Although common ragwort is widespread in the countryside, Oxford ragwort – a perennial originally from hot, dry parts of southern Europe – was introduced more recently and followed the railways. It is superficially similar to common ragwort but is shorter and bushier rather than tall and upright, making a clump 20–30cm (8–12in) high and as wide. It bears flattish-topped clusters of yellow daisies from May to November, and there are distinctive black-tipped scales on the involucre.
HABITAT Railway embankments, walls and wasteland in cities and town gardens; sometimes round field-edges. Throughout the British Isles but less common in the north.

13 Japanese knotweed
Fallopia japonica

This is a tall, striking, thicket-forming perennial, to 2m (6½ft) high, with reddish-tinged or red-spotted, slightly branching, rather zigzag-shaped, cane-like stems. The leaves are large and oval to heart-shaped and are spaced evenly all along the stems. Flowering from September to October, it produces loose, branching, upright sprays of creamy white, dock-like flowers. A close relative, the giant knotweed (*Polygonum sachalinense*), often mistakenly called Japanese knotweed, is often seen – this grows taller, to 3m (10ft) high, with upright, mostly unbranched, cane-like stems and large, heart-shaped leaves. Although the flowers of the giant knotweed are similar in shape and colour to those of the Japanese knotweed, they grow in more tightly packed spikes and appear slightly earlier in the year, from August to September.
HABITAT Throughout the British Isles on wasteland and roadsides.

Japanese knotweed

This distinctive and dramatic but highly invasive plant was originally introduced in Victorian times as a garden plant and has since spread to become a serious pest. It has now hybridized with the larger giant knotweed and also with the cultivated Russian vine (*Fallopia baldschuanicum*) – the original mile-a-minute plant – to produce even more vigorous and fast-growing offspring. All of these plants are posing a real problem for councils and conservation groups: because of their deep underground rootstocks and creeping rhizomes they are incredibly difficult to eradicate. The stems can push up through concrete, and one plant was known to send its rhizomes under 6 lanes of the M25 motorway and emerge the other side to start a new splinter group. Unlike the original Japanese knotweed, the new hybrids are also capable of growing from seed.

16 Common toadflax
Linaria vulgaris

Also known as yellow toadflax, this very attractive wildflower has tall, upright stems, 20–60cm (8–24in) high, with many long, narrow, rather grassy leaves arranged in pairs along them. From July to October, the stems are topped with tall, striking spikes of slender, hooded, yellow, snapdragon-like flowers, each having a long spur at the back.

HABITAT Wasteland, roadside verges and at edges of fields throughout lowland areas in the British Isles.

17 Yarrow
Achillea millefolium

Yarrow is a common wildflower that frequently grows as a ferny-leaved weed in garden lawns, where regular mowing prevents it from flowering. It is a clump-forming perennial, usually 30–45cm (12–17½in) high, with very finely divided, feathery foliage arranged along the upright main stems. From June to August, it is topped with flattish heads of flower made up of many tiny, white, 5-petalled florets; the flowerheads are a favourite courtship arena for red soldier beetles.

HABITAT Throughout the British Isles, on roadside verges, meadows, banks and lawns.

18 Common sorrel
Rumex acetosa

This is a very common, dock-like plant with thick, rather ribbed stems, to 1m (3ft) high, and long, slender, spearhead-shaped leaves that appear to clasp round the stem at their base. It flowers in May and June, producing a loose spray of inconspicuous, off-white flowers at the tip of each main stem; these are quickly followed by green, disc-like seeds, which turn rusty red in autumn; the leaves take on similar shades in late summer. The dry remains of the old stems stay on the plant until late into the following spring, when they are joined by the new growth.

HABITAT Mainly a plant of grassland, but also appears on roadsides, motorway verges, wasteland and allotments as well as in hedgerows, churchyards and overgrown gardens throughout the British Isles.

14 Pineapple weed
Matricaria discoidea

Flowering in June and July, this is a fairly common and easily identified annual or biennial plant that grows low and bushy. It has feathery, thread-like foliage identical to that of mayweed, but the flowers lack petals, consisting only of the yellow 'bump' in the centre. It smells strongly of pineapple when crushed, hence its name.

HABITAT Throughout the British Isles, on wasteland and cultivated ground including allotments and sometimes gardens.

15 Groundsel
Senecio vulgaris

This is a very common and well-known, annual weed of cultivated ground, with weak, branching stems and soft, lobed leaves with irregularly toothed edges. The flowers, which resemble unopened dandelions, are held in loose clusters at the tips of the stems; after they are over, the seedheads look like tiny dandelion 'clocks', which puff away on the breeze.

Groundsel is among the first plants to colonize newly cleared ground, and it can grow, flower and set seed very quickly, giving rise to several generations each season. It flowers and sets seed virtually all year round except in particularly hard winters.

HABITAT Throughout the British Isles in gardens, allotments, parks and areas of wasteland.

Cultivated ground

Domestic houses continue to be built at an alarming rate, but today's gardens are effective havens for wildlife. The 15 million gardens in Britain cover a million acres between them which, along with another third of a million acres of allotments, amounts to a substantial wildlife reserve distributed all over the country. And now that people are gardening with fewer pesticides, all sorts of creatures find safety in gardens, from spiders and beetles to unusual birds and mammals. Experts reckon that urban slow-worms now outnumber their country cousins; 2 million garden ponds have given frogs and newts a big fillip, and creepers on house walls provide safe nesting sites for birds such as spotted flycatchers and wrens. Derelict outbuildings are soon colonized by swallows, which make their mud nests high up at the top of internal walls, and robins will happily rear a brood in the shed, or even an old car. The Chelsea Flower Show made news one year when a blackbird decided to build a nest in one of the exhibits inside the Great Marquee; it was left untouched until the family had flown.

Gardens and allotments produce enormous amounts of food for wildlife. Fast-growing weeds, such as dandelions, groundsel and creeping thistles, quickly set seed and subsequently attract flocks of sparrows and goldfinches. Gardeners digging the ground turn up grubs and worms that are enjoyed by robins and blackbirds, and fallen fruit or berrying shrubs bring in thrushes and redwings to feed in the autumn. The population of blue tits, great tits and greenfinches has increased enormously since gardeners started putting out food for them all year round, but they are not the only species to have benefited – urban squirrels are ingenious at vandalizing bird-feeders to pinch peanuts, and sparrowhawks are now a common sight in towns, where they have discovered that bird tables provide them, too, with reliable meals. People even find wildlife high up on balcony gardens.

Plants that have 'escaped' from gardens have added to our 'feral' plant population, and while purists may tut-tut, some are a benefit, within reason. Buddleia, an 'exotic' imported shrub named after the vicar who discovered it – Adam Buddle, who died in 1715 – took over cracks in brickwork and paving as well as waste ground and bomb sites, and still provides nectar that supports several species of butterfly. There's lots of it just outside Victoria station in London. What with these, and the large range of garden flowers, our urban butterfly, moth and bee population has never had it so good.

Allotments are increasingly popular in towns and cities. In addition to providing food for humans, they can be much-needed havens for all kinds of wildlife.

19 Yellow corydalis
Pseudofumaria lutea

The yellow corydalis is an attractive, small, rather upright-rosette-shaped, annual plant, to 20cm (8in), with smooth, shiny, bronze-green, ferny foliage and short sprays of yellow, toadflax-like flowers from May to August. It was originally a garden plant that 'escaped' into the wild.

HABITAT Mainly in England and Wales, in hot, dry, usually sunny places, mostly on walls, banks and gravel paths in and around gardens.

20 Large-flowered evening primrose
Oenothera glazioviana

Flowering in the evening, this biennial or short-lived perennial has a rosette of elongated, oval leaves, 20cm (8in) long, with pointed tips and off-white midribs that are red on the underside of the leaf. The tall, upright, red-spotted flower stems, to 1.5m (5ft) high, bear a succession of bowl-shaped yellow flowers, 5–7.5cm (2–3in) across, clustered loosely round the tips of the stems throughout much of the summer.

HABITAT Wasteland, especially in towns and cities, particularly in the southern half of Britain.

21 Great mullein
Verbascum thapsus

Also known as Aaron's rod, this tall biennial starts off as a large rosette of oval, felt-like grey leaves from which, in their second year, arises a single, tall, upright, unbranched flower spike thickly clad in leaves decreasing in size up the stem. This is topped with a spike of round yellow flowers opening over many weeks from the bottom upwards during the summer. Other mulleins may be seen – these are usually hybrids and other species that have 'escaped' from gardens and are easily identified by their branching stems.

HABITAT Hot, dry, sunny wasteland, rocky hillsides, downs and chalk grassland throughout the British Isles except northern Scotland.

22 Opium poppy
Papaver somniferum

The opium poppy is a common and widespread, tall, rather upright annual or biennial with waxy, grey-green leaves and thick stems, topped from June to September with a series of large, solitary, poppy flowers up to 5cm (2in) across. The flower colour is variable, but is usually a dull mauve-pink with a darker blotch at the base of each petal. The flowers are followed by large, rounded, pale green, waxy seed capsules.

HABITAT Recently disturbed wasteland and cultivated land including gardens throughout lowland areas in the British Isles.

23 Hemlock
Conium maculatum

This is a tall, upright, poisonous member of the cow parsley family with spotted stems, up to 2m (6½ft), and extremely finely divided foliage – far more delicate and feathery than that of cow parsley. It has white flowers arranged in typical wagon-wheel-shaped heads on branching sideshoots towards the tops of the main stems. In winter plants lose their foliage and dry out to a bare brown skeleton of very regularly spaced stems, which look almost geometrical and persist until the following year.

HABITAT Near water or on damp roadside verges or wasteland; fairly common in the southern half of Britain but much less so further north.

24 Black nightshade
Solanum nigrum

Also known as garden nightshade, this is a faintly sinister-looking, untidy, sprawling, bushy plant. The dull grey-green leaves are almost triangular in shape, and from July to September it bears clusters of small, white, star-shaped, potato-like flowers with a central 'beak', followed by bunches of pea-sized green berries that slowly ripen to black. You may see flowers and both green and black berries on the same plant at the same time.

Black nightshade is sometimes mistakenly called deadly nightshade. Although not as poisonous as its larger, reddish-purple-flowered relative, it should still be treated with caution and the berries should not be eaten. Many years ago it was a common weed in fields of peas grown for canning and the black peas that you occasionally found inside cans at the time were in fact nightshade berries that had slipped through the net. The harvesting and sorting equipment is better today, and modern weedkillers have in any case eliminated the problem.
HABITAT Wasteland and disturbed or cultivated ground including allotments and gardens. Common in England, less so in the rest of the British Isles and not present in most of Scotland.

25 Hairy bittercress
Cardamine hirsuta

Hairy bittercress is a relatively recent addition to the list of common garden weeds and is already fairly widespread. It is a small, fast-growing annual with a rosette of stunted, watercress-like leaves, from the centre of which grows a short, slightly branching flower stem, 15cm (6in) long, tipped with small clusters of tiny, white, 4-petalled flowers. These are followed by slender pods, 1–2cm (⅜–¾in) long, which 'pop', shooting small, hard seeds some distance. It is capable of producing several generations each season.
HABITAT Garden centres, flowerbeds, tubs, greenhouses, allotments and sometimes in permanently damp, bare, open places in the countryside; rarely in the north of Britain.

26 Yellow oxalis
Oxalis corniculata

A well-known and widespread garden weed, yellow oxalis flowers from June to September outdoors but is capable of flowering almost throughout the year in a greenhouse. It is a small, sprawling plant that makes a prostrate mat of weak stems, usually up to 15–30cm (6–12in) wide, bearing small, green, clover-like leaves that close up at night; the leaves turn bright reddish maroon when the plant grows in strong sun. Small, single, yellow, 5-petalled flowers, usually about 5mm (³⁄₁₆in) across, appear on slender, thread-like stems all over the plant, followed by small, knobbly, pea-like pods that split explosively, sending seeds a considerable distance away.
HABITAT Mostly in southern and central England in hot, dry, sunny situations, in flowerbeds, tubs, greenhouses, allotments and sometimes in open ground in the countryside.

27 Fairy ring champignon
Marasmius oreades

This is the common 'fairy ring' fungus, which can be seen almost any time between spring and autumn, growing in circles in short grass. It produces small, buff-coloured toadstools with tough, wiry stems; the gills underneath are the same colour.

Although some other fungi grow in rings, it is a characteristic of this species that the fungi dry up and shrivel in dry weather, then 'rehydrate' when it rains. Fairy rings consist of several concentric layers, like a dartboard – the centre is dry with sparse, sickly grass, then there is a ring of toadstools with a bright green ring of lush, longer grass round the outside. This is because as the fungus spreads outwards its mycelium or 'roots' release nitrogen from the ground, causing bright green grass, then as it advances it leaves impoverished soil behind. This is also very dry because of the waterproofing action of the mycelium threads, which by now have taken over much of the ground, preventing rain soaking in.
HABITAT Throughout lowland areas in the British Isles, in lawns, parks and playing fields.

Also found in urban areas
Common frog/newt (see p.250)
Coot (see p.235)
Feral cat (see p.203)
Ferret (see p.64)
Great crested grebe (see p.225)
Grey heron (see p.225)
Grey squirrel (see p.103)
Gulls (see pp.28–29)
Jay (see p.93)
Magpie (see p.272)
Mallard (see p.229)
Mole (see p.202)
Moorhen (see p.234)
Mute swan (see p.226)
Red-eared terrapin (see p.249)
Reeves' muntjac (see p.102)
Slow worm (see p.199)
Tawny owl (see p.82)

Conservation organizations

BOTANICAL SOCIETY OF
THE BRITISH ISLES
Botany Dept
The Natural History Museum
Cromwell Road
London SW7 5BD
www.bsbi.org.uk

BUTTERFLY CONSERVATION
Manor Yard
East Lulworth
Wareham
Dorset BH20 5QP
www.butterfly-conservation.org

BRITISH MYCOLOGICAL SOCIETY
The Wolfson Wing
Jodrell Laboratory
Royal Botanic Gardens
Kew
Surrey TW9 3AB
www.britmycolsoc.org.uk

BRITISH TRUST FOR
ORNITHOLOGY (BTO)
The Nunnery
Thetford
Norfolk IP24 2PU
www.bto.org

BUMBLEBEE CONSERVATION TRUST
School of Biological &
Environmental Sciences
University of Stirling
Stirling FK9 4LA
www.bumblebeeconservationtrust.
co.uk

THE FORESTRY COMMISSION
231 Corstorphine Road
Edinburgh
Scotland EH12 7AT
www.forestry.gov.uk

THE IRISH WILDLIFE TRUST
Sigmund Business Centre
93a Lagan Road
Dublin Industrial Estate
Dublin 11 1RE
www.iwt.ie

NATURAL ENGLAND
Northminster House
Peterborough PE1 1UA
www.english-nature.org.uk

THE NATIONAL TRUST
PO Box 39
Warrington WA5 7WD
www.nationaltrust.org.uk

PLANTLIFE INTERNATIONAL
14 Rollestone Street
Salisbury
Wiltshire SP1 1DX
www.plantlife.org.uk

THE WILDLIFE TRUSTS
The Kiln
Mather Road
Newark
Nottinghamshire NG24 1WT
www.wildlifetrusts.org

ROYAL SOCIETY FOR THE
PROTECTION OF BIRDS (RSPB)
The Lodge
Potton Road, Sandy
Bedfordshire SG19 2DL
www.rspb.org.uk

THE TREE COUNCIL
71 Newcomen Street
London SE1 1YT
www.treecouncil.org.uk

THE WOODLAND TRUST
Autumn Park
Dysart Road, Grantham
Lincolnshire NG31 6LL
www.woodland-trust.org.uk

Acknowledgements

This book is dedicated to the members of the Wharfedale Naturalists Society, who introduced a small boy to the wonders of natural history.

A book like this cannot be written alone, in spite of John Ruskin's dictum: 'If you want to learn about something, write a book about it.' I also cherish Martina Navratilova's comment: 'Nobody grows old merely by living a number of years; they grow old when they abandon their enthusiasm to learn.' Indeed, nobody knows everything, and the wisest keep on learning. My own knowledge is broad-based and founded on a love of plants and botany, so wildflowers are 'my bag', along with a fair smattering of birds, mammals and invertebrates learned from the age of eight onwards, courtesy of the Wharfedale Naturalists Society. I owe them a great debt of gratitude for their patience and wisdom in encouraging a small boy to develop a love of nature. I was once their youngest member and this year I am still happy to pay my annual subscription 50 years on – they have given me more than my money's worth.

But I have also had the benefit of help and advice from a wide number of people – many of them experts in their chosen field – whom I am happy to acknowledge here. My profound thanks go to Sue Phillips for her invaluable research, to Polly Boyd and Christopher Tinker for their editorial expertise and to Stephen Moss for being not only an able and entertaining series producer but also a natural historian of considerable knowledge, mainly of the ornithological variety. I only hope he has learned as much about wildflowers from me as I have about birds from him. To Jonathan Elphick, Stephen Harris, Peter Hayward, Trevor James and Richard Jones I am hugely grateful for their particular fields of expertise, and without Andrew Barron and Joanne Forrest Smith the book would not have looked nearly so attractive.

I must also thank the small army of producers, assistant producers, researchers, production managers, cameramen and sound recordists, who travelled with me into the wilds of the British Isles – from Shetland to the Channel Islands – for a year and a half in search of the amazing creatures that inhabit our islands. They made the whole adventure tremendous fun, and produced some amazing sounds and images, as well as moulding the work into a coherent whole.

The BBC Natural History Unit this year celebrates its 50th anniversary. I know from my own experiences in making the television series *The Nature of Britain* that it is in good hands. It has been an honour and a pleasure to work with them.

Alan Titchmarsh

Picture credits

KEY

T   Top
B   Bottom/below
A   Above
L   Left
R   Right
C   Centre

ALAMY/blickwinkel 284CR/Michael Grant 282C/Jim Henderson 282TR/Steve Taylor 273TR/tbkmedia.de 24CRB/David Tipling 25/Woodfall Wild Images 199TR/Woodbridge Wildlife Images 27BC.

ARDEA 21BR, 44TC, 65TR, 110CL, 111, 261CR, 292–3/Dennis Avon 301BR, 304BL/Jack A. Bailey 95TL, 242BC/Brian Bevan 250TR/Elizabeth Bomford 281/Mark Boulton 131, 177, 217–8/John Cancalosi Back Cover (BC), 24BL, 100–1, 135TR, 166CL, 226CL, 314BL/Bill Coster 33BR, 230TL/Werner Curth 252CR/John Daniels 172BL, 277TC, 279CR, 296, 301BL, 302TC, 304BR/Johan de Meester 85BR, 115, 152, 181, 230BC, 278TC/David Dixon 110, 120, 123, 180BC, 263TR/Bob Gibbons 74BL, 95TR, 113BR, 156CTC, 157CL, 171 inset, 175BR, 176 insetR, 177, 198BRA, 203BR, 204CR, 207, 208TC, 255TR, 289, 320/Pascal Goetgheluck 312CL, 97/Francois Gohier 58/D. W. Greenslade 274CRB, 310CRA/Steve Hopkin 98CLB, 143TL 170C, 198CRB/Chris Knights 57CR, 66TR, 69CR, 92BC, 102CL, 165BC, 189, 194BL, 224CR, 228BC, 231 inset, 235CR/Jean Michel Labat 123TR/Jens-Peter Laub 237TR/Tom & Pat Leeson 62T/John Mason 142BR, 160–1C, 170CB/John Mason 142, 197TC/Johan de Meester 115TC, 152BR, 181, 197TR/Pat Morris 45TR, 46BC, 47CRA, 48TL, 50BR, 55, 202CRB, 248CRA/George Reszeter 211, 164/Bryan L. Sage 24TR/Steffen & Alexandra Sailer 280CL/Dae Sasitorn 8–9, 11, 18–19, 20BL, 22BL, 133, 158–9, 161BR, 163, 187, 220BL, 267BR/Peter Steyn 191CR/Zdenek Tunka 130, 134/M. Watson 5TR/David & Katie Urry 303 inset/Duncan Usher 15, 67, 136BL, 170TL, 190 TC & BR, 242TL, 254BR, 265TR, 271BC, 300C/Maurice Walker 171/Adrian Warren 148–9/Jim Zipp 25TL, 43TR.

ART DIRECTORS/TRIP 62, 64, 71, 122TC, 147, 246CL, 251C, 252BC/Annie Anderson 157TR/Steve Austin 110TC, 140CR/Nicholas Bailey 83TL/Martin Barlow 63BL/Frank Blackburn 314BR, 103, 109CR, 141BL, 172BR, 179BC/Michal Cerny 306CR/Bob Devine 276BC/Brian Gibbs 82TR, 144CR/Spencer Grant 133 inset, 226TC/Mel Longhurst 99/BCGeorge McCarthy 86BC, 103TL, 232BC, 235CL/Darren Maybury 276CLB/Dave Osborne 154TC/Jim Ringland 96TL, 169TL, 277CLA, 306BR, 310CL/Helene Rogers 70CL, 145 inset, 255CR, 280BC, 290BL/Mark Stevenson 99TL, 103TR/Zdenek Tunka 130BL, 134CL/Bob Turner 145, 203/John Wender 64CR/B. R. Woods 74/Allan Wright 150BC.

BBC 6, 9/Rita Aspinall/BBC cover.

BUMBLEBEE CONSERVATION TRUST/Dave Goulson 142CL.

CORBIS 44/Peter Adams 124–5/Steve Austin/Papilio 199BR/Richard Becker 256TR/Niall Benvie 67TL, 68, 74CR, 82TR, 114,CR 134TR, 152CR, 153BL, 236BC, 298BL, 304C/Robert Canis 256CR/Brandon D. Cole 51CR/Ashley Cooper Back Cover TR, 79 inset, 177/Eric Crichton 152TC/Derek Croucher 16/DLILLC 60–1/Ian Beames/Ecoscene 104C/Frank Blackburn/Ecoscene 282TL/Chinch Gryniewicz/Ecoscene 108TR, 282BC/Sally A. Morgan/Ecoscene 67, 116BCL, 180TL/Robin Williams/Ecoscene 56CR/Natalie Fobes 243TC/B. Borrell Casals/FLPA 84BC, 113TC/Hugh Clark/FLPA 136CR/Tony Hamblin/FLPA 40CR, 90TL, 138TR & BR, 240C & CR, 242TR, 299TL/John Hawkins/FLPA 85/Derek Middleton/FLPA 136/Geoff Moon/FLPA 32/John Tinning/FLPA 321C/Ian Rose/FLPA 322BC/Peter Reynolds 139TC/FLPA 139/John Watkins/FLPA 304TC/Winfred Wisniewski/FLPA 243BC/Martin B. Withers/FLPA 84TR, 132BC, Tony Wharton/FLPA 33BL, 153TL/John Heseltine 215 main/Eric and David Hosking 29TR, 40TL, 134BC, 202BC, 325CR/Hal Horwitz 260TL/Jacqui Hurst 51BC, 214CR/William Manning 250TLB/Michael Nicholson 127BR/Joe McDonald 252C/George McCarthy 41TR, 42TL, 115TR & BL ,121TC, 168CR, 179TL, 180,TR 196TL, 213TC, 261TL, 289CL/Steve

Austin/Papilio 137CRB/Stan Craig/Papilio 135/Dennis Johnson/Papilio 72TL/Pat Jerrold/Papilio 195CR, 116BCR, 170CA/Bryan Knox/Papilio 120TR, 121, 156CR, 182TR/Michael Maconachie/Papilio 118TL, 156BR/Simon Murray/Papilio 289TR/Alastair Shay/Papilio 106CRB/Frank Young/Papilio 322CR/Patrick Johns 262TL/David Paterson 126BL/Clay Perry 109BL/Robert Pickett 210TR, 319CR/Roy Rainford/Robert Harding World Imagery 258–9/Jim Richardson 49/Andy Rouse 146TR, 225TL/Kevin Schafer 34BL/Skyscan 186BL/Jurgen & Christine Sohns 256BR/Jon Sparks 150C, 151BC, 155TL/Dale C. Spartas 229TL, 271TL/Geray Sweeney 264–5/Roger Tidman 28TL, 32BL, 109BR, 194CR, 236CL, 324CR/Sandro Vannini 20–1/Patrick Ward 49/Lawson Wood 51TL, 55TR/Adam Woolfitt 285 main/Markus Botzek/zefa 137CRA/Oswald Eckstein/zefa 170BC/Grace/zefa 284TL/Helmut Heintges/zefa 92TL/Herbert Kehrer/zefa 109TL/Frank Krahmer/zefa 209CR/Fritz Rauschenbach/zefa 83CR/Hans Reinhard/zefa 202T/Christof Wermter/zefa 113/Herbert Zettl/zefa 302CL.

ECOSCENE/Papilio/Dennis Johnson 30CRA.

FISHBOURNE 266BL.

FLPA 318BC, 324TR/Terry Andrewartha 270BR/Andrew Bailey 89BR/Bill Baston 300TL/Leo Batten 260BC, 287BCL/Richard Becker 198BC, 260TR, 284BR, 286TR, 307C, 311CR, 321TL/B. Borrell Casals 142TC, 143CR, 309CR/Neil Bowman 271C, 308CLB/Hans Dieter Brandl 64CR/David Burton 186–7BC/Robert Canis 69BL, 114,TR 117 inset, 198CRA/Nigel Cattlin 65CR, 69, 97CR, 118CL, 206BR, 208C, 209TR, 263CL, 276TL, 277CR & BL, 283TL, 310BR & CL, 313TL, CRB, C & BC, 322TR, 325TC/Robin Chittenden 41BC, 254CL/Hugh Clark 143/Michael Clark 107TR, 143C, 253/Robin Chittenden 41/Chris Demetriou 209BR/Jeremy Early 5BR, 174,TC 293TR, 310TL/Peter Entwistle 5CL, 86CR, 140BR, 141,TL 167,TC 168, 175BL, 176TL, 185TR, 205CR, 273TL, C & BC, 275/Martin Garwood

246TR/Bob Gibbons 72, 175, 283 BC & BCA/Tony Hamblin 103BL, 164BC, 300BC/Paul Hobson 34TR, 178CR, 315TL/S Jonasson 33TC/John Hawkins 83BL, 85TR/Wil Meinderts/Foto Natura 243CR/David Hosking 91BL, 119,BL 183TR/Roger Hosking 91, 191TR, 237BC, 280TC/William J. Howes 221BR/Joan Hutchings 78, 283TR/Mike Lane 36BR, 64TR/Linda Lewis 45BL/Phil McLean 31, 129, 306TC/Derek Middleton 81, 94BL, 104C, 106CRA, 144TR & BL, 147CRB, 166, 170CR, 198TL, 244TR & CRA, 245CRA, 274BL, 279TL & BC, 315BC/Minden Pictures 25BR/Norbert Wu/Minden Pictures 243TCA/Phil McLean Back cover BR, 12, 247TL/Foto Natura Stock 198CL, 199TL, 244BL, 247TR, 287TR/Jan Castricum/Foto Natura 255TC/CIisca Castelijns/Foto Natura 169BR/Frits van Daalen/Foto Natura 68BR, 137TL, 305C/Flip de Nooyer/Foto Natura 82BL, 88TL/Danny Ellinger/Foto Natura 28BL/Philip Friskorn/Foto Natura 86CL/Fred Hazelhoff/Foto Natura 39TL, 172TC/Michel Schaap, Foto Natura 130TC/Hans Chouten/Foto Natura 298TCA/Chris Schenk/Foto Natura 40BL/Wil Meinderts/Foto Natura 245TL & CLA/Piet Munstermann/Foto Natura 248BL/Ben Schrieken/Foto Natura 57TL/G. F. J. Tik/Foto Natura/Minden Pictures 301TC/Do Van Dijck/Foto Natura 42BL, 43BL, 135BC/Frans Van Boxtel/Foto Natura 89/Peter Verhoog/Foto Natura 56BL/Jan Vermeer/Foto Natura 119, 122TR/Wim Weenik/Foto Natura 88TC/Hugo Willcox/Foto Natura 107CR, 202TR/Mark Newman 251BC/Chris Newton 205TL/Maurice Nimmo 52CR, 173BR, 254TR/Andrew Parkinson 204TC/Primrose Peacock/Holt 286BC/Alwyn J Roberts 244CL, 313CRA/Ian Rose 155CR, 178BR, 179TR/Michael Rose 205C, 246C, 249BC, 321BC/L Lee Rue 29TL/Keith Rushforth 110,CR/Alfred Schauhuber/Imagebroker/310CRB/Malcolm Schuyl 223, 233C & BL, 283CRA, 305TC, 307CL/Silvestris Fotoservice 107C, 249BL, 291C/Jurgen & Christine Sohns 58TC, 63TL, 305BL, 311C/Martin H Smith 53, 193/Gary K Smith 33TCA, 204BL, 228TL, 262BR/Sunset 164CL/Mike J Thomas 74BR/Roger Tidman 165CL, 272CR/John Watkins 38, 233CR/Roger Wilmshurst 65BL, 192BC/Winfried Wisniewski/26, 174,BL 257BL/Tony

Published to accompany the BBC television series *The Nature of Britain*, first broadcast on BBC1 in 2007.

Series producer Stephen Moss

Published in 2007 by BBC Books, an imprint of Ebury Publishing. A Random House Group Company

10 9 8 7 6 5 4 3 2 1

The Random House Group Limited Reg. No. 954009

Addresses for companies within the Random House Group can be found at www.randomhouse.co.uk

A CIP catalogue record for this book is available from the British Library.

ISBN 978 0 563 49398 3

The Random House Group Limited supports The Forest Stewardship Council (FSC), the leading international forest certification organization. All our titles that are printed on Greenpeace approved FSC certified paper carry the FSC logo. Our paper procurement policy can be found at www.rbooks.co.uk/environment

Commissioning editor Nicky Ross
Project manager Christopher Tinker
Project editor Polly Boyd
Designer Andrew Barron
Picture researcher
Joanne Forrest Smith
Production controller Antony Heller

Printed and bound in England by Butler & Tanner, Frome.

To buy books by your favourite authors and register for offers, visit www.rbooks.co.uk